6/23

1001 QUOTATIONS
TO INSPIRE YOU BEFORE YOU DIE

1001 QUOTATIONS
TO INSPIRE YOU BEFORE YOU DIE

GENERAL EDITOR ROBERT ARP

FOREWORD BY NIGEL REES

🌐 William Shakespeare is perhaps one of the most
quoted writers in history.

CASSELL
ILLUSTRATED

A Quintessence Book

First published in Great Britain in 2016 by Cassell Illustrated
A division of Octopus Publishing Group Limited
Carmelite House
50 Victoria Embankment
London EC4Y 0DZ
www.octopusbooks.co.uk

An Hachette UK Company
www.hachette.co.uk

ISBN: 978-1-84403-895-4
QSS.1QUO

A CIP catalogue record for this book is available from the British Library.

This book was designed and produced by
Quintessence Editions Ltd.
The Old Brewery
6 Blundell Street
London N7 9BH

Senior Editor	Elspeth Beidas
Editors	Rebecca Gee, Carol King,
	Fiona Plowman, Frank Ritter
Designer	Damian Jaques
Picture Researcher	Hannah Phillips
Production Manager	Anna Pauletti
Editorial Director	Ruth Patrick
Publisher	Philip Cooper

Colour reproduction by Bright Arts in Hong Kong
Printed in China by Printplus Ltd

Contents

Foreword Nigel Rees

There is a type of quotation or saying that, once discovered, you can carry with you for the rest of your life. I will give you an example of 'words to live by' that I have held on to ever since I first heard them. I had a friend who did me a very great service. He told me that he was giving up his job in broadcasting and that I should apply to take it up. This I did. I got the job, and it started my career as a radio and TV presenter. I never let him forget how grateful I was for the tip-off. At his memorial service when he died, one of the people paying tribute remarked how he had always 'kept his friendships in good repair'. The phrase came from a wise saying of Dr Samuel Johnson: 'If a man does not make new acquaintance as he advances through life, he will soon find himself left alone. A man, Sir, should keep his friendship in good repair'. How true this was in my friend's case. It is one of the best possible pieces of advice you can give anybody, and not just because, in this instance, it was of great benefit to me. You will find it in this book.

Because of the work I have done with quotations as a writer and broadcaster over the past forty years, I am sometimes asked, 'Do you have a favourite quotation?' Impossible to answer, but I am glad to find so many of my favourites included here. This book contains 1,001 quotations and sayings that could well shape your response to whatever life throws up and help you deal with it. They have been chosen carefully to provide perceptive views on a wide range of subjects and to help you think about them more deeply. They range from stern admonitions to humorous witticisms. The entries accompanying each quotation give useful information as to its origin and meaning and reflect an up-to-date state of knowledge on the source and occasion of it. It is a tremendous collection and I hope you will find inspiration and benefit from the wealth of comment and advice it contains. 'Words of wisdom' is a phrase all right – you will find plenty of them in this book.

Introduction Robert Arp

We all love quotations – in fact, we seem to be obsessed with them. We'll place them under our email signatures, stencil them at the top of stationery, heat them into ceramic mugs, carve them into marble, spray paint them onto buildings, write them in permanent marker on bathroom stalls, scratch them into classroom desks, post them on Facebook and Twitter, and paste them on billboards. We use them to justify our positions, manipulate them to make our cases, laugh at them, cry at them, become enraged at them, become befuddled by them, feel enlightened by them, include them in our eulogies, ponder them in our darker or brighter moments – even tattoo them on our bodies. Why do we do this? Why do they strike such a chord with us?

One reason is that we humans react to situations in a fairly similar way – we praise justice, condemn injustice, chuckle at satire, feel proud of what we accomplish and sob when tragedy strikes. Combine this with the fact that people undergo similar events in life – birth of a child, death of a loved one, overcoming a fear, withstanding suffering, falling in love – and the result is a commonality of human experience that is expressible and tangible. A person from China can relate to the African proverb, 'The wealth which enslaves the owner is not wealth,' while a person from the Netherlands has no problem understanding the Chinese adage, 'Give a man a fish and he will eat for a day. Teach a man to fish and he will eat for a lifetime.' This is not to say that every person will be able to relate to every other person's experiences, but there are enough people in the world, and enough experiences in life, that someone's words likely will affect another at a particular moment.

We also appreciate quotations because there are times when an erudite person has captured a moment precisely, described a sentiment exactly or justified a position persuasively, in a way that makes us think, 'I couldn't have said it better myself!' Such shared insight can be a source of great satisfaction. As 20th-century star of stage and screen Marlene Dietrich noted: 'I love quotations because it is a joy to find thoughts one might have, beautifully expressed with much authority by someone recognized wiser than oneself.'

Another reason we enjoy quotations is that we can live vicariously through them. Neil Armstrong's remark, 'That's one small step for man; one giant leap for mankind,' still conjures the same sense of momentousness today as it did for the people all over the world who crowded around their television sets to watch him walk on the moon on 20 July 1969. Quotations provide us not only with an emotional connection to key events in history, but also give us an insight into the characters of those involved in them – such as Elizabeth I's statement that 'I know I have the body but of a weak and feeble woman; but I have the heart and stomach of a king.'

Perhaps the most prevailing reason we repeatedly turn to quotations is for their power to inspire us. A man going through a forced career change in midlife may come across Thomas Fuller's observation that 'It is always darkest just before the Day dawneth,' and feel encouraged that a better job is on the horizon. Or a woman, who on the seventeenth mile of a marathon may want to stop running because her muscles are aching so badly that she wants to cry, soldiers on to complete the race after recalling Pelé's inspiring claim that 'The more difficult the victory, the greater the happiness in winning.' Quotations not only impel us, they also compel us – to face our fears, to agree with what someone has said, or even to change our behaviours.

We will often quote someone for the simple fact that what they have said is downright hilarious. Groucho Marx's comment that 'Those are my principles, and if you don't like them. . .well, I have others,' is gleefully clever. Bob Hope's description of television as 'where the movies go when they die,' at the opening of the first televised Academy Awards ceremony, is a classic one-liner. Tina Fey was able to make audiences laugh, as well as laugh at herself, when she claimed, 'Confidence is 10 percent hard work and 90 percent delusion.' And although not a comedian by trade, Gioachino Rossini demonstrated a perceptive wit when he observed that 'Wagner has lovely moments but awful quarters of an hour.'

The great wordsmiths have also tickled many a funny bone. Oscar Wilde once quipped to a customs official that 'I have nothing to declare except my genius,' while Mark Twain opined, 'Go to Heaven for the climate; Hell for the company.' A literary giant in his own right as well as one of the great doctors of the Catholic Church, St Augustine noted in his work *Confessions* (397 CE) that when he was younger he wanted to quit his wicked, womanizing ways, but he asked God for a little extra time: 'Give me chastity and continency, only not yet.'

At one point or another in our lives, most of us have had to cite another's words as a justification for something we have written, or made reference to what some famous person said to prove a point in an oral presentation. Or we have used someone's words to demonstrate an affinity between our viewpoint and theirs. However, we must be careful when we quote, as the act carries with it certain dangers.

Firstly, it is important to make sure that the quotation is reproduced correctly. There are numerous examples of famous misquotes, such as Humphrey Bogart's instruction to 'Play it again, Sam' in the movie *Casablanca* (1942) – he actually simply says, 'Play it.' There is much truth to satirist Ambrose Bierce's tongue-in-cheek definition of 'quotation' in *The Devil's Dictionary* (1911) as 'The act of repeating erroneously the words of another.' This may not be problematic when it comes to idioms or aphorisms, but when someone's words are being used to bolster a position in an article from a medical journal, or to support an argument that will affect public policy or to convince people to subscribe to a certain set of beliefs, it is imperative to ensure the quotation is correct.

It is also essential to make sure that the quotation is attributed to the correct person or source. 'There's a sucker born every minute' was never actually stated by P T Barnum, although for most of the 20th century, people thought he was the originator. In a way that is similar to misquotation, misattribution of trivial quotations may be of no matter. However, it is possible to imagine that a person's career or livelihood could have been derailed because a quotation of consequence has been misattributed to them. 'Be careful,' warned French writer and statesman André Malraux: 'with quotations, you can damn anything.'

Additionally, it is vital when citing a quotation not to quote out of context. Most of us are probably familiar with the claim that 'Money is the root of all evil' but the full quotation by St Paul from the New Testament is actually, 'For the love of money is the root of all evil, which while some coveted after, they have erred from the faith, and pierced themselves through with many sorrows.' There's a huge difference in meaning between these two statements, and biblical scholars are generally in agreement that St Paul's basic point is not that money per se is the cause of evil, but that the 'foolish and hurtful lust' of things in this world that are not really needed to live, ensnare and tempt us to act in ways that lead to our own destruction.

A further reason we must be careful in our usage of quotations is perhaps best summarized by this remark from author A A Milne: 'A quotation is a handy thing to have about, saving one the trouble of thinking for oneself.' Similarly, writer Dorothy Sayers claimed that a 'facility for quotation covers the absence of original thought,' while Ralph Waldo Emerson noted simply, 'I hate quotations. Tell me what you know.' While it is true that much of our knowledge unavoidably comes from memorizing the ideas of others who have come before us – the Pythagorean theorem, the Second Law of Thermodynamics, and countless other theoretical and practical ideas – we still need to internalize these ideas, understand them, grapple with them, critique them and either accept or reject them based upon reasons and evidence that we provide. We need to think for ourselves. Part of what it means to be a fully rational, adult human being is that one thinks critically about the issues, ideas, opinions, positions and claims that people put forward. Quotations usually take the form of a claim that someone is making, and claims are shown to be either true or false with evidence. If there's evidence for a claim being true, we should accept it; if there's evidence for a claim being false, we should reject it; if there's insufficient evidence for a claim being true or false, we should suspend our judgement about it.

The definition of a quotation is something that has changed over time. The English word is a noun derived from the Medieval Latin *quotationem*, meaning 'the act of numbering.' By the end of the 16th century the word had come to mean 'to give as a reference, to cite as an authority,' and by the end of the 17th century meant 'to copy or repeat the exact words of another.' Today, *The Oxford English Dictionary* defines the quotation as 'a group of words taken from a text or speech and repeated by someone other than the original author or speaker,' while *Merriam-Webster* defines it as 'something that a person says or writes that is repeated or used by someone else in another piece of writing or a speech'. The Wikipedia entry on quotation describes one of the uses of a quotation as 'a means of inspiration and to invoke philosophical thoughts from the reader'.

It is this last definition that has informed the selection of quotations that appears in this book. Chosen from throughout history for their insight into a particular field of human endeavour, each of the 1,001 quotations contained within these pages is listed with its originator, source and date, and is accompanied by an insightful review that analyzes the substance and significance of its weighty words. From Aristotle and Confucius to William Shakespeare, Niccolò Machiavelli, Voltaire, Pablo Picasso, Virginia Woolf and Bill Gates, the greatest minds in the world can be found here. No doubt, some of the quotations will inspire you; no doubt, too, some will get you to think deeply about yourself, your thoughts, the world around you and reality as you know it. In the words of British statesman Winston Churchill, 'It is a good thing for an uneducated man to read books of quotations...The quotations when engraved upon the memory give you good thoughts. They also make you anxious to read the authors and look for more.'

Art and Architecture

Business

Perpetual devotion to what a man calls his business, is only to be sustained by perpetual neglect of many other things. **653**

Pleasure is a thief to business. **643**

Politics greases the wheels of business. **669**

Remember that time is money. **645**

Small is beautiful. **674**

Society cares for the individual only so far as he is profitable. **673**

Talk of nothing but business, and dispatch that business quickly. **639**

The best minds are not in government. If any were, business would hire them right away. **677**

The business world contains plenty of successful men who have no brains. **654**

The buyer has need of a hundred eyes, the seller of but one. **640**

The chief business of the American people is business. **657**

The customer is always right. **653**

The man of virtue makes the difficulty to be overcome his first business, and success only a subsequent consideration. **631**

The only place you find success before work is in the dictionary. **660**

The only way I can get you to do anything is by giving you what you want. **661**

The rule of my life is to make business a pleasure and pleasure my business. **648**

The secret of business is to know something that nobody else knows. **679**

The successful man is the one who finds out what is the matter with his business before his competitors do. **669**

The wealth which enslaves the owner is not wealth. **641**

There is only one boss. The customer. And he can fire everybody in the company from the chairman on down, simply by spending his money somewhere else. **682**

To think twice in every matter and follow the lead of others is no way to make money. **642**

When two men in business always agree, one of them is unnecessary. **659**

Work expands so as to fill the time available for its completion. **668**

You can't build a strong corporation with a lot of committees...You have to be able to make decisions on your own. **681**

Your most unhappy customers are your greatest source of learning. **684**

Education

A general State education is a mere contrivance for moulding people to be exactly like one another. **603**

A little learning is a dangerous thing. **594**

All learning is recollection. **578**

All wish to be learned, but no one is willing to pay the price. **585**

An educational system by itself, cannot fashion the whole future structure of a country, but it can make better citizens. **615**

An error doesn't become a mistake until you refuse to correct it. **617**

An original thinker and able teacher very soon attracts a large class and vice versa. **604**

By education most have been misled. **592**

Children enter school as question marks and leave as periods. **620**

Do not say, 'When I have leisure I will study,' for you may never have leisure. **584**

Don't gain the world and lose your soul, wisdom is better than silver or gold. **625**

Education commences at the mother's knee, and every word spoken within the hearsay of little children tends towards the formation of character. **603**

Education costs money. But then so does ignorance. **626**

Education has produced a vast population able to read but unable to distinguish what is worth reading. **614**

Education is...a two-edged sword that can be used either for the progress of mankind or for its destruction. **621**

Education is a better safeguard of liberty than a standing army. **602**

Education is a progressive discovery of our own ignorance. **619**

Education is an ornament for the prosperous, a refuge for the unfortunate. **580**

Education is the guardian genius of democracy. It is the only dictator that free men recognize, and the only ruler that free men require. **600**

Education is what survives when what has been learned has been forgotten. **618**

Education makes a people easy to lead, but difficult to drive; easy to govern, but impossible to enslave. **600**

Education's purpose is to replace an empty mind with an open one. **626**

Genius without education is like silver in the mine. **597**

Give a man a fish and he will eat for a day. Teach a man to fish and he will eat for a lifetime. **577**

How much a dunce that has been sent to roam, Excels a dunce that has been kept at home. **598**

I have learned all kinds of things from my many mistakes. The one thing I never learn is to stop making them. **627**

I have learned much from my teachers, more from my colleagues, and the most from my students. **596**

I have never let my schooling interfere with my education. **607**

I wish you'd go back to your horses. **578**

If you think education is expensive, try ignorance. **622**

Ignorance is bliss. **596**

Improvement makes straight roads, but the crooked roads without improvement, are roads of Genius. **599**

In order to be content men must also have the possibility of developing their intellectual and artistic powers... **612**

It is only the ignorant who despise education. **586**

Just think of the tragedy of teaching children not to doubt. **610**

Learn to live, and live to learn; ignorance like a fire doth burn; little tasks make large return. **602**

Learning by study must be won; 'twas ne'er entail'd from son to son. **594**

Learning is an ornament in prosperity, a refuge in adversity, and a provision in old age. **581**

Much learning does not teach understanding. **577**

Nothing in education is so astonishing as the amount of ignorance it accumulates in the form of inert facts. **607**

Share your knowledge. It is a way to achieve immortality. **627**

Skill comes so slow, and life so fast doth fly, We learn so little and forget so much. **591**

Strange as it seems, no amount of learning can cure stupidity, and higher education positively fortifies it. **624**

Teachers open the door, but you must enter by yourself. **583**

The aim of education is the knowledge, not of facts, but of values. **610**

The foundation of every state is the education of its youth. **588**

The good teacher not only understands the child: he approves of the child. **611**

The highest result of education is tolerance. **605**

The history of scholarship is a record of disagreements. **608**

The life so short, the craft so long to learn. **580**

The object of education is to teach us to love what is beautiful. **581**

The principal goal of education...should be creating men and women who are capable of doing new things, not simply repeating what other generations have done. **616**

The very spring and root of honesty and virtue lie in good education. **585**

To learning and law, there's no greater foe, than they that nothing know. **591**

To pursue education is to be human, to give it up, to be a beast. **583**

To repeat what others have said, requires education; to challenge it, requires brains. **611**

Too often we give our children the answers to remember rather than the problems to solve. **622**

We do not learn for school, but for life. **584**

What is the first part of politics? Education. The second? Education. And the third? Education. **601**

When the pupil is ready, the teacher will appear. **604**

Who dares to teach must never cease to learn. **609**

You always learn a lot more when you lose than when you win. **592**

You can't teach an old dog new tricks. **590**

You will find something more in woods than in books. Trees and stones will teach you that which you can never learn from masters. **588**

Entertainment

Academia is the death of cinema. It is the very opposite of passion. Film is not the art of scholars, but of illiterates. **893**

All good ideas start out as bad ideas, that's why it takes so long. **886**

All the world's a stage, And all the men and women merely players. **842**

Although one may fail to find happiness in theatrical life, one never wishes to give it up after having once tasted its fruits. **852**

Always be a first-rate version of yourself, instead of a second-rate version of somebody else. **867**

Ambition is a dream with a V8 engine. **873**

An actor is at most a poet and at least an entertainer. **888**

Science and Nature

We scientists are clever – too clever – are you not satisfied? Is four square miles in one bomb not enough? Men are still thinking. Just tell us how big you want it! **768**

Why does the universe go to all the bother of existing? **780**

Sports and Leisure

A champion is someone who gets up when he can't. **815**

A lifetime of training for just ten seconds. **812**

Adversity causes some men to break; others to break records. **815**

Because it's there. **802**

Blest leisure is our curse, like that of Cain it makes us wander. **792**

Boxing is the only sport you can get your brain shook, your money took and your name in the undertaker book. **829**

Every strike brings me closer to the next home run. **805**

Football is the ballet of the masses. **810**

I consider myself the luckiest man on the face of the Earth. **807**

I fear not the man who has practiced 10,000 kicks once, but I fear the man who has practiced one kick 10,000 times. **813**

I have found adventure in flying, in world travel, in business, and even close at hand…Adventure is a state of mind and spirit. **811**

I've failed over and over and over again in my life. And that is why I succeed. **829**

Idle hands are the devil's workshop. **786**

Idleness as such is by no means a root of evil; on the contrary, it is truly a divine life, if one is not bored. **794**

Idleness, like kisses, to be sweet must be stolen. **797**

If all the year were playing holidays, To sport would be as tedious as to work. **790**

If everything is under control, you're not going fast enough. **838**

Invention…arises directly from idleness, possibly also from laziness. To save oneself trouble. **817**

[It is] not that you won or lost, but how you played the game. **808**

It is not the mountain we conquer but ourselves. **836**

It's just a job. Grass grows, birds fly, waves pound the sand. I beat people up. **818**

It's not whether you get knocked down; it's whether you get up. **809**

Leadership, like coaching, is fighting for the hearts and souls of men and getting them to believe in you. **827**

Love is the most important thing in the world, but baseball is pretty good, too. **825**

Man is so made that he can only find relaxation from one kind of labor by taking up another. **796**

Nobody cares about the bronze or silver medals. **839**

Nowhere can a man find a quieter or more untroubled retreat than in his own soul. **788**

Oh, that I had wings like a dove! I would fly away and be at rest. **787**

One man practising sportsmanship is far better than a hundred teaching it. **801**

Persistence can change failure into extraordinary achievement. **837**

Retired Leisure, That in trim gardens takes his pleasure. **790**

Sports don't build character. They reveal it. **816**

Sports were theatrical events meant to fill a primal void created by the lack of bloodshed men craved. **839**

The busiest men have the most leisure. **793**

The chase, the sport of kings; image of war, without its guilt. **791**

The five S's of sports training are: stamina, speed, strength, skill, and spirit; but the greatest of these is spirit. **833**

The idea that the poor should have leisure has always been shocking to the rich. **806**

The more difficult the victory, the greater the happiness in winning. **830**

The most important thing in the Olympic Games is not to win, but to take part. **799**

The NFL, like life, is full of idiots. **834**

The nice guys are all over there, in seventh place. **808**

The only ones who remember when you come second are your wife and your dog. **826**

The will to win is important, but the will to prepare is vital. **833**

There is no wisdom without leisure. **787**

There's never enough time to do all the nothing you want. **824**

They think it's all over…It is now. **814**

Time you enjoy wasting is not wasted time. **800**

We're all given some sort of skill in life. Mine just happens to be beating up on people. **816**

What I most surely know in the long run about morality and the obligations of men, I owe to sport. **811**

What is this life if, full of care, we have no time to stand and stare? **799**

When I play with my cat, who knows whether I do not make her more sport than she makes me? **789**

When you win, say nothing; when you lose, say less. **820**

Women are around all the time but World Cups come only once every four years. **835**

Work is not always required of a man. There is such a thing as sacred idleness. **795**

You are never really playing an opponent. You are playing yourself, your own highest standards, and when you reach your limits, that is real joy. **823**

You have to have a real love of your sport to carry you through all the bad times. **832**

You miss 100 percent of the shots you don't take. **821**

Technology

A bad workman blames his tools. **695**

A determined soul will do more with a rusty monkey wrench than a loafer will accomplish with all the tools in a machine shop. **718**

Any coward can sit in his home and criticize a pilot for flying into a mountain in fog. But I would rather, by far, die on a mountainside than in bed. **710**

Any sufficiently advanced technology is indistinguishable from magic. **716**

Everywhere we remain unfree and chained to technology, whether we passionately affirm or deny it. **713**

Genius is one percent inspiration, ninety-nine percent perspiration. **707**

Give me but one firm spot on which to stand and I will move the Earth. **693**

Having found the bomb we have used it. **713**

Here's to the crazy ones: the misfits; the rebels; the troublemakers; the round pegs in the square holes; the ones who see things differently. **723**

I haven't failed, I've found 10,000 ways that don't work. **700**

If I'd asked people what they wanted, they would have said a faster horse. **703**

If you are building a house and a nail breaks, do you stop building or do you change the nail? **700**

If your only tool is a hammer, you will see every problem as a nail. **715**

In the twenty-first century, the robot will take the place which slave labor occupied in ancient civilization. **709**

Invention, it must be humbly admitted, does not consist in creating out of void, but out of chaos. **697**

Man is a tool-using animal…Without tools he is nothing, with tools he is all. **698**

Men of genius sometimes accomplish most when they work the least. **694**

One machine can do the work of fifty ordinary men. No machine can do the work of one extraordinary man. **701**

Our inventions mirror our secret wishes. **715**

Please, no matter how we advance technologically, please don't abandon the book. **727**

Technological progress has merely provided us with more efficient means for going backwards. **709**

Technology is a useful servant but a dangerous master. **702**

Technology is dominated by two types of people: those who understand what they do not manage, and those who manage what they do not understand. **718**

Technology is the knack of so arranging the world that we don't have to experience it. **714**

The important thing to remember is that the Internet is not a new form of life. It is just a new activity. **720**

[The Internet] ought to be like clay, rather than a sculpture that you observe from a distance. **724**

The true creator is necessity, who is the mother of our invention. **692**

The Wright brothers flew right through the smokescreen of impossibility. **711**

We are stuck with technology when what we really want is just stuff that works. **725**

We owe to the Middle Ages the two worst inventions of humanity – romantic love and gunpowder. **702**

What gunpowder did for war the printing press has done for the mind. **699**

When I took office, only high-energy physicists had ever heard of what is called the World Wide Web…Now even my cat has its own page. **721**

Wherever smart people work, doors are unlocked. **726**

You ain't heard nothing yet. **704**

Life & Death

"The Lord blessed the latter part of Job's life more than the former part."

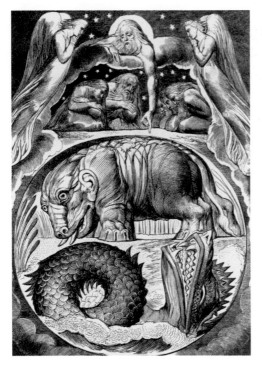

The satanic Behemoth and Leviathan from William Blake's illustrations of the Book of Job.

Book of Job

Chapter 42

c. 700 BCE

This important passage in the Old Testament of the Bible reassures the faithful that they can be rewarded on Earth, as well as in heaven.

When God holds up Job as an exemplary model of behaviour, Satan suggests that this man is good only because he's living a comfortable life – he's rich and has a dutiful wife, sons and daughters. If God were to take away the foundations of Job's happiness, the Devil claims, his base nature would become apparent. God allows Satan to test Job's faith and the Devil afflicts him with a plague of boils. His three friends tell him that he has brought his misfortunes on himself by being sinful ('Job's comforters' is a term now used to describe people whose comments make a bad situation worse).

But Job keeps the faith: he holds hard to the belief that since we receive good from God, we must also be prepared to receive bad things; as he says: 'The Lord gave, and the Lord has taken away; may the name of the Lord be praised.' Moreover, Job is sure that he has done nothing to deserve this treatment and that all will come right in the end. It does; at the end of his trials, Job is amply compensated by God for his patience. JP

"*Fortune favours the bold.*"

Ennius
Annales 257
c. 200 BCE

According to Macrobius, a Roman historian of the 5th century CE, this quotation first appeared in a section (now lost) of work by the poet Ennius – in the original Latin, it read '*Audentis Fortuna iuvat.*'

Virgil used the same words verbatim in Book X, line 284, of the *Aeneid* (19 BCE). If Macrobius's attribution is correct, that does not make the later writer a plagiarist, however: it was probably a literary allusion that the earliest readers and listeners would have recognized instantly, and appreciated; moreover, less than a single hexameter out of an epic poem of nearly 10,000 lines hardly counts as a copycat crime.

Since these earliest occurrences, the notion has appeared repeatedly in numerous works, either unchanged or with the replacement of 'bold' by '. brave. It has been adopted as a motto by numerous families and organizations. It may, of course, be taken at face value: as a straightforward exhortation. Conversely, it might be interpreted as an equivocation, a misleading prophecy: many actions are thought brave only if they are successful; those that end in failure are often rated as foolish whether or not courage was required. JP

◉ The Wheel of Fortune (*Rota Fortunae*) from a 13th-century manuscript of *Carmina Burana*.

"One man's meat is another man's poison."

Lucretius
De rerum natura
c. 100 BCE

The idea that all preferences are relative, and that no generalizations can reasonably be made about them, is probably older than civilization itself. It almost certainly predates Roman poet Lucretius, but it is his version that is widely regarded as the classic instance – and justly, too, because although the sentiment may be commonplace, this is a prime example of true wit, which Alexander Pope defined as 'what oft was thought, but ne'er so well express'd'.

The original line in Latin was '*quod ali cibus est aliis fuat acre venenum*' ('what is food for one person may be bitter poison to others'). Later, the axiom infiltrated most, and possibly all, local languages in the Roman Empire. In English, the oldest recorded occurrence of the expression is in the autobiography of composer Thomas Whythorne (c. 1576). By the early 17th century, the phrase had evidently been reduced to the familiarity of cliché: in 1604, the playwright Thomas Middleton described it as 'that old moth-eaten proverb'.

Another Latin adage that covers the same ground is '*de gustibus non est disputandum*,' which may be loosely translated as 'there's no accounting for taste'. JP

"Carpe diem."

Horace
Odes
13 BCE

Some Latin adages are easy to render in other languages. A few are difficult to translate because they are enigmatic and their exact meaning elusive. '*Et in Arcadia ego*' ('I too am in Arcadia') is a prime example of this type – what exactly does it mean? No one really knows.

Other maxims resist translation because they encompass so much in far fewer words than would be possible in any other language. '*Carpe diem*' literally means 'Seize the day,' yet although that is a common rendering, it fails to convey the rich underlying meaning, which is similar to that of 'Let us eat and drink, for tomorrow we die,' a phrase that occurs repeatedly in the Bible in Isaiah 22, Proverbs 23, and I Corinthians 15.

The basic idea is that we should enjoy the moment and try not to worry about anything that led up to it or that may happen in the future. Some people might think that this is an early form of existentialism – that the past has no bearing on the future and that each moment is hermetically sealed from every other – but Horace was a poet of common sense and normality, not of high-falutin' intellectual concepts. JP

◑ The poet Horace, depicted greeting visitors at his home.

Time is a vindictive bandit to steal the beauty of our former selves.

Raphael
Attributed
1519

A painter whose works are widely held to rival those of Leonardo da Vinci and Michelangelo as the greatest achievements of the High Renaissance, Raphael (Rafaello Sanzio) was born in Urbino, Italy, in 1483. His life was intensely productive – 300 images of the Madonna were merely a fraction of his prolific output – but lamentably brief: he died on 6 April 1520, his thirty-seventh birthday, which was young, even for the period.

The above quotation continues thus: 'We are left with sagging, rippled flesh, and burning gums with empty socks.' To have such a strong sense of physical decay and, by extension, of transience, may seem remarkable in one so young, but, as an artist, Raphael would have had a heightened awareness of the human body and was perhaps able to see decline much earlier than other people, who tend to notice their deterioration only after the process is well established.

Nevertheless, we should not be too surprised that such a feeling should be so strong in one so young. English Victorian poet Matthew Arnold wrote the powerful and pessimistic 'Growing Old' before reaching the age of twenty-seven. **JP**

To thine own self be true.

William Shakespeare
Hamlet
c. 1601

This remark, the importance of which is heralded by the phrase that immediately precedes it – 'This above all' – comes at the conclusion of a fairly long (thirty-line) speech by Polonius to his son, Laertes. The complete passage is full of sensible advice, including the equally famous lines 'Give every man thine ear, but few thy voice' and 'Neither a borrower nor a lender be.'

If the advice is so good, one may wonder why the speaker is almost invariably played in production as an insufferable old bore – but that may be at the heart of the problem of *Hamlet*: that, as the little boy is reputed to have said, it is full of quotations, perhaps too many.

The meaning of this particular remark is clear, and unlike much else in the play, unambiguous: the precept requires that one should never do anything with which one feels uncomfortable, physically, spiritually or morally.

The trick is to recognize such discomfort before the point at which we can no longer extricate ourselves from it. Thus, it is important to 'Know thyself', a motto written up in the ancient Greek temple of Delphi. **JP**

❷ Depiction of a performance of *Hamlet* in an Elizabethan theatre.

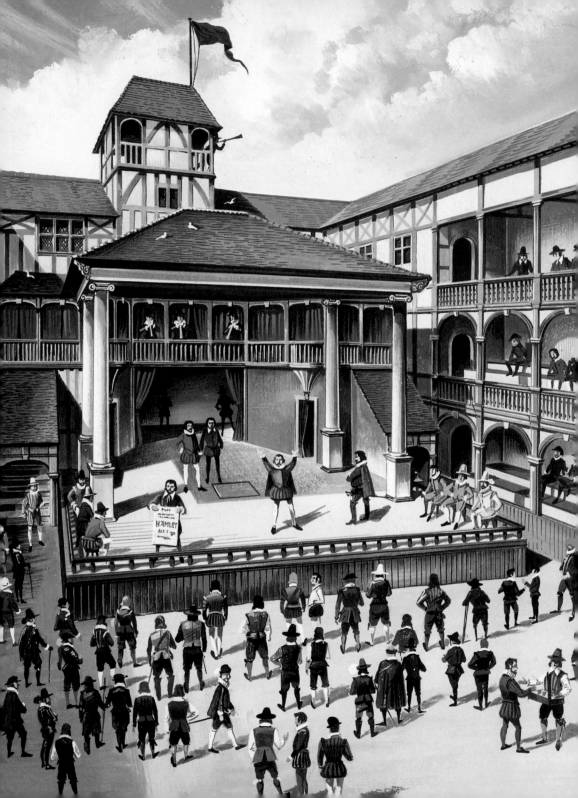

"Death comes equally to us all, and makes us all equal when it comes."

John Donne
Sermons
1621

English metaphysical poet John Donne was a lusty Roman Catholic in his youth, but he later converted to Protestantism and became a deeply devout and pious Church minister in the service of King James I.

This quotation from a sermon in London's St Paul's Cathedral, of which Donne was dean from 1621, was no doubt intended to help his parishioners reconcile themselves to their inevitable fate and to accept that this is the way of all flesh. Such stoicism may appear rather at odds with the wordplay that had led the younger Donne to conclude his 1609 sonnet titled 'Death Be Not Proud' with the defiant line: 'And death shall be no more; Death, thou shalt die.' (This is an allusion to I Corinthians 15 in the New Testament of the Bible: 'The last enemy that shall be destroyed is Death.')

There again, to a person of true faith in any of the Abrahamic religions (Judaism, Christianity and Islam), there is no contradiction here because God's promise of everlasting life means that death is even more transient than human existence on Earth – it is not a destination, as the pessimists fear, but merely a route to eternal glory in heaven above. **JP**

"It is always darkest just before the Day dawneth."

Thomas Fuller
A Pisgah-Sight of Palestine and the Confines Thereof, 1650

Thomas Fuller was an English churchman and historian, and a prolific writer. The Pisgah in the title of this work was the name of a high hill with a commanding view over the Holy Land.

The idea expressed here has become something of a proverbial commonplace, but there is no earlier recorded expression of it. It is unknown whether Fuller coined the phrase or was merely following previously established usage. (In the 1850s, Irish songwriter Samuel Lover claimed, without any supporting evidence, that the expression had been used in Ireland for hundreds of years.)

Among the best-known subsequent versions of the phrase was in 'Dedicated to the One I Love,' a pop song by Lowman Pauling and Ralph Bass, which was a hit for The Shirelles in 1959 and the Mamas and the Papas in 1967 – 'The darkest hour is just before dawn.'

It is worth noting that there is no scientific evidence to support this assertion. It is not necessarily any darker at this time of the night than any other. However, that does not weaken the point, which is metaphorical: it is often just when we think that everything is hopeless that matters begin to improve. **JP**

"Living well is the best revenge."

George Herbert
Jacula Prudentum
1651

In addition to being a highly influential English metaphysical and religious poet, George Herbert was an inveterate collector of idiomatic verbal expressions. His first publication in this area was *Outlandish Proverbs Selected by Mr. G. H.*, in 1640. Twelve years later, he produced an expanded version of this work under the title *Jacula Prudentum*, in which the above quotation first appeared in print.

The underlying meaning is that people should never give their enemies the satisfaction of knowing that they have upset or hurt them; that no matter how great the humiliation to which one has been subjected, one must carry on as if undiminished by hostility and malice – put a brave face on it all.

In his youth, actor Rob Lowe was a Hollywood hell-raiser. Around the time he starred in *The Outsiders* (1983), people said he was going to destroy himself, almost certainly professionally and probably physically as well. But he cleaned up his act, married, had children and thirty years later he told *The Huffington Post* that he'd been inspired to go straight by the thought of the satisfaction he would thereby deny his detractors: 'Living well is the best revenge,' he said. **JP**

"They also serve who only stand and wait."

John Milton
'On His Blindness'
1673

This is the concluding line of Milton's great sonnet, 'On His Blindness,' which opens with the line: 'When I consider how my light is spent.'

When the poet lost his sight in 1652 – doctors had warned him, but he took none of their recommended precautions – he feared that he would be unable to work any longer, and this poem expresses a resignation to what he regards as the will of God – the victim does not rail against his fate. The theological doctrine that underlies Milton's thought process here is that since God is omniscient and omnipotent, there is nothing that we can do that has not been planned and approved by Him; consequently, there is nothing to complain about, because it is all part of a bigger picture, even though we may not as individuals be able to perceive the greater purpose as a whole or even in part.

As events transpired, the next fifteen years were the most productive of Milton's life. During this period he dictated to his amanuenses one of the greatest epic poems in the English language, *Paradise Lost* (twelve books; a total of more than 10,000 lines); its sequel, *Paradise Regained* (four books; a little over 2,000 lines); and a full-length poetic drama, *Samson Agonistes*. **JP**

" The months and days are the travellers of eternity. The years that come and go are also voyagers. "

Matsuo Bashō

Oku no Hosomichi

1689

Matsuo Bashō's *Oku no Hosomichi* – sometimes rendered in English as 'The Narrow Road to the Deep North' – is a work in prose and verse that tells the story of a poet's journey to a cold, inhospitable and even dangerous region of early Edo period Japan. Bashō takes on the role of wandering traveller and priest, exploring both the land and its spiritual history. His book expresses a personal freedom that was almost unknown in the strictly regimented society of its time.

Oku no Hosomichi is one of the most popular works of classical Japanese literature. It is so beloved that when the book's three-hundredth anniversary was celebrated in 1989, millions of fans re-created Bashō's journey.

Much of the appeal of the work lies in its synthesis of travelogue and spiritual quest, and its metaphorical reflections on life. Bashō says that we move through the days and months of our lives in the same way as travellers move through the lands they visit; stopping only briefly, meeting people, making friendships that cannot last forever, and leaving a fleeting remnant of our existence. Our lives are but a transitory exploration of a small corner of Earth. **MT**

" 'Tis impossible to be sure of any thing but death and taxes. "

Christopher Bullock

The Cobler of Preston, a Farce

c. 1716

Endlessly misattributed – frequently to Benjamin Franklin, sometimes to Mark Twain – the earliest version of this famous observation is in Bullock's dramatic farce, in which a shoemaker is duped into thinking that he is a justice of the peace. When a complainant brought before him starts his evidence with the words: 'But I am sure. . . ,' the drunken cobbler interrupts him at once, saying: 'You lie, you are not sure,' and then adding the above remark for good measure.

Today, the line is most often quoted in cynical reference to governments, but in the original, the emphasis is on uncertainty: the judge–cobbler can be certain of nothing – neither his own identity, nor the evidence of his senses. The focus of the phrase here is therefore more philosophical than satirical.

There were two plays entitled *The Cobler of Preston*, both written at around the same time, a year after the Jacobite Rising of 1715. Both are similar and loosely based on Shakespeare's *The Taming of the Shrew*. Charles Johnson's play, a political satire, is better known and widely regarded as the superior work, but it is Bullock's that gave the world this quotation. **LW**

❯ A print of a cobbler's shop (c.1559–91) by Jost Amman.

"You can't make an omelette without breaking eggs."

An Old Woman Cooking Eggs, a painting of 1618 by Spanish artist Diego Velázquez.

French Proverb
Unknown
c. 1740

Originating in French, this proverb was first made famous by François Athanase de Charette de la Contrie, a military commander who led royalist forces against French Revolutionaries in the War of the Vendée, during which tens of thousands were massacred. Defeated and brought to trial in 1796, Charette admitted to causing deaths, but used the above phrase to justify his actions (he was found guilty and shot by firing squad). The earliest recorded use of it in English is dated 1859.

The implication is that there will inevitably be casualties of success. The proverb is often used in political, business or military contexts to explain away regrettable side effects of a chosen course of action – 'collateral damage' – while also indicating that the end result will nonetheless be beneficial.

The phrase is fundamentally flawed, however, resting as it does on the assumption that there is an equivalence between the act of breaking eggs and much more morally dubious processes, such as bombing people by using drones. In cases of the latter, whether defending a monarchy or imposing a new government, the ends rarely justify the means. **LW**

"Whenever you do a thing, act as if all the world were watching."

Thomas Jefferson
Letter to Peter Carr
1785

'Whenever you are to do a thing, though it can never be known but to yourself, ask yourself how you would act were all the world looking at you, and act accordingly.' These are the words of advice that Thomas Jefferson wrote from Paris to his nephew Peter Carr.

While in France, Jefferson learned of the death of his youngest daughter, Lucy, from whooping cough. He insisted that the best way to protect her older sister, Mary, was to have her join him in France and asked that someone responsible should accompany the child.

The person chosen was fourteen-year-old Sally Hemings, a slave. Jefferson was then forty-four years old. He began a relationship with Sally soon after she arrived, and by the time she was sixteen, she was pregnant. It is likely that Jefferson fathered all six of Sally's children. At first sight, the above quotation may seem like advice along the same lines as Jesus Christ's 'Do as you would be done by.' But in the light of Jefferson's personal conduct it could be advice to cover your tracks. Perhaps 'act accordingly' here is coded advice to take steps to avoid violating the so-called 'Eleventh Commandment': 'Thou shalt not get caught.' **LW**

⊘ Thomas Jefferson was the third president of the United States. His words here could be taken more than one way.

"*The Child is father of the Man.*"

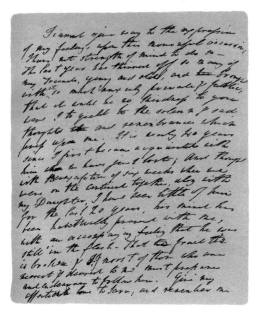

William Wordsworth
'My Heart Leaps Up'
1802

Wordsworth wrote 'My Heart Leaps Up' in 1802; it was first published five years later in *Poems, in Two Volumes*. The poem is also known by the alternative title of 'The Rainbow'.

The basic idea of this simple, nine-line lyric is that the poet liked rainbows when he was young, that he still likes them in adulthood and he hopes to go on enjoying them for as long as he lives. The suggestion is that the preferences of youth – in this case, for the wonders of nature – determine the tastes of maturity.

Nothing original here, perhaps, but the above line is the most widely used exemplar of the paradox – for a moment, the reader may think, 'that's absurd: it's the wrong way round; obviously the man is father of the child'; but then, a moment later, the real meaning dawns.

Another English poet, Gerard Manley Hopkins, later wrote an eight-line verse in which he responded to the Wordsworth original as follows:

"'The child is father to the man."
How can he be? The words are wild.'

But it is clear that Hopkins was joking; he knew perfectly well what 'My Heart Leaps Up' really meant. **LW**

"*A thing of beauty is a joy forever.*"

John Keats
Endymion
1818

The above quotation is the opening line of Keats's long Romantic poem in rhyming couplets about the mythological Greek shepherd who loved, and was beloved by, the Moon goddess, Selene. It continues:

'Its loveliness increases; it will never
Pass into nothingness.'

On first publication, *Endymion* received a critical hammering. Almost none of the reviewers liked it, and their criticisms were scathing. But Keats was undeterred and went on to produce, in the *Poems of 1820*, several of the greatest odes in the English language. After the poet's death in 1821, at the age of twenty-five, *Endymion* was revalued upward. It was no longer seen as an artistic catastrophe but rather as the work of a prentice hand on its way to becoming a master.

Yet readers still struggle with this opening. Although the lines are among the most famous in literature, many people regard them as just unsubstantiated assertion: saying something doesn't make it true. It may be taken as an allusion to the function of memory – that the past is never over; it exists again whenever we call it to mind – but Keats doesn't actually say that. JE

⊘ This painting of Keats (1821–23) is by his friend Joseph Severn, who accompanied the poet on his trip to Rome, Italy.

" With consistency a great soul has simply nothing to do. "

▲ A drawing of Emerson delivering a lecture on philosophy to a gathering in Concord, Massachusetts.

Ralph Waldo Emerson
Essays
1841

The above quotation is taken from the essay titled 'Self-Reliance,' in which Emerson contends that any attempt to reduce existence or experience to a system inhibits thought and creativity ('soul') – that there is no point in trying to develop an all-embracing theory of anything, because in reality, one size never fits all.

The idea is similar to that later expressed in Walt Whitman's 'Song of Myself' (1855):

'Do I contradict myself?
Very well then I contradict myself,
(I am large, I contain multitudes.)'

Here again, the suggestion is that a fulfilled life of the mind is one in which every thought may be subjected to renewed scrutiny at any time.

In a perfect world, there are no prejudices, no predispositions, no idées fixes, no received wisdom. As Emerson also writes: 'A foolish consistency is the hobgoblin of little minds, adored by little statesmen and philosophers and divines.' These sideswipes at groups to whom Emerson felt antipathy are gratuitous, but the basic point remains unweakened – that consistency may render the soul redundant. **JP**

"To strive, to seek, to find, and not to yield."

Alfred, Lord Tennyson
'Ulysses'
1842

When Alfred, Lord Tennyson, published his third book of poetry in 1842, it marked the end of a ten-year period during which the future poet laureate had published nothing. Tennyson's 1833 book of poetry had met with stiff criticism, but the publication of his 1842 work cemented the writer's place as one of the most beloved poets of English literature.

In 'Ulysses', King Odysseus (Ulysses) looks back upon a life of triumph from a place of comfort and boredom. Having returned from the odyssey, and become king of Ithaca, the once-heroic young man now yearns for the challenges of years past, for the conquest of hardships in the struggle that made life worth living.

This final line of 'Ulysses', standing alone, has become a call to perseverance and tenacity, no matter the difficulty. In 2012 it was used as an inspirational maxim to greet the world's athletes at the entrance to the London Olympic village. The preceding lines leave no doubt that Tennyson was referring specifically to bravery in the face of ageing, but the quotation has taken on a life of its own, becoming a call to the human spirit, and a plea never to give up in the face of adversity. **MT**

This portrait of Alfred, Lord Tennyson, was painted in 1880 by John Everett Millais, when the poet was seventy-one years old.

I would rather die of passion than of boredom.

Émile Zola
Au Bonheur des Dames (The Ladies' Paradise)
1883

This is the eleventh of the twenty novels in Zola's Rougon-Macquart sequence, which also includes *Nana* (1880), *Germinal* (1885) and *La Bête Humaine* (1890).

The central character of *Au Bonheur des Dames*, Octave Mouret, runs a women's clothing store. He is a womanizer who dislikes women and pursues them mainly in the hope of deriving material advantage from them. When a friend asks him to explain his approach, Mouret extols unrequited lovers as laudable fighters of bold rearguard actions. When his friend suggests that such behaviour is merely an attempt to forget, Mouret announces that since we will all die, it is better to act passionately than to wait in mute acquiescence for our inevitable demise.

Mouret duly pursues Denise Baudu, one of his employees. Her consistent rejections of his advances inflame him, and his basic contempt for females is gradually eroded by his growing, genuine affection for this one woman in particular. Zola depicts their eventual marriage as a victory for the woman – Mouret thought he would conquer her, but she did that to him. **LW**

◀ Portrait of Émile Zola (1868) by Édouard Manet.

Because I could not stop for Death He kindly stopped for me.

Emily Dickinson
Poems
1890

The narrator in Dickinson's poem could not stop, and neither can we. Being alive involves a particular kind of animation that only death can end. The quotation is a hit because it reverses expectations: death does not come knocking on a door behind which we freeze; instead, it scoops us off the treadmill and lets us rest.

We may believe in immortality, but all we know for certain is that death is both kind and cruel. It lifts us off the tracks we cannot help but travel. That is an act of kindness in light of the idea that we could not tolerate a life of eternal suffering. On the other hand, we fear losing all that we know and love and falling apart, or facing the three possible futures that death may bring: paradise, damnation or nothing. Death is also closer to our everyday experience than eternal activity – it is more familiar. Every day ends with sleep, which is a little death, and bouts of strenuous activity are followed by periods of rest that foreshadow our ultimate destination.

Emily Dickinson never saw this poem published. Death came for her in 1886, when she was fifty-five years old. She foresaw 'a great darkness' while she was still in the midst of living. **LW**

" *Character, not circumstances, makes the man.* "

Booker T Washington
'Democracy and Education'
1896

In a speech to the Institute of Arts and Science in Brooklyn, New York, African American rights campaigner Booker T Washington argued that the iniquities and injustices inflicted on black people in the South adversely affected people of all races throughout the United States and that all Americans should unite to oppose them.

He told his audience that crime damages the criminal as much as the victim:

'Physical death comes to the one Negro lynched in a county, but death of the morals – death of the soul – comes to the thousands responsible for the lynching.'

He then said, of black people in general: 'We are . . . patient, humble. . .We can afford to work and wait. There is plenty in this country for us to do. . .If others would be little, we can be great. If others would be mean, we can be good. If others would push us down, we can help push them up.' He then spoke the words quoted above. The inspiring message was that oppression does not dampen the human spirit; that the more the have-nots are deprived, the better they will be, and the more generously they will behave when their ultimate, inevitable liberation is achieved. **MT**

" *Once at least in his life each man walks with Christ to Emmaus.* "

Oscar Wilde
De Profundis
1897

Wilde wrote *De Profundis* during his imprisonment; it was not published until 1905, five years after his death. The work took the form of an open letter to Lord Alfred Douglas; it was the two men's relationship that had led to Wilde's arrest and conviction.

The beauty of this work is that Wilde abandons the wordplay that had made his fortune – epigrams such as 'The truth is rarely pure, and never simple' – and here writes intelligently and honestly about some of his deepest feelings.

The reference in the above quotation is to the Gospel according to St Luke in the New Testament of the Bible, in which there is a story of two men on a walk from Jerusalem, who are joined by a stranger who asks them what's been in the news recently. They tell him that Jesus has been crucified. The stranger says that that's the fulfillment of a prophecy in the Old Testament. And then he unaccountably disappears. It is only after he has gone that the two men realize that they have been talking to the risen Christ. Wilde appears to be suggesting that everyone finds the truth – 'once at least' – but may not identify it until it has evaded his or her grasp. **JP**

"Whatever you are, try to be a good one."

William Makepeace Thackeray
Attributed
1897

The above quotation appears in *A Boy I Knew and Four Dogs*, a memoir by Laurence Hutton, literary editor of *Harper's Magazine*. The writer recounts his meeting as a small child in the 1850s with the author of *Vanity Fair* during one of his lecture tours of the United States. Thackeray asked the boy what he wanted to be when he grew up, and the boy replied 'A farmer, sir.' And Thackeray (who perhaps didn't have much to say about that occupation) came back with this riposte.

In 1904, extracts from Hutton's book were serialized in the *Boston Herald* newspaper, whose editor cut the words 'try to' from the original. And that's the way the remark has often since been quoted, almost as often as it has been falsely attributed to a host of other big names, most notably Abraham Lincoln, in collections of quotations. There is no compelling evidence that the sixteenth US president ever said any such thing, but the fact remains that almost everyone has heard of him, whereas relatively few people know about Thackeray, and today, almost no one has heard of Hutton. And that's often the way of good remarks: they get pressed into the service of established aphorists. **LW**

A drawing of English novelist William Makepeace Thackeray from *The Maclise Portrait Gallery* (1898).

" *Speak softly and carry a big stick.* "

Theodore Roosevelt
Letter to Henry L Sprague
1900

As the youngest president of the United States, and the only holder of the office to have won a Congressional Medal of Honor, Theodore 'Teddy' Roosevelt was a man of action. The twenty-sixth president radically altered US foreign and domestic policies by breaking up powerful trusts, instituting national regulatory reforms, and ushering in the era of 'big stick' diplomacy.

Roosevelt's first use of what became his catchphrase was in this letter dated 26 January 1900, where he describes it as 'a West African proverb'. His version was an abbreviation: in full, the proverb reads: 'Speak softly and carry a big stick; you will go far.'

He first aired the phrase in public on 2 September 1901 at the Minnesota State Fair. At the time, he was vice president, but eleven days later, President William McKinley was assassinated. On taking over at the White House, Roosevelt was able to put the advice of the proverb into practice and give the maxim a living, breathing embodiment; the big stick he used was the US Navy, one of the largest armed maritime forces in the world. One of his major achievements was to build the Panama Canal, and his soft voice won him the Nobel Prize for Peace in 1906. **MT**

◀ A contemporary cartoon of Roosevelt with his big stick.

" *Just have one more try — it's dead easy to die, It's the keeping-on-living that's hard.* "

Robert W Service
'The Quitter'
1912

British-born Canadian poet Robert Service gained fame with his poems about the rough conditions, and people, of northwestern Canada. Even though Service was a bank clerk and ranch hand on Vancouver Island years after the Klondike Gold Rush, his works earned him admiration and the nickname 'Bard of the Yukon'.

'The Quitter,' of which these are the closing lines, is a poem about the difficulty of facing the hardships that life can throw at us, about persevering in the face of overwhelming difficulty. It is commonly misattributed to geologist Douglas Mawson, leader of the 1911 Australian Antarctic Expedition. In late 1912, Mawson and two fellow explorers met with disaster on a sledge trip into the interior reaches of the southernmost continent. Mawson was the only one to come out alive, finally being rescued in December 1913.

Mawson, perhaps more than most, understood the hardships that mere survival can require. We are all mortal, and age spares us no indignities. Enduring pain, hopelessness and grief in the face of inevitability can be by far the harder path, even when death is the only alternative. **MT**

> ❝ *Two roads diverged in a wood, and I – I took the one less traveled by, And that has made all the difference.* ❞

⬦ Robert Frost was a master of poetry without poeticism, and of the rhythms of natural speech.

Robert Frost
'The Road Not Taken'
1920

Advertisements, songs, episode titles and at least one video game have used these lines as a whole or in part. The poem itself is one of the best known in the English-speaking world, yet many readers misunderstand it. The commonplace interpretation is that this is a paean to triumphant self-assertion. While that is both excusable and even justifiable, there is a certain irony in the vast majority conforming to a particular reading when the subject matter in question is apparently nonconformity.

In the original, neither road is less travelled: both are equally worn. The point is to show that we must choose, and we make up stories later to justify those choices. Yet, the emblem of a fork in the road, and the effect of taking one route rather than another, is deeply resonant.

Our neural pathways are branched like many-forked roads. We ourselves are unique in the paths we take and condemned to react in preordained ways by the limitations of our experience and physiology. We can be self-aware about our choices and mercilessly manipulated by circumstance. The symbol of divergent roads is like the first division of one cell into two, and just as significant. **LW**

"Live fast, die young, and leave a good-looking corpse."

Irene L Luce
Letter to Oscar B Luce
1920

Many versions of this injunction exist, but the first instance of the full statement appears in a letter quoted during matrimonial proceedings covered in the California newspaper the *Riverside Daily Press*. On the basis of Irene Luce's bold and perhaps rash assertion – 'I can't be bothered with a husband...I intend to live a fast life, die young, and be a beautiful corpse' – her husband was granted a divorce.

The context of the quotation reveals a young person's struggle for freedom from convention, which is poignant, given the outcome of the case. The young are well known for romantically trifling with the idea of death, partly because death seems so much more distant to them than it does to older generations. But in the British television series *The Office* (2001) Ricky Gervais gave it a postmodern twist: 'Live fast, sure, live too bloody fast sometimes, but die young? Die old! That's the way.'

Luce's original remark is really about breaking the rules. 'Live fast' is a mantra of youth; 'die young,' or as it was in earlier iterations, 'die fast,' reflects a sense of urgency in an age of uncertainty. Concern about the look of the cadaver reflects a stage of life at which personal appearance counts for everything.

Although the quotation expresses the rebelliousness of youth, Gervais is more percipient. If life is all there is, being a rebel is all very well, but survival is what really matters, and no one should care what it looks like. **LW**

"Things fall apart; the centre cannot hold."

W B Yeats
'The Second Coming'
1920

One of the most anthologized poems in the English language, 'The Second Coming' was written in many versions, but these seven words persist unchanged in each reworking. This particular phrase is followed by: 'Mere anarchy is loosed upon the world,/The blood-dimmed tide is loosed, and everywhere/The ceremony of innocence is drowned./The best lack all conviction, while the worst/Are full of passionate intensity.'

Yeats began the poem in January 1919, with the political and military aftershocks of the Easter Rising of 1916 and World War I (1914–18) still disrupting the social, political and physical landscape of his native Ireland. Respect for authority, the observance of traditions and the cohesion of the old class-dominated social order had been lost, perhaps irrevocably, and the disappearance of a sense of the common good had left a vacuum that was filled only by anger and despair. Yeats himself had reached a critical stage in his life, too. This poem, which marks a significant point in the poet's development, was first published in the US transcendentalist magazine *The Dial*, and it formed part of the book of verse that followed, *Michael Robartes and the Dancer* (1921).

Nigerian author Chinua Achebe used the first three words of the above quotation as the title of a novel, published in 1958, about the disintegration of Western colonialism in West Africa. *Things Fall Apart* echoes the idea in Yeats's original that of all the possible forms of destruction, it is that of a personal sense of continuity which most fundamentally matters. **LW**

> *" This is the way the*
> *world ends*
> *Not with a bang*
> *but a whimper. "*

T S Eliot
'The Hollow Men'
1925

The poem from which the above quotation is taken was published three years after *The Waste Land* and is sometimes regarded as a sort of coda to that work.

However, 'The Hollow Men' is much bleaker than its predecessor. This is by no means to suggest that *The Waste Land* is upbeat and optimistic; nevertheless, the opening lines of that work – 'April is the cruelest month, breeding/Lilacs out of the dead land' – suggest the possibility of regeneration. 'The Hollow Men' has no such optimism; it features 'Shape without form, shade without color' and endeavours to 'avoid speech'; much of its sparse text is deliberately repetitive, and incantatory in a way that may suggest a funeral dirge.

Here, then, in a poem of fewer than 500 words, is encapsulated the central problem of Eliot. Some readers regard his poetry as a much-needed rejection of what Lee Oser has termed 'romantic self-infatuation'; others, while accepting that the overwhelming sense of futility pervading Eliot's verse is a fine representation of the despair felt at the end of World War I, take the less charitable view that it is, in its way, no less egotistical than the most florid verse of the 19th century. **JP**

> *" Candy*
> *Is dandy*
> *But liquor*
> *Is quicker. "*

Ogden Nash
'Reflections on Ice-breaking'
1931

The master of the light verse, who claimed to have thought in rhyme from the age of six, Ogden Nash was one of the most beloved US poets of the 20th century. Upon his death in 1971, *The New York Times* commented that his 'droll verse with its unconventional rhymes made him the country's best-known producer of humorous poetry'. He took on various jobs in his youth, including teaching and staff writing at the *New Yorker*. In 1931 he published his first collection of poems, *Hard Lines*, which included the above verse, which advises on how to behave at a party. The book was an immediate success and made Nash a popular guest on comedy and radio shows. He toured the United States and Britain, giving lectures at universities. He also collaborated with librettist S J Perelmen and composer Kurt Weill on the musical *One Touch of Venus*. Nash's skilful observations of life include: 'People who work sitting down get paid more than people who work standing up' and 'Progress might have been all right once, but it has gone on too long.' **IHS**

❷ Poet Ogden Nash at work at his desk in 1952.

" Human kind Cannot bear very much reality. "

T S Eliot
'Burnt Norton'
1935

This quotation should inspire as well as temper our approach to life and death. Reality is an abyss into which we look with horror, and we must perforce distract ourselves from the enormity of what we face – the emptiness that stretches into eternity before and beyond us – or else we will shatter. In politics, too, we often prefer lies, half-truths, state-sponsored propaganda and wishful thinking to the often hideous truth.

In admonishing humanity for its shortcomings, its failure to shoulder the burden of truth, Eliot has the bird in the poem call 'Go!' three times. We cannot bear reality, and reality does not expect us to bear it. We will collapse, we will avoid, but this is not because we are hopeless. It is simply an acknowledgement of what we are: fallible, falling from birth towards death, falling apart and all the time holding ourselves together with stories and other crumbs of consolation.

Superficially, this line may seem downbeat and negative to the point of nihilism. But Eliot was a committed Christian; he believed in the life everlasting. Thus there is compassion in this observation, a metaphorical hand on the shoulder. **LW**

⚑ T S Eliot in 1959, looking pleased with a volume of his own verse, despite its sometimes lugubrious content.

"*Stop all the clocks, cut off the telephone.*"

W H Auden
'Funeral Blues'
1938

This line begins one of the most emotionally affecting works by the beloved British poet. It has had several incarnations, first as a biting satire, then as a tribute to victims of a sporting disaster and more recently, as a heartbreaking memorial eulogy.

Auden originally wrote this five-stanza poem, which poked fun at a dead politician, for the 1936 satirical verse play *The Ascent of F6*, a collaboration with Christopher Isherwood. In 1938, one stanza was removed, and the poem became part of the libretto for a cabaret, with music by Benjamin Britten. In the same year, the poem appeared in a celebrated anthology, and in 1940 it featured in Auden's collection *Another Time*, as one of 'Four Cabaret Songs for Miss Hedli Anderson'. It has appeared in many Auden anthologies. The poem was the English contribution to a statue commemorating the soccer fans who died in the 1985 Heysel Stadium disaster. This gave the poem a more mournful tone, which was emphasized further by its use in Mike Newell's movie *Four Weddings and a Funeral* (1994); here, it is spoken at a major character's memorial service, and it has often been used as a funeral oration since. **IHS**

British-born W H Auden sitting on a dock near his home in his adopted country of the United States in 1946.

Life shrinks or expands in proportion to one's courage.

Anaïs Nin
The Diary of Anaïs Nin
1939

Success did not come easily or quickly to Anaïs Nin, the Cuban-born, French-raised, US-domiciled author of around thirty works in several genres. She struggled for more than sixty years before the publication in 1966 of her seven-volume feminist diaries finally brought her acclaim. Later, her other works – such as *Delta of Venus*, *Little Birds*, *Henry and June* and *Incest* – made her name synonymous with erotica.

Nin's passionate, bohemian lifestyle, extensively detailed throughout her diaries, gained her a cultlike status among many young women during the late 1960s and for the greater part of the 1970s. Her literary status has not gone unchallenged, however: some critics have deplored her explicitness; a minority have found her work immature.

Nevertheless, even Nin's greatest detractors would be unlikely to deny that she was something of a trailblazer – one of the first women to write openly about physical attraction, a field that had previously been almost the exclusive preserve of male authors. She was thus at least a figure of historical, even if not of literary, importance. **MT**

If you are going through hell, keep going.

Winston Churchill
Attributed
c. 1940

There is no evidence that Churchill ever said this, but of all the people to whom the remark has been attributed, the British wartime prime minister is by far the most famous, and attaching his name to it gives it even more sonority than it might otherwise carry. It is the kind of thing he might have said during the Blitz. (The next most frequent attribution is to US self-help author Douglas Bloch, whose version is that the best advice we can give to those who say they are 'going through hell' is to tell them 'Don't stop!')

The sentiment itself is, of course, as old as the hills. Among the best-known (and best) expressions of it is in Shakespeare's *Macbeth*, where the tragic hero, beset by troubles of his own making, decides that there can be no going back:

'I am in blood
Stepped in so far that, should I wade no more,
Returning were as tedious as go o'er.'

But these lines are hard to quote accurately; the epigram here – Churchill or not, Churchillian or not – is much more readily memorable. **MT**

❯ London burns during the Blitz in 1940.

"Life is either a daring adventure or nothing."

○ Helen Keller (*left*) at a political rally with her secretary and companion, Polly Thompson, c. 1946.

Helen Keller
Let Us Have Faith
1940

At nineteen months of age, Helen Keller was left deaf and blind. In a period when most people assumed that such disabilities would deny anyone a fulfilling life, Keller defied the common wisdom. With the aid of her teacher, Anne M Sullivan, Keller learned to read, write and speak. At the age of twenty-four, she became the first deaf and blind person to receive a bachelor's degree, graduating cum laude from Radcliffe College, Massachusetts, in 1904.

Had Keller never written a word about herself or spoken publicly about her story, her life would have been inspirational enough. But Keller was not only a prolific author, having written a dozen books and numerous articles, she was also a world-renowned public speaker, activist and advocate for people with disabilities.

A woman of deep religious conviction, Keller wrote in *Let Us Have Faith* that she believed that avoiding dangers is no safer than seeking them out and that the timid are just as likely as the bold to meet disaster. For Keller, bravery in the face of seemingly overwhelming disabilities stemmed from her faith. But regardless of its source, her triumph in the face of adversity became an inspiration to the world. **MT**

"Do not go gentle into that good night."

Dylan Thomas
Botteghe Oscure
1951

This is the opening line of Dylan Thomas's most celebrated work, which was written when the poet was in Florence with his family in 1947. It was first published in the above named Italian literary journal and then in a collection of the poet's work, *In Country Sleep, and Other Poems*, in 1952, the year of his father's death.

It is a villanelle, a form more common in French verse than in English, which here consists of five three-line stanzas rhymed ABA, and a closing quatrain rhymed ABAA. The closing line – 'Rage, rage against the dying of the light'– has been interpreted by some as referring to his father losing his sight in old age.

The line has appeared in numerous cultural contexts, from three paintings of the 1950s by Welsh artist Ceri Richards, to innumerable quotations in music, films and plays. It was sung by rock artist John Cale on his 1989 album *Words for the Dying*. In an episode in 2007 of the BBC TV science-fiction serial *Doctor Who*, the time-travelling hero warns playwright William Shakespeare not to use the line because it is 'someone else's'. The line was also quoted by Michael Caine's character in the science-fiction movie *Interstellar* (2014). **ME**

◉ A Welshman, Dylan Thomas was a master of poetry in English and a well-known and popular broadcaster.

"Not all those who wander are lost."

☝ Elijah Wood as Frodo (*left*) and Viggo Mortensen as Strider in *The Lord of the Rings: The Fellowship of the Ring* (2001).

J R R Tolkien
The Lord of the Rings
1954

The above quotation is the second line of a poem that begins: 'All that is gold does not glitter.' In context, it refers to Strider, the ranger who is also a king (Aragorn), and hence greater than his poor appearance makes him seem. The poem represents a means of authenticating the man's character. It is also a kind of initiation verse.

Strider's pilgrimage is the necessary journey of one who has other things on his mind. His aim is to protect what is good from what is evil, no matter where that may lead him. In spite of his rough, wanderer's appearance, the words also denote his passage from outsider to rightful inheritor of a royal crown.

This line was later used in defence of the flower-power generation, the hippy counterculture of the 1960s. It has since been requisitioned by recruiters, adrenaline junkies and even home renters to justify their unwillingness to settle down to a fixed location.

All art is open to interpretation and revaluation, but there can come a point when the original meaning of the art is travestied and lost. It seems unlikely that Tolkien – a conservative, a Roman Catholic and a traditionalist – would have approved. **LW**

"Don't hide your scars. They make you who you are."

Frank Sinatra
Attributed
c. 1960

Well known for a sometimes brittle personality, Frank Sinatra didn't suffer fools gladly, although the warmth that he projected in his delivery of some of the greatest love songs ever written was also expressed in his personal life. He was an outspoken liberal who did much to promote race relations in the entertainment industry, but his past was clouded by an association with organized crime that he found hard to shake off. That, and a reputation for bursts of violence – particularly against intrusive reporters and paparazzi – meant that there were aspects of his past life that he couldn't deny.

There is also an analogy to physical disfigurements in the above quotation. Sinatra bore scars to his face from his birth, a forceps delivery. More concerned with the fate of his mother, the hospital staff laid the new-born infant to one side, his grandmother being the one who revived the baby under a cold tap. The scar on the left of Sinatra's face ran from the corner of his mouth, and as a teenager he was nicknamed Scarface. As a teen idol in the 1940s he tried to cover up the blemish, but by the 1960s he had admitted that, like the dubious aspects of his past, it made him what he was. **ME**

Sinatra hid the scar on the left side of his face for many years, but he later decided that his fans could stand his imperfections.

"You must do the thing you think you cannot do."

Eleanor Roosevelt
You Learn by Living
1960

In 'Fear – the Great Enemy' – a chapter in her successful self-help book *You Learn by Living: Eleven Keys for a More Fulfilling Life* – Eleanor Roosevelt recounts her youth and the sense of trepidation that she felt about the world. Her remedy was to accomplish tasks that caused her anxiety: 'The danger lies in refusing to face the fear, in not daring to come to grips with it. If you fail anywhere along the line it will take away your confidence. You must make yourself succeed every time.' She ends this passage with the above quotation.

The idea of outstaring one's demons isn't new. Among those who'd previously offered similar advice was Ralph Waldo Emerson, who stated in his 1841 essay 'Heroism' that you should 'always do what you are afraid to do'. (To which social reformer Jane Addams later commented: 'To do what you are afraid to do is to guide your life by fear. How much better not to be afraid to do what you believe in doing!') In 1997, Mary Schmich included the line 'Do one thing every day that scares you' in her column for the *Chicago Tribune*, the text of which was later used in Baz Luhrmann's 1999 hit single, 'Everybody's Free (to Wear Sunscreen)'. **IHS**

⊛ Eleanor Roosevelt in 1958, aged seventy-four years old.

❯ Eleanor Roosevelt addresses the 1956 Democratic National Convention in Chicago.

1956
DEMOCRATIC
NATIONAL
CONVENTION

"Not everything that can be counted counts, and not everything that counts can be counted."

W B Cameron
Informal Sociology
1963

This celebrated remark, often erroneously attributed to Albert Einstein, was, in fact, first made by US academic William Bruce Cameron in reference to the limitations of his own subject, sociology.

The remark was much more widely applicable, however, especially after the post-1980s zeitgeist seemed to demand that everything worthwhile had to be measurable and that there was no sphere of human activity that could not be enriched by analysis with graphs and charts.

We like knowing how much we have. Whether it is money, baseball bats or tea bags, an accurate accounting gives us a better understanding of our world and our place within it. Or, at least, it may.

Nevertheless, we also know that there's more to life than counting and more to living than numbers. What price do we put on our satisfaction? How many units of joy does a child provide? How much happiness lives in the bottom of a cup of coffee? If we value only those things that can be counted or measured, we diminish ourselves and the whole of existence. And, perhaps even more importantly, two things that happen at the same time are not necessarily cause and effect. **MT**

"The way to get started is to quit talking and begin doing."

Walt Disney
Attributed
1963

As far as quotations from the business community are concerned, Walt Disney's output was as prolific as that of Henry Ford. He is credited with the creation of countless verbal gems on life, work and commercial practice. And, like the automobile manufacturer, Disney is held responsible for much that he did not say, for the reason that an aphorism with an attribution packs more of a punch than all but the very best of uncredited wisecracks. The above remark is one of his more famous ones, but typically it lacks a verifiable source. Whether or not it is strictly authentic, it resembles many of the no-nonsense statements that Disney made in the course of his career: it sounds like an authentic quotation, even though it might not be one.

Certainly, it encapsulates Disney's vigorous approach to life. He set up his first company at the tender age of nineteen, and at twenty-seven years old introduced the world to Mickey Mouse. His career in the movies was defined by action, constant momentum and invention. As he once said of his company: 'Around here...we don't look backward for very long. We keep moving forward, opening up new doors and doing new things, because we're curious... and curiosity keeps leading us down new paths.' **IHS**

> # *Yesterday is gone. Tomorrow has not yet come. We have only today. Let us begin.*

Mother Teresa
Attributed
1977

Born Agnes Gonxha Bojaxhiu in 1910 in what is today Skopje, Macedonia, Mother Teresa was a nun, the founder of the Missionaries of Charity, and a widely venerated religious figure of the 20th century. The congregation she started dedicated itself to providing hospice care for the sick and dying in India, and for her life's work she received the 1979 Nobel Peace Prize.

Mother Teresa's oft-quoted call came from a discussion she had in Rotterdam, Netherlands, in 1977, with a bishop who asked her opinion about the future of the Church. She replied by quoting a clause of the Constitutions of the Missionaries of Charity, saying that she will 'allow the good God to make plans for the future – for yesterday has gone, tomorrow has not yet come and we only have today to make Him known, loved, and served'. The popularly cited version of the quotation given above lacks the religious context and an imperative has been added. It is less a statement about the future of the Roman Catholic Church, and more a reminder that we can only ever live in the present. If we want to act, we should resolve to begin today, for we can never know what tomorrow holds. **MT**

⊙ Mother Teresa, photographed with children; in 2003 she was beatified 'Blessed Teresa of Calcutta' for her charitable work.

" Life is what happens to you while you're busy making other plans. "

John Lennon
'Beautiful Boy (Darling Boy)'
1980

One of the standout tracks on the album *Double Fantasy* by John Lennon and Yoko Ono – released just three weeks before the former's murder on 8 December 1980 – 'Beautiful Boy' was dedicated to their son, Sean. In the light of Lennon's untimely and tragic death, the song – which starts with John comforting the five-year-old after he has had a nightmare and turns into a heartfelt paean of parental love – took on an even greater poignant significance.

The album went on to be a huge success worldwide, winning a 1981 Grammy Award as Album of the Year. In 1982, Paul McCartney chose the song as one of his all-time favourite tracks when he was a guest on the long-running UK radio show *Desert Island Discs*, and when Yoko Ono appeared on the same show in 2007 it was the only Lennon song that she chose.

The most quoted line from the song – 'Life is what happens to you while you're busy making other plans' – had actually been coined or cited many years earlier, in an article in *Reader's Digest* magazine in January 1957, where it was attributed to journalist Allen Saunders, who produced cartoons in collaboration with various artists. Saunders was best known for his writing for the syndicated US comic strips *Steve Roper and Mike Nomad*, *Mary Worth* and *Kerry Drake*. **ME**

" Twenty years from now you will be more disappointed by the things that you didn't do than by the ones that you did do. "

H Jackson Brown Jr
P. S. I Love You
1990

What do we remember most when we look back on our lives? Our joys? Our successes? The opportunities we missed because we were hesitant? Age and experience suggest it is the last.

Although the above quotation is widely attributed to Mark Twain, it doesn't appear in any of his known writings. It makes no appearance until author H Jackson Brown published *P. S. I Love You*, a book of inspirational sayings. Brown, who achieved greater success the following year with the self-help best seller *Life's Little Instruction Book*, writes of the words of wisdom passed on to him by his mother. Even so, the phrase remains incorrectly identified as a Twain witticism.

Regret can accompany us for a lifetime, and actions we never took can haunt us more than our mistakes. Do we skip taking a trip to save money? Do we stay in the secure but stressful job instead of taking the risk to start something on our own? The wisdom of Brown's mother suggests our fear of failure may haunt us more than failure itself. A risk may not be safe, but even a disastrous adventure can leave us feeling more fulfilled than the dissatisfaction of missed opportunities. **MT**

" A person doesn't have to change who he is to become better. "

Sidney Poitier
The Measure of a Man: A Spiritual Autobiography
2000

Few figures in US popular culture have been as revered as Sidney Poitier. His status as an icon is as much defined by his actions, dignity and charisma off the screen as it is by his on-screen roles.

Starting out on stage, Poitier moved into movie acting with a role in *No Way Out* (1950), but his breakthrough came with his spirited turn as a talented but rebellious student in *The Blackboard Jungle* (1955). He gained further acclaim as a runaway convict chained to a white prisoner, played by Tony Curtis, in *The Defiant Ones* (1958), and in 1963 he became the first African American to win an Academy Award for Best Actor, for *Lilies of the Field*.

A string of standout roles followed, in *The Bedford Incident* (1965), *Guess Who's Coming to Dinner* and *To Sir, With Love* (both 1967). The same year's *In the Heat of the Night* teamed Poitier up with Rod Steiger in a compelling drama about the pursuit of a criminal by two cops with very different views on race and society in the United States. Poitier also directed several films, including *Uptown Saturday Night* (1974) and *Stir Crazy* (1980).

At the same time, Poitier was a key figure in the US civil rights movement, and the above quotation, which appears in his memoirs, attests to his lifelong commitment to standing up for his beliefs. **IHS**

" So often in life, things that you regard as an impediment turn out to be great good fortune. "

Ruth Bader Ginsburg
Interview for *Makers*
2012

Ruth Bader Ginsburg is the second woman to serve as a justice on the Supreme Court of the United States. Prior to her appointment in 1993, she attended Harvard Law School, later transferring to and graduating from, Columbia Law School; served as a law professor at Columbia and Rutgers; was an attorney for the American Civil Liberties Union; and served as judge on the United States Court of Appeals for the District of Columbia after having been appointed by President Jimmy Carter.

When Ginsburg graduated law school in 1959, even her educational achievements and recommendation from Supreme Court Justice Felix Frankfurter couldn't land her the job she wanted. Ginsburg was rejected by a large and well-known New York law firm simply because it had already hired a woman – and, moreover, a black woman – so it didn't feel any further need to demonstrate its 'progressiveness' to the world.

The rejection was fortunate for Ginsburg. She said that had she become an attorney, she likely would have climbed the ranks and retired as a partner. Instead, what she then saw as a failure has allowed her to take a different road, one that led her to becoming a justice of the Supreme Court of the United States. **MT**

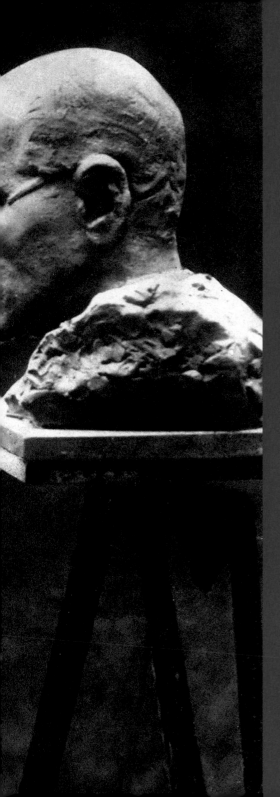

Love &
Relationships

Sigmund Freud's psychoanalytic theory sought to uncover the unconscious urges behind relationships.

"*Many waters cannot quench love, neither can the floods drown it.*"

This Russian icon depicts King Solomon, to whom this book of the Bible was historically attributed.

Unknown
Song of Solomon
C. 1000 BCE

The *Song of Solomon*, or *Songs of Songs*, is a collection of love poems that forms a book of the Old Testament of the Bible. The beautiful and sensuous love poetry has been interpreted by both the Jewish and the Christian communities as a metaphor for God's love for his people.

A religious community, as a body of the faithful, has an inextinguishable love for its object of worship that shines like a flame through whatever deluge of wickedness or cruelty is thrown over it by unbelievers. Floods of force or persecution, offerings of material plenty, even the opportunity for longevity, all pale beside the eternal brightness of this love. Furthermore, the truly faithful will embrace torments and tests since so doing proves to them that their love can endure a storm of trials yet never falter.

But there has been disagreement about what type of love the poem represents. The text has undergone various interpretations. It has also been read as a song about physical love between a man and a woman, famously defended by French theologian and Protestant reformer John Calvin as an example of the divine manifestation of love. **LW**

"Even fools are thought wise if they keep silent, and discerning if they hold their tongue."

Old Testament
Book of Proverbs
c. 700 BCE

This quotation, from chapter seventeen, verse twenty-eight, of the twentieth book of the Old Testament of the Bible, expresses a sentiment that is commonly felt, and frequently expressed in only slightly variant forms, perhaps most famously as: 'It is better to remain silent, and be thought a fool, than to speak out, and remove all doubt,' which is sometimes spuriously credited to US President Abraham Lincoln. It is also cognate with 'Still waters run deep' and 'Empty vessels make most sound,' both of which appear in similar form in many languages.

The Book of Proverbs is attributed to Solomon, the Israelite king of the 10th century BCE who built the first temple in Jerusalem and who is revered in all three Abrahamic religions (Judaism, Christianity and Islam). However, there is no evidence that Solomon actually said or wrote any of the axioms contained in this work. Indeed, the earliest extant versions of the text appeared some three centuries after his death. Wisdom literature – collections of aphorisms, of which the Book of Proverbs is a prominent example – was popular throughout ancient Asia, and a personal name in a title was not then a declaration of authorship, as it is today. JP

The Three Wise Monkeys, of Buddhist origin, show their wisdom by speaking no evil, seeing no evil and hearing no evil.

" No act of kindness, no matter how small, is ever wasted. "

Aesop
Fables
c. 600 BCE

Although none of his works survive, Aesop is widely credited as an author of fables. In the fable of which this is the moral, a mouse caught by a lion begs for its life on the grounds that it may be able to return the favour at a later date. The saying, therefore, is all about reciprocity, or 'the golden rule'. This rule seems to underpin all of our moral codes: do as you would be done by. The twist here is that the inequality in power between mouse and lion, like the insignificance of smiling or opening a door, relative to giving away a financial fortune or setting up a charity, is not as relevant as the acts themselves.

The weak have something to offer the strong precisely because 'weak' and 'strong' are relative terms, just as 'small' and 'great' are unimportant qualities when it comes to action. Action itself – the way of doing a thing, and in particular, whether or not it is done with resentment, or with compassion – is all that matters.

Two things are important about this: firstly, knowing the theory is no guarantor of success. Those who purport to be moral may behave no more, or even less, morally than those who make no such claims. Secondly, some moral codes are so narrow and rigid that they lack compassion entirely: better in that case to have no code at all and just be guided by kindness. **LW**

" Kindness in words creates confidence. Kindness in thinking creates profoundness. Kindness in giving creates love. "

Laozi
Attributed
c. 550 BCE

Laozi was a philosopher in ancient China and widely influential as the reputed author of the *Tao Te Ching* (although, like many ancient texts, this work is sometimes attributed to several individuals). Laozi is consequently regarded as one of the founders of Taoism.

The Tao is a moral code. The above quotation outlines the benefits of three forms of kindness. This is a subject to which the *Tao Te Ching* frequently returns, asserting that the righteous person or saint shows the 'true virtue of kindness' by being kind to everyone – to the kind and to the unkind alike. Elsewhere in the book, kindness is described as one of the Three Treasures (alongside simplicity and humility).

This quotation does not appear in the *Tao Te Ching*, but its aphoristic wisdom gains even greater authority and resonance than it would otherwise have by attribution to Laozi. And even if the philosopher never said or wrote any such thing, the remark is a succinct summary of some key Taoist principles, even if it is not authentic. **JE**

❯ An undated painting of Sakyamuni, Laozi (*centre*) and Confucius.

"Have no friends not equal to yourself."

There are no authenticated images of Confucius, but this is just one of thousands of later artists' impressions.

Confucius
Analects
c. 500 BCE

Confucius was China's most famous teacher, philosopher and political theorist. The above quotation, from *Analects*, chapter one, verse eight, echoes the most important rule of Confucianism, often referred to as 'the golden rule,' which dictates that we should treat others in the way we wish to be treated ourselves. By telling us that the ideal friends are ones who are equal to ourselves, Confucius is also encouraging us to see our friends as equals and to treat them as we'd like to be treated ourselves. Equality was of huge importance to Confucius. Take another of his other maxims: 'In the presence of a good man, think all the time how you may learn to equal him. In the presence of a bad man, turn your gaze within.' This reflects Confucius's belief that the people we associate with have major roles in our lives and that it's important to surround ourselves with those we look up to, and from whom we can learn, because we're unavoidably influenced by their behaviour. The quotation reminds us of the central Confucian tenet that we should learn from those around us, and surround ourselves only with people who can help us to grow, and become better people, avoiding all others. TH

A true friend is one soul in two bodies.

Aristotle
Attributed
c. 335 BCE

Aristotle believed that friendship fell into three categories and could be based on utility, pleasure or goodness. He believed that friendships were of huge importance with regard to personal development, that friendships are what shape our morals, and that the best friends are slightly better – but very similar – versions of ourselves: people we can learn from, and look to for guidance.

This quotation is taken from *The Lives and Opinions of Eminent Philosophers* by Diogenes Laërtius, a Greek author who lived around half a millennium after Aristotle. Its accuracy is therefore gravely in doubt; nevertheless, it has the air of authenticity: it is the sort of thing that Aristotle might have said, and it reflects the worldview that appears throughout his copious extant work.

The quotation suggests that while friends have the ability to improve one another by changing the way they think, they are essentially very similar people, with the same morals, attitudes and values. They might occasionally disagree, or challenge one another's thoughts, but they rarely have serious quarrels and will have the same priorities. **TH**

ARISTOTELI. STAGIRITAE

⬥ A 15th-century CE artist's impression of ancient Greek philosopher and scientist Aristotle.

" The enemy of my enemy is my friend. "

Kautilya
Arthashastra
C. 300 BCE

Also known as Vishnugupta or Chanakya, Kautilya was an Indian teacher, economist, philosopher and adviser to the Mauryan emperor Chandragupta. He is most notable as the author of the *Arthashastra*, a practical handbook for ruling an empire. Written in Sanskrit, it was a pioneering work of political science and economics that was rediscovered in 1915, after having been lost towards the end of the Gupta Empire in the 6th century CE.

The above quotation is one of the key insights in Kautilya's work. In Book VI of the *Arthashastra*, the author contextualizes his thought thus: 'The king who is. . . situated close to the enemy, but separated from the conqueror only by the enemy, is termed the friend of the conqueror.'

The principle of uniting with almost anyone against a common foe has been adopted throughout history by pragmatic politicians, many of whom have used this remark in defence of their actions. During World War II, when questioned about the morality of allying with the Soviet Union against Nazi Germany, British prime minister Winston Churchill is said to have replied: 'If Hitler invaded Hell, I would make at least a favourable reference to the Devil in the House of Commons.' **JE**

" Friendship with a man is friendship with his virtue, and does not admit of assumptions of superiority. "

Mencius
Mencius Book 5, Part 2
C. 300 BCE

In one of the books of philosophical dialogues that bear his name, Mencius – the most important ancient Chinese philosopher after Confucius – states the above in response to one of his interlocutors, Wan Chang, who has just said: 'I venture to ask the principles of friendship.' This quotation is a reminder of the importance of equality, and that believing oneself to be superior to a friend is to threaten the whole relationship. Mencius is warning us that we should choose our friends, and want to spend time with them, because we admire what is good about them. We should be attracted, not to their status or their wealth, but to their virtue. We should never choose friends because we believe them to be people who can help us out as a result of their social connections or their influence. We should never choose friends because we want to boast about knowing them or because we feel that they will open doors for us or improve our lives in a superficial way. Being motivated by such desires will not result in true friendship and will only hurt those around us, and, sooner or later, incur the wrath of the people we have been trying to befriend on false pretenses. **TH**

> # *No guest is so welcome in a friend's house that he will not become a nuisance after three days.*

Plautus

Miles Gloriosus

c. 200 BCE

Titus Maccius Plautus was a comic playwright in ancient Rome. His first plays were produced between around 205 BCE and 184 BCE. *Miles Gloriosus* – sometimes translated as 'the Boastful Soldier' – is one of his most famous works.

Among the common themes in Plautus were servant–master relationships and the meaning of true friendship. The above quotation describes the notion that friends should not be taken advantage of, lest the relationship be strained to a breaking point.

Plautus evidently regarded friendships as delicate social bonds. Even though a friend may make exceedingly generous offers – whether of accommodation, money or something else – the recipient should always be mindful that there are limits to how much of that generosity should be accepted. It is not simply for the givers to let the receivers know when they have accepted more than their fair share of hospitality or other gifts. The recipients also have a responsibility to bear in mind that even the strongest friendships depend on equality and mutual respect and that friendships are most likely to be tested when these boundaries are overstepped. **TH**

⬥ The title page of a 1518 edition of Plautus's comedies, which have been a template for dramatic humour down the ages.

"*To like and dislike the same things, that is indeed true friendship.*"

Salluſtius

This coloured woodcut by Michael Wolgemut in the 15th-century *Nuremberg Chronicle* depicts Roman author Sallust.

Sallust
The Conspiracy of Catiline's War
C. 50 BCE

Sallust was a Roman historian and politician, an opponent of the aristocracy and a supporter of Julius Caesar. This quotation reflects the pessimism with which he viewed friendship. He was heavily influenced by Thucydides, the Greek historian of the 5th century BCE, and firmly believed that true friendships relied upon honesty and impartiality. True friendship, in his opinion, was not simply about keeping friends happy by agreeing with their views. It wasn't about choosing to keep quiet when friends voiced opinions one might not agree with. True friends will respect one another's viewpoints without letting differences in opinion affect the relationship. True friendship, in Sallust's opinion, was about shared but also new experiences, and friends who 'like and dislike' the same things will encourage one another to embark on new adventures, and to try things that they might have previously overlooked or disregarded. Good friends are often described as like 'two peas in a pod,' but this quotation shows that Sallust believed that best friends aren't identical people, but people who have different interests and passions, and it is precisely these differences that strengthen friendships. **TH**

"Prosperity makes friends, adversity tries them."

Publilius Syrus
Sententiae
C. 50 BCE

Publilius Syrus was an Assyrian author of Latin maxims. Legend states that he was brought as a slave to Italy, where his wit and creativity won over his master, who eventually freed and educated him.

This quotation is a reminder that when people are materially successful, their popularity might also increase, albeit not for the right reasons. They may find themselves with many new friends, but these admirers may actually be motivated by a desire for some of the glory or the material benefits. It is also a warning that friends made during times of prosperity may not always be genuine ones, and that the real tests of a friendship are when there are times of hardship. Only the true friends stick with us through good times and bad.

By implication, Syrus is suggesting that we should never become too dependent on friends, because the tougher times are often when they might abandon us. He is also perhaps pointing out that even the toughest experiences can make us better people and can improve our lives by helping us to find out which friends we can really rely on. He may also be hinting that being overly dependent is never a good thing. **TH**

"Love conquers all things; let us too surrender to love."

Virgil
Eclogues
37 BCE

The power of love has long been recognized. Here, in his series of pastoral idylls, Roman poet Virgil gives the idea its finest expression. In this form, it later recurred in the works of many other artists, including 14th-century English poet Geoffrey Chaucer, in whose *The Canterbury Tales* one character, the Prioress, wore a brooch engraved with the legend '*amor vincit omnia*' ('love conquers all'); 17th-century Milanese painter Caravaggio, who used the phrase as the title of his painting otherwise known as *Victorious Cupid*; and 20th-century poet Edgar Bowers, who reinterpreted the phrase all over again in his poem with the same Latin title as that engraved on the Prioress's brooch.

Virgil was keen to point out that surrendering to love isn't always easy, that occasionally love may cause heartbreak and suffering. However, he maintained that these risks were worth taking. The poem further reminds us that, even though we may encounter heartbreak in the quest for true love, we should never forget that, once we have found it, its power is immense. Finding it isn't as simple as we might think – it's something to which we willingly have to surrender. **TH**

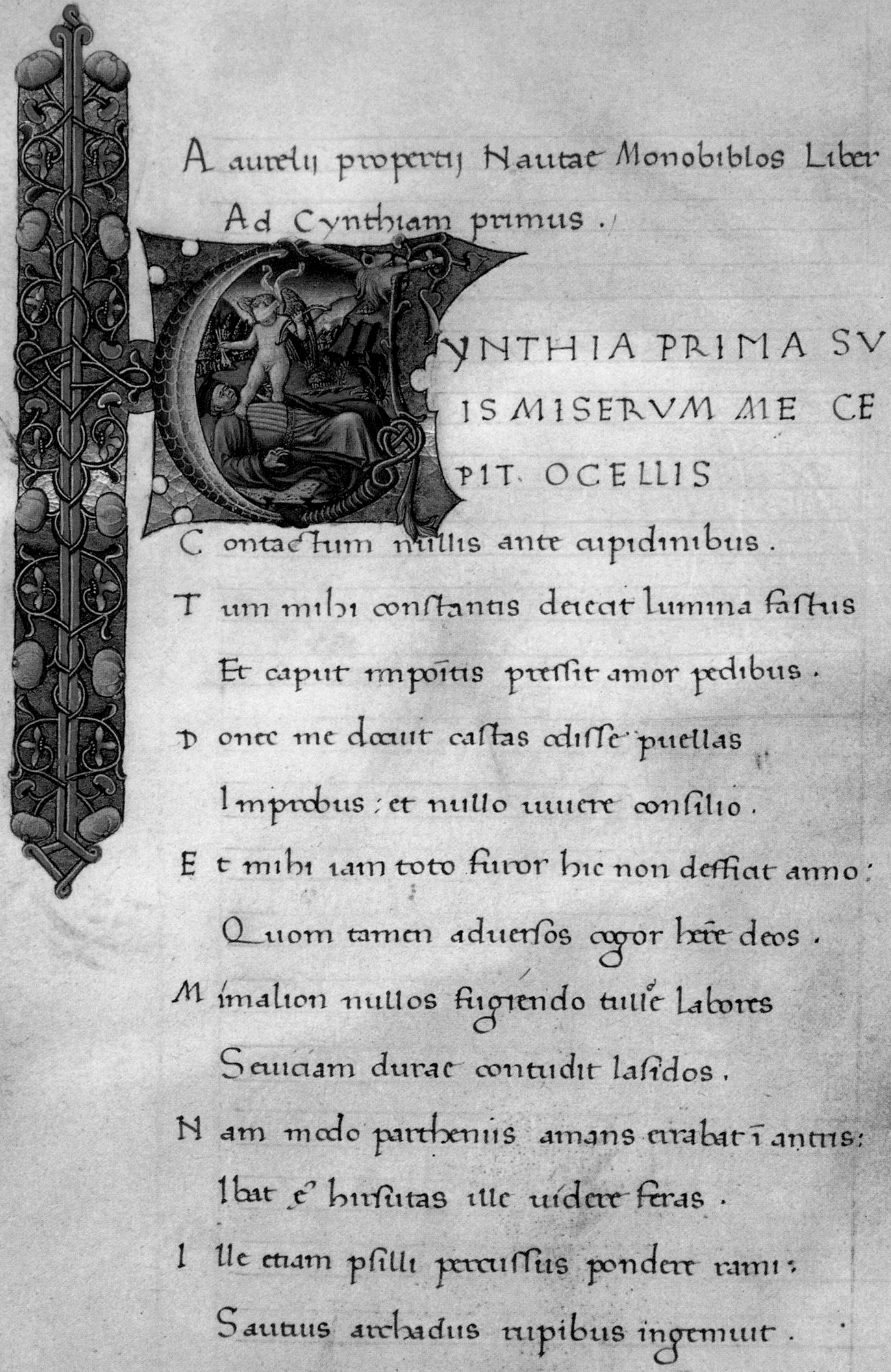

A aurelij propertij Nautae Monobiblos Liber
Ad Cynthiam primus.

YNTHIA PRIMA SV
IS MISERVM ME CE
PIT. OCELLIS

C ontactum nullis ante cupidinibus.

T um mihi constantis deiecit lumina fastus

   Et caput impositis pressit amor pedibus.

D onec me docuit castas odisse puellas

   Improbus; et nullo uiuere consilio.

E t mihi iam toto furor hic non deficit anno:

   Quom tamen aduersos cogor here deos.

M imalion nullos fugiendo tulle labores

   Seuitiam durae contudit Iasidos.

N am modo partheniis amans errabat in antris:

   Ibat et hirsutas ille uidere feras.

I lle etiam psilli percussus pondere rami:

   Sautius archadus rupibus ingemuit.

"*Absence makes the heart grow fonder.*"

Sextus Propertius
Elegies
C. 24 BCE

An Augustan poet and a friend of Virgil, Sextus Propertius came to prominence as a result of his love elegies, which are the source of this proverb regarding love. Propertius's *Elegies* largely concern his tormented affair with an older woman, referred to as Cynthia. Her exact identity is unknown; it has been thought she was either a courtesan or perhaps a married woman. Cynthia's inconsistencies eventually exhausted the poet. Propertius describes journeying to free himself of love's 'burden' and his efforts to recover from the effects of spending too much time with her: '[E]ndless presence reduces the man who's always around.' Yet he mourns her absence, and her distance from him inflames his passions, even after her death.

Intimate relationships are a mix of the needs for either proximity or space. People want to feel understood and appreciated, and to experience physical closeness. They do not want to feel overwhelmed by neediness or suffocated by another's inability to be alone. It is pleasant to be considered a couple, less so when one's individuality is lost. The truth of this ancient adage, therefore, is only partial. Whether absence kindles or quenches depends on the degree of love involved. **LW**

◉ Illuminated opening words from the first book of the *Elegies*.

"*Greater love has no one than this, that someone lays down his life for his friends.*"

Jesus Christ
Gospel according to St John
30 CE

Jesus, who was given the title 'Christ' (meaning 'Anointed One,' or 'Messiah') by his followers, spoke these words while teaching his disciples just before he was betrayed and put to death. He added the command 'to love one another as I have loved you,' and said that in obeying this, they would become his friends. The words have inspired countless acts of heroism and self-sacrifice, both military and civilian. They have also been the inspiration for many works of art, from the American soldier in Jason Bullard's *No Greater Love* series to *Greater Love Hath No Man* by Casey Childs, depicting the murder of Joseph Smith, founder of the Mormons.

In the above quotation, Jesus is both stating a general precept and foreshadowing his own death on the cross. Christians believe that Jesus was the son of God and that he chose to accept his crucifixion, sacrificing himself willingly, and deliberately, out of love for the world, to rescue those who trust in him from the consequences of their sins. The mechanics of this atonement are a mystery, even to believers, but mystery is a key component of faith, and the theme of redemption has run consistently throughout the whole of Christian history. **JF**

> **" Love is patient, love is kind. It does not envy, it does not boast, it is not proud. "**

St Paul
First Letter to the Corinthians
c. 50 CE

This quotation, along with other parts of St Paul's First Letter to the Corinthians, originally written in Greek, is often read at weddings, because the theme is love. However, the love that St Paul is referring to here is not the love between two people, but selfless love among members of a group. Where English has only one word for 'love,' which consequently has to cover many different shades of meaning, Greek has several words. In the New Testament of the Bible, the word 'agape' – unconditional love, such as that of Jesus for human beings, and the Christian love that follows his example – is defined as the highest type of love.

The early part of Paul's letter deals with matters of Church discipline. He then bursts out with an inspired passage extolling 'agape'. If members of the Church could only learn this kind of love – 'a more excellent way' – there would be no need to correct them, for they would find the right path for themselves. St Augustine would express something of the same idea 300 years later when he wrote: 'Love and do as you wish'. JF

◐ *The Marriage of the Virgin* (c. 1500) is attributed to Pietro Perugino.

> **" It is part of human nature to hate the man you have hurt. "**

Tacitus
Agricola
56 CE

A prominent historian during the Roman Empire, Publius Cornelius Tacitus believed that Roman emperors held too much power, and he publicly voiced concerns about corruption. But these particular words are taken from a biography he wrote about his father-in-law, Agricola, a general who led the Roman conquest of Britain. Tacitus had particular admiration for Agricola's brutal assault on Wales and Scotland but loathed the corruption that accompanied it. Tacitus, who was often on the receiving end of the wrath of the emperors he criticized, also saw how those defeated by Agricola were consumed by anger, which he understood to be a coping mechanism. Anger spurred people on to avenge perceived wrongs, while emboldening soldiers on battlefields and helping them to justify their actions. Tacitus also believed that even the most powerful of emperors or the bravest of soldiers occasionally questioned their motives and experienced guilt. After years of observing the bloodshed that resulted from his father-in-law's conquests, and also the ingrained corruption that permeated the highest levels of government, Tacitus concluded that for many, hatred of the defeated was what allowed victors to put aside feelings of guilt and to justify their actions. TH

> " *I don't need a friend who changes when I change and who nods when I nod; my shadow does that much better.* "

Plutarch
Attributed
C. 100 CE

Plutarch was a Greek historian and biographer who also worked as a magistrate. He was known as someone for whom no job was too menial, someone with no airs or graces, who was faithful to his friends, and who disliked excessive praise. He was also known for his criticism of vice, and belief in the importance of virtue, and as someone who was not afraid to criticize some of the most famous Greek and Roman rulers – many of whom he saw as greedy and selfish. These words reflect Plutarch's desire to have only friends who spoke their own minds, were not afraid to voice their own thoughts, and acted how they wanted to act, motivated not by social gains but by a desire to do what was right – in a time when the most powerful were often the most corrupt. He points out that nobody could duplicate and agree with him more closely than his own shadow, but when it comes to his friends, Plutarch seeks something more. He requires not just friendship, but someone who is honest in good times and bad, who will disagree with him and correct him because he or she has his best interests at heart. Plutarch clearly believed that far too few people in his society behaved in this way. **TH**

> " *The friendship that can cease has never been real.* "

St Jerome
Attributed
C. 380 CE

St Jerome was born in 347 in Stridonius, a small town near the head of the Adriatic in what is now Bosnia Herzegovina. His father was a devoted Christian who taught his son at home; he had lessons from the famous pagan grammarian Donatus and the Christian rhetorician Victorinus. After years of travel, Jerome eventually renounced all secular pursuits to dedicate himself entirely to God.

Jerome was a firm believer in the importance of friendship and the trust we must place in our friends. Examining St Jerome's words, it is worth noting his decision to use the words 'can cease' rather than simply 'ceases'. They suggest that he's talking about friendships that feel volatile and fickle and that turbulent relationships that experience extreme lows and highs are often the weakest ones. If we worry that our friendships may fall apart, or that our friends may desert us, then perhaps those friendships are not as genuine as we would like them to be. True friends would not entertain the thought that petty squabbles could threaten their relationship and would never let minor disagreements divide them. If someone feels that they are constantly walking on eggshells when spending time with a friend, and thus avoids being honest, then that friendship is destined to fail. **TH**

" Love is not to be purchased, and affection has no price. "

St Jerome
Attributed
C. 380 CE

St Jerome was best known for his translation of the Bible from Hebrew into Latin – a version that became known as the Vulgate. Many believe that his greatest achievement was the creation of a unified Latin version of the Bible's New Testament, and this accomplishment meant that his words were held in extremely high regard.

Jerome's writings often focused on subjects connected with the Church, and he was someone who was hugely respected and trusted within the religion. He was a firm believer in honesty, and had little time for those who attempted to win over others through flattery. He expressed thoughts of this kind on many occasions: other examples include: 'Beauty when unadorned is adorned the most' and 'Everything must have in it a sharp seasoning of truth.'

Jerome believed that honesty was of the utmost importance, along with an ability to see through the deceptions and distractions created by those wanting to obscure the truth. But in addition to saying that love is not something that can be purchased through flattery or other means, St Jerome was stating that genuine affection should be given freely. Certainly, he was warning people against trying to buy the affections of others, but he was also saying that there was no need for them to do so. **TH**

" Familiarity breeds contempt. "

Proverb
Unknown
C. 400 CE

The origins of this saying are unclear. The concept is sometimes associated with 'The Fox and the Lion,' a fable attributed to Aesop (c. 600 BCE). In this tale the fox is reasonably afraid of the lion at first, but is eventually emboldened to approach the king of beasts.

In this original form, the fable demonstrates merely the idea that becoming more familiar with someone or something allows people to overcome their initial fears. Nothing of the story's initial telling suggests contempt, however: the fox engages the lion in conversation, and the lion responds; he doesn't attack his interlocutor. Contempt was added by Jeffreys Taylor in his *Aesop, in Rhyme with Some Originals* (1820). Taylor embellished the ending – the lion throws the fox into a river to teach him some manners – and linked the saying to the story.

However, the first recorded version of the saying dates to the 4th century CE in St Augustine of Hippo's *Scala Paradisi* (*The Ladder of Divine Ascent*), but the saying is not attributed to him because he describes it as 'a common proverb'.

A similar saying occurs in Geoffrey Chaucer's *The Canterbury Tales* (c. 1387) in 'The Tale of Melibee': 'For right as men seyn that "over-greet hoomlynesse engendreth dispreisynge", so fareth it by to greet humylitee or mekenesse'. ('For just as men say that "over-great familiarity engenders contempt", so fares it by too great humility or meekness.') **LW**

> ❝ *He who has a thousand friends has not a friend to spare, And he who has one enemy will meet him everywhere.* ❞

Ali ibn-Abi-Talib
Sunan Abu Dawud
c. 660 CE

Sunan Abu Dawud is one of the *Kutub as-Sittah* (six major hadiths) collected by Imam Abu Dawud Sulayman. Hadiths are collections of accounts that claim to report verbatim the sayings of the Prophet Muhammad. Ali ibn-Abi-Talib, the source of this quotation, was the cousin and son-in-law of Muhammad. Ali ibn-Abi-Talib's words express the belief that true friends are extremely valuable and are meant as a reminder that we should avoid alienating or offending any of our friends. The quotation is also a warning against making enemies. When we have a falling out with someone, we dread seeing that person, and as a result the person seems to appear everywhere. We cannot avoid them, and they are always in our thoughts, whether it is because we dread a further confrontation or because we feel guilty about what we have said or done that turned them into an enemy.

Today, Ali ibn-Abi-Talib stands as an important figure for both Sunni and Shia Muslims. He is universally regarded as someone who was a true and pious Muslim, devoted to the cause of Islam and motivated only by the desire to spread the Prophet Muhammad's teachings and rule in accordance with the Qur'an. **TH**

> ❝ *And what is better than wisdom? Woman. And what is better than a good woman? Nothing.* ❞

Geoffrey Chaucer
The Canterbury Tales
c. 1387

This quotation is from 'The Tale of Melibee,' the eponymous hero of which is away one day when three thugs break into his house, beat his wife, Dame Prudence, and attack his daughter, leaving her for dead. The bulk of the narrative is a debate between Melibee and Prudence on what actions to take, and how to seek appropriate redress. Prudence counsels caution, reproaches Melibee for some of his more extreme opinions and supports her views with extensive quotations from the Bible and other learned authorities.

The problem with 'The Tale of Melibee' is that, unlike most of *The Canterbury Tales*, it is in prose, and is generally regarded as so long-winded that most modern editions either summarize it or omit it altogether. Nevertheless, a good quotation is a good quotation, regardless of its source, and this one appears in almost all collections of aphorisms. Chaucer's more readable views on women are presented in the so-called 'Marriage Group': 'The Clerk's Tale,''The Franklin's Tale,''The Merchant's Tale' and 'The Wife of Bath's Tale.' **TH**

❯ Geoffrey Chaucer upon a horse in the early 15th-century Ellesmere illustrated manuscript of *The Canterbury Tales*.

Of þrides, than ye han herd bifore
Comprehended in this litel tretys heer
To enforce with, theffect of my matiere
And though I nat the same wordes
As ye han herd, yet to yow alle I pray
Blameth me nat, for as in my sentence
Shul ye nowher, fynden difference
ffro the sentence, of this tretys lyte
After the which, this murye tale I write
And therfore herkneth what þt I shal say
And lat me tellen, al my tale I praye

Explicit

Heere bigynneth Chaucere

yong man called . . .
. . . on his wyf that
which that called . . .
. . . for his desport is
his wyf and eek his doghter hath . . .
the sores Whan faste yschette thre . . .
and setten laddres to the walles of
been cried, and setten his wyf
fyue mortal woundes in fyue . . .
hir feet, in hys handes, in hir eyes
and leften hir for deed and wenten
tourned was in to his hous, and . . .
. . . man rentynge his clothes

"Love is a thing as any spirit free."

Geoffrey Chaucer
The Canterbury Tales
c. 1387

These words express Chaucer's belief that love itself is powerful, a force that cannot and should not be controlled or contained. In order to understand the quotation further, it is important to see it in context. The sentences that follow read: 'Women, of kind, desire liberty, and not to been constrained as a thrall; And so do men, if soothly I say shall.' Chaucer acknowledges that neither men nor women wish to be controlled and constrained, and that both wish to be free, but he is not saying that love is impossible. What he believes is that love should not imprison or restrict and that it is not possible to control love. Chaucer devoted time to pondering the concept of true love and how love is changed by marriage. In *The Canterbury Tales*, the author is preoccupied with examining the social practices of those living within the institution of marriage.

It should be noted that whatever Chaucer's views about love, his scepticism about marriage was voiced at a time when marriage was viewed primarily as a transaction to enhance economic status. In that context, it is unsurprising he believed that the truest examples of love are found outside of that union. **TH**

"It is safer . . . to be feared than loved."

Niccolò Machiavelli
The Prince
1513

The name of Niccolò Machiavelli has acquired almost exclusively bad connotations: a Machiavellian is an unscrupulous politicker; 'Old Nick', a shortened form of his forename, is a term for the Devil. But many people who have read *The Prince* take the view that the author was a pragmatist and a recorder of observed behaviour, rather than an evil provocateur.

The above remark illustrates the point. These eight words are usually the only ones quoted from a passage that reads in full: '. . .a question arises: whether it be better to be loved than feared or feared than loved? It may be answered that one should wish to be both, but, because it is difficult to unite them in one person, it is much safer to be feared than loved, when, of the two, either must be dispensed with'.

So this is no unreserved endorsement of despotism; on the contrary, the author plainly believes that it is good to be loved. But love can be exploited by others, and those who give it should not leave themselves unprotected and vulnerable. **JP**

❯ A 16th-century portrait of Machiavelli by Santi di Tito.

"To God I speak Spanish, to women Italian, to men French, and to my horse – German."

⚉ *The Emperor Charles V on Horseback* (c. 1548), by Titian, depicts the most powerful man in the world in the mid-16th century.

Emperor Charles V
Attributed
c. 1530

Although there is some debate about who originally uttered these words, it is believed to have been Charles V, Holy Roman Emperor. The quotation expresses traditional ideas that Spanish is the language of God, Italian the language of love and French the language of diplomacy. Charles V's contribution was to suggest that German, being a gruff, guttural language to outsiders' ears, was particularly suitable for giving orders. German is traditionally perceived to sound harsh, but it was Charles V's reference to addressing an animal that was deliberately insulting to the Germans.

The quotation offers an insight into how the different European languages were viewed historically, and are still regarded today, albeit to a lesser extent. Aside from the insult to the Germans, the words express the huge respect Charles V had for the Spanish territories. Those in South and Central America were a huge source of power and wealth, and their importance increased throughout his reign, during which time he sanctioned conquests of the Inca and Aztec Empires. For this reason it is perhaps understandable that he seems to have had most respect for the Spanish language. **TH**

" *Gestures, in love, are incomparably more attractive, effective and valuable than words.* "

François Rabelais
Gargantua and Pantagruel
c. 1532

Although François Rabelais always was, and remains, best known for his bawdy jokes and songs, the above quotation suggests that the French novelist had a softer side, revealing his belief that, while fine words are easy to utter, gestures are infinitely more important, and mean much more.

Perhaps the author was here referring to the huge number of common phrases, if not clichés, reeled off by people in love, and suggesting that if something is being said simply for the sake of it, there is no point in saying it at all. People hoping to confess their love may have a vast compendium of phrases at their disposal, but a gesture requires more thought if it is to be personal, and will therefore be of greater value.

Although *Gargantua and Pantagruel* – a five-volume series of novels – was regarded by many as obscene, and was condemned by the clerics of the Paris university of the Sorbonne, it was a huge success – Rabelais was clearly able to tap into human emotions, and to analyze human nature. After *Gargantua and Pantagruel*, he wrote nothing for eleven years, and today the series is regarded as his finest work. **TH**

◮ The engraved frontispiece of *Gargantua*, the second novel of Rabelais's series, in an edition dated 1537.

" There goes more to marriage than four bare legs in a bed. "

John Heywood
The Dialogue of the Effectual Proverbs . . .
c. 1549

This proverb refers to the belief that a successful marriage requires more than lust and physical compatibility. Several other proverbs dating back to the 16th century address the same issue. One – 'Marry in haste and repent at leisure' – seems similar in its warning against setting too much store by the physical aspect of marriage, while another – the somewhat politically incorrect 'A deaf husband and a blind wife are always a happy couple' – humorously sets out the conditions for successful relations between the sexes.

Heywood was a prolific author of short dramatic pieces, and a composer of music at the court of Henry VIII, king of England. He remained staunchly Roman Catholic throughout Henry's break with the Church of Rome, and seems to have escaped persecution, although it may be significant that, shortly after the accession of Elizabeth I in 1558, he moved to Belgium, where he lived until his death aged at an advanced age no earlier than 1575.

Among the proverbs recorded in this collection are several that remain in common usage to this day, including 'Rome was not built in one day.' **TH**

" All's fair in love and war. "

John Lyly
Euphues: The Anatomy of Wit
1578

Today, English poet, playwright and politician John Lyly is best known for his didactic romance, *Euphues: The Anatomy of Wit* – the term 'Euphues' being a derivative from a Greek word meaning 'graceful and witty'. However, while he is credited with the above quotation, he did not write it in the way that it is commonly worded today. What he actually wrote was: 'The rules of fair play do not apply in love and war' – the universal axiom that appears here evolved over the subsequent centuries.

The first appearance of the quotation in its now-familiar wording is in Francis Edward Smedley's novel *Frank Fairleigh* (1850), which documents the life of a young schoolboy. Here, the quotation reflects the belief that there are no boundaries when it comes to protecting those you love or wreaking revenge on those you hate. However, critics have pointed out that, although true love might justify any sacrifice, the idea that people should do whatever they need to in order to win a war is much more controversial – as is the common use of the saying as a justification for bad behaviour. **TH**

❷ Fairness in love and war is a theme of the movie *For Whom the Bell Tolls* (1940), based on the novel by Ernest Hemingway.

" Ring out your bells! Let mourning shows be spread. For love is dead! "

Philip Sidney
'A Dirge'
1582

Sidney was an English poet, scholar and soldier. Many of his works are dark and brooding, perhaps influenced by what he saw on the battlefields. Among these, the sonnets collectively named *Astrophel and Stella* focus on the love of a man named Astrophel for a woman named Stella – characters many people believe he based on himself and a woman named Penelope Devereux.

Among Sidney's other poems is one titled 'A Dirge', also about Astrophel and Stella, in which he laments Stella's forthcoming marriage to another man. The poem starts with the quotation and continues with a series of gloomy, funerary images: weeping neighbours, Trentalls (prayers for souls in purgatory) and the mistress's 'hart' itself transformed into a tomb. However, Sidney subsequently learns that the marriage is compulsory, and so does not imply his loss of her love. He writes, 'Love is not dead, but sleepeth. In her unmatched mind. . .' Thus, while 'love is dead!' is a brooding, pessimistic take on the concept of love, the author ends by stating that perhaps it is not dead after all. In other words, Sidney was vowing never to lose hope that one day his love for Penelope might be reciprocated. **TH**

" A rose by any other name would smell as sweet. "

William Shakespeare
Romeo and Juliet
c. 1594

In William Shakespeare's famous dramatic tragedy, Romeo and Juliet fall in love at a masked ball. However, their affair must remain a secret because he is a Montague and Juliet is a Capulet, and the two families are fierce enemies.

The above quotation, which appears in Act II of the play, is part of a speech in which Juliet states that it does not matter to her if Romeo is of a rival family or not. She rejects nominal differences, asking: 'What's in a name?' and answering herself immediately with: 'That which we call a rose by any other name would smell as sweet.'

Juliet further notes that Romeo would be himself (and as perfect) by any other name and bids Romeo to abandon his name and take hers instead. In essence, Juliet is making the claim that one's family background and labels have no relation to one's essence – Romeo's name is irrelevant to his perfection, and roses would be what they are, irrespective of what name they have. One implication of this argument is that it advocates loving people for who they are, without regard for the labels that are put on them by others. **JE**

> An unattributed painting of the star-crossed lovers.

"The course of true love never did run smooth."

William Shakespeare
A Midsummer Night's Dream
c. 1595

The relationship between Lysander and Hermia in the comedy *A Midsummer Night's Dream* is extraordinarily turbulent from the outset, and this quotation perfectly encapsulates the essence of the couple's unpredictable, volatile partnership. Hermia's father, Egeus, has declared his wish that his daughter should marry another suitor, Demetrius, rather than Lysander, so it is hardly surprising that Demetrius should be the inspiration of the above remark by Lysander. If Hermia disobeys her father's command, she will have to face the law of Athens, and the consequence for her will be either death or consignment to a nunnery. Lysander's words are offered to Hermia as a comfort, and he compares the course of love to that of a road or a river. She interrupts him more than once, but he goes on to list further examples of situations that can prevent the smooth flow of a relationship, including overbearing friends, and differences in class and age.

His words are offered as reassurance that such obstacles are merely bumps in the road experienced by most people in love, and the fact that these obstacles have been placed in their path does not mean that their love is not true. In just one line, Lysander acknowledges that they may have adversities to overcome, but also reminds her that their love cannot be defeated. **TH**

"The gentle mind by gentle deeds is known. For a man by nothing is so well exposed, as by his manners."

Edmund Spenser
The Faerie Queene
1596

Although the medieval code of chivalry had died out around a century before Spenser's epic poem, the poet used that Arthurian mythology to craft an allegorical commentary on the aristocracy of the late 16th century. Since courtesy is an essential virtue of chivalry, courteous deeds can be rightly judged as evidence of a 'gentle' mind. In Spenser's time, 'gentle' was commonly equated with 'noble,' implying that genuine courtesy could be expected only among the nobility. But Spenser also describes discourteous knights, and one in particular is shamed by a fellow knight whose pure courtesy is displayed in 'every act and word'.

Spenser frequently remarks on the courtesy of eloquence; using words to provide consolation is itself a gentle deed of a gentle mind. Therefore, this quotation is not the platitude that 'actions speak louder than words'. Rather, good manners reflect good will towards others. For this very reason, Spenser decried the tendency among Elizabethan nobles to feign virtue in an effort to be well regarded. However, precisely because such behaviour is recognized as self-serving, it cannot be a sign of a genuine concern for others. **TJ**

"Who ever loved, that loved not at first sight?"

Christopher Marlowe
'Hero and Leander'
1598

The Greek myth of the doomed lovers Hero and Leander is a famous illustration of the conventional wisdom that the first few seconds of a meeting dictate whether or not the chemistry between two people is right. Recognizing who a person wants to spend time with is widely believed to take place instantly. These lines are often attributed to William Shakespeare, but actually come from Christopher Marlowe's epic poem, which was completed after his death in 1593 by fellow poet and dramatist George Chapman.

Marlowe's murder in a tavern brawl at the age of twenty-nine years cut off the career of a glittering wit and intellect. Shakespeare was affected enough to pay homage to Marlowe's words through Phoebe, a shepherdess in *As You Like It* (1599), who prefaces them with: 'Dead shepherd, now I find thy saw of might;/"Who ever lov'd that lov'd not at first sight?"' It is Marlowe, the master of insight, whom Shakespeare acknowledges here, imitation being the height of flattery. Shakespeare also refers to Marlowe's death through another character, the court jester Touchstone. Shakespeare may have known that Marlowe was killed for apostasy on the authority of a rigidly narrow-minded Church, sanctioned by a state that could not understand his verse. **LW**

"Adversity makes strange bedfellows."

European Proverb
Unknown
c. 1600

This proverb of unknown provenance points out that it is often in the most trying of circumstances that people who otherwise might never have formed a bond will join together. It is more of an observation than advice, because it is also a reminder that the people in question may part ways very quickly once the moment of adversity is over.

Over the centuries, the proverb has emerged in different forms, including the version 'Politics makes strange bedfellows,' but the point remains the same. The proverb is also a reminder that even in the darkest times, we should look for positive interpretations of our predicaments. During these moments, we might meet and get to know people whose paths otherwise might never have crossed our own, and it is often these people, those with whom we have shared trauma, who are able to help us through future times of adversity. In other words, adversity gives rise to empathy, and shared experiences foster understanding of what other people are enduring, and might continue to endure.

The above quotation has some parallels with the phrase 'strength in numbers' because sometimes, in the toughest times, the people who offer the most support are the ones who are experiencing exactly the same emotions. **TH**

"Love all; trust a few, Do wrong to none."

William Shakespeare
All's Well That Ends Well
1605

Spoken by the Countess of Roussillon, whose role George Bernard Shaw described as 'the most beautiful old woman's part ever written,' the above quotation appears at the beginning of one of Shakespeare's 'problem' plays. According to E K Chambers's 1930 chronology, it is the playwright's twenty-fifth dramatic work and sits between *Troilus and Cressida* and *Measure for Measure*. The line is spoken to Bertram, the countess's son, in the opening scene of Act I, which is set in Roussillon, then a province of Spain, now one of France. The young count bids farewell to his mother as he leaves to take his place in the court of the king of France, where he will assume the role of the monarch's ward and attendant. His destination is what prompts Bertram's mother to issue her guiding words, for any aristocrat would know what lay in wait for an unsuspecting courtier. The French court was a place of intrigue and excitement, but also of danger. The French king from 1589 to 1610 was Henry IV. As benevolent as he may have been, Henry knew too well the machinations of rulers, having previously been Henry of Navarre, and narrowly escaped death, along with thousands of his fellow Protestants, in the St Bartholomew's Day Massacre of 1572. **IHS**

"He who laughs last, laughs longest."

Unknown
The Christmas Prince
1608

While this proverb dates back to Tudor England, its authorship did not, as one might have imagined, have anything to do with Shakespeare. It first appeared in print in a play, *The Christmas Prince*, that was first performed in Cambridge, England, in the early 17th century. The lines that are the origins of the phrase are actually worded as follows:

'Laugh on laugh on my friend
He laugheth best that laugheth to the end.'

The purpose of the saying is to urge caution against claiming victory too soon, and against making assumptions about an outcome. It is a reminder that complete satisfaction may be expected only when a result is known for sure, while those who do not wait, and who act too quickly, may discover, to their discomfiture, that their reaction is premature.

The proverb is also reflective of a commonly held belief in Tudor England: that people prepared to wait patiently for justice, and wait calmly for the outcome of a certain situation, will always get the most satisfaction – what was commonly referred to as 'the last laugh'. The proverb warns against cockiness and is a reminder that patience will be rewarded – a belief strongly held in the 17th century. **TH**

"*Shall I compare thee to a summer's day?*"

William Shakespeare
Sonnets
1609

This opening line is the most frequently quoted part of Sonnet 18, probably the best known of Shakespeare's 154 sonnets. The answer to the question is affirmative; a comparison follows, and summer comes off the worse from it: the addressee is 'more lovely and more temperate' than the season. The sonnet concludes:

'So long as men can breathe, or eyes can see,
So long lives this, and this gives life to thee.'

The poet is claiming that the addressee will be immortalized by his verse – writers and artists throughout history have claimed that their work cheats transience and captures moments for eternity.

Sonnet 18 answers its own rhetorical questions, but raises at least two others. One relates to line ten – 'Nor lose possession of that fair thou ow'st' – is the last word an abbreviated form of 'ownest' or of 'owest'? Or (most likely) did Shakespeare intend to suggest both?

The other abiding question is that of whether the person addressed is male or female: it might be one or the other, but again it could be both; the possibility of variant readings is one of the things that turns verse into poetry. **JP**

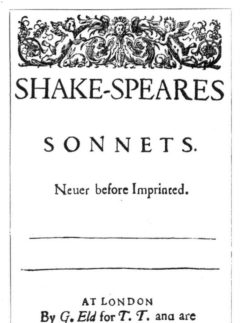

SHAKE-SPEARES

SONNETS.

Neuer before Imprinted.

AT LONDON
By *G. Eld* for *T. T.* and are
to be folde by *Iohn Wright*, dwelling
at Chrift Church gate.
1609.

◬ The title page of the 1609 edition of Shakespeare's work.

> " *There is no greater glory than love, nor any greater punishment than jealousy.* "

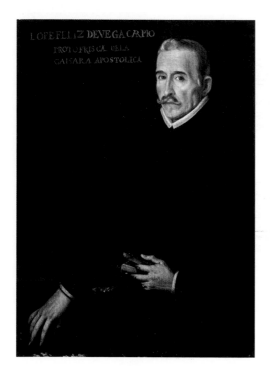

Félix Lope de Vega
La Dorotea
1632

To state simply that Félix Lope de Vega y Carpio was a Spanish playwright gives little hint of his prodigious output, which, although subsequently exaggerated, is known to have been greater than that of almost any other author in world history. He wrote 1,800 plays, most of them full length, and some of which are known to have gone from the tip of his pen to live performance in the course of a single day; around fifty of these works remain extant. He also wrote twenty-one large volumes of nondramatic works, including poetry and prose.

Although rightly acclaimed as a mature masterpiece, *La Dorotea* is to some extent a puzzling work – although presented in dialogue form, it is not a play but a thinly veiled slice of autobiography that describes the two main women in the dramatist's life, and his disputes with his contemporary playwright Luis de Gongora. The story centres on Dorotea's love for Fernando, a poet. Their relationship is strong, but they are driven apart by sexual jealousy. After Fernando walks out, Dorotea makes a suicide attempt before meeting another man, Don Bela. Fernando returns to Dorotea, finds her with Don Bela and kills him. **TH**

> *A mighty pain to love it is,*
> *And 'tis a pain that pain to miss;*
> *But of all pains the greatest pain*
> *It is to love, but love in vain.*

Abraham Cowley

Anacreontiques

1633

Anacreon (c. 582–485 BCE) was an ancient Greek lyric poet who wrote entertainingly on a wide range of subjects, both frivolous and profound. Little of his work survives, but later poets in other languages have emulated his distinctive manner in their own writings.

Among the most celebrated imitators of Anacreon was English poet Abraham Cowley, who pretended that verses such as those from which the above quotation is taken were authentic translations of some newly rediscovered originals. They weren't, and no one was fooled; it was merely a literary conceit, not an attempt at deception.

Indeed, most of Cowley's output was in the style of someone else: *Pindaric Ode* in the manner of another great Greek lyric poet; *Poetical Blossoms* in that of Edmund Spenser, author of *The Faerie Queene*; and *The Mistress*, in the metaphysical style of John Donne. Such self-conscious affectation was popular during the poet's lifetime, but subsequently fell from favour. The poem of Cowley that is most widely esteemed today is 'On the Death of Mr Crashaw,' in which emotion, for once, got the better of artifice. **TH**

⊘ The original caption of this engraving of Abraham Cowley (1633) draws attention to the poet's youthful appearance.

"When love is not madness, it is not love."

⊘ Undated portrait of Spanish playwright and priest Pedro Calderón de la Barca. His book denotes that he is a man of letters.

Pedro Calderón de La Barca

El Mayor Monstruo Los Celos (*Jealousy, the Greatest Monster*), c. 1637

Calderón was an enormously prolific Spanish playwright whose three main modes were comedies and tragedies for secular audiences, and religious works written for performance in churches. Within these forms various themes recur, and the most dominant of them become leitmotifs. Among the most striking of these are that life is but a dream, and the persistent idea that, even if all amatory involvement is not a form of insanity, it may reasonably be mistaken for the same.

The work from which the above quotation is taken is a rather didactic drama that seeks to demonstrate that jealousy is the most destructive of all the negative feelings that lovers can experience. In *Othello*, William Shakespeare called it 'the green-eyed monster, which doth mock the meat it feeds on'. As soon as one partner begins to doubt the other, no reassurance is possible: he may ask her if she is faithful to him; she may answer in the affirmative, but now that he is suspicious, he will not believe anything she says. When she realizes that she is not believed, she may decide that she might as well commit the crimes for which she is regarded as guilty anyway. **JP**

"Fair Daffodils, we weep to see You haste so soon."

Robert Herrick
"To Daffodils"
1648

In the famous poem of which these are the opening lines, Robert Herrick, a 17th-century English cavalier poet, refers to the perennial plant of the Amaryllidaceae family as a metaphor for transience. At the start of the second and last stanza, the poet observes:

'We have short time to stay, as you,
    We have as short a spring.'

Spring here represents youth, which comes and goes all too quickly, like the daffodils. The sentiment may not be original, but it is here elegantly expressed. And if we were to deprecate poems about death – on the grounds that we all know that we are going to die, and there's nothing profound in such thoughts – we would banish some of the most popular and widely quoted works in the whole of world literature.

Herrick often returns to this theme, perhaps most famously in the following stanza from 'To the Virgins, to Make Much of Time':

'Gather ye rose-buds while ye may,
    Old Time is still a-flying,
And this same flower that smiles today
    Tomorrow will be dying' **TH**

⬧ The cavalier poet Robert Herrick, a detail of an illustration (c. 1800) by A S Hartrick.

" *Tact is the art of making a point without making an enemy.* "

⊘ Engraving of Sir Isaac Newton, taken from a 1702 portrait by Godfrey Kneller.

Isaac Newton
Attributed
c. 1650

Sir Isaac Newton, English physicist, mathematician, astronomer, philosopher and theologian, was a man of many achievements. He built the first telescope and conducted extensive studies on the speed of sound, but many people are unaware that he was also very religious. He wrote more on biblical hermeneutics, and religion in general, than on science and mathematics.

The above quotation reflects his belief in caution, and that we should always aim to express our thoughts without offending or riling others. The ability to show tact has been emphasized since the earliest proverbs, including this one from the Bible: 'A gentle answer turns away wrath, but a harsh word stirs up anger.'

Newton was a firm believer that a gentle approach and good communication were essential when it came to building relationships. He believed that by making his point tactfully he allowed others to speak, and this gave him the opportunity to learn from others and understand their points of view. This is reflected in another quotation of his, which reminds us of the importance of learning from others: 'If I have seen further than others, it is by standing upon the shoulders of giants.' **TH**

> # *The more we love our friends, the less we flatter them; it is by excusing nothing that pure love shows itself.*

Molière
Le Misanthrope
1666

Jean-Baptiste Poquelin, the dramatist known by his stage name of Molière, was one of the early masters of comedy in Western literature. This quotation stresses the importance of honesty, even if it is sometimes brutal, and that there is more to true friendship than flattery and paying compliments.

Molière here suggests that those who do not genuinely care for one another often use flattery to get what they want, and that flattery is rarely heartfelt. Genuine friends will be honest all the time, and never turn a blind eye to their loved ones' faults or errors: their praise is genuine, and their criticisms are well meant.

Friends want the best for one another, and often it is only our intimates who can see our faults. In turn, friends recognize that criticism from genuine friends is given only because of genuine concern, not a desire to put someone down. Molière is showing that, although criticism may be hard to take, the silver lining is that it is a sign of true friendship, and that only true friends with a genuine love for one another will be truly honest with both their compliments and their criticism. This in turn strengthens relationships. **TH**

◬ An 1870 engraving of an early production of Molière's play *Le Misanthrope*, after a drawing by G Staal.

"True friendship is never serene."

Marie de Rabutin-Chantal
Letters
1675

French aristocrat Marie de Rabutin-Chantal was most famous for her long, detailed letters (more than 1,000 of them) to numerous recipients, most notably her daughter Françoise-Marguerite. Widowed at age twenty-four, after her husband was killed in a duel over another woman, Marie never remarried and devoted much of the rest of her life to *belles lettres*.

Her prolific output may have given her some solace in her grief, but it also, as it turned out, had commercial value. Her letters were copied and widely circulated, not because they were scandalous, but because they were full of sound advice, and (more importantly at the time) well written. She was aware, almost from the start of her enterprise, that her letters were semipublic documents, and she wrote them accordingly, with one eye on the addressee, and the other on posterity.

Thus the above quotation is aimed not merely at the named recipient of the letter, but at the world at large. Marie was keen to remind her readers that true friendship is not simple and will never be free of conflict or turmoil. The sentiment is commonplace, and what goes for friendship applies equally to true love, the course of which, as Shakespeare wrote in *A Midsummer Night's Dream* (c. 1595–96), 'never did run smooth'. **TH**

"There is no disguise which can hide love for long where it exists, or feign it where it does not."

Duc de la Rochefoucauld
Maxims
1678

François, Duc de La Rochefoucauld, was a French nobleman and a soldier who fought with distinction for his country, but was severely wounded, so withdrew from the battlefield to begin a new life as a writer.

His reputation in his second career rests on the work from which the above quotation is taken – a large collection of often fairly cynical apothegms about humanity and the human condition.

Many people quote La Rochefoucauld on a wide range of subjects – he's the after-dinner speaker's perennial go-to source – but in a short story titled 'The Little Hours' (1939), Dorothy Parker created a protagonist who expresses the tenable view that a relentless aphorist is rather a bore, and who wonders how many people have ever read La Rochefoucauld 'without a middleman' – in other words, who have got their quotations directly from the source, rather than read someone else who has quoted the *Maxims*.

The above quotation asserts that love – or the absence of love – is unmistakable. **JP**

❷ La Rochefoucauld warns King Louis XVI of revolutionary action.

> # *"Friendship is the golden thread that ties the heart of all the world."*

JOANNES EVELYN ARMIG.
REG. SOCIETATIS SOC.

◬ John Evelyn was, with Samuel Pepys, one of the most famous English diarists of the 17th century.

John Evelyn
The Life of Mrs Godolphin
1680

John Evelyn was a public servant in England after the restoration of the monarchy in 1660. He is best known today for his diaries, which remained unpublished until 1818 but are among the most important historical documents of the period.

It appears that Evelyn had a great gift for friendship, and he formed two particularly strong bonds of affection. One was with Samuel Pepys, the other celebrated diarist of the era. The two men met at the start of Charles II's Second Dutch War (1665–67), during which Evelyn was serving on a commission for the care of the wounded, and Pepys was a navy official. They remained close until the latter's death in 1703. Evelyn's other great bond was with Margaret Blagge, a maid of honour at the royal court, whom he first met in around 1670. She was thirty-two years his junior, and his affection for her may well have been nothing other than paternal. In 1675, Blagge was secretly married to Sidney Godolphin, a future Lord High Treasurer of England. After she died in childbirth in 1678, Evelyn was moved to write her biography; it is from this powerfully emotional work (first published in 1847) that the above quotation is taken. TH

Love ceases to be a Pleasure, when it ceases to be a Secret.

Aphra Behn
The Lover's Watch
1686

Aphra Behn was the first Englishwoman known to have earned a living as a writer. She was the author of several plays and works of prose fiction, together with a small body of poetry. She is of abiding interest as a protofeminist, because one of her works, *Oroonoko* (1688), addresses themes of slavery, race and gender.

The Lover's Watch is a slight but charming book of verse and prose that presents an etiquette template for suitors. It suggests ways of passing those seemingly interminable periods when the loved one is absent, and offers consolation to women who are worried about the temptations to which the objects of their desire may succumb when they are far away. It advises that the mornings be spent in 'agreeable reverie' and that the time of greatest danger is between five and six in the afternoon, when the loved one may receive or pay 'dangerous visits,' during which there may be encounters with rival suitors.

Some books of manners are weakened by excessive prescription. Behn makes no such errors here: her touch is unfailingly light, and her observations are invariably laced with gentle irony. **JP**

◭ A painting of Aphra Behn (c. 1670) by Baroque portrait painter Sir Peter Lely.

"Time, which strengthens friendship, weakens love."

"There are no secrets that time does not reveal."

Jean de La Bruyère
Les Caractères ou les Moeurs de ce Siècle
1688

Jean Racine
Athalie
1691

The masterpiece of French literature from which this quotation is taken was ostensibly a translation of the work of ancient Greek philosopher Theophrastus. But La Bruyère was more than a classical scholar – he was also an acerbic satirist. And his real targets were not pre-Christian Athenians; they were some of his richest and most powerful contemporaries.

The unique and lasting appeal of *Les Caractères* is that it starts with Theophrastus's general observations about ill manners and then gives particular examples of them in French life. And since La Bruyère worked at the court of Louis II de Bourbon, many of the instances of bad behaviour that he held up to ridicule – avarice, depravity, dissimulation, sycophancy, rustic coarseness – were attributable to royalty and ministers of state.

La Bruyère was careful to deny that any of the vices he portrayed belonged to any particular person, but readers thought they could identify some of the author's targets, and his works became best sellers.

Perhaps predictably, this made La Bruyère many enemies among those who thought, rightly or wrongly, that it was they who were being ridiculed. **TH**

In this play, the title character, widow of the king of Judah, believes that she has eliminated all the rest of the royal family and that her power is unassailable. But she is mistaken, and the past comes back to punish her.

The sentiment is often encountered in literature – Chaucer's 'Murder will out' in *The Canterbury Tales* is a famous earlier example – but although the notion may be attractive to optimists, romantics and writers seeking plausible denouements to their fiction, there is abundant evidence that the reality is not quite so clear-cut.

The development of DNA testing has enabled police to reopen cold cases, and to apprehend criminals who have escaped justice for more than half a century. Conversely, at the height of the early 21st-century fashion for researching family history, many US people who were keen to trace their lineage to George Washington (or whomever) found that public records went back no earlier than the time of their great-grandparents. For these researchers, few maxims could be further from the truth than Racine's suggestion. **TH**

❷ A 19th-century poster for a production of Racine's play.

M. DE MAX
ET Melle DELVAIR

DE LA COMÉDIE-FRANÇAISE DANS:

ATHALIE

D'APRÈS LA TRAGÉDIE DE JEAN RACINE
ADAPTATION ET MISE EN SCÈNE DE M. MICHEL CARRÉ

PAUL BERTHON

S.A.P.F.

S.A.P.F.

S.C.A.G.L.

S.C.A.G.L.

SÉRIE D'ART PATHÉ FRÈRES

Heaven has no rage, like love to hatred turned, Nor Hell a fury, like a woman scorned.

William Congreve
The Mourning Bride
1697

The version of this quotation most often encountered is 'Hell hath no fury like a woman scorned,' but here is the original text on which the well-known proverb is based. Uttered at the close of Act III of English Restoration dramatist William Congreve's play *The Mourning Bride*, it is part of a dramatic speech given by Queen Zara on learning that the man she has fallen in love with, Alphonso, the son of a powerful king, had secretly married another woman, Almeira, against his father's wishes. Almeira is the mourning bride of the title because she and her husband were parted by a shipwreck. The plot of the play is a complicated one in which all three characters have been forced to conceal their true feelings through fear of what Alphonso's father would do if he learned the truth. Zara herself has had to feign an attraction to Alphonso's father to protect her beloved, and so is doubly furious to discover that all the dissembling she has undertaken has been for nothing.

The Mourning Bride ends with Zara's suicide and was Congreve's only tragedy. He has always been better known for his comedies: *The Old Bachelor*, *Love for Love*, *The Double-Dealer* and *The Way of the World*. JP

Vendetta in a Harem (1854) by Italian painter Federico Faruffini – note the knife in the hand.

To err is human;
to forgive, divine.

Alexander Pope
An Essay on Criticism
1711

Pope's *Essay,* from which this remark is taken, uses rhymed couplets to set out some requirements of good writing, and satirize bad literary practice. The *Essay* was influenced by Horace's *Ars Poetica.*

Although the context here is light-hearted, the underlying concept has greatly exercised theologians and intellectuals for at least 2,000 years – namely, the power of the monotheistic deity, a being who knows everything, including the future, and can do anything. Although mystery is an important part of faith – in other words, that there should be matters that are beyond comprehension, which mortals have to take on trust – that has not stopped intellectuals hypothesizing about the ramifications of God's omnipotence, especially the overriding question: if God is good, can foresee disaster and can prevent it, why doesn't He do so?

Some writers tied themselves in knots thinking about it – John Milton, for example, evidently found Satan a more attractive character (in strictly artistic terms) than God. Others were more like Pope: German poet Heinrich Heine, for example, is reputed to have said: 'God will forgive me; that's His job.' **TH**

◉ Jesus shows forgiveness to a sinful woman in this painting by 18th-century Danish artist Hendrick Krock.

"Laugh at your friends, and if your friends are sore, So much the better, you may laugh the more."

Alexander Pope
Epilogue to the Satires
1738

This rather puzzling couplet may be clarified to some extent by referring to the two lines that immediately precede it. The lines assert that we should not laugh at fools, lest we make them angry, nor at our enemies, because our laughter will do nothing to make them friendlier towards us, and will only exacerbate the situation. Thus, by a process of elimination, of all the people we know, the only ones remaining that we can laugh at are our friends.

But is it right to laugh at people we love? Pope takes – or, within the context of the poem, affects to take – the view that real friends will let us laugh at them and will take it in good stride, because they are confident that they can trust us. Conversely, by definition, any friend who takes offense cannot be a true friend, and so laughing at them serves the useful purpose of revealing them in their true colours.

But that is not the only way in which the text can be interpreted. The lines equally may be taken to mean that your friends' discomfiture when you first laugh at them should make you laugh even more. Such pleasure in another's discomfiture would be what is known in German as *schadenfreude*.

The above lines are an example of a quotation that has become well known and popular despite being imperfectly understood, largely due to their becoming detached from their original context. **TH**

"Be just before you're generous."

Eliza Haywood
The Female Spectator
1745

Eliza Haywood (née Fowler) was an English actress and a prolific poet, playwright and author of romans à clef (novels in which famous celebrities of the period are depicted in easily seen-through disguises). She also wrote realistic novels, including *The History of Jemmy and Jenny Jessamy* (1753), and, most famously, *Love in Excess* (1720), a romance about a lothario who cleans up his act and learns morality.

Haywood's largely satirical views of humankind are thought to have been at least partly the reason that she came under attack from Alexander Pope. Provoked by her writings, he was rude about her in his poem *The Dunciad* (1728). Her fame also seems to have reached Jonathan Swift, author of *Gulliver's Travels*, to similar effect. In a letter of 1731, Swift wrote: 'Mrs Haywood I have heard of as a stupid, infamous, scribbling woman, but have not seen any of her productions.'

From April 1744 to May 1746, Haywood published *The Female Spectator*, the first periodical in English to be written by a woman. The magazine was protofeminist in its focus on the iniquities attendant to the state of matrimony. It also dealt with child-rearing, education and, less seriously, with matters of etiquette. Haywood contributed to it under four pseudonyms, and the articles purported to originate in letters from readers, another innovation. Haywood recognized that there was much in society that was unfair to women, and she encouraged her readers to recognize that it need not always be so.

Haywood describes the quotation above as 'an old saying'. It may well be, but this is its earliest recorded usage, and the reason for the present attribution. **LW**

> *If a man does not make new acquaintance as he advances through life, he will soon find himself left alone. A man, Sir, should keep his friendship in constant repair.*

Samuel Johnson
Attributed
1755

The above quotation appears in *The Life of Samuel Johnson* (1791) by James Boswell, who devoted much of his life to recording the wit and wisdom of Dr Samuel Johnson, poet, novelist, critic and compiler of the first comprehensive dictionary of the English language.

Johnson had a trenchant view on almost everything, but was admirably willing to admit when he was wrong. When a woman asked him why he had incorrectly defined 'pastern' as 'the knee of a horse' (in fact, it's the part of the leg between the fetlock and the top of the hoof), he replied: 'Ignorance, madam, pure ignorance.' In this quotation, Johnson takes a typically unconventional view. It is much more common to encounter the suggestion that a few friends, usually those made in youth, are enough to last a lifetime. But Johnson turns this platitude on its head and puts forward a whole new aspect: that for one reason or another (geographical separation, death, poverty, immobility) we might lose touch with our oldest intimates. More than that, Johnson notes that friendships are not adamantine – like anything else, they are subject to forces of decay and need regular maintenance. **TH**

> *Drive out prejudices through the door, and they will return through the window.*

Frederick the Great
Letter to Voltaire
1771

The correspondence between Frederick the Great, the third king of Prussia, and French philosopher Voltaire lasted for forty years. In 1736, at the age of twenty-four (Voltaire was forty-two), Frederick wrote him his first letter in which he spoke of 'the numberless beauties in your works' and begged to be included in the number of people 'whom you find worthy of your instruction'.

It is difficult to imagine Frederick the Great, the supremely successful military commander who turned Prussia into a great united power, to be the same young man who built a garden lavishly furnished with erotic statues, who surrounded himself in court with literary dilettantes, and who courted Voltaire. But Frederick, who drew admiration for sharing the hardships of war with his fellow officers, and could never be accused of reigning from a position of safety, also grew to admire all things French and was inspired to copy the luxurious court of Louis XIV. He was, to a certain extent, an enlightened man in an age of enlightenment, who wanted to cultivate the 'manners and morals' of his own people, and to encourage political and social tolerance.

In his correspondence with Voltaire, he complained about the prejudices he was facing, and expressed personal dissatisfaction with his circumstances. Doubtless he deserved some sympathy, and Albert Einstein is said to have remarked, much later, that, 'It is harder to crack prejudice than an atom.' **TH**

> ❝ *I love the man that can smile in trouble, that can gather strength from distress, and grow brave by reflection.* ❞

The cartoon *Wha Wants Me* (1792) by Isaac Cruikshank portrays Paine as a radical revolutionary for hire.

Thomas Paine
The American Crisis
1776

This quotation, from the first in a series of essays written by Thomas Paine titled *The American Crisis*, was a rallying cry for Americans after their long withdrawal through New Jersey to the Delaware River during the American Revolution (1775–83). The soldiers were tired and lacking in provisions, but Paine praises them for their orderly retreat. He goes further, saying that although there is a 'summer soldier' and 'sunshine patriot', the true soldier shows his fortitude when challenged not by 'trifles' but by serious distressm – 'the harder the conflict, the more glorious the triumph'. He reiterates that 'little minds shrink' and what we gain easily we do not value.

Paine's beliefs were to be sorely tested. Although *Common Sense* (1776), his pamphlet in defence of American independence from England, earned him the title of 'Father of the American Revolution', it was not without its critics, and his later comments on the funding of the Revolution were controversial and led to him being denied high political office. Although Paine never abandoned his convictions, his friends ostracized him for his outspoken criticism of Christianity and he died abandoned by most of them. **TH**

"*He who praises everybody, praises nobody.*"

Samuel Johnson
Lives of the Poets
1779

Samuel Johnson's quotation above – that if one praises everything, then nothing has value – should be the universal motto for critics. As a critic, Johnson himself was strongly opinionated. His book *Lives of the Poets* included critical appraisals of more than fifty poets, many of whom lived in the 18th century. The book was drawn from a series of articles that began to appear in 1740; from these, Johnson established a pecking order of the poets most deserving of our attention.

The opening statement of Johnson's preface to *The Plays of William Shakespeare* (1765) makes it clear that we should praise only the great rather than shower everyone with acclaim: 'That praises are without reason lavished on the dead, and that the honours due only to excellence are paid to antiquity, is a complaint likely to be always continued by those, who, being able to add nothing to truth, hope for eminence from the heresies of paradox; or those, who, being forced by disappointment upon consolatory expedients, are willing to hope from posterity what the present age refuses, and flatter themselves that the regard which is yet denied by envy, will be at last bestowed by time.' **IHS**

⊙ Johnson (*right*) helped to found the Literary Club in 1764; here he talks with poet and fellow member Oliver Goldsmith (*left*).

" *Your body is the church where Nature asks to be reverenced.* "

Marquis de Sade
Juliette
1791

The quotation above sums up the morally inverted philosophy of Donatien Alphonse François, Marquis de Sade. Sent away at the age of six to be educated by an uncle, the boy was introduced to sex by a corrupt abbot. At Jesuit school, at ten, he experienced beatings.

He wooed the daughter of a wealthy magistrate, but her father made him marry the older, plainer sister. He eventually ran off to Italy with the younger sister when the authorities lost patience with his behaviour, which included beating prostitutes and kidnapping local children to satisfy his paedophilia. His wife forgave him, but his mother-in-law, Madame de Montreuil, did not. She went to the king, Louis XV, on whose direct order Sade was imprisoned without trial; he spent around twenty-seven years in custody.

Imprisonment gave Sade time to write. The quotation here is uttered by the abbess Madame Delbène, who seduces and depraves the thirteen-year-old anti-heroine, Juliette. Juliette goes on to enjoy wealth and happiness – obtained by a life of vice, robbery and murder – in contrast to her sister, Justine, who suffers terribly by trying to live virtuously. **LW**

" *[Marriage] is the tomb of love.* "

Giacomo Casanova
Histoire de ma Vie
c. 1797

Giacomo Casanova was a Venetian adventurer and author who wrote and translated under a number of different pen names, and at the end of his life produced his best-known work – *Histoire de ma Vie* (*Story of my Life*) – in French. It is a great adventure story, revealing him to be a notorious gambler, soldier, enthusiastic traveller and linguist who sometimes worked as a spy for Venice, practiced the magical arts, and was occasionally thrown into prison for his misdeeds.

He is best remembered for the many confessions he made in his memoir about love:

'The chief business of my life has always been to indulge my senses. . .I felt myself born for the fair sex, I have ever loved it dearly.'

But the above quotation makes clear his opinion on the sacrament of marriage. However, it should be acknowledged that he lived and died a Christian and that his attitude to the women he seduced was always one of courtesy. He was kind and attentive, never violent. In this respect, his behaviour was very different from that of most of the nobility of the time, who indulged in selfish casual affairs, their marriages being made for financial profit or social climbing. **TH**

"Fate chooses our relatives, we choose our friends."

Jacques Delille
'La Pitié'
c. 1803

These words express a sentiment echoed in the familiar adage that you can choose your friends, but you cannot choose your family. Whether or not they reflect the true feelings of French poet Jacques Delille is not clear. Certainly, his life was not an abundantly happy one. Born near Clermont-Ferrand in central France, he was illegitimate but became a prodigious scholar, translator and teacher of the classics. Though refused entry to the Académie Française at the age of sixteen because he was too young, he became such a respected translator that he was nicknamed 'the French Virgil'. He seems to have been a lonely figure, though, making his home in Switzerland and Germany, and dying almost blind in Paris.

Delille is better known today for his translations than for the poetry he wrote. The above quotation comes from his work, 'La Pitié: Poeme en Quatre Figures,' which contains a number of slightly sad lines suggesting his personal loneliness – for example, '*Les fruits les plus doux sont les fruits que l'on sème soi-même*' ('The sweetest fruits are fruits that are self-sown'), and '*Les vrais plaisirs sont ceux que l'on doit à soi-mêm*' ('The true pleasures are those that one finds oneself'). **TH**

◬ *Jacques Delille and his Wife* was painted by French portraitist Henri-Pierre Danloux in 1802.

> " *They sin who tell us love can die; with life all other passions fly; all others are but vanity.* "

Robert Southey
The Curse of Kehama
1810

English poet Robert Southey began writing *The Curse of Kehama* in 1802 but did not finish the epic poem until 1810. Its origins can be traced back to his schooldays, when he suffered from the terrible insomnia that inspired many of his greatest works. The epic poem, divided into twelve books, tells the story of an evil priest known as Kehama. The poem is influenced by Hindu myths and Zoroastrianism, which in turn reflect the expanding British commercial interests in India during Southey's lifetime. There are repeated references that evil allows for the shaping of good. In this particular quotation, the poet is disputing the belief (a belief that he describes as a 'sin') that 'love can die'.

Although Southey was never to enjoy the success or fame of his contemporaries Samuel Taylor Coleridge and William Wordsworth, he worked hard all his life to write poetry and prose, the latter gaining more admiration than the former. A generous man, Southey supported his own family, the widow of fellow poet Robert Lowell, and the widow and family of Coleridge.

It was typical of his fair-minded outlook that he wrote: 'No distance of place or lapse of time can lessen the friendship of those who are thoroughly persuaded of each other's worth.' **TH**

> " *It is a truth universally acknowledged, that a single man in possession of a good fortune, must be in want of a wife.* "

Jane Austen
Pride and Prejudice
1813

This is one of the most famous opening lines in world literature. Taken in isolation, the words are not particularly memorable, but within the broader context of the novel as a whole, it becomes apparent that Austen is here establishing both the main theme – the quest for a suitable life partner – and her ironic tone.

In fact, it's hardly necessary to read on in order to detect a certain archness. People object to being told that they cannot disagree with any proposition, no matter how reasonable; thus, from the start, the reader is gently goaded into challenging the words on the page. Once suspicions have been aroused, it becomes hard to take the next phrase at face value. Indeed, the objection is raised: why would a man with plenty of money need someone else to help him spend it? He might, of course, but it doesn't follow that he will.

As it turns out, it's the women who pursue the men, hoping to secure socially advantageous marriages. Mrs Bennet is anxious to find husbands for her five daughters – Jane, Elizabeth, Mary, Kitty and Lydia. **JP**

❯ The front cover of an 1883 edition of the novel.

PRIDE AND PREJUDICE

BY JANE AUSTEN

871

GEORGE ROUTLEDGE & SONS.

66 *To love for the sake of
being loved is human,
but to love for the sake
of loving is angelic.* 99

Alphonse de Lamartine

Graziella

1849

Alphonse de Lamartine was principally a poet; his most celebrated work was *Méditations Poétiques* (1820). He was also a distinguished historian who wrote a popular study of the Girondins (antimonarchists during the French Revolution). As a politician he headed the Second Republic in France for a short time in 1848.

The above quotation is taken from a novel loosely based on the author's affair with the granddaughter of an Italian fisherman. Their relationship ends when he returns to France; they exchange letters for a while, but then he learns of Graziella's death at age sixteen. The novel closes with a poem, *'Le Premier Regret'* ('The First Regret'), dedicated to her memory.

Graziella first appeared as a part of *Nouvelles Confidences*, a mixture of fact and fiction. The work was subsequently published on its own, and later adapted once for the stage and three times for the cinema, most recently in 1955 in a version directed by Giorgio Bianchi, starring Maria Fiore in the title role and Jean-Pierre Mocky as the Frenchman Alphonse. **JP**

◀ A portrait of Lamartine (1839) by Henri Decaisne.

66 *We loved with a love that
was more than love.* 99

Edgar Allen Poe

'Annabel Lee'

1849

'Annabel Lee' is the last poem that Poe completed before his death in 1849. It consists of six stanzas, three of six lines, one of seven lines, and two of eight lines; the rhyme scheme differs slightly in each stanza.

The poem returns to one of Poe's thematic preoccupations: the love of a man for a woman who dies. It is thought to have been written in memory of his wife, Virginia, who died in 1847 after a five-year battle with tuberculosis. But this work is perhaps less pessimistic than his earlier efforts. Whereas in 'The Raven,' for example, the lovers are parted forever by death, here we are told:

'. . .neither the angels in Heaven above
   Nor the demons down under the sea
Can ever dissever my soul from the soul
   Of the beautiful Annabel Lee.'

'Annabel Lee' has inspired and been alluded to in numerous subsequent works: Joan Baez and Stevie Nicks are among the singers who have performed musical settings of the poem; a 2009 full-length feature film adaptation was directed by Michael Rissi.

The potentially sinister implications of being together forever are highlighted in Clint Eastwood's directorial debut movie, *Play Misty for Me* (1971), in which a mad, Poe-quoting female fan tries to kill a disc jockey. **JP**

"Our most intimate friend is not he to whom we show the worst, but the best of our nature."

Nathaniel Hawthorne
Notebooks
c. 1850

⊘ A photograph of US novelist and writer Nathaniel Hawthorne that he used as a form of visiting card.

Nathaniel Hawthorne was a US novelist known for his 'dark romanticism'. He was descended from the first Puritans to emigrate from England. Given his background, it is not surprising that the roots of Hawthorne's work are moral themes, allegorical tales of sin, guilt and evil. The deeper psychological themes of his writing later drew praise from Henry James and D H Lawrence.

The above words about friendship are found not in Hawthorne's actual work but in his preparatory notes for essays and short stories. They were discovered by his son, Julian, and mentioned in volume 1 of the latter's *Nathaniel Hawthorne and His Wife: A Biography* (1884). The notes are serious in tone. The writer seems to be saying that our intimate friends deserve to be shown the best of our qualities rather than being privy to our faults and forgiving them. Hawthorne's friend and contemporary Ralph Waldo Emerson said: 'It is one of the blessings of old friends that you can afford to be stupid with them,' and German philosopher Friedrich Nietzsche declared that 'Love is blind; friendship closes its eyes.' Does Hawthorne's comment on the relationship with our friends run counter to these sayings? **TH**

'Tis better to have loved and lost than never to have loved at all.

Alfred, Lord Tennyson

In Memoriam A. H. H.

1850

These words were written not about the end of a love affair but about a bereavement. Arthur Henry Hallam (A. H. H.) was a poet and contemporary of Tennyson who died of a stroke while in Vienna with his father in 1833, at the age of twenty-two. Tennyson and Hallam met at Cambridge University in 1829, and the two men quickly became friends, spending Christmas together at Tennyson's home in Lincolnshire, where Hallam fell in love with Tennyson's eighteen-year-old sister, Emily. Her clergyman father disapproved and banned Hallam from the house, but the couple resumed their relationship after the old man died. Hallam was much loved by all who knew him, judging by the outpouring of grief on his death. Tennyson took seventeen years to complete the 133 stanzas in memory of his friend.

The quotation inspires us to remain hopeful at a time of despair. Rather than feeling that it would have been better never to have known the beloved person, Tennyson sees the love in itself as worthwhile and fruitful, and not negated by the subsequent loss. The death of Hallam has been seen as contributing to the melancholia and nostalgia of Tennyson's later poems. JF

⬥ This oil-on-canvas portrait of Alfred, Lord Tennyson, was painted in 1864 by George Frederick Watts.

“ *How do I love thee? Let me count the ways.* ”

Elizabeth Barrett Browning
Sonnets from the Portuguese; 'Sonnet 43'
1850

Sonnets from the Portuguese is a famous collection of forty-four love sonnets; of these, 'Sonnet 43' is one of the best-known poems in the English language. It was written by the prominent Victorian poet Elizabeth Barrett Browning, and the quoted line is its opening. All the poems in the collection adhere strictly to the sonnet form. Initially Barrett Browning was reluctant to publish 'Sonnet 43' on the grounds that it was too personal. However, her husband, Robert Browning, urged her to reconsider, and she did publish it.

After the question that drives 'Sonnet 43,' the poet goes on to list the ways in which she loves the person in question, her husband. Some critics have pointed out that the word 'count' suggests a calculating nature and a callous approach to describing love. However, it can be argued that the question suggests actual disbelief that her love could be questioned, and the detailed list of answers that follow demonstrate the intensity of her feelings. Barrett Browning had married against the wishes of her tyrannical father. Her earlier literary work before she met her husband was not successful, but *Sonnets from the Portuguese* was a triumph and showed the happiness Robert Browning brought into her life. **TH**

◑ A colour lithograph portrait (1840) of Elizabeth Barrett Browning.

“ *They loved each other beyond belief – she was a strumpet, he was a thief.* ”

Heinrich Heine
New Poems
1852

These words from the poem '*Ein Weib*' ('A Woman') appear in the 1938 English translation by US poet Louis Untermeyer. At only sixteen lines long, the poem expresses much in a short space. It tells the story of a love affair that ends when the man, a career criminal, is arrested for stealing. He writes to his woman from prison, imploring her to visit him, but she is hard-hearted and ignores his request. Even when he is executed, she shows no sympathy – she merely quaffs a glass of red wine and laughs at his fate.

Heinrich Heine was born in 1797 in Düsseldorf, Germany, and educated at the universities of Bonn and Göttingen before finally settling in 1831 in Paris, France, where he spent the last twenty-five years of his life. He was devoted principally to his art and to radical politics, but his life was not without romantic entanglements. His most significant love affair was with Crescence Eugénie Mirat, whom he nicknamed 'Mathilde'. A French shop assistant half his age, she was illiterate, spoke no German and had no intellectual interests. Nevertheless, they married and lived together, apparently contentedly, until Heine's death in 1856 at the age of fifty-eight. **JP**

Above all do not appear to others what you are not.

🔊 Mathew B Brady's portrait of Robert E Lee on his porch in Richmond, Virginia, in 1865, after the American Civil War was over.

Robert E. Lee
Letter to George Washington Custis Lee
1852

Robert E Lee was a US soldier who commanded the Confederate Army of Northern Virginia during the American Civil War. This quotation comes from a letter he wrote before the War broke out in 1861. Lee penned the letter in April 1852 from his home in Arlington, Virginia. He wrote it to his eldest son, George Washington Custis, who was then nineteen years old and studying at the US Military Academy at West Point, New York.

Lee had also attended West Point, graduating second in his class. In the letter he advised his son on how to behave, also saying: 'You must study to be frank with the world, frankness is the child of honesty and courage. Say just what you mean to do on every occasion, and take it for granted you mean to do right. . .Never do a wrong thing to make a friend or keep one. The man who requires you to do so is dearly purchased at a sacrifice. Deal kindly but firmly with all your classmates. You will find it the policy which wears best.'

In September of the same year, Lee was appointed superintendent of the academy at West Point. His advice to his son bore fruit: Custis graduated first in his class in 1854, and he later served under his father as a major general in the Confederate Army. CK

Life is a flower of which love is the honey.

Victor Hugo
Les Misérables
1862

This quotation comes from *Les Misérables* by Victor Hugo, the 19th-century French Romantic poet, dramatist and novelist. Hugo's sweeping historical novel is set against the backdrop of Revolutionary Paris and centres on the story of escaped convict Jean Valjean. It touches on themes of love, compassion, justice, redemption and forgiveness. Hugo was deeply critical of the social injustice, poverty and rigid class structure he observed in French society, which could turn innocent individuals into beggars, criminals and prostitutes. His writing explores how the lives of individuals play out in the context of wider political and historical events.

The transformation of Valjean from hardened criminal to respected citizen exemplifies Hugo's belief in love and compassion. Repeatedly in the novel love begets love and compassion begets compassion. Myriel's act of kindness sets Valjean on the road to redemption and it is only by learning to love others that Valjean makes something of his life. This quotation is a reminder of nature's eternal ongoing cycle and of the primacy of love in the human life cycle. It was a message that appealed to Hugo's readers: his death in 1885 brought two million mourners onto the streets of Paris. **TH**

◈ The enduring popularity of Victor Hugo's novel has seen numerous adaptations for film, television and stage.

> " *Have a heart that never hardens, and a temper that never tires, and a touch that never hurts.* "

Charles Dickens
Our Mutual Friend
1865

From Dickens's last completed novel, this quotation is part of an admiring description of the character Lizzie Hexam, who endures poverty, loneliness and other hardships. The daughter of a boatman who makes his living by robbing corpses found in the River Thames, Lizzie sacrifices her own prospects to help her brother. Her father is wrongly accused of murder, and dies, and she must also contend with the advances of her brother's violent teacher while secretly loving a man whose upper-class status makes him unattainable.

In these circumstances, Lizzie could develop a hostile or a cynical attitude, hardening her heart against further disappointments. Or she could lose control of her temper, become angry and resentful, and cease caring about others. Instead, she steadfastly refuses to be downcast, and it is only by maintaining her generous nature that she eventually finds the happiness she deserves. Lizzie's goodness inspires goodness in others, and serves as an exemplar to counter the cynicism that may sometimes be observed in real life. **TJ**

❹ Stained-glass window in the Dickens Museum in London.

> " *A difference of taste in jokes is a great strain on the affections.* "

George Eliot
Daniel Deronda
1876

Daniel Deronda is a novel by Mary Ann Evans, a British author who used the pen name George Eliot. It was her last novel, the only one set in contemporary Victorian society, and it is a story that combines moral comment and social satire. As a girl, Evans was a voracious reader and later, in her twenties, she came under the influence of Charles Bray, a rich manufacturer, philanthropist and freethinker. Early in her career, Evans worked as a journalist and editor, but when she started to write novels she adopted the name George Eliot in order to distinguish her work from the 'frivolous plots' of contemporary lady novelists whose work she had criticized in her reviews.

George Eliot wrote seven novels, of which *Daniel Deronda* was her most shocking and controversial. In the background of the novel is an examination of the position of Jews in British and European societies in the 19th century. The passage from which the above quotation is taken is part of a conversation between Daniel Deronda and Sir Hugo Mallinger. The latter's attitude to marriage is shallow, and he makes jokes that the more serious-minded Daniel does not find funny. It is at this point that Eliot makes her very shrewd observation on jokes as an aside. **TH**

"All happy families are alike; each unhappy family is unhappy in its own way."

Leo Tolstoy
Anna Karenina
1877

This quotation, the first line in Leo Tolstoy's epic novel, raises questions about the nature of success. Psychologists and anthropologists, chaos theorists and economists have all played around with this idea. The 'Anna Karenina principle' describes a situation in which every one of a number of conditions must be met in order for a particular circumstance – say, a happy family or a habitable planet – to come about. Avoidance of every deficient factor makes for a fragile state of affairs.

Aristotle concluded that not only families but all 'men are good in but one way, but bad in many'. The ways to unhappiness are broad and various but the way to happiness is hard and narrow: this is the essence of Christian philosophy. Tolstoy did not entirely fulfil the promise of this pronouncement, either in his own family or in his fictional work. The happiness of many relationships founders in that most dangerous of zones: sex. We find happiness in acts of solidarity or concurrence, but lose it in fear and boredom. We are not like Russian nesting dolls, fitting together by conforming to a certain standard. We are more like migrating geese, going in the right direction when we are attuned to ourselves. **LW**

◉ Kieron Moore and Vivien Leigh in *Anna Karenina* (1948).

◉ Leo Tolstoy with his wife and family in 1887.

"Marriage is like life . . . it is a field of battle, and not a bed of roses."

Robert Louis Stevenson
Virginibus Puerisque and Other Papers
1881

The essays collected under the title *Virginibus Puerisque and Other Papers* by the author of *Kidnapped* (1886), *Treasure Island* (1883) and *The Strange Case of Dr Jekyll and Mr Hyde* (1886) are full of pithy quotations about the battle of the sexes, and this is the most famous of them.

Stevenson here treats his chosen subject, marriage, lightheartedly, but not frivolously. He notes among his contemporaries a reluctance to take the plunge into matrimony, and adduces reasons in support of their hesitancy. He wonders why people ever marry, and rejects out of hand the suggestion that they do it 'for love,' because he regards love as no more than a slight preference rather than a powerful motivational force. A man and a woman may 'choose' each other, but there is no strong reason why they might not, in other circumstances, have chosen differently, or indeed have made no choice at all and remained contentedly single.

Stevenson described marriage as 'terrifying,' both in prospect and in reality. He conceded that there was no reason that marriages need be unsuccessful, but maintained that success in marriage required constant work. He also said: 'These notes, if they amuse the reader at all, will probably amuse him more when he differs than when he agrees with them; at least they will do no harm, for nobody will follow my advice.' **JP**

"Love is like measles; we all have to go through it."

Jerome K Jerome
Idle Thoughts of an Idle Fellow
1886

Idle Thoughts of an Idle Fellow is the title given to a collection of humorous essays by Jerome K Jerome. It is the author's second published work and it helped to establish his reputation. Typically, the book is dedicated to his idle companion: not a favoured human being, but his pipe. The work is written in the same frivolous vein as his much-loved novel, *Three Men in a Boat* (1889), although it has never attracted as much acclaim. The comparison of experiencing love to having measles is typical of Jerome's light-hearted style. By drawing a parallel with a disease that is relatively easy to overcome in childhood but is more painful in adulthood, the writer suggests that love comes easily to the young but is a complicated matter for older people.

Jerome K Jerome was born in 1859 in Walsall, Staffordshire, and was forced to leave his school studies after the early death of his parents. Thereafter followed unsuccessful attempts at acting, journalism and teaching, before he produced *On the Stage – And Off* (1885), a memoir of his work in the theatre, and *Idle Thoughts of an Idle Fellow*. *Three Men in a Boat* appeared soon after his marriage to Georgina Marris in 1888; the book had been inspired by the honeymoon they had taken on the River Thames. The book is full of comic situations involving three male companions, mixed in with accounts of the history of the region. It was an instant success and is still in print. **TH**

This is not a letter. It is only my arms round you for a quick minute.

Katherine Mansfield
Letter to Leslie Beauchamp
1915

Kathleen Mansfield Beauchamp was born in Wellington, New Zealand. At the age of nineteen she left her home country and settled in the United Kingdom. She travelled in Europe between 1903 and 1906 and began to write short stories under the pen name Katherine Mansfield. She briefly returned to New Zealand, but found it provincial, and after two years returned to London.

Mansfield was a member of several literary groups that included Virginia Woolf and D H Lawrence. One such was that of Lady Ottoline Morrell, who maintained literary salons in both her London house and her country retreat, attended by intellectuals from all walks of life. She was particularly interested in the work of young artists and writers and kept up many lengthy correspondences, including one with Mansfield, about whom she wrote: 'as a companion she was intoxicating …she wasn't a fraud – she was more of an adventuress'.

The quotation above comes from a letter from Mansfield to her beloved younger brother, Leslie, who was serving on the Western Front and was killed later that year. In her poignant letter, words are called upon to reduce the physical distance between them. **TH**

◉ Virginia Woolf once remarked that Katherine Mansfield had produced 'the only writing I have ever been jealous of'.

Love is to me that you are the knife which I turn within myself.

⊙ Kafka cuts a dapper figure as he poses for a photograph in Prague c. 1910.

Franz Kafka
Letter to Milena Jesenská
1920

Franz Kafka was a German novelist from a Jewish family who lived in Prague. He had a lonely childhood but was nevertheless dominated by his overbearing father. He rarely attended the synagogue and declared himself an atheist while in his teens. In 1907 he began work in the insurance industry and although he was successful and quickly promoted in several establishments, he resented the fact that it reduced the time that he had for writing.

Kafka was a shy man, sensitive but lacking in confidence, and many of his books focus on themes of alienation and conflict. He description of love as 'the knife which I turn within myself' confirms that he found it to be a contradictory and painful emotion. His attitude towards books was equally troubled. To Oskar Pollak, his close childhood friend, he maintained that we should read only books that 'wound and stab us'. He declared: 'A book must be the ax for the frozen sea within.' It has been claimed that Kafka had a schizoid personality disorder, for an anguished entry in his diary of 1913 talks of 'the tremendous world in my head' that is 'ripping' and 'tearing in me'. *The Metamorphosis* (1915) is one of his works that is often cited as proof of his illness. **TH**

" *The tragedy of love is indifference.* "

William Somerset Maugham
The Trembling of a Leaf
1921

The above quotation is from the short love story titled 'Red,' usually published as part of the collection titled *The Trembling of a Leaf*. William Somerset Maugham clearly subscribed to the belief that having a lover who is merely satisfactory and does not awake passion is the worst kind of relationship. Indifference was, in his opinion, the death knell of any relationship, worse than 'death' or 'separation'.

It could well be that he spoke from experience. Although he was homosexual, he was married to Syrie Wellcome, with whom he had a daughter, but they divorced in 1929. Syrie cited her husband's relationship with secretary Frederick Gerald Haxton as a contributing factor. Haxton was, in fact, Maugham's lover. As the writer was a homosexual man married to a heterosexual woman, the marriage was doomed to be indifferent at best. His relationship with Haxton was passionate, even tumultuous, but for Maugham, this was preferable to indifference. Some of Maugham's most memorable words are about his own experience of indifference and unrequited love: 'I have most loved people who cared little or nothing for me.' TH

⬙ Playwright and novelist William Somerset Maugham was one of the most renowned authors of his era.

"A bore is a man who, when you ask how he is, tells you."

Bert Leston Taylor
The So-Called Human Race
1922

Bert Leston Taylor had little time for bores. 'Bore' or 'bored' appears frequently in the posthumous collection *The So-Called Human Race*, a volume of essays, light verse and miscellaneous material. The wit in the above quotation is dependent on understanding that bores fail this basic test of self-awareness.

Taylor was most certainly not a bore. He had myriad interests, from classics to politics, from golf to natural history. His central interest, however, was good writing. He never believed that he could make a good enough musician to contribute in that field, but he knew how to coin a phrase and to tell a story, and this was the world in which he worked. He was as critical of himself as he was of any of the writers he had to read or edit, and while his appraisals may have been elegantly and even humorously expressed, they were devastatingly accurate. The secret to being a bore is to tell everything, as Voltaire said. This was an adage that Taylor stood by: draw only the main lines; let the story speak for itself. He did not hate people, but he did hate the way they failed to see what fools they were. This was his genius, and why a phrase like this is so enchanting. **LW**

"Life without love is like a tree without blossoms or fruit."

Kahlil Gibran
The Prophet
1923

Kahlil Gibran is the third best-selling poet in the world, after Shakespeare and Laozi. His work has been translated into forty languages – not bad for a man who actually considered himself to be more of a painter.

Born on 6 January 1883, in Lebanon, and educated in Beirut, Paris and Boston, Gibran used painterly imagery in his work to convey his philosophies of life, love and spirituality. Gibran pulled together teachings from Eastern Christianity, Islam, Buddhism, American transcendentalism and Lebanese folklore to create his own universal 'Anthem of Humanity'. From his most famous work, a book-length prose poem, the above quotation suggests that love fertilizes life. This can be interpreted literally, in terms of procreation, or figuratively, suggesting the necessity of love for nurturing creativity and productivity. Romantic in both style and philosophy, Gibran goes on to suggest that 'love without beauty is like flowers without fragrance, and fruit without seeds'.

Gibran fans have included Swiss psychoanalyst Carl Jung and US singer Elvis Presley. **EP**

❯ Kahlil Gibran at around the age of thirteen years.

"The great question that has never been answered . . . is, 'What does a woman want?'"

Sigmund Freud
Letter to Princess Marie Bonaparte
1925

Freud wrote the above words in a letter to Princess Marie Bonaparte, who had been consulting him concerning her own frigidity. A sexually adventurous woman, the Princess was nevertheless failing to reach sexual fulfillment and she had already embarked on a life-long programme of serious research into the subject. In later life she translated Freud's work into French and was to practise as a psychoanalyst herself.

Freud was genuinely frustrated by his inability to understand women. In his paper 'The Psychical Consequences of the Anatomic Distinction Between the Sexes' (1925) he wrote: 'Women oppose change, receive passively, and add nothing of their own'. As Donna Stewart, chair of women's health at the University Health Network, points out, 'Freud was a man of his times. He was opposed to the women's emancipation movement and believed that women's lives were dominated by their sexual reproductive functions.'

Freud believed that women should be subservient (he described his wife of many years, Martha, as a good housewife), so it may be that he failed to understand only women prepared to challenge his views. **TH**

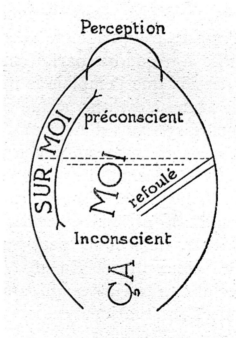

⬣ A diagram by Sigmund Freud of a psychological system.

◀ A portrait of Sigmund Freud that appeared on the cover of *Vu* magazine, 20 July 1932.

" The deepest definition of youth is life as yet untouched by tragedy. "

Alfred North Whitehead
Adventures of Ideas
1933

The above quotation is from Alfred North Whitehead's last major work on philosophy, which takes as its subject the development of civilization. In the chapter titled 'Peace,' Whitehead not only offers this stark definition of 'youth' but also contemplates the entire life-phase of youth. Observing first that 'youth is too chequered to be termed a happy period,' he concludes that ,the memories of youth are better to live through, than is youth itself'. Whitehead also examines the important process by which youth progresses to maturity.

Today, Whitehead's philosophy remains influential in the areas of education and ecology. He was responsible for the school of thought known as 'Process Philosophy,' which argues that we should see the world 'as a web of interrelated processes of which we are integral parts, so that all of our choices and actions have consequences for the world around us'. From the holism of these basic ideas came his beliefs about education.

One of his best-known pronouncements was that 'knowledge does not keep any better than fish [does]'. In other words, we should avoid 'multi-disciplinary education' that is content to put forward scraps of unrelated information, and which encourages uncritical parroting by the pupil. Instead, we should foster 'trans-disciplinary education,' which presents children with general principles and helps them make connections between all the different aspects of the world. **TH**

" When a lady chooses to change her mind, a gentleman would consider it no more than her privilege, and not badger her about it. "

Noel Langley
The Land of Green Ginger
1937

The work from which the above quotation is taken was the third novel by a South African writer who moved to Britain in 1935. Noel Langley's previous works had been whimsical comedies for adults: *Cage Me a Peacock* (1935) was set in ancient Rome; *There's a Porpoise Close Behind Us* (1936) was about English theatre folk. *The Land of Green Ginger* was a magical children's story about Abu Ali, son of Aladdin and future emperor of China.

The last named work was a success and prompted MGM movie studios to hire Langley to go to Beverly Hills and write the screenplay of L Frank Baum's novel *The Wonderful Wizard of Oz* (1900). Langley hated the resulting movie – his script was much altered and partly rewritten by several other hands – but he loved California and remained there for the rest of his life. He wrote an amusing novel about Hollywood – *Hocus Pocus* (1941) – and became a US citizen in 1961.

The idea that women are at liberty to change their minds, because that's what women do, does not originate here – it was a standard sexist stereotype of the period – but here Langley gives it eloquent and memorable expression. **JP**

Experience shows us that love does not consist in gazing at each other but in looking together in the same direction.

Antoine de Saint-Exupéry
Terre des Hommes (*Wind, Sand and Stars*)
1939

At first glance, it might appear that the above quotation is referring to the love of a couple. In fact, it is more about comradeship and the shared goals of people who find themselves in the same situation. Antoine de Saint-Exupéry was a writer, poet, journalist and aristocrat. He was also a pioneering aviator, and much of his writing focused on aviation. *Terre des Hommes* (*Wind, Sand and Stars*) is a philosophical memoir that deals with a number of themes, including friendship, death, heroism and the quest for truth. The book's main event is an accident that the author and his navigator, André Prévot, had in the Libyan Sahara in 1935; the pair almost died of thirst.

It is impossible to mention Saint-Exupéry without reference to his novella *Le Petit Prince* (*The Little Prince*; 1943). The same crash gave rise to its opening, in which a pilot is marooned in the desert, whereas the ending echoes Saint-Exupéry's description of the death of his brother at the age of fifteen. In this story, the Little Prince does a lot of gazing, but it is not this sort of gazing that the above quotation refers to. This is a comment springing from the experience of a pilot who found himself stranded with his navigator in the Sahara. **TH**

◭ Watercolour illustration from *The Little Prince* (1943) by Antoine de Saint-Exupéry.

"*Hell is other people.*"

Jean-Paul Sartre
Huis Clos (No Exit)
1944

This line, which at first appears banal, as well as misanthropic, expresses a central tenet of the philosophy of existentialism. Sartre would sometimes deny that he was an existentialist, and later substantially altered his philosophy. Yet, those acts of repudiation and revision exemplify his own early theory of human relations, as described in 'Being and Nothingness,' the influential 1943 essay in which individuals are characterized as radically free, in the sense of being fully responsible for what they become as a result of their own choices. Since we are always free to choose differently in the future, our identities can never be fixed by what we have done in the past. But this pure, positive freedom to continually forge our own personal identities is constantly negated by the mere presence of other people, because their recollections of what we have done restrict their perceptions of what we might be in the future.

Sartre believed that this process of mutual objectification was practically insuperable and inescapable. However, elements of this idea have since emerged in the theory of 'learned helplessness,' so it may be a remediable psychological problem. TJ

In human relationships kindness and lies are worth a thousand truths.

Graham Greene
The Heart of the Matter
1948

Graham Greene is regarded by many as the greatest writer of the 20th century. A large number of his works were Catholic novels in which he explored moral and political issues and commented on the complex and often ambivalent nature of human relationships. The above quotation is one such example. Greene often wrote about the issue of truth, and it seems that he did not place a high priority on it. Here, in *The Heart of the Matter*, he states that being kind is more important than being honest, especially if honesty results in offense.

Greene was once criticized for always writing novels about the struggle between good and evil, for creating characters who are flawed, and he replied that he was unable to write about pure faith and goodness. The gloomy realism that pervades his work perhaps comes from his own life experience. He suffered from depression as a child and struggled with religion, converting to Roman Catholicism when he married. As a spy for the British MI6, he travelled widely, and his books are set in countries such as Mexico, Argentina, Cameroon and the Congo. The term 'Greeneland' was coined to refer to these hot and sometimes poor backgrounds. **TH**

⬥ Photographed at his London home, Graham Greene featured in *Picture Post* magazine in 1954.

"*If you expeᛦ nothing from anybody, you're never disappointed.*"

◉ Although Plath seems relaxed here as she works outdoors, she could never escape her inner turmoil.

Sylvia Plath
The Bell Jar
1963

Sylvia Plath was well known for her bleak outlook on life, a stance that could not be reflected more clearly than in the above quotation from *The Bell Jar*. Written just before she died, it was her only novel that was published in her lifetime, and, poignantly, it describes a woman slowly becoming insane. The quotation reflects Plath's reluctant belief that those closest to her would always let her down. She also wrote much 'confessional' poetry that drew on her deepest private emotions.

Even as a child Plath was clinically depressed, but a crucial event happened after her third year at university, when she was a guest editor at *Mademoiselle* magazine. The magazine had arranged a meeting with Welsh poet Dylan Thomas, someone whom Plath admired and had described as 'loving more than life itself', but she was devastated not to be invited. She waited outside his hotel in the hope of seeing him, not knowing that he had already left. A few weeks later she slashed her legs in what many saw as her first attempt at suicide. She married poet Ted Hughes in 1956, but he had an affair and left her on her own with their two children. In the very harsh winter of 1963 she committed suicide. **TH**

> # I know enough to know that no woman should ever marry a man who hated his mother.

Martha Gellhorn
Letter to Sandy Gellhorn
1969

Mothers are traditionally seen as nurturers. They have a huge effect on their children's lives, shaping their personalities and characteristics, so one suspects that Martha Gellhorn had a very good reason to make the barbed comment that was written in a letter to her adopted son, Sandy Gellhorn.

Gellhorn was the third wife of the troubled US novelist Ernest Hemingway, and sure enough, her husband had professed a deep hatred of his mother. Hemingway had deeply resented the fact that his mother had forced him to stay indoors and learn the cello, rather than allow him to explore the great outdoors with his father, who had still managed to teach him how to hunt and fish. Hemingway was receiving treatment for his depression when Gellhorn first met him; he was experiencing one of his most troubled periods. Gellhorn was in little doubt that the cause of his disorder was his fractured relationship with his mother.

However, Gellhorn herself was not the ideal partner, according to Hemingway. He did not enjoy the frequent absences caused by her journalistic work – she was one of the greatest war correspondents of the 20th century and covered the whole of World War II – and in 1945 he left her for another woman. Could this explain the extreme bitterness of her words? **TH**

> # They fuck you up, your mum and dad. They may not mean to, but they do. They fill you with the faults they had And add some extra, just for you.

Philip Larkin
'This Be the Verse'
1971

It may not be the kind of language that one would expect from an unassuming librarian, but a surly dissatisfaction burned within Philip Larkin long before it burst forth in the sardonic profanity of his most famous poem. First printed in the August 1971 edition of *New Humanist* magazine, the poem found a permanent home in Larkin's final collection of verse, *High Windows* (1974).

The poem's expletive-laden, nursery-rhyme simplicity remains tailor-made for perking up dull English literature classes for disgruntled teens, although Larkin was almost fifty years old when he penned his forceful meditation on the shortcomings of parenthood, concluding with a morose injunction not to have any children.

After leaving Oxford University with a promising degree and aspirations of becoming a novelist, Larkin had instead become a librarian and lived as a bachelor in the working-class suburbs of Hull in northeast England. Stark meditations on the preoccupations of British proletarian life, flickering with contempt, pervade his modest body of work. 'Deprivation is for me what daffodils were for Wordsworth,' Larkin explained in *Required Writing* (1977). **EP**

"It is the most violent people who go for love and peace."

John Lennon
Playboy magazine
1980

In this famous response during a long interview in *Playboy* magazine, held two months before his death, John Lennon ruminated on the theme of goodness being restitution for earlier sins and repaying a debt to society – the greater the sinner, the greater the saint.

Reflecting on 'Getting Better,' a track from the album *Sgt. Pepper's Lonely Hearts Club Band* (1967), Lennon said that the lines 'I used to be cruel to my woman/I beat her and kept her apart from the things that she loved' were autobiographical. He continued: 'I was a hitter. I couldn't express myself, and I hit. . .That is why I am always on about peace, you see. It is the most violent people who go for love and peace.'

In his later years, Lennon did, indeed, become a great proponent of both, not least in the weeklong 'bed-in' that he and Yoko Ono held in the Amsterdam Hilton Hotel shortly after their marriage in 1969.

On 10 December the *Philadelphia Inquirer* reported that Lennon had ruefully admitted that, 'I really thought that love would save us all.' Two days earlier, he'd been shot dead by a deranged assassin. **JP**

◀ Newlyweds John and Yoko in bed in the Netherlands in 1969.

"It was inevitable: the scent of bitter almonds always reminded him of the fate of unrequited love."

Gabriel García Márquez
Love in the Time of Cholera
1985

The above quotation, the opening sentence of the novel, refers to the reactions of an elderly doctor, Juvenal Urbino, who is called to the death of a sick friend. He realizes that the old man has committed suicide – 'the scent of bitter almonds' refers to cyanide, which is present in bitter almonds – but he does not intend to make the cause of death public. A young doctor accompanying him is disappointed not to be able to study the effects of cyanide on the human body, but Dr Urbino points out that he will undoubtedly have many more chances in the future to examine the bodies of people who have committed suicide because of love.

After discovering the suicide, Dr Urbino goes home but soon afterwards dies as a result of a fall. It is at this point that the novel moves back fifty years to the youth of the doctor and his marriage to the beautiful Fermina. The many guises of love – futile, unrequited, youthful, timeless – permeate the novel, but Gabriel García Márquez gives us hope that it can be found even in our darkest hour, for Fermina is reunited with her first love, Florentino, and the two seventy-year-olds spend what remains of their lives together. **TH**

"*Nobody dies from lack of sex. It's lack of love we die from.*"

⊘ Multi-award-winning author Margaret Atwood, seen here in 1988.

Margaret Atwood
The Handmaid's Tale
1985

Canadian author, environmentalist and feminist Margaret Atwood often portrays female characters dominated by patriarchy. She insisted that *The Handmaid's Tale* is not science fiction but 'speculative fiction', because it portrays a scenario that is possible. However, the novel is set in the future and tells the story of a dystopian world known as Gilead, which is run by a strange religious group and where women are forbidden to read.

The narrator is a character called Offred, who is kept as a concubine by the ruling classes in the group in order to allow them to reproduce. The book describes a society in which certain relationships are forbidden and sex is merely a tool for reproduction. Although Offred's aunt maintains 'love is not the point', for Offred love is, in fact, the most important thing. She is not only missing her family, but also commenting on the lack of love within Gilead. She confirms this later with: 'There is nobody here I can love, all the people I could love are dead or elsewhere.' And later still, when the Commander tries to justify Gilead's regime, he asks, 'What did we overlook?' Offred's simple answer is: 'Love.' **TH**

"This is what I know for sure: love is all around."

Oprah Winfrey
What I Know for Sure
2014

By some measures Oprah Winfrey has been rated the most influential woman in the world. What is certain is that the African American talk-show host, actress, producer, philanthropist and media owner is a powerful woman who has the ear of both politicians and the public. She revolutionized the talk-show format with her award-winning *The Oprah Winfrey Show* that included the inspirational stories of individuals who overcame adversity. Her own rags-to-riches tale – she was born into poverty to a teenage single parent and has worked hard to become a multibillionaire – is an inspiration to others. Winfrey shares some of the secrets of what makes her a success in her book *What I Know for Sure*, in which she passes on her insights on love and happiness.

In the above quotation Winfrey explains her belief in many kinds of love, not just romantic love. She writes that the notion of romance leads many women to mistakenly think they are incomplete without a lover; they may also have preconceived ideas of what a potential lover will be like and what a loving relationship is. Winfrey asserts that love comes in various forms. All a woman needs is to be open to the possibility. **CK**

Oprah Winfrey speaks during a media conference in Sydney, Australia, in 2010 ahead of taping *The Oprah Winfrey Show*.

Literature

> **"Among all men on earth, bards have a share of honour and reverence, because the Muse has taught them songs, and loves the race of bards."**

Homer
Odyssey
c. 800 BCE

Homer's *Odyssey* is, after only his *Iliad*, the second-oldest work of Western literature, and a keystone of human art. The epic poem tells the tale of Odysseus and his band of warriors who, after having participated in the decade-long Trojan War, return to their home of Ithaca.

When Odysseus and company reach the island of Scheria, they find themselves in the hospitable company of Alcinious, king of Phaecians. While being treated to the monarch's generosity, Odysseus listens to the songs of Demodocus and is so moved that he is compelled to cover his own face with his cloak to hide his tears. Odysseus offers Demodocus a choice cut of meat, saying that the songs affected him deeply and that the bard is truly blessed by the Muses to have such an ability.

In Greek mythology, the nine Muses – Calliope, Clio, Erato, Euterpe, Polyhymnia, Melpomene, Terpsichore, Thalia and Urania – were the source of creativity and inspiration. It is only through the songs of the bards, Homer tells us, that humanity experiences artistic beauty, tragedy or inspiration. It is for those experiences, bestowed upon them by the Muses, and upon us by them, that we love our artists so. **MT**

> **"A great book is a great evil."**

Callimachus of Cyrene
Fragment 465
c. 250 BCE

Callimachus was a poet and scholar who was born to a prominent family in Cyrene, near the present-day city of Shahhat in Libya, which was then part of the ancient Greek empire. He was educated in Athens, and lived most of his life as a scholar at the Royal Library of Alexandria in Egypt.

Callimachus's works and teachings influenced Greek and Roman poets for hundreds of years. During his tenure in Alexandria, he surveyed the library's entire collection of books in order to create the *Pinakes*, a work that is widely considered to be the earliest example of a library catalogue or bibliography.

The meaning of the quotation above is unexpectedly literal: Callimachus is referring not to the book's cultural importance but merely to its size. Alternately translated as 'A big book is a big misfortune,' the quotation is principally a critique of what Callimachus viewed as unnecessarily long-winded works. He had little love for epic poems, such as Homer's *Odyssey*, and preferred brief, tightly structured, refined expressions. Claiming that he had received guidance from none other than the god Apollo, who had visited him in a dream, Callimachus advised his pupils in poetry to write concisely and to the point.

A big book, for Callimachus, was far from impressive. It was a source of frustration, reliable evidence of poor writing, and something unlikely to yield inspiration or wisdom. For him, if something was worth saying, it deserved to be written down succinctly. **MT**

If you have a garden and a library, you have everything you need.

Cicero
De Divinatione (On Divination)
44 BCE

Marcus Tullius Cicero was born into a wealthy Roman family – part of the equestrian order, at the lower end of that ancient society's aristocratic class – and served as a politician, consul and lawyer. He was also a philosopher and a highly accomplished orator. Following the rediscovery of his letters by Petrarch in the 14th century CE, Cicero's views on the world and civic affairs influenced the European Renaissance. Many of his writings were preserved and venerated by the early Church, which honoured him as a righteous pagan.

Of these writings, Cicero's two-part philosophical treatise, *On Divination*, is key. It is one of the few texts to detail the workings of Roman religion of the time. Comprised of a dialogue between Cicero and his brother, Quintus, Book I deals with Quintus's defense of divination, while Book II finds Marcus offering up a refutation from a philosophical stance.

The above quotation stresses that we should identify what is important in life, not be bogged down in inconsequential matters, and eschew the pointless activities or possessions that can only hinder the process of living a good and happy life. **IHS**

⊘ Illustration of Cicero putting one of his legal arguments to the people in the Forum of Rome.

> # *Against the disease of writing one must take special precautions, since it is a dangerous and contagious disease.* "

Peter Abelard was a medieval French scholar whose lasting fame derives from his love for his brilliant student, Héloïse.

Peter Abelard
Letter to Héloïse
1125

In 1115 a woman known only as Héloïse became a pupil of Peter Abelard, a prominent theologian and philosopher, in Paris, France. They fell in love, and the affair became legendary after the publication in 1616 of their collected letters. The correspondences detailed a tortured relationship: infatuation; secret love and marriage; Abelard's mutilation at the hands of Héloïse's vengeful uncle; the couple's separation and entry into holy orders (he became a monk, she a nun); and, finally, their epistolary reunion, more than ten years later.

Héloïse and Abelard coexisted largely in secret, and their involvement might have passed into obscurity had the letters not survived, along with Abelard's memoir, *Historia Calamitatum* (*The Story of My Misfortunes*).

Today, the quotation above is seen as a statement about the seductive allure of the act of writing itself rather than as a caution against the danger of writing letters while in love and separated from the object of desire. Whatever our subject matter, we are alone with our thoughts when we write, and what might be harmless recollection, distraction or fantasy can turn into unhealthy preoccupation, or even obsession. **MT**

"The lady doth protest too much, methinks."

William Shakespeare
Hamlet
c. 1600

In this English verse tragedy, which some critics regard as the greatest play in any language, the title character suspects that his father, the king of Denmark, has been murdered by his uncle, Claudius, who, only two months later, occupied the throne and married Hamlet's mother, Gertrude. Determined to prove Claudius's guilt, Hamlet orders an actors' touring company to stage a play that he has amended as a reconstruction of the events as he believes they occurred.

Hamlet watches his suspect throughout the performance for signs of guilt. As the play-within-the-play, entitled 'The Murder of Gonzago,' unfolds, one of the characters remarks that she would never remarry if her husband died. At this point, Hamlet asks Gertrude how she likes the production, to which she responds: 'The lady doth protest too much, methinks.' Hamlet suspects her of some collusion with Claudius and the comment further damages his relationship with his mother. Not long afterwards, Claudius takes offence, and walks out of the performance. Hamlet's worst fears have been confirmed and his way forward is clear – he must kill his stepfather, the regicide usurper. JE

◉ This view of an 18th-century production of *Hamlet* depicts the scene in which Hamlet confronts his mother.

> " *The desire to have many books, and never to use them, is like a child that will have a candle burning by him all the while he is sleeping.* "

Frontispiece of an early reprint of this popular and, in its time, highly influential book.

Henry Peacham
The Compleat Gentleman
1622

The book from which this remark is taken was required reading for any young man of the period who aspired to become a courteous, well-rounded member of society. The work contained practical advice on everything from travel, to what to read, to how to hold a conversation of substance while keeping it light enough so that everyone could have an enjoyable time.

Peacham originally wrote his guide in an effort to secure the patronage of the Earl of Arundel by providing the earl's son with advice on ways of gaining acceptance, and feeling at ease, in polite society. The book was later printed and well received, making Peacham rich and famous and giving a generation of young Englishmen practical guidance as they strove to improve themselves.

Like other humanists of the time, Peacham believed that improvement was possible through the application of reason. However, where etiquette was concerned, he drew a sharp distinction between affectation and the real thing. He deplored the former and believed that the good manners of a gentleman should be effortless and never obtrusive. Indeed, good conduct should come as second nature. MT

Shakespeare is not of an age, but for all time! "

Ben Jonson
To the Memory of My Beloved, the Author
1623

Ben Jonson and William Shakespeare were rival English playwrights during the late 16th and early 17th centuries. They were about equally popular during their lifetimes, and Jonson may even have had an edge at the box-office. But posterity has looked more favourably on Shakespeare, most of whose works are still performed regularly, while all but a couple of Jonson's playscripts (*The Alchemist* and *Volpone*) are now strictly the province of library habitués.

The two men seem to have known each other personally, and although Shakespeare never mentioned Jonson in his writing, Jonson made plenty of comments about his rival. It was Jonson who coined the sobriquet 'Swan of Avon,' and he who reported the testimony of actors that Shakespeare 'never blotted a line'. That Jonson then added 'Would he had blotted a thousand' suggests an ambivalence that comes out more clearly in his admission elsewhere that he had loved Shakespeare 'on this side idolatry'. But in the above quotation, Jonson seems to have been able to set aside envious feelings and praise Shakespeare (then long dead) unambiguously – and prophetically. **MT**

⬥ Portrait of Ben Jonson, painted in around 1617 by the Flemish artist Abraham van Blijenberch.

> # "Reading maketh a full man, conference a ready man and writing an exact man."

Francis Bacon
Essays
1625

Francis Bacon was a great English philosopher, lawyer, statesman and scientist who reputedly died of pneumonia after trying snow as a refrigerant of meat.

In his essay titled 'Of Studies,' Bacon gives his much-quoted view on some of the main uses of literacy. Two of the terms he used are less familiar in context today than they were in his time. 'Conference' means, broadly, what we would now term 'discussion': the idea is that people can and should test the validity of their thoughts by talking them over – conferring—with others. 'Exact' means considered, accurate and precise in one's choice of phrase. It is all too easy to be clear in our own minds what we mean, only to have it pointed out by others that we may have said something substantially different from what we intended.

If, for example, we say, 'We regret the need for increased gun control,' does that mean that we support the aims of the US National Rifle Association or oppose them? By writing such statements, preferably before we say or publish them, we can see more clearly whether they are themselves clear or, like this example, either deliberately obscure or devoid of effective meaning. JP

> " *The reading of all good books is like conversation with the fineſt men of paſt centuries.* "

René Descartes
Discourse on the Method
1637

French philosopher René Descartes was so influential in the development of rationalism, and remains so strongly associated with it, even today, that the philosophy is often alternatively known as Cartesianism, and its adherents as Cartesians.

Descartes is famous for his axiom "*Cogito ergo sum*" ("I think, therefore I am"), which purports to prove that anyone who thinks that he may not exist has, by the very fact that he thinks he might not, demonstrated that he, in fact, does. By the twenty-first century, this was a phrase that was more widely quoted than agreed with, and is sometimes parodied as "I think, therefore I think I am."

Descartes's *Discourse on the Method* aims to set out only those things that we know to be true and about which we need have no doubts. While the above statement is not pontifical—Descartes is not suggesting that this is one of life's certainties—we may nevertheless doubt whether the word "conversation" is appropriate here: living readers may learn from dead writers, but it's hard to imagine any reciprocal benefit. Not all quotations are clever; some are merely memorable. Nevertheless, we often see writers of the past responding to authors of older vintage. **JP**

> " *Books are not absolutely dead things, but do contain a potency of life in them to be as aĉive as that soul was whose progeny they are.* "

John Milton
Areopagitica
1644

Areopagitica is one of the most eloquent and indignant defences of free speech in any language. Milton reused the title of a work on the same subject by Athenian orator Isocrates of the 5th century BCE. (The Areopagus was an open-air court of appeal in ancient Athens.)

During the English Civil War (1642–51), Milton supported Parliament against the Royalist forces of King Charles I, but the future author of *Paradise Lost* felt unable to remain silent after that legislative body passed an Ordinance for the Regulating of Printing, also known as the Licensing Order of 1643, which required writers to obtain government permission before their works could be published. *Areopagitica* was consequently published as a pamphlet, without a license, in defiance of the censorship that the author opposed.

The central idea in the above quotation is the same as that expressed by the Roman poet Horace in *Odes* III, 30: '*Non omnis moriar*' ('I shall not wholly die'), but live on – in the sense of being known to future generations through a body of work – always assuming, as Milton could not, that the work in question could be published at all. **JP**

"My little friend Grildrig, you have made a most admirable "panegyric upon Yourself and Country, but from what I can "gather from your own relation & the answers I have with "much pains wringed & extorted from you; I cannot but con- "-clude you to be, one of the most pernicious, little-odious- "reptiles, that nature ever suffer'd to crawl upon the surface of the Earth."

The KING of BROBDINGNAG, and GULLIVER.

_Vide Swift's Gulliver: Voyage to Brobd

> **Satire is a sort of glass wherein beholders do generally discover everybody's face but their own.**

Jonathan Swift
A Tale of a Tub
1704

This quotation is taken from 'The Battle of the Books,' the prologue of *A Tale of a Tub*, a wide-ranging satire on almost everything. The prologue was Swift's contribution to a debate that was raging about whether modern knowledge had surpassed, and consequently outmoded, the wisdom of earlier writers.

Swift depicts an armed engagement between books divided into two forces – one ancient, the other modern – in a library and cleverly leaves the outcome unresolved. (He does, however, give some insight into his private view, in a digression that depicts the ancients as bees that gather and create, and the moderns as spiders that kill and devour their victims.)

Swift made no attempt to define the genre of which he was a consummate master, but he does here identify one of its most prominent characteristics. It is an idea that found new expression in the 1970s, when British abstract painter Howard Hodgkin was asked whether the subjects of his portraits recognized themselves. 'No,' the artist reportedly replied, 'but their friends do.' **JP**

◀ An 1803 illustration based on the text of Swift's *Gulliver's Travels*.

> **Of all those arts in which the wise excel, Nature's chief masterpiece is writing well.**

John Sheffield, Duke of Buckingham
Essay on Poetry
1723

This poem in rhyming couplets was a popular success on its first publication. Unlike many works that tackle the subject of good writing, it is not satirical about inferior material – the duke saved that for his *Essay on Satire*, which was circulated anonymously. Many people believed that to be the work of John Dryden, who was beaten up by thugs of the Earl of Rochester because of the criticism of their master that it contained.

But neither does the *Essay on Poetry* give the reader much of an idea about how to write well. It suggests various authors whose styles an aspiring writer might wish to emulate, but the names are unsurprising – Homer, Horace, Virgil, John Milton: the usual suspects.

In *A History of English Literature*, French critics Émile Legouis and Louis Cazamian summarized Buckingham's work as 'a very creditable grouping together of average qualities. . .a clear and pleasant exposition of sensible ideas with a limited scope'. That seems a reasonable assessment of a work that is more about good manners in writing – ways to avoid offending or boring the reader– than instruction that could possibly turn poetasters into world figures. **JP**

"No entertainment is so cheap as reading, nor any pleasure so lasting."

◬ An 18th-century portrait of Lady Mary Wortley Montagu, painted by the Venetian Bartolomeo Nazari.

Lady Mary Wortley Montagu
Letter to the Countess of Bute
1753

Lady Mary Wortley Montagu was an eccentric English aristocrat who became renowned for her literary output. Her face was scarred by a youthful attack of smallpox, and she later helped to introduce into Britain the use of inoculation against that disease, as she had seen it practised successfully in Turkey.

Her fame was founded originally on a series of adaptations of Virgil's *Eclogues*, which she reset in London. She went on to create a considerable body of original material, including a play, *Simplicity*, and numerous essays, the best of which present her radical feminism. She collaborated briefly with Alexander Pope (the two later had a falling out; he satirized her in *The Dunciad*) and wrote scathingly about Jonathan Swift.

Also significant are the letters she wrote from Brescia, Italy, to her daughter, Mary, Countess of Bute, most of which contain detailed, elegant accounts of her simple life and re-creations, such as the one identified in the above quotation. However, her lasting reputation is based on the fifty-two letters she wrote about her time in Constantinople, where she lived for several years while her husband, Edward, served as British ambassador. JP

" Writing, when properly managed ... is but a different name for conversation. "

Laurence Sterne

The Life and Opinions of Tristram Shandy

1759

This is a famous quotation, but it is unclear whether the germ of its wisdom relates to writing in general or merely to the work in which it appears. *Tristram Shandy* purports to be the autobiography of the title character, but the narrator gets so distracted by incidental details that grab his attention along the way that he never gets very far – it is not until volume three of the work that Tristram gets around to telling the reader about his birth.

At one level, this structure is Sterne's elaborate joke. At another, it is a more accurate reflection of the true nature of life than is commonly, or perhaps ever, encountered elsewhere in literature or art – there are so many distractions, and the imagination is so diverse, that single-mindedness is a dream rather than an ambition.

The above quotation is generally used in support of the notion that people who wish to attain a good, readable prose style should 'write as they speak'. This is sound advice insofar as it may discourage authors from putting more highfalutin' language on the page than they would use in discussion, but many would argue that normal conversation has unnecessary repetitions and fillers that need to be edited out to achieve good prose. **JP**

" You write with ease to show your breeding, But easy writing's curst hard reading. "

Richard Brinsley Sheridan

Clio's Protest; or, The Picture Varnished

1771

We write to inform, to entertain, to record and to correspond. Through the symbolic expression of language, we can communicate across space and time. Historically, writing was the tool of only the educated and the wealthy. When literacy is a social marker, the ability to write complex compositions with ease becomes the hallmark of the elite. At the same time, dense prose does not make for easy reading.

In the posthumously published collection of poems, Sheridan jabs at those who write to impress rather than to express. He was barely twenty years of age when he wrote the work, so he must have been preoccupied with establishing his own reputation. As an aspiring playwright, he considered efficient expression and distillation of experience into art important. In the above couplet, Sheridan identifies himself as a person with the ability to write complexly, while simultaneously bemoaning such practice as counterproductive.

Today, Sheridan's quotation may serve as an admonition to academics, intellectuals and anyone who uses writing as thinly cloaked braggadocio: stop blowing your own trumpet and get to the point! **MT**

"When a man is tired of London, he is tired of life."

Samuel Johnson
Attributed
1791

This may well have been Dr Johnson's final view of the English capital city, but it was not his original, or perhaps his only, one. In his first published poem, 'London' (1738) – an imitation of a satire by Roman poet Juvenal – he had written at length about his admiration for any man (here, probably, his friend the poet Richard Savage) who moved out into the countryside, away from all the hazards of the urban environment, such as dens of vice, ruffians, thieves and avaricious lawyers. Much later, Johnson regretted the poem, both for its form (he had grown to dislike classical imitations) and its content, saying that 'there is in London all that life can afford'.

The above remark was recorded by James Boswell in his *Life of Samuel Johnson* (1791). On 20 September 1777, the two men had been discussing whether Boswell's enthusiasm for the city would be as great if he lived there all the time, rather than occasionally visiting Johnson from Scotland. On another occasion, Johnson told Boswell that, 'there is more learning and science within the circumference of 10 miles [16 km] from where we now sit [in a house near Fleet Street], than in all the rest of the world'. JP

◖ Portrait of Samuel Johnson (1757) by influential English painter Joshua Reynolds.

◖ Central London during Dr Johnson's lifetime.

"If a book is well written, I always find it too short."

Jane Austen proved that you don't need to have an eventful life to be a great writer.

Jane Austen
'Catharine, or, The Bower'
1791

Many people have reported similar feelings, not only about literature but about all forms of art: of wishing that a symphony were longer or that they didn't have to move away from a great painting in a museum.

Austen pursued writing from an early age, penning a number of short, humorous works throughout her teenage years, including this partially completed short story when she was aged sixteen. Though light-hearted, 'Catharine, or, The Bower' reveals glimmers of the more serious tones and themes that Austen would explore further in the works of her maturity.

Austen published most of her works anonymously, and she died relatively unknown. She received little critical recognition or fame during her lifetime, but her works are widely renowned today. Her appeal extends across the globe, prompting many fans to reread her novels every year and eagerly await any new film or television version of the stories they know almost by heart. Austen died when she was only forty-one, leaving behind a handful of novels and a world of enchantment. For her readers, though, her legacy is strong and enduring and they wish there were more of it. **MT**

"Dreams, books, are each a world; and books, we know, are a substantial world, both pure and good."

William Wordsworth
'Personal Talk'
1806

In this quotation, taken from the poem 'Personal Talk,' Wordsworth rejects the chatter of feigned relationships, the supposed glory of social success and industrial progress. He sees no need for the distractions of a busy life; rather, the beauties and adventures to be found in nature, coupled with the imaginative world of literature, prove to be enough to return us to childlike joy and wonder.

Wordsworth helped to usher in the Romantic Age of literature, and his ode to solitude, introspection and imagination reflects the creative individualism of the movement. While the Enlightenment had elevated reason and understanding to a preeminent place in human endeavours, the Romantics, in reaction against their predecessors, sought a return to passion and awe. Certainly this involved the more obvious dramatic symbols and stories portrayed in much Romantic art and literature, but it was equally embodied by solitary contemplation sitting by the fire. Deepening ourselves proceeds from our own personal contemplation, and it unites our own journey with appreciation of the creative depths found in great artists of the past. **JD**

"I wandered lonely as a cloud."

William Wordsworth
Poems in Two Volumes
1807

The poem of which this is both the title and the opening line was inspired by a walk that Wordsworth took in the Lake District of England with his sister, Dorothy, during which they saw:

'A host, of golden daffodils;
Beside the lake, beneath the trees,
Fluttering and dancing in the breeze.'

The image is one of the most indelible of Romantic poetry, and 'I Wandered Lonely as a Cloud' has become Wordsworth's best-loved and most popular poem. That was not the general view when it was first published, however. Samuel Taylor Coleridge, Wordsworth's great friend and collaborator on *Lyrical Ballads* (1798), objected to what he regarded as its 'bombast,' and Lord Byron went much further, calling the work 'puerile'. Regardless of any judgement as to its worth, the poem provides a valuable insight into Wordsworth's overall philosophy and artistic credo. For him, the daffodils were beautiful to behold, but no less beautiful to recall afterwards. The final stanza reads:

'For oft, when on my couch I lie
In vacant or in pensive mood,
They flash upon that inward eye
Which is the bliss of solitude.'

Wordsworth wrote elsewhere that poetry derives from 'emotion recollected in tranquillity'; this is an outstanding example of what he meant. **JP**

"The man who never looks into a newspaper is better informed than he who reads them."

Thomas Jefferson
Letter to John Norvell
1807

⊘ A French engraving of 1825 depicts a man monopolizing all the papers at the Café Momus, Paris, France.

The above quotation was part of Jefferson's reply from the White House to the future editor of the *Baltimore Whig*'s inquiry about 'the manner in which a newspaper, to be most extensively beneficial, should be conducted'.

Jefferson began by suggesting that any such publication should restrain itself by confining its coverage to 'true facts & sound principles only'. But he believed that this was a counsel of perfection, and continued: 'Yet I fear such a paper would find few subscribers. It is a melancholy truth...Nothing can now be believed which is seen in a newspaper. Truth itself becomes suspicious by being put into that polluted vehicle...He who reads nothing will still learn the great facts, and the details are all false.'

From this we may deduce that the third president of the United States was no lover of the fourth estate. But he was not in favour of censorship; on the contrary, in a letter of 1787 to Virginia statesman Edward Carrington, he asserted: 'Were it left to me to decide whether we should have a government without newspapers, or newspapers without a government, I should not hesitate a moment to prefer the latter.' **JP**

"Mad, bad and dangerous to know."

Lady Caroline Lamb
Diary
1812

Lady Caroline Lamb was a midrank novelist during the 18th century in England, but she is most remembered today for her short and scandalous love affair with Romantic poet Lord Byron. By the time she met Byron in 1812, she had been married for seven years. Byron had recently become famous following the publication of the first two cantos of his long poem 'Childe Harold's Pilgrimage.' Like many other women, Caroline was entranced by the hero's passion and restlessness, and sent Byron her own homage to Childe Harold. It was only later, after first seeing Byron at a ball, that Caroline reportedly noted in her diary that he was 'mad, bad and dangerous to know'.

Caroline may have coined the phrase some time after Byron ended their affair, but she was right about how dangerous he was: their affair ruined her reputation in society. Even at that early stage of his career, at age twenty-four, Byron's prodigal life closely mirrored that of his Childe Harold creation. Byron's 'mad and bad' reputation preceded him when he met Caroline, and his subsequent literary version of the Don Juan myth reinforced his image as a world-weary antihero. TJ

◭ An undated oil painting of Lady Caroline Lamb by English portraitist Thomas Phillips.

"Beauty is truth, truth beauty, that is all ye know on Earth and all ye need to know."

Leaned forward with bright drooping hair

⊘ The illustrated title page of a 19th-century edition of the works of Keats.

John Keats
'Ode on a Grecian Urn'
1820

These lines conclude the famous poem in which Keats lets his fancy roam at the prompting of the illustrations decorating a piece of ancient pottery. Who are the people depicted? Where are they going? What music are they listening to?

T S Eliot considered that this ending spoiled an otherwise beautiful poem. Certainly, its meaning is not obvious. Both beauty and truth are subjective, so the idea that one can 'know' them in any intellectually cogent sense is widely regarded as untenable. The matter is further complicated by the fact that the lines appear in quotation marks – who or what is supposed to be saying this, and to whom? Is it the poet to the urn, the urn to the poet, the poet and/or the urn to the reader?

If 'Ode on a Grecian Urn' has a 'message', it seems to be that great art should make the mind wander on to related matters that are not encompassed by the work itself – that art is self-contained, yet hints at the wider world. The conclusion seems to be that readers, listeners or viewers should not be concerned that there are no satisfactory answers: there may be felicity in not knowing, because mystery is fascinating. **LW**

"Season of mists and mellow fruitfulness!"

John Keats
'To Autumn'
1820

This, the opening line of a poem in Keats's verse collection *Poems of 1820*, differs from most of the other quotations in the present volume because it contains neither precept nor wisecrack – it is merely a description of the autumn. However, the line is so vivid and memorable that it is often repeated and is known to many millions throughout the English-speaking world.

Keats wrote 'To Autumn' after an evening stroll through the English countryside. The poem consists of three eleven-line stanzas, rhymed ababcdedcce or ababcdecdde, and is a tour de force of vivid imagery and onomatopoeia. The first section is a description of harvest time. In the second stanza, and the opening part of the third, Autumn is personified, and apostrophized (that is, addressed directly): 'Who hath not seen thee oft amid thy store…?'). The poem ends with more vivid description of nature's beauty and bounty.

If 'To Autumn' has a flaw, it may be that it has no intellectual component – the lines are merely descriptive, and Keats sees no reason to interpret what he sees or draw any wider conclusion. However, most people regard such criticism as being as churlish and pointless as deprecating Picasso for his failure to be Rembrandt. This is one of the most popular poems in the English language because its appeal is emotional. **MT**

"If you but knew the flames that burn in me which I attempt to beat down with my reason."

Alexander Pushkin
Eugene Onegin
1825

Alexander Pushkin, Russia's greatest poet and the foundational figure of Russian literature, established himself as a literary force early in life. He published his first poem at the age of fifteen and had become a popular and critically acclaimed poet by his mid twenties.

Written in rhymed verse, and first published as a serialized novel between 1825 and 1832, *Eugene Onegin* tells the love story of the eponymous hero and Tatyana Larin. When first they meet, the young, shy and impressionable Tatyana falls instantly in love with Onegin, only to have her affections rebuffed by the brooding aristocrat. By the time the two meet again, several years later, Tatyana has become a composed, confident, married woman, and it is now Onegin's turn to fall hopelessly in love with her. He pours his heart out to her, but, just as he had once rejected her, so she now spurns him, and Onegin is left to live a life of despair.

Onegin first confesses his love for Tatyana in a letter, one to which she does not reply. She then ignores the many letters he sends her after that. The tragedy of *Eugene Onegin* is that of a man who is insufficiently proactive to take charge of his own destiny. **MT**

> " *Achilles exists only through Homer. Take away the art of writing from this world, and you will probably take away its glory.* "

François-René de Chateaubriand
Les Natchez
1826

⊘ A 19th-century portrait of Chateaubriand by Anne-Louis Girodet de Roucy, a pupil of Jacques-Louis David.

Chateaubriand's lush, poetic prose style, and his veneration of the beauty of the natural world, helped to usher in Romanticism to French literature. Chateaubriand came from an aristocratic family, and in 1791 he fled to America for a time during the French Revolution. While in America, he explored cities and wilderness alike, and reportedly spent a month with Native Americans while recuperating from an injury.

The natural beauty of North America captured Chateaubriand's imagination. When he returned to France in 1792, his experiences there stayed with him, and later became the inspiration for several novels set in the American wilds. In the preface to one of these, *Les Natchez*, Chateaubriand reflects on the importance of writing, style and storytellers and of identifying the points at which fact and fiction intersect. How much of Julius Caesar's fame is derived from his own writings, and how much from words written about him by others? What do we know about the fictional hero Achilles other than what the poet Homer tells us? And do we know anything other than what we glean either from personal experience or from written accounts? **MT**

> " *God be thanked for books. They are the voices of the distant and the dead, and make us heirs of the spiritual life of past ages.* "

William Ellery Channing
'Self Culture'
1838

William Ellery Channing was a US clergyman who became known as 'the apostle of Unitarianism.' He was a lifelong activist against what he regarded as the greatest evils in the world – slavery, drunkenness, poverty and war.

The above quotation is taken from his lecture on the nature of culture and education, in which he spoke of ordinary, working people who, because of their needs, knew little more than the requirements of their trades or businesses allowed them to know. Channing asked how the average, well-intentioned person with a job and a family could ever hope to be the cultural equal of the wealthy or of those who have the time and the resources to learn everything they can.

In Channing's view, the answer lay in books. Books allow people to delight in imagination, to share insights and to reap the wisdom of recorded words passed down the generations. Books, if universally available, dismantle the barriers of poverty and low status to the acquisition of knowledge. Books make culture and education available to all who use them, and may enlighten anyone who is literate and willing to turn a page. **MT**

◆ Channing was a great 19th-century American champion of social reform.

"The pen is mightier than the sword."

⊘ Portrait of Edward Bulwer-Lytton, after an engraving of 1873.

⊘ Writer Gloria Steinem demonstrates the power of words with a phrase used by numerous protest movements in the 1960s.

Edward Bulwer-Lytton
Richelieu
1839

Edward Bulwer-Lytton was a British politician, poet, novelist, dramatist and critic. The above quotation is from his play about the influential cardinal during the reigns of the French kings Louis XIII and Louis XIV.

The sentiment is commonplace and is expressed proverbially in every language. Its earliest-known occurrence in writing is in Assyria in the 7th century BCE. Later, it recurs frequently, in the ancient Greek drama of Euripides, in the Bible and in many other places. The exact form of words is not the same in every instance, of course – it may be 'tongue' and 'blade' or 'mind' and machine gun – but the idea is always that brawn is no match for intellect.

There is a very similar remark in Robert Burton's *The Anatomy of Melancholy* (1621) – 'From this it is clear how much the pen is worse than the sword' – but Bulwer-Lytton is easier to quote because his statement is categorical, whereas Burton's may invite the response 'How much is that?' But that is a question that still may be worth asking. The basic idea is possibly true; or it may, alternatively, be wishful thinking; and it might just be a way for writers to justify their existence. **LW**

"There was no possibility of taking a walk that day."

Charlotte Brontë
Jane Eyre
1847

Charlotte Brontë's *Jane Eyre* was a commercially successful, innovative and groundbreaking work of prose fiction. Despite her talent and ability, the author was obliged to publish under the male pseudonym 'Currer Bell.' The novel, written entirely from a female perspective, caused a scandal when it was first published, for it was the tale of a woman insisting on making her own way through the world rather than submitting to a man's care and protection.

Brontë used many of her personal experiences to give the book a compelling realism. *Jane Eyre* begins with the narrator-protagonist confined indoors with no other option available to her. Although it is the wind and cold that keep Jane from taking a walk, the limitations that they impose on her are emblematic of other, more cultural shackles. Jane, like her creator, must overcome the restrictions of class, gender and family, and struggle to outgrow society's narrow definition of a woman. To find love and happiness, and to maintain true autonomy, Jane must make hard choices. And, in the end, she succeeds, not because she permits a man to marry her, but because she marries him. **MT**

"Call me Ishmael."

Herman Melville
Moby-Dick
1851

'Call me Ishmael' is one of the most famous opening lines to a novel, and it continues to reverberate in English-speaking culture today. In just one instance, the *Variety* review of Ron Howard's movie *In the Heart of the Sea* (2015), a fictional account of the events that inspired Melville's novel, opens with a humorous variation on the original line, 'Call me indifferent.'

Melville imbues his narrator with a tinge of ambiguity from the outset. He does not tell us that his name is Ishmael; instead, he asks us to call him that. Is this character someone whose recording of events may not be as balanced as we would hope for? Is he, in short, a reliable or an unreliable narrator?

Myth – the blurred area between fact and fiction – lies at the heart of Melville's epic tale, alongside a deconstruction of class in the 18th century and a documentary-like account of life aboard a whaling ship. One theme of the novel is perception and the difficulty in identifying reality and truth. Ahab, the captain obsessed with killing the titular beast, is larger than life, and Melville employs a wide variety of styles – from prose, poetry and songs to Shakespearean stage directions and asides – to flesh out his world. **IHS**

❯ Whale hunting in *Moby-Dick*, in an illustrated edition of 1956.

> " *The reason why so few good books are written is, that so few people can write that know anything.* "

Walter Bagehot
'Shakespeare, the Man: an Essay'
1853

Walter Bagehot was a banker, journalist and man of letters in 19th-century England. US President Woodrow Wilson once said of him that he clarified 'the thought of his generation'. Bagehot edited *The Economist* magazine for seventeen years, expanding the publication's influence on policymakers and its coverage of both political and social issues. He wrote extensively on government policy, economics and literature.

In this essay, Bagehot declared that a first-rate imagination must come from great experiences, and great experiences must come from curiosity and an eagerness to explore the world. He said that far too many writers spend their lives reading, writing and editing, and doing little else. They learn too little of the world, and live too little of the life they try to examine.

Bagehot believed that, although the best writers devote themselves to their craft, they must not do so at the expense of experience. Study can bestow skill, but such skill is not synonymous with wisdom, much less with insight. To Bagehot, writing well is one thing, but having something to say, something borne of experience and understanding, is entirely another. **MT**

> " *I celebrate myself, and sing myself.* "

Walt Whitman
Leaves of Grass
1855

The quotation above is taken from 'Song of Myself', a poem in the above-named collection. In the poem Whitman goes to great lengths to describe the subject he knows more intimately than any other: himself. Yet the work is not an exploration of narcissism, but of humanity – the poet always wrote about himself for the benefit and edification of everyone.

Leaves of Grass was something of a life's work for Whitman. He revised the collection several times in the course of his career, with the final version being released in 1892, the year of his death. Although Whitman eschewed common poetical conventions, such as formal stanzas, and rhymed or metered prose, 'Song of Myself' has its own musical, rhythmic and almost chant-like voice. Although he is now recognized as 'the father of free verse,' Whitman caused a sensation when he first released the collection, although it was the content rather than the form of the poems that caused dismay. Conservative critics were quick to decry the poems' occasionally erotic imagery as indecent.

'Song of Myself' has since become a cornerstone of US poetry, a blend of the emotional appeal of Romanticism with transcendental optimism and self-reliance. Whitman created a persona that expanded and progressed beyond itself, beyond the singular 'I.' The self revealed by the poem is at one with the nation, its people, humanity and the whole of nature. **MT**

It was the best of times, it was the worst of times.

Charles Dickens
A Tale of Two Cities
1859

This is the first part of the opening sentence of one of the best-selling novels in history. The work concerns the period after the French Revolution of 1789, during which the people of Paris faced a most uncertain, and dangerous, future. The Revolution had started out with the most laudable motives – to put an end to the old regime of corruption and injustice and to create in its place a world of freedom, equality and fraternity. But the dream of liberty had soon changed into the nightmare of the Reign of Terror, which was within the living memory of the first readers of *A Tale of Two Cities*. Thousands were guillotined: some of the early executions, including those of the king and queen, Louis XVI and Marie Antoinette, were generally accepted as part of a necessary purge, but the arrests soon became indiscriminate, and many innocent people were killed.

The true meaning of the above quotation can be gleaned by reading on. The sentence continues: '. . .in short, the period was so far like the present period'. Dickens recognized that we are always simultaneously in both the worst and the best of times: circumstances will always nourish both knaves and angels. **LW**

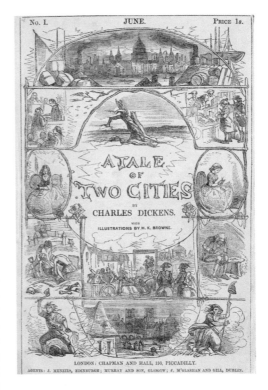

⬥ *A Tale of Two Cities* was first published in serialized form; this engraved title page is from the first part of the first edition.

"If I can stop one heart from breaking, I shall not live in vain."

US poet Emily Elizabeth Dickinson (c. 1846).

Emily Dickinson
Untitled poem
1865

Emily Dickinson spent much of her life in quiet contemplation. Her personal contacts were mostly limited to her closest family members and friends. But in that cloistered seclusion, she created a body of poetic work that has become an influential, indelible part of the American cultural landscape.

Dickinson made little effort to see her poetry published or shared it with anyone other than those who were closest to her, and she gained no fame until the posthumous publication of her almost 1,800 untitled poems. Eschewing conventions such as punctuation, capitalization and structural constraints, Dickinson's work is poignant, trenchant and highly complex while superficially simple. She wrote about religion, nature, life, love, our sense of self and mortality.

In the above quotation, Dickinson reflects on how the value of life can hinge on our usefulness to others. If we can shield a single person from the wrench of heartbreak, or alleviate another's despair, our own lives have some value. For the famously reclusive poet, it is a sweeping recognition that we are validated by our social nature and by our ability to help one another. **MT**

" Prose is for ideas, verse for visions. "

Henrik Ibsen
'Rhymed Letter for Fru Heiberg'
1871

The addressee of this epistle is Luise Heiberg, a leading Danish actress who did much to get the controversial work of Norwegian playwright Henrik Ibsen performed in Copenhagen. She had told him that she regretted being too old to play the new women in his plays herself (she was born in 1812, so was thirty-eight when Ibsen completed his first work, *Catiline*). Ibsen was grateful for her support and described her as someone who had turned her substance, 'rich and free,' into great art.

The ideas referred to in this quotation concern the upgrading of women in society, which several of Ibsen's plays – notably *Pillars of Society* (1877) and *A Doll's House* (1879) – are about. Ibsen is suggesting that, like legal documentation or scientific thought, politically innovative ideas such as his are best set out in prose, clearly and concisely, without the use of metaphor, simile or any other intrusion of figurative language. Otherwise the style might distract the reader's attention from what is being said, or otherwise cloud the issue.

It is hard to find exceptions to this rule, and easy to find examples of poems that are diminished by the author's desire to expound a theory. **MT**

⚫ Norwegian playwright Henrik Ibsen (1892).

> ## *Idle youth, enslaved to everything; by being too sensitive I have wasted my life.*

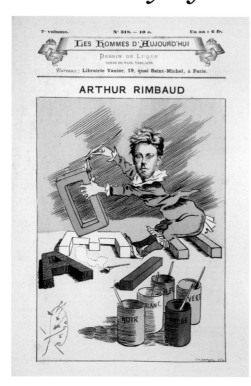

Arthur Rimbaud
'Song of the Highest Tower'
1872

French poet Arthur Rimbaud pioneered a compositional style induced by a deliberate 'derangement of the senses,' which was aided by his frequent use of absinthe. This produced many poems with a hallucinatory, and often indecipherable, quality that contrasts with some short and simple works of the same period, such as the poem from which the above quotation is taken, the meaning of which is transparent.

Only a year later Rimbaud had become disillusioned with his poetic ambitions, and now described 'Song of the Highest Tower' as an expression of embittered world-weariness. The quotation is clearly a commentary on his own addictive overindulgence. More important, however, is the irony that youthful idleness and oversensitivity had been the catalyst for such feverish and disordered activity, only to end in a yearning to recover the earlier innocence of youth. Rimbaud soon tired of his bohemian lifestyle and abandoned poetry altogether. But his heightened sensibility yielded the sober reflectiveness of experience in these few lines, which have proved to be an accurate summation of youthful recklessness, longing and regret. **TJ**

One must be a wise reader to quote wisely and well.

Amos Bronson Alcott
Table-talk
1877

Table talk is a literary subgenre, a form of memoir, in which the author records impromptu comments by a noted individual in an informal setting (often at meals). The form dates as far back as German religious reformer Martin Luther, whose collected comments were published in 1566. Other subjects have included John Milton, Samuel Johnson, Johann Wolfgang von Goethe, Napoléon Bonaparte, Ludwig van Beethoven, Samuel Taylor Coleridge, George Bernard Shaw and Adolf Hitler.

Amos Bronson Alcott was a transcendentalist and a friend of Ralph Waldo Emerson. As an educator Alcott was opposed to corporal punishment and believed that it was possible to create a utopian society, which he attempted to do at Fruitlands, a small community in Massachusetts. It failed, but Alcott's desire for humanity to improve itself continued through his campaigning for a better universal education system. It was not good enough to be able to read; it was necessary to have the best opportunities and resources available to learn. Alcott's views were regarded as unconventional, even dangerous. His second daughter, Louisa May, reflected on her childhood in her novel *Little Women* (1868). **IHS**

◬ Wood engraving (1875) of US teacher and transcendentalist Amos Alcott, father of children's book author Louisa May Alcott.

"Beauty is mysterious as well as terrible. God and the devil are fighting there, and the battlefield is the heart of man."

Fyodor Dostoyevsky
The Brothers Karamazov
1880

Originally published in serial form, *The Brothers Karamazov* is a vastly ambitious novel that examines a host of themes. Simultaneously, it is a philosophical exploration of faith in the face of doubt, of the nature of free will and morality, of human suffering and redemption, and of the role of the family. It is also a drama about a father, his sons and a patricide. Written in the final years of Fyodor Dostoyevsky's life, it is widely regarded as the author's crowning achievement and one of the finest novels ever written.

The above quotation comes when the hot-blooded, eldest Karamazov brother, Dmitri, drunkenly confesses to the mild-mannered, youngest brother, Aloysha, of the lustful urges in his heart. He laments that he is little more than an insect, a creature motivated by nothing more than sensual lust.

For Dmitri, beauty can never be understood, at least not by men; for them, it is a riddle that has always been, is now and always will be. Men's failure to comprehend it makes them chase opposites – they need chaste maidens but pursue loose women. He believes it drives even the best of men to seek both the ideal perfection of the Virgin Mary and to indulge in the wanton carnality of Sodom. In the heart of those like Dmitri Karamazov, there exists a conflict between base urges and divine aspirations that will never cease until the day they die. **MT**

"I have nothing to declare except my genius."

Oscar Wilde
Attributed
1882

Irish poet and dramatist Osacar Wilde arrived in New York on 2 January 1882, but his ship was held in quarantine until the following morning, which would have given him plenty of time to prepare what he had to say before the gathered throng of press journalists. Arthur Ransome, an early biographer of Wilde, said that the above words were uttered in response to the waiting customs officials, but he does not attribute them as a direct quotation. This may appear surprising, in view of the large number of Wilde's witticisms that were directly quoted in the press: he gave about a hundred interviews during this lecture tour.

Nevertheless, the phrase rings with Wilde's signature self-belief and timing – it sounds authentic, even if it isn't. There is no doubt, either, that at the heart of Wilde's project was the determination to promote the aesthetic philosophy for which he was renowned. He frequently employed poetic licence to craft a quip and was decades ahead of his time in manipulating the media to achieve fame, whether through celebrity or notoriety. He managed this successfully for a while, but eventually his extroversion led him to his downfall.

The phrase is not so much about personal vanity as a recognition of the capacity to tune in to truth and to articulate both through living and language. If he had not kept declaring his vision in such moving and inventive ways, he would have bored himself and certainly not challenged and amused the rest of us so vividly. The remark has since become one of Wilde's most famous wisecracks. When it was quoted by Frank Harris (*My Life and Loves*) in his 1918 profile of the author, it became enshrined in the canon of Wildeana. **LW**

A writer is not a confectioner, a cosmetic dealer or an entertainer. He is a man who has signed a contract with his conscience and his sense of duty.

Anton Chekhov
Letter to M V Kiseleva
1887

Trained as a physician, Chekhov found fame first as a playwright and later as a writer as his short stories received widespread acclaim. Today, his legacy is that of one of the most important dramatists and short-story writers in history. As a young doctor, Chekhov initially turned to writing to earn additional income, writing mostly short, comedic works. Later he turned his eye towards more serious topics. His works examined people without complex or convoluted plots, often hinging upon seemingly trivial events to explore the passions, motivations, and unconscious desires of his characters.

Entertainment? Distraction? Amusement? Escapism? For Chekhov, writing was nothing so facile; it was an act of self-reflection, discovery and even treatment. Writers have an obligation to understand reality and present it with unflinching honesty. No lens of wish fulfillment must obscure the world from the writer's vision. No work must avoid the truth, regardless of how painful or disturbing it might be. A writer looks at the human condition in the same way as a doctor examines a patient, or a scientist explains his or her findings. To do anything less is to do a disservice to nature. **MT**

⊙ A digitally coloured portrait of Anton Chekhov in 1901, three years before his death from tuberculosis at age forty-four.

"What a comfort a Dictionary is!"

Lewis Carroll

Sylvie and Bruno Concluded

1893

The sequel of *Sylvie and Bruno* (1889), *Sylvie and Bruno Concluded* was the final novel published in Lewis Carroll's lifetime. While the story meanders through playful children's scenes, and grown-up social commentary, it explores alternate and parallel worlds, challenges accepted notions of character and blurs the line between reality and fantasy – just as the author had done in his most famous works, *Alice's Adventures in Wonderland* (1865) and *Through the Looking-Glass* (1871).

The above quotation is spoken by the Other Professor, a clumsy, bookish character. According to Sylvie, this is the only thing he says to her throughout an entire banquet, for most of which he is asleep. In the midst of shifting realities, strange poems, fragmented plots and cultural criticism, Carroll reminds us of our search for stability, reference and authority in our understanding. Whether language can truly be trusted is another matter. After the banquet, the Other Professor recites a strange poem titled 'The Pig Tale,' introduced as a work he has never recited before and will never recite again. **JD**

◐ An illustration from Carroll's *Alice's Adventures in Wonderland* (1865).

"Tread softly because you tread on my dreams."

W B Yeats

The Wind Among the Reeds

1899

These words conclude 'Aedh Wishes for the Cloths of Heaven,' one of thirty-seven poems in the above collection. The addressee is taken to be Maud Gonne, the actress and Irish nationalist who was the unrequited love of the poet. Upon first encounter the work seems to be a relatively commonplace poetic trope – a suitor throws himself upon the mercy of his loved one – and the memorable and euphonious lines are often quoted.

However, closer inspection may reveal some uncertainties. The eight-line verse opens with:

'Had I the heaven's embroidered cloths. . ."

Are these cloths literal (all the fabric in the world) or figurative (powers of poetic expression)?

Yeats then writes:

'. . .I, being poor, have only my dreams;
I have spread my dreams under your feet.'

What does he mean by 'poor'? Does he mean that he lacks material wealth, and consequently, all he has to spread beneath his loved one's feet are dreams rather than expensive fabrics? Or does he mean that he doubts his own abilities as a poet? If the latter, is this genuine modesty or a stylized pose? **LW**

"Literature is a luxury; fiction is a necessity."

G K Chesterton
The Defendant
1901

In his essay, 'A Defence of Penny-Dreadfuls,' Chesterton asserts that in the past the educated classes simply ignored 'vulgar' literature, but they have come to take pride in despising and distancing themselves from it. But this elevated position causes us to miss something central to the creative arts: 'The simple need for some kind of ideal world in which fictitious persons play an unhampered part is infinitely deeper and older than the rules of good art, and much more important.' While 'penny dreadfuls' (cheap novels) may not meet the often-contrived standards of high literature, their importance should not be underestimated, as they are the 'actual centre of a million flaming imaginations'.

Throughout his work, Chesterton sought to bring out the truth of a subject, even when it was paradoxical. Here, stories that fall short of the standard-bearing literature of a given time may still embody a mythos that transcends any particular work. They are the necessary expression of our creative exploration. While the condensation of human yearnings into 'higher' types of literature provides us with masterpieces, the source of such works remains connected to a common, universal and vital ancestry. JD

"A book must be the axe for the frozen sea within us."

Franz Kafka
Letter to Oskar Pollak
1904

It was only after his death that Czech author Franz Kafka was hailed as one of the most original, imaginative writers in literary history. Some of his short stories had been published before his death in 1924, but he had an ambivalent attitude towards his own writings and instructed his close friend, Max Brod, to burn everything he had written. Brod ignored those instructions.

Kafka's doubts about the merits of his early writings can be seen in the letters he wrote schoolmate Oskar Pollak. In this letter of 1904, the serious depth of Kafka's literary ambitions is perfectly expressed. Kafka had just read 1,800 pages of the diaries of German poet Christian Friedrich Hebbel, and while he 'wrestled' with the content, he realized that it was akin to his struggle with his own conscience. This constant struggle was to become a recurring theme in much of Kafka's published work while the metaphor of the axe and the sea reflects the new Freudian ideal of exposing the hidden depths of the unconscious. In that respect the metaphor can also be seen as anticipating the Surrealist movement. TJ

❯ Text and sketches in one of the diaries kept by Franz Kafka.

…leser …noch einmal …Sohlen in Ver-
…igung stehn. Es ist das natürlich nicht alles,
…und eine solche Sache ich frage brauch ich nicht nur
…den. Aber jeden Tag soll mindest eine Zeile
…gegen mich gerichtet werden wie man die
…Rohre jetzt gegen den Kometen richtet. Und
…wenn ich dann einmal vor jenem Satze erscheine
…und hergehetzt von jenem Satze so wie ich
…B letztes Weihnachten gewesen bin und wo
…so weit war, dass ich mich nur noch …
…Konnte und wo ich wirklich auf
…der letzten Stufe meiner Leiter schien, die
…ruhig auf dem Boden stand und an
…der Wand. Aber was für ein Boden, was für
…eine Wand! Und doch hielt jene Leiter nicht,
…drückten sie meine Füsse an den Boden,
…holen sie meine Füsse an die Wand.

" *The worst tragedy for a poet is to be admired through being misunderstood.* "

Jean Cocteau works on a mural in the Lady Chapel of the Notre Dame de France church in London (1959).

Jean Cocteau
Le Coq et l'Arlequin (*The Cock and the Harlequin*)
1918

Why do we create art? Among other reasons, we seek to express ourselves and to connect with one another around the universal themes of our humanity. Cocteau was a distinguished creative in multiple arts, including poetry, literature, theatre and film. His views on poetry often point to the ability of art to speak for itself, without the running commentary and clarification of the artist: 'An artist cannot speak about his art any more than a plant can discuss horticulture.' And yet, within one's ineffable art, there is a deep desire to be understood. Elsewhere Cocteau wrote: 'The poet never asks for admiration; he wants to be believed.'

Danish existentialist philosopher Søren Kierkegaard intimated something similar: 'What is a poet? An unhappy man who conceals profound anguish in his heart, but whose lips are so fashioned that, when sighs and groans pass over them, they sound like beautiful music...Behold, therefore would I rather be a swineherd on Amager [a remote Danish island] and be understood by the swine than a poet, and misunderstood by men.' Cocteau would likely rather have joined Kierkegaard on Amager than be admired through being misunderstood. **JD**

We must wash literature off ourselves. We want to be men above all, to be human.

Antonin Artaud

Les Oeuvres et les Hommes (*The Works and Men*)
1922

French theatre producer Artaud was a leading light in the development of the Theatre of Cruelty, a theory of drama that influenced many subsequent playwrights, from Samuel Beckett to Edward Albee. Artaud used the term 'theatre' to mean more than stage production: it was any intellectual or psychological awakening. Likewise, 'cruelty' was not unkindness in the conventional sense, but any relentless stimulus that makes its recipients reassess their previous assumptions.

The above quotation is central to Artaud's thinking. Implicit in his statement is the premise that literature is nonessential, something that can be removed from us, and, indeed, should be discarded in order that we can achieve greater self-realization. This may be true – one may think that one has encountered certain people who have become so engaged with fiction that they can process their own experience only by reference to imaginary creations. However, the notion that without literature we will somehow be 'human' in a way that we were not before flies in the face of the rather more popular and widespread notion that culture banishes barbarism. **JP**

⊘ Antonin Artaud in the role of French revolutionary Jean-Paul Marat in the movie *Napoleon* (1927), directed by Abel Gance.

"A rose is a rose is a rose."

Gertrude Stein
Geography and Plays
1922

This phrase, which would recur in several of Gertrude Stein's works, first appeared in the poem 'Sacred Emily', written in 1913 and published in the above collection. Stein returned to it deliberately, sometimes to suggest circularity, similarity and interconnectedness, and at other times to 'caress' and 'address' the noun.

In another Stein poem, 'The World is Round', a girl named Rose thinks upon her name and her identity – would she still be who she is if she had been called something different? In the poem 'As Fine as Melanctha', Stein relates the rose to the beginning of civilization. In *Four in America* (1947) – her study of Ulysses S Grant, Wilbur Wright, George Washington and Henry James – Stein wrote:

'Now listen! I'm no fool. I know that in daily life we don't go around saying is a…is a…is a…Yes, I'm no fool; but I think that, in that line, the rose is red for the first time in English poetry for a hundred years.'

Stein means that the use of the word 'rose' had once conveyed the idea of the flower, but that with overuse it had been reduced to just another thing that one would expect to find in a nature poem: a word that had lost its primary, literal meaning; she sought to restore it. **JD**

"To read a newspaper is to refrain from reading something worthwhile."

Aleister Crowley
The Spirit of Solitude
1929

Occultist writer Aleister Crowley embodied the key tenet of Thelema, the religion he founded: 'Do what thou wilt shall be the whole of the Law.' He flouted conventional morality and announced that the world had entered an epoch of self-realization, self-determination and self-actualization. In the midst of this grand pursuit, Crowley disdained the news media and their attempts to characterize his thought and behaviour. He regarded newspapers as 'canned chatter', in contrast to serious writing, which, he wrote, required 'effort of intelligence.' Crowley believed that events can only truly be understood with background and perspective, and thus newspapers are either downright deceptive, or, because of the pressures of publication, forced to exaggerate and misreport. The lambasting that flowed from British papers concerning his libertine lifestyle only exacerbated his critical position. The popular press labelled Crowley 'the wickedest man in the world', and by the 1930s he had entered into numerous legal disputes with parties whom he felt had libelled him. **JD**

❯ English writer and occultist Aleister Crowley in 1921.

" A poem is never finished, only abandoned. "

Paul Valéry
Au Sujet du Cimetière marin
1930

French poet and philosopher Paul Valéry made the above remark in reference to his reexamination of his poem '*Le Cimetière marin*' ('The Graveyard by the Sea,' 1920). He considered how finishing a work always involved some 'accidental' factor, such as 'weariness, satisfaction, the need to deliver or death'. Elsewhere, he wrote about how the artist's perfectionism led to abandonment in the light of the impossibility of true 'completion.'

Valéry found no natural, obvious end point in artistic activity: while the objective may be to 'complete a personal expression,' the way in which that happened was never in the artist's complete control, and very few artists returned to their previous work without seeing improvements or alterations that they wished they had made.

Valéry also related the tension between completion and abandonment to the process of personal development that occurred in artistic production. He wrote: 'For, in relation to who or what is making it, it can only be one stage in a series of inner transformations.' The products of an artist's work are evidence of something larger that is going on in artistry; for Valéry, artworks are the expression of humankind's ongoing personal journey. An artist's works are 'a magnificent and wonderfully ordered expression of his nature and our destinies.' JD

" To be amused by what you read – that is the great spring of happy quotations. "

C E Montague
A Writer's Notes on His Trade
1930

Charles Edward Montague was a British journalist and author whose writing addressed war, media and literary criticism. While disillusioned by much of his worldly subject matter, Montague still provided a positive account of reading that encouraged internalization and appreciation: 'reading again and again, in all sorts of moods, with an increase of delight every time, till the thing read has become a part of your system and goes forth along with you to meet any new experience you may have'.

Montague served as chief leader writer for the *Manchester Guardian* and was initially critical of British involvement in World War I. However, his belief in the necessary defeat of German militarism eventually led him to serve in intelligence and as an armed escort for VIPs visiting the battlefield. The brutal realities of war received harsh treatment in some of his most influential work, including *Disenchantment* (1922) and *Rough Justice* (1926). Still, Montague explored more uplifting themes in other writings, and his literary views ultimately presented an optimistic philosophy of language as inspiration: 'Each word's evocative value or virtue, its individual power of touching springs in the mind and of initiating visions, becomes a treasure to revel in.' JD

> # *There is no surer foundation for a beautiful friendship than a mutual taste in literature.*

P G Wodehouse
'Strychnine in the Soup'
1932

Read on its own, Wodehouse's comment in this short story may seem just another testament to the shared interests of soul mates. In context, however, it shows the English humorist's insightful style, comic characters and sharp wordplay. The main characters, Cyril and Amelia, are strangers who happen to be sitting next to each other at a performance of a play entitled *The Gray Vampire*. For Cyril, it is love at first sight, although it takes him until the first intermission to open up a conversation. He does so upon realizing that Amelia is absentmindedly clutching his right leg. As she embarrassingly relinquishes the 'handful of his flesh,' they muse about their common love of mystery plays and novels. It is at this point that the narrator makes the above remark.

Wodehouse was a prolific, pragmatic and profitable writer. He never considered himself an 'artist' in any elitist sense, and his works playfully explore relationships across a host of contexts and situations. His comment on friendship founded upon shared tastes is less about an intuitive, high-minded understanding of beauty, but more a recognition that, even in sharing the simplest of things, one life can resonate with another. JD

◈ P G Wodehouse at his adopted home in New York State on the day in 1974 that he was knighted by Queen Elizabeth II.

"Literature is news that stays news."

Ezra Pound
ABC of Reading
1934

As time rolls on we become increasingly inundated with mountains of information from countless sources. Numerous advances in technology only expand our easy access to facts, opinions and reports, and, in the midst of all the 'noise,' we often struggle to find the clarity of a truly meaningful message for our lives. US poet and critic Ezra Pound's sentiment that literature 'stays news' postulates something that transcends the din and chatter of merely temporary interest and replaces it with something that makes a lasting impression and resonates across time and place. More than ever, it is a definition that rings true in the contemporary day and age.

Pound was famously connected to political debate and social commentary – 'news' in the situated historical sense – especially as an expatriate American living in Italy up until and during World War II. His anti-Semitism, coupled together with his attacks on the United States in general – and on President Franklin D Roosevelt in particular – spread freely throughout his letters, papers and Italian radio broadcasts, and eventually, led to his conviction on charges of treason at the end of the war – this was news that stayed news and in the present day is better forgotten. Meanwhile, however, throughout his time spent in Italy and his subsequent imprisonment at St Elizabeth's Hospital in the United States, he was producing his most profound and transcending poetry *The Cantos*, exceptional literature that would stand the test of time. **JD**

"Literature is the most agreeable way of ignoring life."

Fernando Pessoa
The Book of Disquiet
1935

One of Portugal's most influential writers of the 20th century, Fernando Pessoa was an author, critic, translator and spiritualist. His poetry and prose provide us with an escape into a solitary and creative existence, stretching beyond the facade of mundane restraints and desires. Pessoa elaborates: 'Music soothes, the visual arts exhilarate, the performing arts (such as acting and dance) entertain. Literature, however, retreats from life by turning it into slumber.' This dreaming of literature is shown throughout Pessoa's writing. He takes us on a journey in which we are less concerned with finding our true selves than with overcoming the constraints of identity.

In addition, Pessoa pushed past the assumed boundaries of real life through his use of pseudonyms, which he himself characterized as 'heteronyms,' totalling more than seventy distinct personas. These heteronyms had various backstories, styles and personalities of their own. Pessoa's publications under his own name used an 'orthonym,' as he distanced himself from his work as an author. He wrote *The Book of Disquiet*, an influential fictional journal, under the semiheteronym 'Bernardo Soares'; it was ultimately compiled after Pessoa's death in 1935. In the world of literature it is a familiar quip that the four greatest Portuguese poets of modern times are Fernando Pessoa. **JD**

> ❝*After love, book collecting is the most exhilarating sport of all.*❞

A S W Rosenbach
A Book Hunter's Holiday
1936

Abraham Simon Wolf Rosenbach was a scholar and bookseller based in Philadelphia. Such an apparently humble title falls far short of describing the high-level dealings Rosenbach engaged in as he helped to facilitate the acquisition of many literary masterpieces during the first part of the 20th century. His eponymous company helped to assemble extensive collections of rare manuscripts, including those of the Huntington Library, Los Angeles, and the Folger Shakespeare Library, Washington, DC. The dramatic competition between these two institutions to build their collections often saw Rosenbach as a central figure researching, bidding upon and securing manuscripts for his wealthy buyers.

For Rosenbach, collecting was equal parts calling and sport. The British called him 'the Invader', due in part to his ability to secure early and original English manuscripts for his US collectors and in part to his brash attitude to the 'sport' of collecting. However, Rosenbach was far more than a shrewd, competitive middleman for rich collectors, and he retained a deep appreciation for the works he helped to collect. His own essay collection *A Book Hunter's Holiday*, subtitled *Adventures with Books and Manuscripts*, celebrated and promoted the investment in literature as a worthy (and economic) human endeavour. Rosenbach showed the world that love and triumph need not be mutually exclusive pursuits. **JD**

> ❝*That is part of the beauty of all literature. You discover that your longings are universal longings, that you're not lonely and isolated from anyone.*❞

F Scott Fitzgerald
Attributed
1938

This quotation comes from *Beloved Infidel: The Education of a Woman*, a memoir by Fitzgerald's lover, Hollywood gossip columnist Sheilah Graham. It was published in 1958, eighteen years after the novelist's death. The notion that literature shows us that our travails are not unique, and that we do not suffer alone, has been expressed in various forms since at least the time of Plato.

Throughout his works, Fitzgerald explored the tensions between the romantic and the tragic, and the role of the imagination in people's relations with one another – how much of our perception is accurate, and how much of it is prejudice or predisposition, merely in the eye of the beholder? The remark takes on added poignancy in the light of Fitzgerald's own life, which was marked by alcoholism, depression and a persistent sense that his work failed to measure up to his own and everyone's high expectations. The reality of his own personal struggles, along with those of his wife, Zelda, with mental illness, adds another level of significance to his view that literature provides us with an opportunity to feel less lonely and less isolated, and to make a universal connection in our common humanity. **JD**

"*Show me a hero and I will write you a tragedy.*"

● Mia Farrow as Daisy Buchanan and Robert Redford as Jay Gatsby in the movie of Fitzgerald's *The Great Gatsby* (1974).

F Scott Fitzgerald
'Notebook E'
1940

The above quotation, from 'Notebook E', edited by Edmund Wilson in 1945, was written in 1940, the year of F Scott Fitzgerald's death. Fitzgerald was the darling, and the voice, of the Jazz Age, the legendary era of hedonism in the United States in the 1920s. And yet, as Fitzgerald's novels highlighted, the gaiety was also a hollow comfort – little more than a sheen that glossed over a malaise in society, the soullessness of which was merely exacerbated by the constant rounds of parties.

Jay Gatsby, the hero of the author's acclaimed 1925 novel, is the archetypal Fitzgerald hero. Although he projects the image of a man who enjoys life, with people never happier than when they're invited to one of the renowned parties at his residence in the fictional town of West Egg, Gatsby is a ghost, a man tortured by failure and unfulfilled desires. Heroes are mostly defined by events, often tragedies. Their emergence can mollify the pain felt by victims of that event or by society at large. But the heroes of Fitzgerald's worlds have nothing by which they can define themselves. And so their heroism is little more than an act, a veneer that they wear like armour, which eventually tarnishes. **IHS**

I did not come here to solve anything. I came here to sing, and for you to sing with me.

Pablo Neruda
'Let the Rail Splitter Awake'
1948

It is probable that many of us have had similar experiences in conversation with confidants: when we seek nothing more than a listening ear, and a sympathetic soul, we are given advice, critique and analysis. To rejoice with those who rejoice, and to mourn with those who mourn, can be difficult in the midst of our pragmatic desire to resolve problematic situations. Neruda's poetic plea for resonance and personal connection seeks to transcend the mundane preoccupations of everyday life and calls upon the power of our shared humanity to deal with the struggles we all face at one time or another.

The above quotation forms the closing lines of the long poem at the heart of Neruda's collection *Let the Rail Splitter Awake and Other Poems* (1950). It refers to far more than simply personal issues. Neruda wrote about the hope for peace, justice and good that wells up within all people facing oppression across the world, invoking the spirit of US President Abraham Lincoln, and dreamed of a better world, in which love would 'pound the table', and bloodshed would cease. His concluding refrain calls us to feel his passion and to respond in kind. JD

◭ The Chilean Neruda on a visit to Prague, in what was then Communist Czechoslovakia, in 1949.

" *It was a bright, cold day in April, and the clocks were striking thirteen.* "

George Orwell
Nineteen Eighty-Four
1949

This is the opening sentence of one of the most influential novels in the English language, which describes a totalitarian state known as Airstrip One (formerly Britain) in the superstate of Oceania. In it, all thought is subservient to the Party line, controlled by the euphemistically named Ministry of Truth. Other governing bodies with equally contradictory names are the Ministry of Peace (conducting a never-ending war), the Ministry of Plenty (in charge of rationing), and the Ministry of Love, which oversees the suppression and torture of dissidents. The story concerns the doomed attempts of the protagonist to gain a little freedom.

The book gave the world a number of terms and concepts, including 'doublethink,' 'newspeak,' 'Room 101,' and 'Big Brother.' The adjective 'Orwellian' has come to describe the secretive aspects of authoritarian regimes. Orwell –whose real name was Eric Blair – was a committed democratic Socialist, disillusioned with the authoritarian left as manifested under Soviet Communism. It was a theme he had already explored in the allegorical work *Animal Farm* (1945) and would continue to espouse until his death in 1950 at the age of forty-six. **ME**

Poetry is the language in which man explores his own amazement.

Christopher Fry
Time
1950

A golden age of drama in verse was inspired by the work of Marlowe and Shakespeare, but in the 19th century, theatrical plays employing poetry as a primary mode began to wane as conversation pieces, and prose rose to prominence. But for a period in the mid-20th century, verse-drama was revived in the work of T S Eliot and Christopher Fry. Plays such as Eliot's *Murder in the Cathedral* (1935) and Fry's *The Lady's Not For Burning* (1948) and *Venus Observed* (1950) brought poetry back into the mainstream of British theatre.

In his poetic plays, Fry used romantic rhetoric in response to his personal calling to speak with a distinctive voice. The way in which Fry voiced 'his own amazement,' as he called it, was inspired by his Christian faith and an optimistic humanism. These shaped Fry's magnanimous creativity; he was at peace with a world that could, despite its conflicts, reveal both truth and goodness. He once stated: 'In prose, we convey the eccentricity of things, in poetry their concentricity, the sense of relationship between them: a belief that all things express the same identity and are all contained in one discipline of revelation.' JD

⬥ Christopher Fry on the set of the movie *Ben-Hur* (1959). He was one of the team of contributors to its screenplay.

" When in doubt, have a man come through the door with a gun in his hand. "

Raymond Chandler
Saturday Review of Literature
1950

One of the most celebrated names in popular fiction, Raymond Chandler wrote novels – such as *The Big Sleep* (1939), *Farewell My Lovely* (1940) and *The Long Goodbye* (1953) – that have become classics of the genre of 'hard-boiled' detective literature. Along with Dashiell Hammett, Chandler raised the standard of crime writing to a level where it was considered an intrinsic part of the American literary tradition. His wisecracking, hard-drinking private detective hero Philip Marlowe was played on screen by a number of actors, including Humphrey Bogart, Robert Mitchum' and Dick Powell.

The above quotation is taken from an essay entitled 'The Simple Art of Murder', in which Chandler discussed detective fiction in the wider context of general literature, citing his contemporary Hammett ('the ace performer') as the prime representative of the movement, with his mastery of the 'American language.' The essay was first published in *The Atlantic Monthly* of December 1944, but it was in a later, revised version of the text that this sentence first appeared. Also in 1950, the same title was used for a collection of Chandler short stories that pre-dated *The Big Sleep*. **ME**

◒ Raymond Chandler was a classic writer in a populist medium.

◗ Publicity still for *The Big Sleep* movie (1946), starring Humphrey Bogart and Lauren Bacall.

"No bad man can be a good poet."

Boris Pasternak
Letter
1956

This statement by the Russian poet and novelist, author of *Doctor Zhivago* and winner of the 1958 Nobel Prize for Literature is characteristic: Boris Pasternak believed that humanity, friendship and the love of art and beauty will ultimately vanquish bitterness and hatred.

However, he also took the view that one has to 'pay for the right to live on one's own spiritual reserves'. This 'no pain–no gain' attitude is sometimes observable in people trying to carry on a normal existence under dictatorships, but for those who never lived through Stalin's terror or similar atrocities, the above quotation may appear to take wishful thinking to an incredible extreme. Of course, the epithets are subjective, but it is all too easy to think of poets who were regarded as proficient artists but defective personalities: Lord Byron was described as 'mad, bad and dangerous to know'; a friend told Frost, 'You're a good poet, Robert, but you're a bad man.'

The idea that goodness in art reflects goodness in the creator of that art is certainly charitable and ignores or discounts the possibility that the virtue may be a stylized affectation, an imitation of an emotion. **LW**

◀ Pasternak on hearing that he had won the Nobel Prize.

"Creative ideas do not spring from groups. They spring from individuals."

Alfred Whitney Griswold
Address at Yale University
1957

Alfred Whitney Griswold was a staunch defender of intellectual and academic freedoms when they were threatened by McCarthyism and the House Un-American Activities Committee. Notably, Griswold positioned Yale as an opponent of the National Defense Education Act, which required beneficiaries of government funding to disclaim belief in the overthrow of the US government.

The freedom to think and explore played a central role in Griswold's view of education. Rather than succumb to the lowest common denominator of Orwellian 'groupthink,' he encouraged the personal intellectual and creative journey that a liberal education could best foster: 'There are certain things in a man that have to be won, not forced; inspired, not compelled. Among these are many, I should say most, of the things that constitute the good life.' When it comes to the greatest achievements of human culture, Griswold asked: 'Could *Hamlet* have been written by a committee, or the *Mona Lisa* painted by a club?' They could not. Instead, 'The divine spark leaps from the finger of God to the finger of Adam' and inspires all human achievement in every area: law, science, art and politics. **JD**

" Poetry is a way of taking life by the throat. "

Robert Frost
Attributed
1960

Poet and playwright Robert Frost was one of the best-loved and the most critically acclaimed US poets of the 20th century. This was recognized with four Pulitzer Prizes for Poetry and a Congressional Gold Medal. Frost perceived life to be confrontational to the core. Historically, he wrote at an intersection when traditional verse forms were being challenged by modern poetic sentiments. Frost chose a way of expression that was unique and influential, using a common vernacular to explore themes ranging from the contemplation of nature in the midst of pastoral New England to existential questions that revealed a dark and troubled world. During his pursuit of thoughtful engagement and confrontation with living, he evoked beautiful and bold imagery, thereby conveying the deepest human need to find meaning and significance in our confrontation with life.

The above quotation, which comes from Elizabeth S Sergeant's book *Robert Frost: The Trial by Existence* (1960), conveys the poet's notion of writing, conceptualization and artistic expression themselves as modes of engaging life and asserting our will. The act of creation is as powerful and adaptable a tool as any practical instrument used in humans' pursuit of purpose. The challenge to understand ourselves demands more than merely existing, more than passively observing our lives go by. It demands intention, struggle and passion as we wrestle with our own mortality. Frost was a poet who, in summary, had a 'lover's quarrel with the world'. **JD**

" There is nothing outside of the text. "

Jacques Derrida
Of Grammatology
1967

Born in Algeria, Jacques Derrida was a French philosopher who controversially contended that writing is not the visible, legible representation of speech but a separate entity; and, moreover, that the need to express our ideas in writing both influences, and restricts, our thoughts and our capacity to think. The above quotation is mistranslated. In *Of Grammatology*, Derrida wrote '*Il n'y a pas de hors-texte,*' meaning, 'There is no outside-text.'

Texts, in Derrida's view, are not authoritative and incontrovertible – 'It's there, in black and white' – but open to innumerable different interpretations, most of which are legitimate. We may return to a book and understand it differently from the first time we read it; neither response is necessarily wrong – each may merely reflect a process of 'infinite play' between people, words, space and time. Derrida quotes Michel de Montaigne: 'We need to interpret interpretations more than to interpret things.' What significance, if any, should we attach to an author's use of the word 'refugee' when he or she could have used the word 'migrant'?

All this might sound complicated, but at the heart of Derrida's work is a useful insight into how we communicate. We need to realize that words are not solid, unchanging building blocks of meaning that can be constructed into a permanent representation of what is out there. Words are in some ways uncontrollable and shift like the contours of sand dunes; like sand dunes, they respond to exterior factors, changing in their nuances of meaning over time. **LW**

> *"A perfect poem is impossible. Once it had been written, the world would end."*

Robert Graves
The Paris Review
1969

Robert Graves was a 20th-century British poet, novelist and critic, best known for his historical novel *I, Claudius* (1934), and his history of poetic mythmaking *The White Goddess* (1948). In an interview in *The Paris Review*, from which the above quotation is taken, he said that what made true English poets was that they drew from '[a] source in the primitive. In the prerational'. While this aligns with his work in the classics, and his ongoing interest in mythological themes, the exploration of the primordial source of our creativity also reveals how the currents running beneath our rational selves are deeper than we know.

One of the themes that Graves hits upon in his critical thought is the universalizing tendency of philosophy and its antithesis to poetry. 'Philosophy is antipoetic. Philosophize about mankind and you brush aside individual uniqueness, which a poet cannot do without self-damage.' In relation to the impossibility of perfect poetry, perhaps we can interpret Graves's thought in terms of our individual humanity. Were we to perfect our creative expression to the point of objective and abstract exactness, we would do away with the world as we know it to be: flawed, unique and beautiful. That world would end, and so would poetry along with it. **JD**

> *"I speak and speak, but the listener retains only the words he is expecting. It is not the voice that commands the story: it is the ear."*

Italo Calvino
Invisible Cities
1972

Calvino's acclaimed novel takes the form of an imaginary conversation between Kubla Khan and Marco Polo. Unable to travel widely, the ageing Khan relies on itinerant merchants to describe life in the outposts of his empire. Polo tells stories about the cities – all of them variations of his beloved Venice – through objects he acquired there during his travels. However, the tales are often strange and unworldly. They also become platforms for the exploration of art, humanity and, particularly, linguistics. Polo and Khan have no common language, but the latter draws meaning from the objects, and his understanding is filtered through his own prior knowledge and life experience.

In the late 1960s Calvino was invited by Raymond Queneau to join Oulipo, an experimental writing group that included Claude Lévi-Strauss and Roland Barthes, key exponents of Structuralist and Poststructuralist thought. They had a profound impact on Calvino's subsequent work, as evidenced by the above quotation, which suggests that the meaning that readers glean from a particular text is significantly influenced by their prior expectations. **IHS**

"*A writer should have the precision of a poet and the imagination of a scientist.*"

Vladimir Nabokov
Strong Opinions
1973

What are the components of a literary style? In the above quotation, Nabokov turns the tables on us by playing with traditional stereotypes, causing us to think in fresh terms about poetry and science. Associating precision with the poet, and imagination with the scientist, he blurs the lines between style and substance, prompting us to reconsider the nature and power of literature. For some this makes Nabokov difficult – more interested in aesthetic style and structure than in plot and character. Russian poet Yevgeny Yevtushenko once declared that he could 'hear the clatter of surgical tools' in Nabokov's prose. For others this is what makes Nabokov one of the all-time greats.

The juxtaposition is at home in the man himself. Nabokov was a keen lepidopterist and thus had a foot in the camp of science as well as that of art. In his study of the mimicry of butterflies, he mused: 'I discovered in nature the nonutilitarian delights that I sought in art. Both were a form of magic, both were a game of intricate enchantment and deception.' Nabokov found beauty and enlightenment in the means and ends of both worlds. **JD**

The possession of a book becomes a substitute for reading it.

Anthony Burgess
Napoleon Symphony
1974

In 1971, Burgess's 1962 novel *A Clockwork Orange* was turned into a successful and highly controversial movie, starring Malcolm McDowell and directed by Stanley Kubrick. Burgess subsequently suggested to Kubrick that they collaborate on a film biography of Napoleon Bonaparte. Kubrick was interested at first, but when he saw Burgess's first draft of the script decided that the project was not for him. The author went on alone and produced a novel that was stylistically experimental in its attempt to re-create in English prose the four movements of Beethoven's *Symphony No. 3* (1804). The composer had originally intended to dedicate this work to Napoleon, whom he regarded as a great champion of democracy, but when Napoleon had himself crowned emperor, Beethoven was disgusted and scratched Napoleon's name off the dedication page of the score. The work was subsequently entitled *Eroica*.

Napoleon Symphony is set mainly in Egypt. The above quotation expresses a common concern among writers and educators: that books need do no more than furnish a room, and that more people buy them – or, at least, acquire them – than read them. **JP**

◬ Anthony Burgess was a famous British novelist who regretted not being better known as a classical composer.

> " *Books are the carriers of civilization. Without books, history is silent, literature dumb, science crippled, thought and speculation at a standstill.* "

Barbara W Tuchman
American Academy of Arts and Sciences bulletin, 1980

Tuchman wrote these words before the technological revolution that was sparked by the advent of the World Wide Web. Today, one might argue that the Internet has at least partially replaced books as a repository of knowledge, but the Internet is somewhat ephemeral (links get cut; websites disappear) and lacks the substance of books. With books, we know where we are at the point of entry. Some are educational; others are escapist. By contrast, the Internet is more like a jungle – few, if any, well-trodden paths, and a cacophony of sound: bright voices sometimes audible, but at other times drowned out by a whirlwind of not necessarily informed opinion. The elitism of researched authorship is vital if we are to discern where knowledge lies. Just as we would not expect a car mechanic to perform open heart surgery, we know that, for a considered view of anything, we need to read books – and not just any books.

Not only are books the strongholds of civilization as knowledge, they also help to define the conditions for civilized behaviour. Personal computers may serve some of the same functions as books, but they will never entirely supersede them. **LW**

> " *A classic is a book that has never finished saying what it has to say.* "

Italo Calvino
L'Espresso
1981

Does a work speak to something bigger than its time and place? Does it pave the way for us to confront the deepest concerns of our humanity? Italo Calvino considered his style to exist in a space between poetry and prose, and for many (stretching all the way back to Aristotle) the poetic is that which speaks to something universal and eternal rather than the merely momentary. For Calvino, classics not only have a memorable personal impact, but they also tap into both the individual and the collective unconscious.

A significant practical implication that Calvino himself advocates is that we should return to the classics from our youth when we are adults. In the *L'Espresso* newspaper article from which the above quotation was taken, Calvino suggests that great works of literature always have more to give, and we should never think that we have finished with them. He writes: 'There should therefore be a time in adult life devoted to revisiting the most important books of our youth. Even if the books have remained the same (though they do change, in the light of an altered historical perspective), we have most certainly changed, and our encounter will be an entirely new thing.'

It is in part because classics have spoken, but even more so because they continue to influence and speak to the way our personal and collective histories unfolds, that we read and reread them. **JD**

You can't use up creativity. The more you use, the more you have.

Maya Angelou
Interview for *Bell Telephone Magazine*
1982

This quotation originally appeared in *Bell Telephone Magazine*, in the first in a series of celebrity interviews entitled 'It's the Thought that Counts.' Maya Angelou's life included four years, as a child, during which she did not speak at all as a consequence of abuse. But once she'd found her voice, the wellspring of her creativity was opened, and flowed throughout the rest of her life: over a fifty-year career, she wrote seven volumes of autobiography, three books of essays and several books of poetry, as well as plays, movies and television shows.

Angelou is here suggesting that ideas breed ideas. Perhaps we should not worry if one of our brainwaves is hijacked by others and used without acknowledgement, because there are plenty more where the missing one came from. Even if you never use it, if you've got it in the first place, you'll always have it.

And, of course, also present here is the implication that success breeds success: as soon as Angelou's first book, *I Know Why the Caged Bird Sings* (1969), became a hit, publishers were after her subsequent works: her creativity was further lubricated by commercial demand and kept up to speed by demanding deadlines. **LW**

◬ Maya Angelou at the Cheltenham Literary Festival in England in 2005.

> *Ever tried. Ever failed. No matter. Try again. Fail again. Fail better.*

Samuel Beckett
Worstward Ho
1983

For Samuel Beckett, failure was the ultimate goal of art. As he wrote in *Three Dialogues*: 'To be an artist is to fail, as no other dare fail, that failure is his world and the shrink from it desertion.' His works play constantly with failure of narrative, dialogue and language itself.

Failure is not an end point; it is an essential part of a cyclical process. Beckett failed again and again during his writing, as is evident from his manuscripts. Only the faintest hope glimmers in the darkness of this quotation. The secret is to do things differently. Innovate, engage in the evolutionary process without knowing which direction is the right one. There is only trial and error, and there is no ultimate point at which you will reach the utopia of success. If you are lucky, one failure will be marginally less devastating than the one before. No matter. Have compassion. Do not balk at the impossible absurdity of life: like Beckett, we must learn never to succumb to the misery that failure threatens, but keep plugging away. That is the tragicomedy of this quotation, and the beauty of Beckett's mind. **LW**

❮ Beckett (*left*) directs his play *Waiting for Godot* (1953) in Berlin.

> *Write what you know. That should leave you with a lot of free time.*

Howard Nemerov
Inside the Onion
1984

The sardonic wit of Howard Nemerov parodies the commonplace 'Write what you know,' but is this really the devastating commentary on human knowledge it appears to be? These words come from the prolific pen of a novelist, essayist and poet whose work as a university professor required him to write a great deal, and left little time for other pursuits.

Taking 'Write what you know' literally leaves us with little to say. The Socratic paradox ('I know one thing: that I know nothing') should render us dumb. Yet even Socrates meant only that we can be confident in nothing for certain, except the power of the imagination. Nobel Prize-winner Mario Vargas Llosa said that he could not say for certain what was true and what was fictional in his work. This is because writing is, according to William Trevor, not to express oneself, but to escape oneself, the act of transposing what you know to other settings, and the empathy this generates makes a whole, new, truer thing. Nemerov, in his biting way, was being ironic: writing what you know will keep you to the limits of where you are. Better to go beyond that, and explore the unknown, and to take advice less seriously. **LW**

> " *You can't get to the truth by writing history; only the novelist can do that.* "

Gerald Brenan
Times Literary Supplement
1986

Gerald Brenan was born in Malta in 1894 into an Anglo-Irish family with strong military connections. At the age of eighteen, he set out from England with a friend on an epic journey on foot to China. They made it only as far as Bosnia, but nevertheless managed to cover some 2,400 km (1,500 miles). Brenan then joined the army at the outbreak of World War I, serving in France. In 1919 he moved to Spain, where he lived, intermittently, for the rest of his life.

Brenan was an avowed Hispanist and his burgeoning writing career was accompanied by his interest in Spanish culture. His first couple of novels and a nonfiction work were atypical of his later work, but the publication of *The Spanish Labyrinth: An Account of the Social and Political Background of the Spanish Civil War* (1943) established his reputation. This book remains a key text in understanding Spanish history and culture during this period.

The above quotation is an odd statement by someone whose most famous work as a writer was a factual account of a country in the midst of a devastating conflict. It stands in contrast to his acclaimed body of work, but it is perhaps an acceptance that, although the historian can report on events, it is the novelist's job to make sense of it all. **IHS**

> " *Every writer hopes or boldly assumes that his life is in some sense exemplary, that the particular will turn out to be universal.* "

Martin Amis
The Observer
1987

Martin Amis is perhaps not a writer whom you would automatically regard as exemplary. Privileged, well-read and insightful – but also on occasion rebarbatively acerbic – he displays few immediately apparent signs of having been an example to others. But not all examples are paragons of virtue; the awful warning can be as instructive as the golden rule. Amis often attempts to provoke moral outrage by offering fictional worst-case scenarios, which may be aesthetically revolting – deliberately so, because they attempt to instil in readers some of his own sense of revulsion and indignation.

Amis himself purports to be promoting a 'harmonial' view of the world (but this may be further attitudinizing). He seeks to point out in his work a 'coarsening of the culture' stemming from 'brutal Philistinism.' It is this that he sets out to tackle as a writer, using gross caricature and satire.

Modern fiction, according to Amis, tends towards the autobiographical. That certainly seems to be true of his. Perhaps it is a juxtaposition – of hypersensitivity to beauty, combined with a sense of the grotesque – 0that most effectively characterizes his work. **LW**

"*Life itself is a quotation.*"

Jorge Luis Borges
Attributed
1987

In *Cool Memories*, French sociologist Jean Baudrillard reports that the Argentine author made the above remark during a lecture in Paris. The idea is certainly provocative, and at first glance, also paradoxical. Life itself is no more a quotation than Paris is a person. One possible interpretation is that individual lives, like quotations, inspire and provide examples for us to follow. All lives are, to some extent, modelled on those that have gone before – children may rebel against their parents, but their reaction is a reference to an antecedent, and thus also a sort of quotation. Every work of art is either consciously inspired or unconsciously influenced by something else, and therefore in that sense a quotation.

When we say things, we may influence other people. We may seek a particular effect – 'Be quiet!' – or stimulate others, whether intentionally or not. Exactly how we do this is the most interesting aspect: we can give them an idea, fully formed; alternatively, we can sow seeds that will grow into their own ideas or at least encourage them to think for themselves. 'Life itself is a quotation' is an example of the latter: it is food for thought, and therefore inspirational. **LW**

⊙ Borges at home in Buenos Aires in 1983 at the age of eighty-four. He had been completely blind since he was fifty-five.

"*Wit invents; inspiration reveals.*"

⊘ Octavio Paz with his wife, Marie-José, pictured in New York City in 1990 after he was awarded the Nobel Prize in Literature.

Octavio Paz
Sor Juana, or, The Traps of Faith
1988

Octavio Paz was a Mexican poet, essayist, cultural critic and diplomat who was awarded the Nobel Prize in Literature in 1990. In his writing, always characterized by wit and humour, he addressed a wide range of subjects – politics, religion, music, art – but most of all he wrote about the Mexican psyche and the contrast between Mexico's ancient civilizations and the influence of the country's Spanish colonists. His poetry would deal with eroticism and love, as well as modern art.

In 1988, in the biography *Sor Juana, or, The Traps of Faith,* one of his most highly regarded works, Paz introduced readers beyond Latin American shores to the works of Sor Juana Inés de la Cruz. A Mexican poet and scholar of the 17th century, Sor Juana abandoned court life at the age of twenty and entered a convent, where she spent the rest of her life. Although Paz's book ostensibly concerns Sor Juana and her influence on Spanish writers, it is also about Mexico, Paz himself and his views on poetry. The quotation above draws an important distinction, identifying wit as the defining feature of baroque poetry and naming inspiration as the heart of romantic poetry. **HJ**

"People who are strangers to liquor are incapable of talking about literature."

Mo Yan
The Republic of Wine
1992

The novelist Mo Yan is controversial for a number of reasons. His pseudonym, meaning 'don't speak', derives from his parents' instructions to him during the Cultural Revolution. He knew starvation under a totalitarian regime, yet his novel *The Republic of Wine* does not critique the regime itself – although it was written three months after the massacre at Tiananmen Square.

Mo implies that talking about literature requires wit and wisdom, and that requires a dissolution by alcohol of the sanctimonious, schoolmarmish spirit in which it is often discussed. Yet the passage in which this quotation appears admonishes the correspondent for admiring literature at all. Its statement that 'liquor is literature' is bizarre and sounds like something that would be said under the influence. Mo even has his protagonist say that he wrote these words when he was 'good and drunk and you must not take them to heart'.

Perhaps the quotation above was never meant to be anything more than a provocation. Liquor and literature have often been intimately interwoven, and overindulgence may free up an understanding of the disciplined clear-thinking literature demands, but Mo's intoxicated vision does nothing to clarify the issue. **LW**

"Stories of imagination tend to upset those without one."

Terry Pratchett
The Ultimate Encyclopedia of Fantasy
1998

British author Terry Pratchett wrote these words in defence of the fantasy genre, which, he said, 'still trails clouds of disapproval'. Yet the statement itself is like whining in front of bullies: they immediately taste blood. Few would accuse Pratchett, in particular, and fantasy writers, in general, of lacking imagination, but what Pratchett really objected to was those who claim that fantasy writing is not real literature.

There is nothing wrong with the imaginations of those who gather at Discworld conventions. They are no different, in essence, from those who join Mensa after doing an IQ test: the effect is to put them with like minds. Yet not all 'stories of the imagination' are equal. J R R Tolkien is a heavyweight, but Pratchett's 'stories of the imagination' are jocular. And, unlike the stories of T H White or C S Lewis, Pratchett's do not alter something in us. There is something light-hearted about the wild outlandishness of his worlds, and even the names he gives his characters are frequently tongue-in-cheek. He seldom took himself too seriously, except perhaps in the above quotation, where he was trying to provoke people who have a fixed idea of what good writing was to reconsider their prejudices. Naturally, not every reader will come down on his side. **LW**

> ## *I just write what I wanted to write. I write what amuses me. It's totally for myself.*

J K Rowling
The New York Times
2000

'I never in my wildest dreams expected this popularity,' J K Rowling told reporter Alan Cowell as she travelled on a train dubbed 'the Hogwarts Express' to promote the newly published *Harry Potter and the Goblet of Fire*.

She said she never had an audience in mind for the magical fantasy. But she always knew what she wanted, and she refused to be diverted from her greater purpose, or to dilute her vision to accommodate the whims of fans or editors, such as the one who suggested that she bring an American exchange student to Hogwarts to appeal to her growing US audience.

Even after her enormous financial success with Harry Potter, Rowling went back to the modest Edinburgh café in which she had started the story of the schoolboy wizard, and there began work on a new crime series. And when she'd finished the first volume of this new enterprise, she published it under a pseudonym, Robert Galbraith, in order that her work should be judged on its own merits rather than as the latest offering of an established author – she is still writing for herself. **EP**

◀ J K Rowling receiving an honorary degree in 2006.

> ## *Literature is humanity talking to itself.*

Norman Rush
Mortals
2003

Ray Finch, the hero of sorts of Rush's thriller-cum-existential-treatise, is a teacher of English at an Anglican school in Botswana who also happens to be a contract agent for the CIA, and whose job it is to report to the Pentagon on 'persons of interest.' Set in the early 1990s, *Mortals* is told entirely from Ray's perspective. We find out everything about him from his views on all manner of intellectual matters to details of his professional and intimate relationships, and even his personal hygiene. The chapter titled 'I Would Like to Reassure You About My Penis' has him taking a bath over the course of thirty-odd pages.

The detail is extraordinary, and the effect immersive. If spy novels have historically been regarded as something different from, and not quite, literature, then Rush's aim seems to have been to bridge that gap. His novel is full of learned allusions to great writers of the past, and Ray himself is an artrfact of a bygone era. He sees himself more in line with his heroes from classical literature and poetry, worlds that he prefers to the one he lives in. As such, rather than learn from the mistakes of history, Ray is more likely to look to literature to find the right path. For him, literature is less an entertainment or a distraction from life than it is a guide through it. **IHS**

> " *Books are the perfect entertainment: no commercials, no batteries, hours of enjoyment for each dollar spent.* "

Stephen King
Entertainment Weekly
2007

⬆ Stephen King may not be a highbrow author, but he thinks deeply about his craft.

Stephen King is an enormously successful writer. It makes sense for him to advocate reading, since books are his bread and butter. However, King puts books above all other entertainment options for serious reasons, in spite of several of his own works having gone on to form the basis for hit movies.

Books are interactive, in the sense that they require more input than simply watching a screen. On the other hand, they do not ask us to complete mission quests in the way that some video games do. Instead, they allow us to escape for a few moments, in a unique combination of author's directive – the story – and our own imaginations. Not only is the technology of a book pretty straightforward, but the act of reading, once mastered, becomes second nature. King makes it clear that he thinks people should buy books to read, but the simplicity of his approach is deceptive. He is immensely literary, and he recognizes that writing is a compulsion – perhaps even a pathology – rather than a lifestyle choice; he is also aware that literacy itself opens up worlds and experiences to people who might otherwise be confined by circumstance to just a single view. **LW**

Everybody does have a book in them, but in most cases that's where it should stay.

Christopher Hitchens
Slate.com
2008

Christopher Hitchens was a raconteur par excellence, a self-professed contrarian, unapologetically opinionated, and one of the finest essayists in the English language. Friends testified to his ceaseless energy for writing, no matter the hour of the day or the level of liquor consumed. Even as he succumbed to esophageal cancer, Hitchens penned a moving account of his illness, its effects and his unwavering antitheism. He was born to be a writer – a talent he cherished, but one that he knew was not shared by everyone who picked up a pen.

In London, Hitchens fell in with a legendary Friday lunch group that included Martin Amis, Ian McEwan and Clive James. He and Amis were employed by the *New Statesman* and became the scourge of writers they felt were not entitled to be in print. Their friendship cemented their reputation as enfants terribles of the London literary scene. Amis moved on to fiction while Hitchens's favoured form was the essay. Hitchens was as much at home covering a story for *Vanity Fair* as he was writing for *The Nation*. And no topic was off limits – from politics and war, to being waterboarded in order to satisfy himself that it was a form of torture. **IHS**

⊙ Christopher Hitchens at his home in Washington, DC, in February 2011.

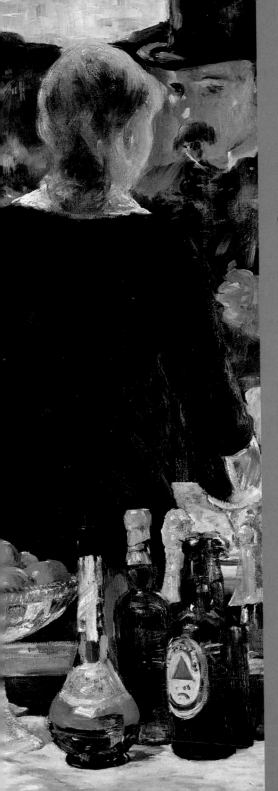

Art & Architecture

"*An arch never sleeps.*"

Indian Proverb
Unknown
c. 799–684 BCE

A symmetrical composition of two halves, an arch uses the principle of 'balanced tension' to ensure that the structure of which it is a part remains standing. An arch is constantly load-bearing – hence, metaphorically, it cannot relax, and it never sleeps.

In the arch of a stone bridge, the overall weight is transferred into thrusts contained by abutments at either end of the arch. Thus, the load is distributed evenly throughout. Leonardo da Vinci described the arch as 'two weaknesses which together make a strength'.

The concept of the arch is thought to have originated in Mesopotamia (modern Iraq). From there it spread to the rest of the world. The greater the load that an arch has to bear, the stronger it must be – this mechanical truism lends itself to figurative interpretations: the greater the burden of responsibility that a person has to bear, the stronger he or she becomes.

This proverb was originally Tamil. The basic idea is easily adaptable – anything inanimate can be said to never sleep. Neil Young used a variant as the title of a 1979 album. But while an arch is beneficial, Young's sleepless one – rust – was a metaphor for complacency. **BDS**

An illustration of an iwan (a vaulted space that opens on one side to a courtyard) at a mosque in India.

The Taj Mahal in Agra, India, took twenty-one years to build.

" Neither natural ability without instruction, nor instruction without natural ability, can make the perfect artist. "

Vitruvius

De Architectura (On Architecture)

C. 20 BCE

Vitruvius was the greatest Roman writer on architecture. His ten-volume masterpiece dealt with every aspect of building. Among the topics he covered were: architecture in general, urban planning, symmetry, style, materials, temple construction, civic amenities, private residences, floors, hydraulics and the supply of water to human habitations.

One of Vitruvius's fundamental tenets was that human-made structures should appear as organic as natural ones: houses should blend in with their surroundings as easily as beehives or birds' nests. The author also maintained that every building must be solid, useful and beautiful – these three criteria became known as the 'Vitruvian virtues.'

The above quotation, from Volume One of *De Architectura*, leads into a list of desirable qualities for the proficient architect: 'Let him be educated, skilful with the pencil, instructed in geometry, know much history, have followed the philosophers with attention, understand music, have some knowledge of medicine, know the opinions of the jurists, and be acquainted with astronomy and the theory of the heavens.' It's a big ask. **JP**

" Painters and poets . . . have always had an equal licence in bold invention. "

Horace

Ars Poetica (The Art of Poetry)

C. 19 BCE

Horace – Quintus Horatius Flaccus – was the son of a freed slave. He fought under Brutus at the Battle of Philippi (42 BCE), and after returning, defeated, to Rome, became acquainted with the poets Varius and Virgil. He later became one of the great lyric poets of his age, heavily influenced by Hellenistic aesthetics.

The above line is usually quoted without context, as if it were a categorical assertion of a universal truth. But Horace was too subtle a writer to deal in absolutes, and his opinions are almost always nuanced, and not infrequently ambivalent.

Evidently, Horace took the view that creativity should be at liberty to explore the unknown, to move outside conventional boundaries. However, *Ars Poetica* emphasizes as paramount the need for self-discipline and cautions that artists need to be constantly mindful of their own limitations. Stylistically, there are rules that should never be broken. For example, one should not, Horace said, pair 'snakes with birds' – in other words, mix metaphors. The wine flagon on the potter's wheel should not become, in error, a water jug. Horace also suggested that if you want your play to have a second performance, 'it should not be either shorter or longer than five acts'. **BDS**

"Paintings are the Bible of the laity."

Gratian
Attributed
1150 CE

Little is known of the life of Gratian, the Italian Benedictine monk born in Tuscany near the end of the 11th century CE. We know that he was a lecturer, and that he wrote the *Concordia discordantium canonum*, a treatise that sought to harmonize religious contradictions and their inconsistencies with the civil legal code. We know, too, that out of that substantial work, canon law was born as a bold, new discipline, distinct from traditional theology, a discipline that provided later popes with concrete foundations upon which their decrees would be founded and rendered applicable throughout the ever-broadening Roman Catholic world.

Gratian's best-known aphorism reflected the times in which he lived. Literacy was a rarity outside of the Church in the 11th and 12th centuries; indeed, religious leaders discouraged its spread in order to retain control of information and its interpretation. Images – including stained-glass windows and the profusion of reliefs on Europe's great cathedrals – were considered a primary source of information for a largely uneducated and illiterate laity. Paintings with religious themes were used evangelically, to spread the gospel and to encourage discussions and interpretations of biblical events. Icons and other images were all considered to be 'scripture for the illiterate,' capable of lifting the minds of ordinary men and women out of earthly concerns into heavenly realms. **BDS**

"I saw the angel in the marble and carved until I set him free."

Michelangelo
Attributed
c. 1494–95

According to Michelangelo – the great Renaissance painter, engineer, poet and sculptor – every piece of stone already contained within it a figure, and it was the responsibility of the sculptor to chip away at it until that hidden image was revealed or liberated from its rocky confinement.

The angel to which the artist was referring in this quote is one of two that can be found in the Basilica of San Domenico in Bologna, Italy, kneeling at the foot of the saint's tomb, a commission for which the young Michelangelo was paid thirty ducats by his patron.

The basilica itself was a massive undertaking, constructed over 500 years, starting from the early 13th century, and contributed to by a multitude of artists. In 1494 Michelangelo carved three figures for the basilica: an angel, kneeling and holding a candlestick; a statue of San Petronio, Bologna's patron saint; and a figure of San Procolo, the 4th-century martyr, a sculpture that closely resembles the statue of David that would come ten years later, in 1504.

In Michelangelo's mind, blocks of stone contained 'every thought the greatest artist has,' a universe of potential forms and ideas. And what went for marble applied *a fortiori* to creation as a whole – beneath superficial exteriors, beauty lies concealed. **BDS**

> *Painting is poetry which is seen and not heard, and poetry is a painting which is heard but not seen.*

Leonardo da Vinci
Notebooks
c. 1500

The intellectual battle between poet and painter goes back to antiquity – the struggle between, on the one side, the visual artist, who tries to impart a spiritual dimension with the brush, and, on the other side, the poet, who seeks to inspire and to be remembered through words alone. Leonardo da Vinci believed that the painter inhabited a loftier plane than the bard: he considered the eye was of a nobler sense than the sense of 'mere' hearing. He argued that though a deaf man could benefit greatly from gazing upon a painting, a blind man could never gain the same benefit from hearing a poem because '[h]e has never seen anything of the beauty of the world'. The deaf man, according to da Vinci, having lost his 'less noble sense', will nevertheless understand the art of the painter and what the artist is seeking to represent.

Da Vinci studied anatomy and physiology so that he could better represent, in paintings, what he saw in the world. In *Trattato della pittura* (*A Treatise on Painting*), a collection of manuscripts compiled after his death, he is quoted as having said that paintings represent the essence of nature more than words ever could. **BDS**

◬ This self-portrait (c. 1512) by Leonardo da Vinci is thought to have been made when the artist was in his mid-fifties.

◁ Cecilia Gallerani, painted by Leonardo da Vinci (c. 1489).

"*It is not bright colors but good drawing that makes figures beautiful.*"

⬤ *The Penitent Magdalene* (1555–65) – Titian at the height of his artistic powers.

Titian
Attributed
c. 1570

Tiziano Vecelli (Titian) was a central figure in the 16th-century Venetian school of the Italian Renaissance, and one of the most versatile painters of his era. Referred to by his contemporaries as a 'sun amidst small stars' (a reference to the final line of Dante's *The Divine Comedy*), Titian had a lifelong fascination with colour, with his most memorable works beguiling products of loose brushwork; subtle tones; and vivid, earthy tones. Titian's use of only a very few primary colours – combined with his perfection of the art of oil painting using a mixture of egg and oil – freed the brush from being a tool used to describe only volumes, details and surfaces into a medium through which light could be interpreted via colour – the art of *colorito*.

In each picture, Titian's use of translucent colour glazing – applying more than thirty glazes, one over the other, and putting down a mass of colour—laid the foundation of the image that was to come. The above quotation, however, makes it plain that he was aware that the use of bold colours alone did not make an artist, and that while malachite green or yellow ochre are surely vivid, 'one must know how to use them'. **BDS**

It is crooked wood that shows the best sculptor.

African Proverb
Unknown
c. 1600

In Africa, as all over the world throughout recorded history, proverbs have always been used to convey important truths about almost every aspect of existence, from everyday exchanges on the street to important tribal, regional and governmental meetings. In African society, in particular, it is common for a person first to speak a proverb and then to follow it with an explanation of its meaning. The use of proverbs is also widely associated with, but is not the sole preserve of, older people.

'It is crooked wood that shows the best sculptor' – which, like most proverbs, comes with no actual source or originator attached to it – means that, often, people's true abilities are not revealed until they are presented with a testing dilemma.

Many African proverbs are tied to the land and to the creatures that inhabit it. For example, 'The best way to eat an elephant in your path is to cut him up into little pieces' is a humorously imaginative way of saying that problems are best tackled bit by bit. 'A roaring lion kills no game' means that nothing can be achieved simply by talking about it. **BDS**

⬤ It is not only African proverbs that are inspired by the continent's flora and fauna: this is a lion napkin ring.

A painting is complete when it has the shadows of a god.

Rembrandt
Attributed
1665

Although this remark is almost invariably attributed to Rembrandt, there is no incontrovertible evidence that he ever said it. Nevertheless, even if it is apocryphal, it is well invented: the Dutch master's use of light and shadow became increasingly sophisticated from the late 1620s, when he began experimenting with different ways of depicting light as it falls onto an object from a distance. To create these areas of intense, focused light required immersing his paintings in large areas of shadows – especially the corners, foregrounds and backgrounds – so that each painting's centrally lit themes, often clustered together, draw in the viewer's eye.

Details too were sacrificed in favour of expanses of darker tones. In *A Woman in Bed* (1647), the light entering the subject's bedroom from the left adds a tantalizing degree of realism to her upper body, thanks to the contrasting deep shadows that dominate the work. Rembrandt's light is selective. It touches only what he wants you to see. But the light would not be so bright were it not for the shadows that surround it. **BDS**

◐ *A Priest at an Altar* (c. 1631–32) is thought to be by Rembrandt.

Architecture aims at Eternity.

Christopher Wren
Attributed
c. 1680

A mathematician and a scientist long before he turned his attention to designing buildings, Christopher Wren was in the vanguard of a new generation of English architects who regarded architecture as a means of expressing a vision, a philosophy – even of glimpsing the nature of God. The contemporary architect Frank Gehry claimed as much too, when he proclaimed: 'Architecture should speak of its time and place, but yearn for timelessness.'

Eternity. Timelessness. Buildings that are more than the sum of their parts, based on more than simply form and function. Wren looked beyond the cutting of stone and the laying of foundations and saw the greater whole. In the aftermath of the Great Fire of London in 1666, inspired by the Baroque splendours of Paris, Wren set about giving solid form to his visions, and in the process transformed London's skyline.

His son, Christopher, author of *Parentalia; or, Memoirs of the Family of the Wrens* (1750), attributed the above remark to his father, who achieved his lofty goal of eternal architecture in part with his 'wedding cake'-style of church steeples, and above all with his masterpiece, the post-Fire reconstruction of St Paul's Cathedral. **BDS**

"[Architecture] is music in space, as [if] it were a frozen music."

Friedrich von Schelling
Philosophy of Art
1802

Born in 1775 in the town of Leonberg, Germany, Friedrich von Schelling was academically successful from a young age. While attending the prominent Tübinger Stift (an Evangelical-Lutheran seminary), he developed close friendships with two prominent future philosophers, Georg Wilhelm Friedrich Hegel and Friedrich Hölderlin.

Schelling's work focused on the natural sciences, the arts and the philosophy of religion. He was a prolific writer and lecturer throughout his life. In time he became notorious for the fluctuation of his thoughts, which was taken as inconsistency, but more recent interpretations of his works have led some critics to hail him as one of the most influential thinkers of the German Idealist movement.

Schelling saw a work of art as complex and powerful, being a set (finite) object capable of providing us with the potential for limitless (infinite) thoughts. He saw beautiful architecture as rhythmic, eliciting emotion and attitude, even though it is positioned and static. Schelling's description of architecture as frozen music was ahead of its time, like much of his work. Indeed, his vision of architecture as a fusion of sight and sound influences many architects today: no longer do they merely create buildings; they now try to imagine how every one of our senses will be affected by the spaces they design. **GG**

"Beauty is only the promise of happiness."

Stendhal
De L'Amour (On Love)
1822

Marie-Henri Beyle – better known as Stendhal, author of *Le Rouge et le Noir* (*The Red and the Black*, 1830) – participated in the Realist and Romanticist literary movements of the 19th century. Lively and eccentric in his behaviour and thought, he used more than one hundred diverse pseudonyms, many with comic overtones. The only book he published under his real name was a history of painting.

De L'Amour, the source of the quotation above, is a serious analysis of the progression a person goes through when falling in love. Stendhal wrote the work to address the heartbreak he experienced when his love for Mathilde, Countess Dembowska, was not reciprocated. Stendhal referred to the progression as 'crystallization,' a transformative process of four steps: the first step, admiration, is followed by acknowledgement, then hope and finally delight. Stendhal saw falling in love as an instinctive process, one that has little, if anything, to do with an individual's will.

Stendhal's words suggest that being in the presence of beauty, be it that of another person or a work of art, reminds us of our own potential for happiness. Each of the four steps of crystallization produces its own sense of joy. Thus, when someone is at the admiration step of the process and beginning to fall in love, he or she will see the object of affection as beautiful and will anticipate happiness to come from that beauty. **GG**

> *Ancient sculpture is the true school of modesty. But where the Greeks had modesty, we have cant . . .*

Thomas Love Peacock
Crotchet Castle
1831

Thomas Love Peacock, referred to by close friends, including the poet Percy Bysshe Shelley, as the 'laughing philosopher,' was born to Samuel Peacock, a London glass merchant, and Sarah Love in 1785. Samuel passed away a few years later of 'poor circumstances,' and it remains unclear what exactly caused his demise.

In 1805, Peacock published *Palmyra and Other Poems*; the collection was well received. It was around this time that Peacock fell in love with and became engaged to Fanny Falkner. Unfortunately, the relationship foundered due to meddling by one of Fanny's relatives. Peacock's poem 'Newark Abbey' speaks of this experience.

His first novel, *Headlong Hall* (1816), set the pattern for the works that followed: they were all conversation novels with little action. Peacock enjoyed poking fun at his peers and the absurdity of his day's norms and practices. His love for humour and satire is evident in his sixth and penultimate novel, *Crotchet Castle*, and ever present in the descriptions of the quirky fixations of its protagonist. Indeed, it is this character, Mr Crotchet, who delivers the above quotation. Using Mr Crotchet as his mouthpiece, Peacock attempts to shame his contemporaries for their lewdness, weaknesses and sanctimonious thoughts, and for their failure to embrace the natural joys and pleasures that existence offers. **GG**

> *There is no better deliverance from the world than through art; and a man can form no surer bond with it than through art.*

Johann Wolfgang von Goethe
Maxims and Reflections
1833

Goethe, considered the greatest German literary figure of the modern era, was a man of inexhaustible talents. Aside from his legendary writings, including his famous *Faust* (1808), he was a poet, scientist and artist.

Of all the children born to Goethe's parents, only he and his sister survived. The losses of these children, and the professional frustration of his lawyer father, resulted in Goethe being the fortunate recipient of a superb early education. Goethe enjoyed a huge exposure to languages – Latin, Greek, French, Italian, English and Hebrew – as well as to the arts, and his passion for drawing and theatre continued throughout his life. At the age of sixteen he left home to study law in Leipzig. Although his time there was fruitful for his writings, he ended up leaving the city without a degree.

Maxims and Reflections contains some 1,400 items and provides a wealth of insights into Goethe's thoughts and ideals. The quotation expresses his ardent belief in the power of art to help our minds transcend our mundane and painful existences. Even more important, art simultaneously pulls us back into the world and encourages us to engage with and respond to it. **GG**

Art is beauty, the perpetual invention of detail, the choice of words, the exquisite care of execution.

Théophile Gautier
La Revue des Deux-Mondes
1841

Théophile Gautier published the above quotation in *La Revue des Deux-Mondes* (*The Review of the Two Worlds*), a literary magazine that is still published. The original purpose of the magazine, begun in 1829, was to create a cultural, political and economic bridge between the United States and France (the New World and the Old).

It was following an introduction to Victor Hugo that Gautier, an aspiring painter at that time, turned to literature. Gautier had begun writing poetry at an early age, but the bulk of his writings were contributions to literary journals. While producing both literary writing and travel literature, Gautier was able to meet a wealth of influential arts patrons. In his writings he could express his personal preferences in art and culture.

This quotation both hints at the effort that Gautier expended on his most famous romantic ballet, *Giselle* (1841), and alludes to the complexities of any art form. By calling attention to detail, he exhorts the viewer to go beyond the 'big picture' of an artwork and appreciate its constituent elements. By concentrating on the richness of the detail, the viewer is able to embrace the artwork and so become a part of it. **GG**

> "*The artist who aims at perfection in everything achieves it in nothing.*"

Eugène Delacroix
Journal
c. 1850

Thought to have been the illegitimate son of the French statesman Talleyrand, Delacroix studied at the Lycée Louis-le-Grand in Paris, immersing himself in the classics and winning recognition for his drawings. He was greatly influenced by the works of Guérin, Rubens and Géricault. Despite being ridiculed by the public and French government for his first major painting, *The Barque of Dante* (1822), Delacroix led the French Romantic school. Nine years on, another of his paintings, *Liberty Leading the People* (1831), was similarly derided by the ruling French officials; deemed to be an inflammatory piece, it was removed from public view.

The quotation above speaks of the high standards that Delacroix set for himself, because the artist achieved perfection across multiple domains of artistic expression. Perhaps it was his belief that perfection is unattainable that drove him to create flawless pieces. In any event, his gift for brushstroke techniques and use of optical colour effects influenced many Impressionist artists and inspired many Symbolists. Delacroix was also an acclaimed lithographer who illustrated works by Shakespeare, Walter Scott and Goethe. GG

A self-portrait by Eugène Delacroix (c. 1837).

"Ornamentation is the principal part of architecture, considered as a subject of fine art."

⬢ An accomplished artist himself, Ruskin produced this fine watercolour study of the Baptistery, Florence, in 1872.

John Ruskin

Lectures on Architecture and Painting

1854

The quotation above comes from a lecture delivered in Edinburgh in 1853 by the highly influential British art critic and theorist John Ruskin. Here, in the first of a very popular series of public lectures he gave on architecture and painting, Ruskin proposed that a great architect must be a great sculptor or painter.

To place Ruskin's lecture in context, the critic was concerned by a drop in standards that was affecting all the arts. The Industrial Revolution had changed Britain dramatically, particularly in the growth of a mass market of consumers, and the introduction of mass-produced goods for them. Ruskin believed that this had resulted in a welter of shoddy, inferior goods, unlike the handcrafted objects of earlier times, and that artisans' skills had been devalued by the arrival of goods manufactured in factories. Espousing the Gothic Revival, he had an interest in the medieval period and advocated a return to craftsmanship in all branches of the decorative arts and architecture. Ruskin not only asserted his views through writing and teaching, he also actively sought to change society, inspiring the Art Workers' Guild in 1884 to raise the status of the decorative arts. **CK**

The art of art, the glory of expression and the sunshine of the light of letters, is simplicity.

Walt Whitman
Leaves of Grass
1855

Walt Whitman is often referred to as the father of free verse. Born into a poor family, he began to support himself early, working for several newspapers while also attempting to publish his poetry and fiction.

The above quotation comes from Whitman's famous collection of poetry, *Leaves of Grass*. Throughout his life, Whitman often faced questions about his personal life and the homosexual undertones of the collection. *Leaves of Grass* was considered obscene by some at the time of its publication.

Leaves of Grass was first printed at Whitman's own expense in 1855. The initial printed versions cited no author, with only a portrait of Whitman on the title page. It was only when Ralph Waldo Emerson and others spoke highly of the collection that Whitman's status was elevated to that of a prominent literary figure.

The above quotation shows Whitman's drive to recognize individuality, celebrate potential and see the beauty in common things while at the same time exploring the mysteries of identity. He celebrates simplicity and truth and warns against the negative effects of superfluous embellishments. **GG**

◭ The frontispiece of early editions of *Leaves of Grass* featured only this engraved portrait of Walt Whitman; no name was added.

" *Every artist was first an amateur.* "

Ralph Waldo Emerson
Letters and Social Aims
1875

Ralph Waldo Emerson, a prominent US lecturer, poet and essayist, has become known as the father of transcendentalism. He grew up in a very sociable household devoted to the intellectual and religious growth of all its family members. This early exposure to literature, religion and the arts certainly prompted Emerson's philosophical discoveries. His formal education, at Boston Latin School and then Harvard College, strengthened the already sound scholarly foundation he had gained at home.

The quotation above could be Emerson's 'call to arms'. He wanted individuals to exert their artistic and intellectual passions and not have their souls' powers of expression inhibited by fear of failure. Emerson offered individuals the freedom to embrace the amateurs within themselves while reminding the outside world of the value and the potential of the amateur.

The quotation comes from a collection of essays that Emerson, his daughter Ellen Tucker Emerson, and his son Edward Waldo Emerson produced collaboratively. Scholars have noted that Emerson's sermons and lectures became increasingly rich and influential over time, partly due to the generosity with which Emerson shared his thoughts regarding his own professional and personal development. **GG**

" *Conciseness in art is essential and a refinement. The concise man makes one think; the verbose bores.* "

Édouard Manet
La Grande Revue
1882

The French painter Édouard Manet has come to be regarded as a father figure to the Impressionists. Known for his avant-garde ideas, he never exhibited with the group, but he was influential, encouraging artists such as Claude Monet, Pierre-Auguste Renoir and Edgar Degas to paint scenes from modern life.

Manet made the above remark late in his life. One of his friends, the painter Pierre-Georges Jeanniot, visited him in January 1882 while he was painting what was to be his last major work, *A Bar at the Folies-Bergère* (1882). Jeanniot later related that the model, a pretty girl, was posed behind a table loaded with 'bottles and victuals'. Manet was by then ill and fragile, suffering from syphilis and rheumatism, but he gave Jeanniot advice on art and painting, stressing the need to be concise. He also advocated looking for the main light and shadow when painting a face, saying that the rest would come naturally. Bridging Impressionism and realism, Manet promoted form as much as content, believing that content may be portrayed realistically through precise form. **CK**

❯ Detail of Édouard Manet's *A Bar at the Folies-Bergère* (1882).

> *"Poetry surrounds us everywhere, but putting it on paper is, alas, not so easy as looking at it."*

Vincent van Gogh
Letter to his brother, Theo
1883

Dutch Postimpressionist painter Vincent van Gogh wrote more than 800 letters, most of them to his younger brother, Theo, an art dealer, who supported Vincent financially and emotionally in his adult life. These private exchanges reveal the nature of the relationship between the siblings, their friendship and their quarrels. They act as a chronicle of van Gogh's life: his daily routine and his failed love affairs. The correspondence also reveals most of what is known about the artist's thoughts: his depression, spiritual beliefs, ethics and theories of art. His letters have been lauded for their literary merit, particularly his expressive capacity when grappling with the notion of imperfection.

Van Gogh trained as a minister before deciding in 1880 to become a painter of the working classes. A largely self-taught artist, he struggled to capture the beauty of the everyday world around him in the Dutch countryside. He saw the extraordinary in the ordinary and attempted to honour the stark realities of peasant life by acknowledging the nobility of toil and making it the subject of his art. **CK**

◀ Vincent van Gogh's *Road with Cypress and Star* (1890).

> *"Every artist dips his brush in his own soul, and paints his own nature into his pictures."*

Henry Ward Beecher
Proverbs from Plymouth Pulpit
1887

Dubbed the 'most famous man in America' by the biographer Debby Applegate, Henry Ward Beecher had a fantastical and controversial life. He was best known for his support of the abolition of slavery and for his innovative oratorical style. Despite being considered one of the less promising of all the Beecher children, he became as famous as his sister, Harriet Beecher Stowe, author of the novel *Uncle Tom's Cabin* (1852).

Henry Ward Beecher was the first and most prominent pastor of the famous Plymouth Church in Brooklyn, New York. There, he routinely addressed congregations of up to 3,000. In addition to his sermons, Beecher joined the lecture circuits in both the United States and Europe. His touring promoted his popularity and increased his personal wealth.

In the above quotation, Beecher clearly expresses his celebration of individuality, stating that people must dig deep into their own subconscious in order to create. By reaching into the soul, the individual is freed to make art unhindered by conventional wisdom or constrained thought. What is created is representative of the individual's internal and external views of nature. **GG**

" *As the sun colours flowers, so does art colour life.* "

John Lubbock
The Pleasures of Life
1887

From his youth, politician and scientist John Lubbock was influenced by Charles Darwin. Darwin lived nearby and became Lubbock's lifelong friend and mentor. In addition to Darwin, other prominent intellectuals and scientists frequently visited the Lubbock household.

Fortunate in his relationship with Darwin, the academic influence of his family, and the quality of his friends, Lubbock excelled in areas as diverse as business and science. His career was a catalogue of significant accomplishments in politics, science and banking. Lubbock became one of the best-known men in England and a great public educator.

The meaning of the quotation above is quite simple, but it makes a strong comment on the value of nature and art. Lubbock points out that without the energy of the sun, the flowers will fail to display their splendid beauty, and suggests that the same occurs with art and humans. Art nurtures our minds, showing us the path to reach our fullest potential. By appreciating and surrounding ourselves with art, we gain the energy to be fully engaged in living, which enables us to increase our understanding of the world around us. **GG**

> " *Architecture should be at the head of the arts, not at the foot of the professions.* "

Reginald Blomfield
Architecture
1892

Reginald Blomfield was born in Bow, Devon, England, in 1856. His first love in life was sculpture, but ultimately he became one of the best regarded architects and architectural historians of the 19th century. He was equally celebrated as an illustrator. Blomfield was to become a part of the Arts and Crafts Movement, joining forces with William Morris. Although Blomfield collaborated with contemporaries in both the horticultural and art worlds, he was not averse to making bold and frank criticisms of their work when the spirit moved him to do so. Blomfield's love of historical architecture prepared him for the work he would ultimately do in architectural preservation, and he is credited with opposing demolition of many churches in London, as well as of Waterloo Bridge.

In the quotation above, Blomfield attempted to reassert the paramount importance of architecture at a time when he suspected that it was being taken for granted. He wanted readers to appreciate the complexity of architecture and to acknowledge that it encompasses the study of multiple disciplines – the sciences, economics, arts and human relationships. His claim that architecture is the supreme art form is not incredible: after all, most people spend more of their time in buildings than in books. **GG**

> " *Art is the only serious thing in the world. And the artist is the only person who is never serious.* "

Oscar Wilde
Maxims for the Instruction of the Over-Educated
1894

Wilde was at the height of his fame when he wrote this. An outspoken and flamboyant figure in London's artistic circles, he was known for his irreverent humour and individualism. A proponent of aestheticism, which espoused the notion of art for art's sake, he promoted sensuality in all its forms – including the decorative arts – and thus flew in the face of conventional Victorian morality. His use of wit often served a purpose – here, to call attention to the role of the artist in society, the value of refinement in design, and the sublime nature of art. His subversive humour sought to advocate craftsmanship in an age of mass production.

This remark first appeared in a short collection of aphorisms published anonymously in the weekly *Saturday Review*. In this article, Wilde examined the value of friendship, the nature of beauty, and the stifling quality of narrow-minded public opinion. A few years later Wilde found out how harsh public opinion could be when he was jailed for gross indecency. His notoriety has added to his reputation as an agent provocateur, but he was a serious artist, who held up a mirror to contemporary society, casting light on its hypocrisy. **CK**

"In art, there are only two types of people: revolutionaries and plagiarists."

Paul Gauguin
Letter to *Le Soir* newspaper
1895

⊘ A page from Paul Gauguin's *Noa Noa: Voyage to Tahiti* (1901).

⊘ Paul Gauguin's *Self-Portrait with Halo and Snake* (1889).

Postimpressionist artist Paul Gauguin had become disillusioned by a lack of success in his native France, so he travelled to Tahiti in search of inspiration. There, he developed an interest in the indigenous culture and was keen to establish himself as a potter. On his return to France, he still struggled to sell his work. At this time he created a ceramic figurine, *Oviri* (1894) – meaning 'wild' or 'savage' – depicting a Tahitian goddess with two wolf cubs. He was primarily a painter, but he had been taught by ceramicist Ernest Chaplet. When Gauguin submitted *Oviri* to the Société Nationale des Beaux-Arts salon in April 1895, it caused a sensation. Reports vary, but he was either expelled or was only allowed to remain after Chaplet threatened to withdraw his own work unless Gauguin's remained. Gauguin wrote an outraged letter to *Le Soir* bemoaning the state of modern ceramics. He saw himself as a revolutionary, but he was also keen to take advantage of the scandal, getting whatever publicity he could to help him to make a living. Nevertheless, Gauguin was one of the first artists to see beauty in the art of indigenous peoples – a fascination that was later shared by Pablo Picasso and led to Primitivism. CK

"A painting in a museum hears more ridiculous opinions than anything else in the world."

Edmond de Goncourt
The House of an Artist
1898

If Paris in the late 19th century witnessed a storm of artistic creativity, the Goncourt brothers, Edmond and Jules, lived in the eye of it. Born into minor aristocracy, which gave them both ample pensions, they lived the bohemian life and surrounded themselves with all manner of artists and creatives. Their journals of the Parisian beau monde, written between 1851 and 1896, remain some of the most important accounts of that era. They were also novelists, contributing much to the development of the naturalist novel. As art critics, their specialty was 18th-century French painting – they were indifferent to current trends, particularly the Impressionists, with the exception of Edgar Degas.

Edmond de Goncourt was a renowned wit and displayed a marked talent for withering bon mots. The above quotation reflects the common experience of people who have listened to random opinions on the merits, meaning and characteristics of paintings. Erudition and inanity may go hand in hand, and the society Edmond moved through with such ease would have provided him with a plentiful supply of both, if not an excess of the latter. **IHS**

"Every time I paint a portrait I lose a friend."

John Singer Sargent
Attributed
c. 1900

Exactly when the American John Singer Sargent, the most successful portrait painter of his generation, made the above remark is unclear. Nevertheless, it is attributed to him in British landscape painter Christopher R W Nevinson's memoir *Paint and Prejudice* (1937), and in art critic Edward Lucie-Smith's book *The Private John Singer Sargent* (2007).

Sargent's portraits attracted criticism in his early career, but by 1900 he was set up as a leading society portrait painter at an international level, with studios in London, New York City, and Boston. Sargent's skill lay not just in his technique but also in his ability to depict the psychology of his sitters. This is most evident in works that were not commissioned, the relatively intimate portraits he made of his circle of friends – writers, singers, actors and dancers – because he felt no need to flatter them. Sargent's feelings about the character of a sitter are sometimes evident too. The wry, almost bitter, quotation is an acknowledgement that sometimes people find it hard to accept themselves as they are. In 1907, sick of portrait painting, Sargent decided to give up his studios and focus instead on murals and landscape studies. **CK**

❯ *Lady Agnew of Lochnaw* (c. 1892) by John Singer Sargent.

> " *All healthy emotion, all strong emotion lacks taste. As soon as an artist becomes human and begins to feel, he is finished as an artist.* "

🔊 Thomas Mann provided readers with an early-20th-century take on the life of the artist.

Thomas Mann
Tonio Kröger
1903

A novella written when Mann was just twenty-five years old, *Tonio Kröger* is a largely autobiographical account of the author's life from his school days to adulthood. The hero feels distant from his parents – an artistic mother and a merchant father – and regards his own insights into the human condition as more profound than theirs while at the same time envying what he perceives as their innocence. As an adult, Tonio achieves success as a writer, but when he returns to his hometown, he is mistaken for a criminal. This experience influences his eventual conclusion that artists need to set themselves apart from emotion. Tonio eventually comes to terms with his feelings of isolation, which he refers to as 'a very chaste bliss'. The character, like his creator, occupies a void, somewhere between art and life.

Thomas Mann's friend, Erich Heller, the Bohemia-born essayist and Germanist, regarded *Tonio Kröger* as an effective expression of the concept that all artists, in order to express themselves effectively, must set themselves apart from mundane reality and avoid emotion. 'To be an artist,' Mann wrote, 'one has to die to everyday life.' **BDS**

Freedom from ornament is a sign of spiritual strength.

Adolf Loos
'Ornament and Crime' speech
1908

Austrian-born modernist architect Adolf Loos wrote this line in 1908. Two years passed before he uttered it in public, in a speech in Vienna in which he revealed his dislike for ornamentation and presented arguments for how it was hindering development. Nor was what Loos called the 'ornament disease' confined to architecture. He said that red velvet clothing made the wearer look like a 'buffoon', a 'fairground monkey'.

Freedom from ornamentation lowers an item's cost. Plain white crockery is cheaper than ornamental crockery, and so the poor man can save more money. And modern man has the spirituality that comes from art, which has taken the place of ornaments in its capacity to provide joy. Changing tastes in ornamented objects lead to their premature devaluation. The upshot of this is that they require replacing more rapidly than less ornamented objects. Ornamentation requires that man has to work longer hours in order to create the embellishments that we think we want – 'panting in slavery to ornament,' Loos called it – and that is a waste of labour, of health and of lifestyle. Loos saw how less work could mean more time to pursue joy and to seek spiritual fulfillment. **BDS**

⊙ Completed in 1930, the Villa Müller in Prague, Czech Republic, is one of the most utilitarian of Loos's modernist creations.

> **What I dream of is an art of balance, of purity and serenity ... something like a good armchair.**

Henri Matisse
Notes of a Painter
1908

Matisse first found fame as the unofficial leader of Les Fauves (The Wild Beasts), whose aggressive brushwork, use of nonnaturalistic colour, and bold use of line caused a stir when they exhibited at the Salon d'Automne in Paris in 1905. His reputation grew, and he opened a school in Paris. His friendly rivalry with Pablo Picasso for leadership of the French avant-garde led him to write what became his personal manifesto, *Notes of a Painter*, which was first published in the weekly magazine *La Grande Revue*.

Matisse wrote the above line after Picasso had received a hostile reception for his radical Cubist painting *Les Demoiselles d'Avignon* (1907), which depicted prostitutes in a brothel in Barcelona. Matisse was distancing himself from such works. His philosophy was that art should appeal to all, elevate the spirit and rest the mind. He wanted art to be uplifting. Some denounced this credo as superficial and bourgeois, because it demanded art that was recreational rather than subversive. But Matisse remained adamant that art should be grounded in everyday life. **CK**

🔘 Henri Matisse at home in Vence, southern France, in 1949.

> **I obey nature, I never presume to command her. The first principle in art is to copy what one sees.**

Auguste Rodin
Conversation with Paul Gsell
1910

French sculptor Auguste Rodin saw nature in the human form, but unlike most of his peers – who put their models on pedestals and then told them to strike particular poses – Rodin never sought to command people in such a way. Instead, he allowed his models to walk about, to do what they felt like doing – and then, if and when they took on an interesting perspective – he would start trying to capture it and reproduce it. Far from commanding his models, Rodin seemed to be at their whim, a master who waited upon his servants' commands. He considered that those who orchestrated their models into poses committed 'violence to nature,' treated human beings as though they were 'puppets' and risked the creation of lifeless, artificial art.

In Rodin's view, the only demand that should be made of any model was that, having once produced an interesting pose, he or she should be able to 'conform to the memory of the pose' – in other words, to re-create whatever it was that first grabbed the sculptor's imagination. The principle, therefore, is to copy nature, because, to quote Rodin again, 'There is no recipe for improving' it. **BDS**

"All great painters were less or more Impressionists. It is mainly a question of instinct."

A detail from Monet's *Water Lilies* (c. 1915–26) – a series of paintings depicting the artist's garden in differing light conditions.

Claude Monet
Letter to Sir Evan Edward Charteris
1910

Claude Monet was at his happiest painting the French countryside, putting his brushes quickly to his canvases before the sunlight on which he depended so much shifted, and it was his *Impression, Sunrise* (1872) that gave the Impressionist movement its name. It was therefore perhaps fitting that he outlived all the great Impressionists: Sisley died in 1899; Pissarro in 1903; Cézanne in 1906; Degas in 1917; and Renoir in 1919. Monet – arguably the greatest of them all – died in 1926, and in the latter stages of his life, he wrote a letter to Sir Evan Edward Charteris, the English lawyer and biographer of painter John Singer Sargent, in which he acknowledged, humbly: 'My only virtue is to have painted directly in front of nature, while trying to render the impressions made on me by the most fleeting effects.' Monet also wrote that, in his opinion, all great painters were Impressionists, and the only things that separated them and gave them each their own voice and style were their individual instincts.

The quotation ends: '. . .and much simpler than [John Singer] Sargent thinks'. Monet said he never 'became' an Impressionist, but 'always was one'. **BDS**

A drawing is simply a line going for a walk.

Paul Klee
Diary
1911

Swiss-born painter Paul Klee excelled at creating exquisite canvases of Symbolist, abstract and Expressionist art that might seem childlike in their simplicity. Indeed, Klee greatly admired the clarity and freedom he saw in children's drawings. The artist created delicate, minimalist paintings and had a lifelong interest in handwriting and calligraphy. He understood better than most how starting a line marks the beginning of transferring form and content to paper. Writing needs to conform to certain principles in order to be decipherable, but Klee recognized how its merging of concept and gesture can result – just as painting does – in the expression of individual sensibilities. He used pictorial symbols such as signs, arrows, and hieroglyphs to blur the traditional boundaries that separate writing and the visual arts.

In Klee's mind, the line goes for a walk on its own; it is not 'taken' for a walk, which is how it is often misquoted. So any such line drawing has a refreshing playfulness about it – a doodle of sorts. It should also have an aimless quality to it, which adds a touch of surrealism to an already eclectic recipe. **BDS**

⊘ Paul Klee photographed in his studio in 1939. The artist explored an expressive language of pictorial symbols and signs.

"*Art has nothing to do with taste; art is not there to be tasted.*"

A portrait of Max Ernst, pioneer of the Dada movement and Surrealism, taken in 1962.

Max Ernst
Volksmund newspaper
1912

Max Ernst – the self-taught, German-born painter, sculptor and graphic artist – was a pioneer of Dadaism and Surrealism who developed provocative ways of making art to express the modern condition. He never held art critics in particularly high regard. Nor did he consider art to be something that should ever be judged. To be a judge of art – a 'critic' – is, Ernst suggested, a 'pleasant occupation,' because no matter what you say, you never have to worry about whether you are right or wrong, and your words will never require revision. When a critic talks about the lack of ability of an artist, all he or she is really saying is that the work is not to his or her taste. And therein lies the absurdity. Ernst knew full well, as all artists do, that 'art has nothing to do with taste'; it is not laboured over by artists simply so that it can be critiqued by others who lack the courage to ever put brush to canvas.

It is not for anyone to say that frottage (the technique of taking a pencil and making a rubbing over an uneven surface, which Ernst himself pioneered) or grattage (the scraping of paint over canvas to reveal the imprint of objects underneath) is tasteful or not. It simply is. **BDS**

The artist is not born to a life of pleasure. He must not live idle; he has a hard work to perform . . .

Wassily Kandinsky

The Art of Spiritual Harmony

1914

Modernist Russian painter and art theorist Wassily Kandinsky had a passion for painting that was matched only by his belief that artists must be free to express themselves outside stifling societal norms, using abstract forms and concepts that have no reference to the material world around them. He promoted and defended his notion of artistic freedom in *The Art of Spiritual Harmony*, first published in English in 1914. For Kandinsky, 'the artist was prophet', not 'born to pleasure' but one who bears an almost Old Testament-like, burdensome cross: to provide people with radical new ways of seeing and interpreting their world, to 'cry in the wilderness' of 'common' art, so that others might understand.

Painting was certainly, for Kandinsky, a 'hard work to perform'. Geometric shapes needed to be unravelled and understood, as did the psychology and language of colour and how it should be independent of form. Kandinsky's pioneering work was geometry carefully and methodically expressed as theory – a prophetic, pure world of circles, half circles, zigzags, straight lines, angles and curves – in which he distilled the emotional and spiritual power of art. **BDS**

⊘ Kandinsky, seen here at work on a canvas, believed that art should aspire to be as abstract as music.

"The position of the artist is humble. He is essentially a channel."

● Piet Mondrian in his workshop in New York, 1942.

❷ *Composition A* (1920) is an early example of Mondrian's pure geometric abstraction using primary colours, black and white.

Piet Mondrian
De Stijl journal
1917

Dutch painter Piet Mondrian began as a landscape artist painting the trees, fields and windmills of his native Holland. However, over time, he found such representational depictions intolerable as he moved through various stylistic periods that produced the almost Pointillist *Mill in Sunlight* (1908) and the Cubist-influenced *Still Life with Gingerpot II* (1912). By 1914 curved lines had been virtually eliminated from his work, which was gradually evolving into a signature mix of black geometric lines and bold primary colours. Mondrian believed that artists were merely channels, or vessels, for use by a higher source, and that the emotion inherent in beauty was too easily obscured by the object. He therefore eliminated the object entirely, leaving only lines and primary colours that contained in their various assemblages the perfection of balance he was seeking.

In 1917 he cofounded the De Stijl (Dutch for 'the Style') movement, which involved the total rejection of visual reality – art 'held back' by the temperament and pride of the artist. Mondrian called his new austere style of abstract art Neoplasticism. It used only 'the straight line and the clearly defined primary colour'. **BDS**

> *Art must not be concentrated in dead shrines called museums. It must be spread everywhere.*

Vladimir Mayakovsky
'Shrine or Factory?' address
1918

In the early 20th century, Vladimir Mayakovsky was a young Bolshevik activist in the Soviet Communist Party. He distributed propaganda leaflets and helped to smuggle female political prisoners out of prison. He was arrested several times before being held in solitary confinement for eleven months in Moscow's Butyrka prison, where he wrote his first poems. 'Revolution and poetry got entangled in my head and became one,' he said. After his release, he realized he could never be a serious revolutionary, and left the Party. He studied at the Moscow School of Painting, Sculpture and Architecture, where he met Futurist David Burliuk. Futurism was an artistic movement, originating in Italy in 1909, which celebrated the speed and technology of the machine age. The idealism of the Futurists captured Mayakovsky's imagination. His belief that museums were 'dead shrines' reflected his desire to bring 'art into life' and to the workers – on the streets and in the factories. In a bid to create a new, relevant and topical art, many artists called for the destruction of museums and libraries. **SH**

◀ Mayakovsky at his exhibition '20 years of Mayakovsky's works.'

> *Life isn't long enough for love and art.*

William Somerset Maugham
The Moon and Sixpence
1919

The above quotation comes from a novel loosely based on the life of stockbroker-turned-Postimpressionist painter Paul Gauguin, who quit his middle-class existence to devote himself to painting. The French artist left his wife and five children to indulge his passion, and in later life he went to Tahiti in the South Pacific Ocean. The colourful work that he produced there, with its simplified, linear forms, paved the way for Primitivism.

Maugham's protagonist is a middle-aged English stockbroker, Charles Strickland, who also abandons a family and career in order to pursue his interest in painting. Maugham depicts Strickland as a callous individual, indifferent to the suffering of those around him to such an extent that his mistress commits suicide after he abandons her. However, Strickland is indifferent to his own comfort, too: he is sufficiently oblivious to his physical surroundings and well-being that he is prepared to suffer hunger and privation for as long as he is free to paint.

The novel's narrator asks Strickland if he has been in love since he became an artist, and Strickland replies that he has no time for both love and art – one has had to go, and the sacrifice has been love. Maugham creates a selfish character in Strickland: one who gives up everything for his art and becomes strange, and obsessive, as a result.

The title of the novel comes from the proverbial expression that someone was so busy striving for the moon that he did not see the riches at his feet. **CK**

" I paint with my prick. "

Pierre-Auguste Renoir
Attributed
c. 1919

Pierre-Auguste Renoir's colourful statement has been regarded both as a crude riposte to a question about how, in his failing health, and with arthritic hands, he continued to paint and, more allegorically, as a way of defining what motivated his artistic drive, passion and creativity. Various women were muses throughout his life, and there is little doubt that some of his desires are visible in his canvases: for instance, his breakthrough painting, *Lise with a Parasol* (1867), which depicts his then lover Lise Tréhot and was shown to great acclaim at the 1868 Paris Salon. Moreover, by the end of Renoir's life, the Freudian notion that everything is motivated by sexuality, whether it be overt or sublimated, had taken a firm grip on Western thought.

It has also been suggested that the above remark is merely a mistranslation of 'It's with a brush that I make love,' which appeared in Albert André's biography *Renoir* (1919). However, the film director Jean Renoir's acclaimed 1958 memoir, *Renoir, My Father*, cites the cruder version, claiming that it was intended to shock a respectable company of diners in the painter's home town of Les Collettes in Provence in the South of France.

D H Lawrence also referred to the remark in *Lady Chatterley's Lover* (1928). As for when it was said, an exact date remains speculative, at best. However, if we are to follow Jean Renoir's account, it is likely to have been near to the end of the artist's life. **IHS**

" Art is a spiritual function of man, which aims at freeing him from life's chaos. "

Kurt Schwitters
Manifesto Proletkult
1923

The avant-garde art movement Dada emerged as a reaction to the horrors of World War I, when many artists, believing that traditional art was the product of a corrupt society, began using unconventional materials and irreverent subject matter. German artist Kurt Schwitters joined Berlin Dada in 1918. He used discarded rubbish, such as bus tickets and fragments of newsprint, to create three-dimensional collages that he called 'Merz.' He took the word from one of his collages that included, on a torn piece of newspaper, the German word *kommerz* ('commerce'). The word '*Merz*,' like Dada, was intentionally nonsensical. Schwitters also wrote and performed abstract poems, sounds without words, while an enthusiasm for typography led him to open his own successful advertising agency.

Overall, Schwitters rejected the fundamental negativity of Dadaism. In this quotation he expresses his belief that by enabling us to explore and invent, the basic act of creating art liberates us from life's complications and miseries. **SH**

> ❯ Photomontage portrait of Kurt Schwitters (c. 1924) by El Lissitzky.

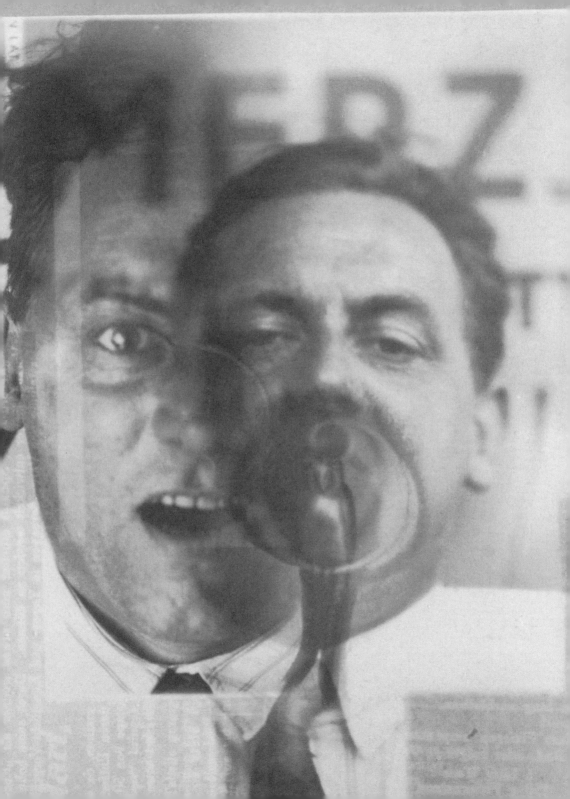

"A house is a machine for living in."

Le Corbusier
Towards an Architecture
1923

When Swiss-French architect and urban planner Charles-Édouard Jeanneret-Gris (better known as Le Corbusier) wrote 'a house is a machine for living in,' his words were always going to be open to misinterpretation. Far from houses evolving into cold, impersonal, industrial-like spaces, Le Corbusier envisaged buildings that were complex and visually stimulating, incorporating the best technological innovations to enhance our standard of living.

One of the finest examples of this modernist push towards purist design is the Villa Savoye in Poissy, northwest of Paris, which he designed with his cousin, Pierre Jeanneret. Completed in 1931, Villa Savoye is the 'machine' Le Corbusier refers to here. Its modular design is the result of his love of mathematics. The villa featured built-in furniture, open interiors, ribbonlike horizontal windows, abstract sculptural lines and a deliberate lack of ornamentation. A blending of industrial functionalism with aesthetic purity, it embodied what he called the 'precision of architecture,' with facades that were 'skins' gloriously freed from load-bearing concerns – a new movement defined by precision. **BDS**

"Art, it is said, is not a mirror, but a hammer: it does not reflect, it shapes."

Leon Trotsky
Literature and Revolution
1924

Of all the revolutionary leaders who rose to prominence in Russia in the early 20th century, none showed the same degree of interest in art as Leon Trotsky. His writings on the subject included *Culture and Socialism* (1927) and the work from which this quotation is taken. Trotsky wanted to use art to bring artists into the revolution, to convince them that art must, in fact, become 'revolutionary'– not just in artistic terms, but politically, to help fight for the liberation of all humanity.

Trotsky likened art galleries to concentration camps. He wanted to remove art from gallery walls and bring an end to 'exhibitions,' a concept with capitalist overtones. He felt that art should be organically linked to architecture and sculpture: 'I want paintings to be connected not by cords but by their artistic significance to walls or to a cupola, to the purpose of a building' and not hung up 'like a hat on a hat stand'. Trotsky believed that socialism had the potential to produce the greatest art of all, the art of life itself, portraying the struggles taking place on the broader canvas of the streets. **BDS**

❯ Leon Trotsky and his wife with Frida Kahlo (*centre*) in 1937.

"One piƈture is worth ten thousand words."

Fred R Barnard
Printers' Ink trade journal
1927

This phrase appeared in a 1927 edition of *Printers' Ink*, an American trade publication for the advertising industry. The words featured in a headline written by advertising manager Fred R Barnard, who labelled them as originating from an ancient Chinese proverb. (He had used a similar phrase – 'One look is worth a thousand words' – in an ad six years previously, when he attributed it to a Japanese philosopher.) That attribution myth was eventually disproved by the anthologist Burton Stevenson, although not before most Americans were crediting the phrase to Confucius. Barnard defended his white lie, saying that he labelled it as a Chinese proverb because he thought that people would take it more seriously. (And the present volume is full of good remarks that have been wrongly attributed to famous people, in an effort to give them additional 'weight.')

Why Barnard used this idiom in his advertising copy, however, is clear: it reminds us how complex ideas can be conveyed via a single image. The thought behind this popular phrase had, of course, been expressed much earlier by others, including by Russian writer Ivan Turgenev in *Fathers and Sons* (1861): 'The drawing shows me at one glance what might be spread over ten pages in a book.' **BDS**

"Art is born of humiliation."

W H Auden
Attributed
1927

Auden made this remark to Stephen Spender when they were both students at the University of Oxford. They met in the fall of 1927, when Auden was in his final year, and Spender was a freshman. Auden had a reputation among his fellow undergraduates as an intellectual to be respected. Spender was keen to meet the man he had heard so much about, and was introduced to him at a luncheon party given by a mutual friend. Spender recounts in his autobiography, *World Within World* (1951), the meeting, their initial friendship and the advice Auden gave him.

Spender recalls showing Auden some of his poetry, but, receiving little encouragement, remarked that perhaps he should switch to prose. Auden firmly opposed the idea, saying: 'You must write nothing but poetry.' Spender quizzed Auden as to why he thought his poetry could possibly be any good. Auden replied: 'Because you are so infinitely capable of being humiliated. Art is born of humiliation.'

The compliment was double-edged, but it helped to forge a longstanding friendship between the two men, and in 1928 Spender hand-printed the first edition of Auden's *Poems*. Spender later went on to encourage the young Dylan Thomas into a poetry career. **CK**

Art, like morality, consists of drawing the line somewhere.

G K Chesterton
Illustrated London News magazine
1928

Art in all its forms is inextricably connected to life and either carries with it the burden of societal norms, existing within its boundaries, or transgresses them in order to question their validity. G K Chesterton's quotation here is unequivocal in its position on the role of art. After discussing the perennial question of whether art is amoral, the author takes a stricter stance, suggesting that art must be held accountable and bear responsibility for the outcome of responses to it. He may be attitudinizing, and the remark is of little use to artists as guidance, but he was paid to be provocative.

A generalist with a remarkably wide range of interests – and a hugely popular novelist, thanks to his *Father Brown* detective series – Chesterton wrote with passion and insight and was unafraid to explore the nature of paradox, even within his own belief system. He was a self-proclaimed 'orthodox' Christian who would eventually convert from the Church of England to Roman Catholicism; his faith informed his moral outlook. He believed that everyone and everything should be responsible for their actions, and in a 1920 article, he had applied a similar stricture to political systems. **IHS**

⊘ G K Chesterton in the garden of his home in Beaconsfield, England, in the 1930s.

"*A house can have integrity, just like a person, and just as seldom.*"

Ayn Rand was an American writer from St Petersburg, Russia, whose novels discussed her philosophy of 'rational selfishness.'

Ayn Rand
The Fountainhead
1943

In Ayn Rand's worldview, a building should be a symbol of individualism, and every individual should strive to stand out from the crowd. Rand believed that society's development could be stymied only by conformity and community – by the notion that the collective, one mass with no discernible difference between its members, is capable of advancing in any positive way.

The cult of the individual lies at the heart of Rand's philosophy. Her breakthrough novel, *The Fountainhead*, tells the story of Howard Roark, an architect who rejects the conventional wisdom that compromise is in the best interests of society and is willing to destroy everything in order to ensure that his vision remains pure. His nemesis is Ellsworth M Toohey, an architecture critic who champions the bland over the inspired.

Rand's aim was to examine 'individualism versus collectivism, not in politics but in a man's soul'. Roark is Rand's idealized everyman – what she believed every human should be. *The Fountainhead* reflected the ideas of objectivism that was central to her philosophical belief system – that human happiness could be achieved only through rational self-interest. **IHS**

"We shape our buildings, and afterwards our buildings shape us."

Winston Churchill

Speech to the House of Commons, London
1943

British prime minister Churchill was speaking here on the subject of how best to go about the reconstruction of the Commons Chamber after its destruction by German incendiary bombs during World War II. Churchill had been arguing that the old rectangular shape of the chamber – which pitted political parties against each other 'face-to-face' – should be kept. It had been an 'adversarial' design, necessary for rigorous debate, which was the essence of British parliamentary democracy. The great statesman believed that changing to a semicircular chamber would affect time-honoured parliamentary processes; no longer would 'crossing the floor' in plain view be the dramatic gesture it was, and the general behaviour of politicians would be altered.

Churchill's words reminded the House that while a building is a static object, which remains as it was built, it also has the potential to shape the way humans behave by virtue of how its form interacts with those who live or work in it. It also, by extension, has the capacity to change the way people feel about the built environment that surrounds them, and in rare instances, perhaps even how a nation is governed. **BDS**

⬥ Winston Churchill at work building a wall at his house, Chartwell, near Westerham, Kent, in 1930.

"*Less is more.*"

⬆ Mies pictured behind a model of his twin twenty-six-storey apartment buildings (1951) on Lake Shore Drive, Chicago.

▶ Farnsworth House, Illinois (1951) a house designed by Mies.

Ludwig Mies van der Rohe
Attributed
1947

Over time, this phrase came to be linked to German architect Ludwig Mies van der Rohe. But, as is revealed in *Mies van der Rohe* (1950) by Philip Johnson, it was said to him by his boss; also, it appeared in English poet Robert Browning's 1855 dramatic monologue 'Andrea del Sarto' ('Well, less is more, Lucrezia').

In 1907, when Mies was in his early twenties, and working for industrial architect Peter Behrens in Berlin, he was asked to design the facade for the west courtyard elevation of the AEG turbine factory. In the course of his work, Mies decided to show Behrens his drawings. The older man cast his eyes over the emerging designs, then looked up at his young apprentice and proclaimed the immortal phrase: 'Less is more.'

Mies liked the phrase so much that he inadvertently made it his own, as he continually sought to define the modernist ethic. He took Behrens's initial idea of restraint much farther, however, reducing his designs down to minimalist rectilinear forms and pure lines. Even Mies's furniture designs employed cantilevers to enhance their sense of lightness. This was an architecture born of new materials in a new technological age. **BDS**

"If you could say it in words there would be no reason to paint."

Edward Hopper
Time magazine
1948

Edward Hopper came from a reasonably prosperous family in New York State and was free to pursue his interest in art and develop his talent from a young age. He enjoyed his education and it was only when he began to earn a living that he began to face difficulties as an artist. From 1905 until the mid-1920s he worked in advertising as an illustrator, all the time wishing that he could focus on his painting. Three visits to Europe renewed his passion for painting, but on his return to the United States he was obliged, again, to work as a freelance illustrator, with the added burden of having to traipse around New York City in search of work. It was only in 1931, when museums began to pay large sums for his works, that his years of frustration ended.

As might be suspected from the quotation above, Hopper rarely indulged in small talk and was renowned for his monumental silences. He understood the desperation and latent violence of many city dwellers, but despite that – or because of it – he excelled as a realist artist. His often solitary subjects are depicted as expressionless in urban, partially lit, nocturnal environments. To look into a Hopper painting such as *Nighthawks* (1942) is to experience an emotional bleakness that words would struggle to deliver. **BDS**

"I think an artist has always to be out of step with his time."

Orson Welles
Attributed
1953

Orson Welles – the man who said 'I started at the top and worked my way down,' alluding to his masterpiece *Citizen Kane* (1941) and the string of films that followed, none of which matched the critical acclaim or indeed the quality of his first endeavour – always felt a little out of step with mainstream America. The actor, writer and director was never embraced by Hollywood's studio system, making a mere thirteen feature films over the course of his career, many of which were heavily edited or not released at all. Welles spent the greater part of his professional life battling against an industry he alienated with the release of *Citizen Kane*, which painted an unflattering picture of the influential newspaper publisher William Randolph Hearst.

As if to compound his woes, Welles believed that being a good artist meant that one had to live a life in isolation. He hated the idea of having to be 'with it' in an industry that requires meetings and lunches, fawning over producers, networking, constantly seeking financial support for projects and making endless compromises. Moviemaking is a collaborative art form, which in the 1940s and 1950s did little to reward maverick filmmakers who wanted the degree of artistic control that Welles always sought. **BDS**

" *You shouldn't talk about art, you should do it.* "

Philip Johnson
'The Seven Crutches of Modern Architecture' lecture, 1954

Philip Johnson, the US architect, architectural critic and master of Postmodern design who founded the Department of Architecture and Design at New York's Museum of Modern Art in 1930, never liked talking about art, which was for him a metaphor for architecture. He never considered the two disciplines to be intellectual pursuits, nor did he think that they could be 'learned', any more than one can learn to write a melody or paint a portrait. He thought that art and architecture classes in universities were a great waste of time and that these subjects should be studied in the streets and 'gutters' rather than in debates and tutorials, which he regarded as death to creativity.

Imagine, then, the irony Johnson must have been aware of when he gave a now-famous informal talk to a group of architecture students at Harvard University in December 1954, in which he used hundreds of words to rail against the excessive use of words. 'We have to descend to the world around us,' he explained, 'if we are to battle it.'

The battle he refers to is not just one of words either, but drawings, too. Johnson despised the idea that architectural drawings were somehow a form of 'pre-architecture' and not, as he preferred to think of them, the 'Crutch of Pretty Drawing.' **BDS**

" *It took me four years to paint like Raphael, but a lifetime to paint like a child.* "

Pablo Picasso
Quoted by Herbert Read in a letter to *The Times*, 1956

When Picasso was developing Cubism, he looked to African and Native American societies for inspiration. For him and other artists of the early 20th century, the 'primitive' art of these cultures had an energy that was raw and primal. Modernists were attempting to create radical new art forms and ideas, and they were drawn to these traditions because they were largely unaffected by Western influences. Similarly, Picasso looked to drawings made by children. He recognized that children perceive reality in a different way to adults: they open up all their senses to experience the world. He believed that every child is an artist, so the problem is how to remain an artist once childhood is left behind. The difficulty artists face is trying to reconnect with that creative innocence and to paint without self-judgement.

Although artists can study and learn techniques at art academies – how to paint like Old Masters such as Raphael – they also need to recapture the curiosity, simplicity and innocence of childhood. Picasso understood that regaining that childlike perception of the world as an artist is crucial if one is to truthfully portray the complexity of the world. **BDS**

"A painting that doesn't shock isn't worth painting."

Marcel Duchamp
'The Creative Act' lecture
1957

French Surrealist artist Marcel Duchamp was a controversial figure of the European avant-garde. In an interview with Pierre Cabanne in 1966, he explained the statement he had first made in his 1957 lecture. Duchamp believed that an artist can exist only if he is 'known,' and to become known means that one must produce great works. Paintings that are everyday interpretations, which fail to experiment with new techniques, rarely rise to become a 'great' work capable of defining an artist and his or her era or of making a lasting impact on society. Duchamp thought 'great' works a rarity and that in the life of any good artist, even given a lifelong output, there will only be 'four or five' works that are really significant. 'The rest,' he said, 'is just everyday filler.'

By paintings that 'shock,' Duchamp meant those groundbreaking works that change the way we view art – paintings like Picasso's proto-Cubist masterpiece *Les Demoiselles d'Avignon*, with its depiction of prostitutes wearing primitivist African masks, and Seurat's *A Sunday Afternoon on the Island of La Grande Jatte*, a gigantic pointillist canvas composed of tiny dots of colour that ushered in a new era of Postimpressionism. These were the 'shocks' that Duchamp longed to see. **BDS**

"Any authentic work of art must start an argument between the artist and his audience."

Rebecca West
The Court and the Castle
1957

Dame Rebecca West was a British journalist, novelist and writer, who was better known during her lifetime for her journalism, criticism and commentary than for her novels, which included *The Return of the Soldier* (1918). As a spokesperson for feminist and socialist causes, and as a commentator, she wrote for various newspapers and journals, including *The New Republic*, *New York Herald Tribune*, *New Statesman* and *The Daily Telegraph*. She also reported on the Nuremberg trials of war criminals (1945–46) for *The New Yorker*.

In a book of literary criticism, *The Court and the Castle*, which examines the relationship of religious and political ideas in literature, West argues that a good artist must stimulate a lively dialogue with his or her audience. In West's mind, the authenticity of an artist can only be proved by this interaction or argument taking place. If, for example, a painting inspires little or no reaction from the viewer, or a novel leaves the reader placidly disengaged, then the artist or author has not met the requirements of his or her vocation. **SH**

❯ The formidable woman of letters Dame Rebecca West.

Noble life demands a noble architecture for noble uses of noble men.

Frank Lloyd Wright
The Living City
1958

Frank Lloyd Wright was perhaps the greatest modern American architect, and certainly one of the most influential. He designed 1,141 structures (532 of which were completed); wrote twenty books, as well as numerous articles; and developed the Prairie School style of architecture – buildings characterized by long horizontal lines, accentuated overhanging eaves under flat or hipped roofs, and uncompromisingly solid construction and craftsmanship. His talent for innovation was enough to set him apart from most other architects of his period, but it was his belief in architecture's power to enrich social, political and religious life that led him to write about the 'nobility' of architecture, a viewpoint that drew deeply on his own philosophy concerning the interconnectedness of life, nature and buildings.

Wright even went so far as to link a lack of culture (and good architecture) to the fall of civilizations. He believed that noble architecture encourages noble men to meet inside noble spaces, and guides nations towards noble causes. 'Maybe we can show government,' he wrote optimistically, 'how to operate better as a result of better architecture.' **BDS**

⬙ Wright photographed at the entrance to an old family chapel on his Taliesin estate, Wisconsin, in 1957.

⊙ The First Christian Church (1971–73) in Phoenix, Arizona, designed by Frank Lloyd Wright.

"*Abstract art is a product of the untalented, sold by the unprincipled to the utterly bewildered.*"

Al Capp
Attributed
c. 1961

Famed for creating the long-running comic strip *Li'l Abner*, Al Capp kept around sixty million readers entertained for more than forty years with his acerbic observations on greed, corruption and social injustice. He also worked as a correspondent for the *Daily News* syndicate and was a radio and TV commentator. By the 1960s his liberal views had become more conservative, and he was perceived by many as bitter and disillusioned.

Capp's forthright opinions emerged in his own life as well as through his cartoons and media persona. In 1961 he reportedly assessed abstract art in a newspaper article with the above quotation. The satirical article debated what a future 'library of creative art' should preserve. Two years later he repeated it when interviewed on the TV programme *Youth Wants to Know*. The next day, several newspapers reported his words. Capp's abhorrence of abstract art remained constant throughout his life. He labelled it all as 'incomprehensible messes' and declared that no abstract art should be exhibited in museums, suggesting that TV commercials should be displayed instead. In 1966 he described abstract art as 'the product of diseased minds'. **SH**

⊘ The cartoonist and humorist Al Capp (*centre*) in his New York offices in the 1950s.

Good artists copy; great artists steal.

Pablo Picasso
Attributed
c. 1965

This quotation is widely attributed to Spanish artist Pablo Picasso. However, it is unsourced. But because Steve Jobs, US technology entrepreneur and cofounder of Apple, cited the quotation as being by Picasso, the attribution appears to have stuck. In an interview about the creation of the Apple Macintosh, Jobs said: 'Picasso had a saying – "good artists copy; great artists steal" – and we have always been shameless about stealing great ideas.' The Macintosh operating system, with its graphical user interface (GUI), came out of the ideas hatched at the innovation arm of the Xerox Corporation, Xerox's PARC in Palo Alto, California. In 1989, Xerox's PARC sued Apple for what it deemed unlawful use of Xerox copyrights in Apple's Macintosh and Lisa computers, but it lost the case.

The sense of the aphorism is that great artists draw on the best of what has gone before, and build on it, rather than restarting from scratch. Picasso himself looked to the Old Masters, re-creating a series of works based on Velázquez's *Las Meninas* (1656). Likewise, as an innovator and marketer, Jobs learned from masters in his industry and then developed something new. **CK**

Picasso at his home in Cannes, France, c. 1960, wearing one of his customary striped shirts.

" *Objective painting is not good painting unless it is good in the abstract sense.* "

Portrait of Georgia O'Keeffe at her home in Abiquiu, New Mexico, in 1971.

Georgia O'Keeffe
Some Memories of Drawings
1974

Renowned for their distinctive synthesis of representation and abstraction in paintings of rocks, landscapes, shells, animal bones and flowers ('I hate flowers – I paint them because they're cheaper than models and they don't move!'), the paintings of Georgia O'Keeffe are deeply personal and show an intimate connection to the landscapes of the American Southwest. When Alfred Stieglitz, the photographer and promoter of modern art, first saw O'Keeffe's early charcoal drawings in New York in 1916 he exclaimed: 'At last, a woman on paper!'

The so-called 'Mother of American Modernism' never understood objective painting (the painting of things as they are): 'It is surprising to me to see how many people separate the objective from the abstract.' She thought that painting was only worthwhile when the object was transformed through abstraction. The intangible elements of her own life were best expressed by abstraction, and the same, she felt, was true of nature. She would paint distant mountains only to notice, when finished, that they looked like the shells and pebbles she had on the table at home. 'I have things in my head,' she said, 'that are not like what anyone taught me.' **BDS**

"How much does your house weigh?"

Richard Buckminster Fuller
Explorations in the Geometry of Thinking
1975

How environmentally efficient is a building? That is what architect, designer, inventor, author and visionary Buckminster Fuller is asking here. He believed that the design of buildings, towns and cities should develop in tandem with a commitment to the world around us.

Massachusetts–born Fuller was twice thrown out of Harvard, and then served in the US Navy in World War I. After the conflict, he practised as an architect, and his life was comparatively uneventful until 1922, when the death of his daughter and the collapse of his affordable housing construction company almost brought him to ruin.

He decided to spend the rest of his life doing as much as he could for the benefit of humankind. He took any jobs to care for his family, while also developing his creative ideas. Of these, the Dymaxion House was key to his thinking about architecture. This design could be mass-produced; was affordable, easily transportable and environmentally efficient; and could both harness the elements and protect itself from them. The first version of the house was built in 1945. It weighed only 3,000 pounds (1,360 kg), compared to 150 tons (134 tonnes) for the average conventional home. **IHS**

⬛ American systems theorist Richard Buckminster Fuller at Cinema Sound in New York City in 1975.

"Drawing is the honesty of the art. There is no possibility of cheating. It is either good or bad."

◔ Salvador Dalí drawing Laurence Olivier as Richard III. The subsequent portrait in oils was completed in 1955.

Salvador Dalí
People magazine
1976

A skilled draughtsman who attended drawing school as a child, artist Salvador Dalí regarded drawing as far more than simply the means of outlining larger, more important artworks. For Dalí, a drawing consisted of the external representation of a thought process, and he used the act of drawing to explore, give shape to and develop his ideas. His technical skill advanced rapidly, and his father organized a display of his son's charcoal drawings in their home when Salvador was aged just thirteen. What Dalí appreciated about drawing was its immediacy; its quality is instantly apparent, whereas paintings may be reworked until all spontaneity is lost.

Dalí loved to share his gift with others and teach them the art of drawing. In his later years he conducted an annual international drawing course at his adopted hometown of Cadaqués on Spain's Costa Brava. It was there that he was once overheard uttering the quotation above to one of his young students.

Dalí's autobiographical works, *The Secret Life of Salvador Dalí* (1942) and *Diary of a Genius* (1963), contain a wealth of miniature drawings that testify to the imagination and skill of the Surrealist master. **BDS**

Great art picks up where nature ends.

Marc Chagall
Time magazine
1985

In 1906, when Chagall was still a teenager, he ran away from his native Belarus and went to St Petersburg, where he enrolled in the Zvantseva School of Drawing and Painting. One night, while drifting off to sleep, he was stirred by what he thought to be a rustling of wings. He felt pins and needles in his forehead. His bedroom, he said, then filled with an ethereal blue light, and he looked up to see an angel above his bed. The angel hovered for a moment, then ascended up through the ceiling, taking the strange blue light with it. This event had a cataclysmic impact upon a lifetime of art that was still to come. No wonder, then, that he would go on to one day claim that 'Great art picks up where nature ends.'

Chagall was Jewish and was fascinated by Hebrew Scriptures contained in the Tanakh – a canonical collection of Jewish texts, which he considered 'the greatest source of poetry that has ever existed'. Though Chagall was an early modernist who dabbled in Cubism, he remained a traditionalist, preferring figurative art to abstraction. He always looked beyond the natural world and drew inspiration from the spiritual, mystical and fantastical themes of Jewish folk culture. **BDS**

⌼ Marc Chagall stands outside his villa at St Paul-de-Vence, southeastern France, in 1957.

" Architecture should speak of its time and place, but yearn for timelessness. "

Frank Gehry
In *Home* by Kim Johnson Gross
1993

Architects never tire of using the word 'timeless' when discussing the single most coveted attribute any building should possess. 'Timelessness' is intended to mean that a building will outlast trends and fleeting fashions. Buildings survive if they make a difference and solve problems. They also survive if they are adaptable and flexible, if they meet the needs of people, and are not built merely as a reaction to an architectural style. They remain relevant if they integrate within the environment, and improve after decades of weathering.

Frank Gehry, as a Canadian-American, Pritzker Architecture Prize-winning architect, knows that timelessness does not simply 'happen.' His sweeping, sculptural, flamboyant forms not only reflect the bold spirit of experimentation in which he works, but they also achieve context in, and harmonize with, their settings. His Guggenheim Museum in Bilbao, Spain, for example, has helped to revitalize the Basque city economically. Indeed, what could be more timeless than the regeneration of a region through the commissioning of innovative, eye-catching, monumental architecture such as this great edifice? **BDS**

◀ Gehry's Walt Disney Concert Hall in Los Angeles, California.

" A city's architecture is always a bit like a constructed, psychological version of its people. "

Jacques Herzog
Süddeutsche Zeitung magazine
2002

Swiss architect Jacques Herzog believes that when architecture is created in rapport with the people of the city in which it is to be built, it has the capacity to reflect their personalities, psychology and values. A perfect example of this is the Elbphilharmonie (2017) – a conglomerate of concert halls, restaurants, bars, apartments and a hotel – in Hamburg, Germany. Many Hamburg residents have long felt their cityscape to be incomplete, particularly around the renowned harbour area, which they felt was disconnected from the rest of the city. Herzog was determined to give the people what they wanted. 'I'm not aware of any other city in the world,' he said, 'that is carrying out a project. . .that will so thoroughly redefine the city.'

Herzog spoke of how the project was 'carried up from the people,' who communicated with him about their needs and ideas. The towering structure of the Elbphilharmonie, located in the social and cultural heart of the area, opens up views over the whole city. Above all, the concert hall with its vertically arranged seating reflects the confidence of Hamburg's populace, rather than simply that of its architectural creator. **BDS**

History

" The superior man acquaints himself with many sayings of antiquity and many deeds of the past, in order to strengthen his character thereby. "

Fuxi
I Ching
before 1000 BCE

The Chinese classic *I Ching*, originally a set of oracles or divinations, but now seen mainly as a wisdom book, has been subject to many interpretations and theories. Confucius, the Chinese philosopher, studied it (wearing out three copies in the process) and wrote text commentaries on it that greatly influenced later Confucianist ideas. It is still consulted by those who seek wisdom in difficult situations, even on occasion by Far Eastern governments. Western interpreters, too, have been fascinated by its occult mystery and profundity.

This quotation recommends historical knowledge as a basis for contemporary decision-making. People of noble character and superior understanding believe they can achieve self-improvement from the sayings and actions of admirable people of the past. This presupposes a culture in which innovation is not a particularly welcome phenomenon, for change often requires thinking 'outside the box' rather than learning from our predecessors. However, the context here is clearly spiritual or moral rather than intellectual or technological. Human nature does not change much, and we can always learn from the heroes of the past. **JF**

" You can't step twice in the same river. "

Heraclitus
Attributed
500 BCE

The above quotation is attributed to Heraclitus by Plato in his dialogue *Cratylus*, which is named after a philosopher of the 5th century BCE who was an ardent proponent of Heraclitean thought. Plato's text is a discussion between Socrates, Cratylus and another Athenian philosopher, Hermogenes. The last two ask Socrates for his views on the nature of language, with specific reference to the notion of naming. The above quotation occurs in an exchange between Socrates, who suggests, 'I have thought of a swarm of wisdom,' and Hermogenes, who replies, 'What is it?'

Socrates elaborates: 'I seem to have a vision of Heraclitus saying some ancient words of wisdom as old as the reign of Cronus and Rhea, which Homer said too.' When pressed, Socrates responds, 'Heraclitus says, you know, that all things move and nothing remains still, and he likens the universe to the current of a river, saying that you cannot step twice into the same stream.'

The suggestion is that life is in a permanent state of flux, and so we must adapt to that change. The expectation of stasis is a failure to understand the mutating nature of the world. The great merit of this aphorism is that it confounds the reader's initial expectations. At first, one almost certainly imagines that a river is an unambiguous symbol of permanence and eternity. It is only when one comes to think about it that one realizes the truth of the deeper insight. **IHS**

❯ A portrait of Heraclitus (1628) by Hendrick Terbrugghen.

> ## "Do nothing secretly; for Time sees and hears all things, and discloses all."

Sophocles
Hipponous
C. 468 BCE

The above quotation is taken from one of the numerous plays by the ancient Greek dramatist that survive only as fragments.

The earliest known version of the story on which this tragedy was based featured in the work of Hesiod, a poet of the 8th century BCE. It concerned Hipponous, king of Olenus in Achaia (part of the modern Peloponnese), who discovers that his daughter, Periboea, is pregnant by an unknown father. Disgusted, he sends her away to Oenus, king of Calydon in Aetolia, with instructions that she should be killed. Oenus, however, recently widowed, takes pity on the young woman and eventually marries her.

The dramatic possibilities of this bare outline are, of course, numerous: the most pressing question concerns the paternity of the unborn child. Classical scholars believe, on the balance of probabilities, that it was Oenus, and that this revelation would have been the peripeteia (unexpected reversal) of the play. Whether that was Sophocles's resolution of the plot is unknown because most of the text is lost – it is thus perhaps mildly ironic that the most quotable extant line should imply that everything will come out in the end. **JP**

> ## "The absence of romance in my history will, I fear, detract somewhat from its interest."

Thucydides
The History of the Peloponnesian War
431 BCE

In the above words, ancient Greek historian Thucydides sarcastically expressed his intention to distinguish his work from the fanciful stories of the poets, and also from the anecdotal and sensationalist accounts offered by his predecessor, Herodotus. His subject was the Peloponnesian War between the Peloponnesian League, led by Sparta, and the Delian League, led by Athens. His aim was to present a reliable history of the war, based on contemporary eyewitness testimony, including his own. He served Athens as a general from 424 to 423 BCE and was then exiled among the Peloponnesians, so he observed events from both sides. He intended his account to be both accurate and useful to those seeking to learn from the past in order to understand the future. The account ends more than six and a half years before the end of the war, most probably due to his death.

Some historians take Thucydides's words at face value, advocating austere and impersonal objectivity, whereas others consider the Thucydidean approach as partaking as much of 'romance – rhetoric, artistry and even partisanship – as any rival approach, if not more so. **GB**

"Whoso neglects learning in his youth, loses the past and is dead for the future."

Euripides
Phrixus
C. 425 BCE

Born in Athens around 485 BCE, Euripides is known to have written about ninety tragedies, of which only nineteen have survived. The most famous are *Medea*, *Hippolytus* and *The Trojan Women*. His plays reimagine Greek myth, generally with dark undertones. He knew some of the 5h-century philosophers, including Socrates, personally, so his works also contain philosophical dialogue. He created strong female characters who were not only victims, but also initiated action

The above quotation comes from a play, which survives only as a fragment about a young man thwarting his wicked stepmother's plan to kill him. The idea that it is important to study in one's youth (as opposed to leaving it until retirement, for example) is an interesting, but not uncontroversial, one. Modern psychologists believe that the brain is at its most 'plastic' when young and that learning at that point will produce the greatest and most enduring effects; the past, or history, can be most easily internalized and become an integral part of the student's world view. Whether youthful learning is as essential as Euripides implies is a moot point, but it certainly lays foundations for the future. **JF**

"Even God cannot change the past."

Agathon
Attributed
C. 425 BCE

This observation from Athenian tragic poet Agathon is attributed to him by Aristotle in *Nicomachean Ethics* (c. 350 BCE). Literally translated from the Greek, it reads, '. . .the one thing that even God cannot do is to make undone that which has been done'. The idea engenders debate among theists (people who believe in a god): if God is absolute, and can change anything he wishes to alter, how can it make sense to restrict his omnipotence?

Events occur according to probabilistic natural laws, and these are dictated by time's arrow, which flies in one direction only. Logicians point out that therefore the past cannot be changed without creating the absurd possibility of a future in which happenings both could and could not occur.

Scientists have made various attempts to posit nonlinear time, in which past events divide at every possible alternative to create an infinite number of futures. However, what has happened – word, deed or act – is etched indelibly into the fabric of the universe, and this quotation is a warning.

Nevertheless, the 'text' (as it were) of any act can be as fragile as the beat of a butterfly's wing and is always open to rereading. People may not be able to change past events, but historians frequently rewrite them. **LW**

"Every advantage in the past is judged in the light of the final issue."

Demosthenes
First Olynthiac
349 BCE

Demosthenes was a prominent Greek statesman and public orator of ancient Athens.

In a powerful speech, Demosthenes urged the people of Athens to provide military support to the city of Olynthus against a threatened attack by the forces of Philip II of Macedon (father of Alexander the Great). Among the great orator's supporting arguments was that failure to act would be impious, suggesting ingratitude to the gods, who had given them the wherewithal and the opportunity to do so.

Demosthenes's argument failed to convince the Athenians, however. Later the same year, he delivered two further addresses on the same subject, as a result of which the people were partially persuaded, but their aid to Olynthus was inadequate and failed to save the city from defeat by Philip in 338 BCE. Demosthenes was later in the Athenian delegation sent to negotiate a peace treaty with the Macedonians and reportedly collapsed from fright on meeting their king.

The sentiments underlying this remark find echoes in many other well-known quotations. One of these is 'The proof of the pudding is in the eating,' a medieval English proverb. Another is George Orwell's 'History is written by the victors.' **GB**

In a short while the generations of living creatures are changed, and like runners relay the torch of life.

Lucretius
De rerum natura (On the Nature of Things)
c. 50 BCE

In this great Latin verse epic, the poet Lucretius sets out the principles of Epicureanism, one of the four major philosophical systems of the Hellenistic age in which he lived. Epicurus held that matter consisted of discrete, solid and indivisible particles – atoms – and the above quotation occurs at the beginning of an explanation of how atoms account for observed phenomena. Lucretius invokes the metaphor of a relay race to explain how material objects can persist through time, even though the atoms of which they are composed come and go.

Neglected if not forgotten during the Middle Ages, *De rerum natura*, and Epicureanism in general, were rediscovered during the Renaissance and influenced the revival of atomism during the Scientific Revolution that began in the 16th century. Later philosophers elaborated on Lucretius's explanation of how material objects consisting of atoms can persist through time. In *An Essay Concerning Human Understanding* (1689), John Locke suggested that a plant continues to be the same plant 'as long as it partakes of the same Life, though that Life be communicated to new Particles of Matter vitally united to the living Plant'. **GB**

⊘ This illustration is taken from an illuminated 9th-century manuscript of the great didactic poem by Lucretius.

"To be ignorant of what happened before you were born is to be ever a child."

Cicero
Orator ad M. Brutum
46 BCE

Marcus Tullius Cicero was a Roman statesman, orator and philosopher. He is widely considered one of Rome's greatest orators, and had considerable stylistic influence on the Latin language. Cicero was also influential in introducing many chief schools of Greek philosophy into Rome and created significant new Latin terminology for important philosophical concepts.

In *Orator ad M Brutum*, a text on oratory and rhetoric, Cicero discusses (among other topics) the appropriate use of history in human thought. In the above quotation, he is arguing that maintaining ignorance of the past prior to one's own existence is a childish choice and perhaps a barrier to achieving one's full potential. In addition to acquiring knowledge of our own past, Cicero advises us to learn from prior generations. This further applies to both the good lessons (what were the successes that we should emulate and learn from?) and the bad (what were the errors and tragic mistakes?) and is applicable at an individual level and to groups as a whole. In short, Cicero cautions us to learn not only from our own contextual past, but also to look to prior eras for lessons that are applicable to our own. JE

"I came, I saw, I conquered."

Julius Caesar
Attributed
C. 46 BCE

Gaius Julius Caesar was a Roman statesman, author and general, who was notable for his military conquests. After triumphing in a civil war, he ruled the Roman republic for two years before his assassination in 44 BCE at the hands of a group of rebellious senators, who feared the rise of a dictatorship.

Caesar's career was important in the start of Rome's shift from republic to empire. After the civil wars that followed Caesar's death, his adopted heir, Octavius, became the first Roman emperor and assumed the regnal name of Augustus.

'I came, I saw, I conquered' (in Latin, '*Veni, vidi, vici*') is reputed to have originally featured in Julius Caesar's letter to the Roman Senate in which he reported his quick and decisive victory in 47 BCE over Pharnaces II of Pontus at the Battle of Zela (Zile in modern Turkey).

However, the original text, if it ever existed, has not survived, and the earliest reference to it is by Appian of Alexandria, a historian who lived more than a century after the events he described. Consequently, the remark was not definitely uttered by Caesar, but it is universally credited to him and is one of the Latin phrases that survives in the original. JE

❷ Caesar's forces besiege Alesia, a town in Gaul (modern France).

QVANTA STRA
GE VIRVM SVBLI
MIS ALEXIA CESSIT
CÆSAREIS AQVI
LIS. PICTA TABEL
LA NOTAT

" Time, the devourer of all things. "

Ovid
Metamorphoses
8 CE

From *Metamorphoses*, one of the most influential works in Western culture, the above quotation reminds us that we cannot escape the ravages of time. It chews through everything we are and all that we possess. The phrase heralds impermanence and is reminiscent of the Zen Buddhist notion that all of existence, without exception, is transient and in a constant state of flux. All will be dissipated under the corroding effects of time.

Our culture, too, is a devouring one, focused on consumerism, on an insatiable hunger for possessions. Time devours our most precious relationships and possessions and we, in the rush to outwit time, devour the very earth to shore up our synthesized world. This shows the absurdity at the heart of our culture, which encourages us to believe that our children matter and that we have an obligation to protect them, but which at the same time urges us to compete with one another and conspicuously consume. We know that our possessions will be dispersed as soon as we die, but this does not stop us from hoarding whatever we can for as long as we can and justifying our compulsion as inheritance. Ovid said that nothing would survive the teeth of time except his poem – not even the Roman empire. Perhaps his foresight is what gives these words their power. **LW**

" I wish the Roman people had but a single neck. "

Caligula
Attributed
C. 37 CE

If the account of the historian Suetonius in *The Twelve Caesars* is to be believed, the Roman emperor Caligula was sadistic, depraved, vindictive and without any redeeming features. Caligula uttered the above words when he was angry with a crowd at the Circensian games for applauding a contestant he opposed, with the implication that if his wish were granted, he would gladly behead the Roman people with a single blow. A later Roman historian, Cassius Dio, suggested that Caligula's assassination by a force of his bodyguards was ironically a reversal: it was then the emperor who had a single neck. But Suetonius, the major source of information about Caligula, is not necessarily reliable. Caligula may have been indulging in grim irony, rather than dreaming of genocide.

Classically educated writers often invoke Caligula's words in castigating those they regard as tyrants. A famous example occurred in 17th-century England, when a court established by Parliament was trying King Charles I on the charge of treason. Explicitly comparing Charles to Caligula, the lord president of the court told him that 'could you but have confounded [the representation of the people by Parliament], you had at one blow cut off the neck of England'. Found guilty, Charles was himself beheaded. **GB**

" Virtue extends our days: he lives two lives who relives his past with pleasure. "

Martial
Epigrams
80–102 CE

Martial was a satirist and poet. Although he was not the first Roman poet to use an epigrammatic style in his works, he is often considered to be the 'father of the epigram,' for his skill in developing the literary genre of epigrams. His technique relies on short, satirical poems, in particular, with a joke in the last line, and he is best known for his twelve books of *Epigrams*, published in Rome between 80 and 102.

In Martial's *Epigrams*, we find the above quotation, whose subject is the Roman general Marcus Antonius Primus. The writer comments on how 'the happy Antonius Primus,' having lived his life well and peacefully, does not fear being closer to death, and 'not one day of his brings remorse or an unpleasant reflection – there is nothing he would not want to remember. Consequently, having lived a virtuous existence, Primus has lengthened his life in that he is always able to enjoy the memories of the life he has lived (and the experiences that resulted from it). In short, Martial's words mean that living life virtuously is like living two lives, because one can always remember and enjoy one's own past without feelings of regret. **JE**

" Every instant of time is a pinprick of eternity. "

Marcus Aurelius
Meditations
c. 167 CE

Marcus Aurelius was Roman emperor from 161 to 180 and is also notable as a Stoic philosopher. His *Meditations*, written in Greek, were not intended for publication or a wide readership; they were merely notes he kept for reflection and self-improvement. As a consequence they are set down as aphorisms rather than as a systematic treatise.

Among the major themes of the *Meditations* is cosmic perspective. The influence of Greek philosopher Epictetus (c. 55–135) is apparent throughout the work, particularly in its repeated emphasis on the impermanence of everything (where change is a constant) and in the advice to suspend one's initial impressions of experiences and things in order to see them as part of the whole, which is identified with God in Stoic philosophy.

The above quotation expresses the notion that what we experience, in the context of the Universe, is never more than transient, fleeting and temporary. The author goes on to state that '[a]ll things are petty, easily changed, vanishing away' and further discusses how all things – even those we perceive as unpleasant or painful – are still parts of God. In other words, it is important to acknowledge that everything is both temporary and part of a greater, divine whole. **JE**

> # *If history records good things of good men, the thoughtful hearer is encouraged to imitate what is good.*

This 11th-century illumination shows a scribe, widely thought to be Bede, at work in a monastery.

Bede
Ecclesiastical History of the English Nation
731 CE

Born in 673, Bede, at age seven, became an oblate (a junior rank of monk) under Benedict Biscop, founder of the monastery of St Peter in Wearmouth, England. Two years later, Bede moved with his mentor to a new monastery at Jarrow, where he lived until his death in 735. He became a deacon and later a priest, but his main interest was always in scholarship. His great work, the *Ecclesiastical History of the English Nation*, completed in 731, covered English history from Roman times to the conversion of the Anglo-Saxons to Christianity in Bede's own lifetime.

Monasteries in 7th-century England were part of a wide network of cultural exchanges covering the Mediterranean world as well as northern Europe, which gave Bede contacts in Rome and other important early medieval cities, as well as across England.

Bede's assertion here is that accounts of virtuous behavior will encourage others to behave in a similar manner. This seems unobjectionable as far as it goes, but the reader may wonder if the opposite applies equally: do descriptions of nefarious conduct inspire copycat crimes, or turn good people into sinners? JF

"When I want to understand what is happening today or try to decide what will happen tomorrow, I look back."

Omar Khayyám

On the Necessity of Contradiction in the World

1120

Omar Khayyám, a Persian polymath, made important discoveries in science and mathematics that are often overshadowed by his poetry and religious/philosophical thought. In the West his best-known poem is the 'Rubaiyat' ('Quatrains'), thanks mainly to the 19th-century English translation by Edward FitzGerald. In *On the Necessity of Contradiction*, a work of philosophy, Khayyám explored the idea that we know today as determinism, which states that what has happened in the past governs absolutely what happens in the future, leaving little or no room for free will. Khayyám broadly held to this view, but without taking it to extremes.

This quotation therefore needs to be seen within its deterministic context. Many philosophers and historians have exalted the role of history as a way of understanding the present, and often as a way of avoiding repetition of the mistakes of the past. But from a determinist viewpoint, what will happen tomorrow can be directly predicted from what happened yesterday, if you have enough information. The 1919 Treaty of Versailles, for example, which punished Germany for World War I, created the conditions that allowed Hitler's rise to power in 1933. **JF**

⬙ Omar Khayyám, as imagined by early 20th-century American artist and photographer Adelaide Hanscom Leeson.

" *Kill them all. God will know his own.* "

An illustration of the massacre and pillage of Béziers by the troops of Simon de Montfort.

Arnaud Amalric
Massacre at Béziers
1209

The Latin version of the above quotation – '*Caedite eos. Novit enim Dominus qui sunt eius*' – was reportedly uttered by a Cistercian monk, Arnaud Amalric, as a strategic response to the knowledge that there were many of his own faith among the heretics besieged, then massacred, at Béziers, France. In order to believe it, we must first have faith in an afterlife in which we are either saved or damned, and, secondly, that 'collateral damage' is acceptable as a by-product of our quest to defend our faith. We need not concern ourselves with the blood of unbelievers.

This is the mind-set of the fundamentalist, and we are familiar with the dangers of this self-absolution. The most horrific crimes against humanity (and beyond) are thus justified as a regrettable, but never unjustifiable, means to some utopian end. If this quotation is to inspire us, it needs to do so in a special way: as a warning of the consequences of believing that we have a hotline to heaven, that responsibility for our decisions and actions lies beyond us, or that we can justify hypocrisy or intolerance on the basis that the reckoning for our deeds in this life will take place in the next. **LW**

"Whoever is responsible for another's becoming powerful ruins himself."

Niccolò Machiavelli
The Prince
1513

Machiavelli's name has come to denote the devious scheming by which ruthless political leaders seek to obtain and secure power. This legacy is almost exclusively due to some of the advice dispensed in *The Prince*. Machiavelli had earlier served as a statesman in the Florentine republic, and this book was probably an attempt to find favour with the ruling Medici dynasty. In any case, his lasting influence follows, not from any exhortation to commit immoral acts, but from how the pursuit and preservation of political power require prudent judgement.

The above quotation expresses a 'general principle' that Machiavelli illustrates with the case of French king Louis XII, who sought to expand his realm by forging alliances with powerful neighbours. However, the strategy was self-defeating, because many of Louis's less powerful allies then saw him as a threat, and turned against him. In describing such counterproductive effects as the workings of a general principle, Machiavelli's insight into the dynamics of power relations has evolved into realpolitik and game theory while also finding application in competitive business strategies. **TJ**

⊙ A portrait of Machiavelli from c. 1510. In a letter of 1513, he described *The Prince* as a 'whimsy.'

"And as time requires, a man of marvellous mirth and pastimes and sometimes of as sad a gravity – a man for all seasons."

Robert Whittington
Vulgaria
1520

Preceded by 'More is a man of angel's wit and singular learning. . .I know not his fellow. For where is the man ...of that gentleness, lowliness and affability?', the above quotation was originally part of a passage for students to translate into Latin. It was a description of Thomas More, the English statesman and author of *Utopia* (1516).

Whittington took the phrase 'a man for all seasons' from Dutch humanist Desiderius Erasmus's *In Praise of Folly* (1511), which was written in Latin. 'Seasons' here does not refer to spring, summer, fall or winter, but to occasions. Whittington is complimenting More on his flexibility, a quality which, as it turned out, did not extend as far as enabling him to swear allegiance to Henry VIII as head of the Church of England. More was consequently convicted of treason, and beheaded in 1535.

More subsequently became the subject of Robert Bolt's celebrated play *A Man for All Seasons* (1960), and the entire description of More appears as one of the epigraphs to the script. The film version of the work, released in 1966, won six Academy Awards, including Best Picture, Best Director (for Fred Zinnemann), and Best Actor (for Paul Scofield as More). **GB**

"The day is gone, and yet I saw no sun; And now I live, and now my life is done."

Chidiock Tichborne
'Tichborne's Elegy'
1586

When the young poet Chidiock Tichborne wrote the above words in a letter to his wife, he was imprisoned in the Tower of London. He was a member of the Babington conspiracy, a plot to assassinate the Protestant Queen Elizabeth I and replace her with her cousin, Mary, Queen of Scots, a Roman Catholic. The conspirators were sentenced to death for their treason, and the day after Tichborne wrote his letter he was carried to central London and publicly hanged, drawn and quartered.

This poem, also known by its first line – 'My prime of youth is but a frost of cares' – is an elegy. Originally applying to a broader range of verse, the term 'elegy' came to refer to poems written in response to the death of a person, typically involving not only mourning and praising the dead, but also seeking solace. Famous elegies in the narrower sense include John Milton's 'Lycidas' (1637); Thomas Gray's 'Elegy Written in a Country Churchyard' (1751); Percy Bysshe Shelley's 'Adonaïs' (1821), about the poet John Keats; Walt Whitman's 'O Captain! My Captain!' (1865), about Abraham Lincoln; and Allen Ginsberg's 'Kaddish' (1959), about his mother.

'Tichborne's Elegy' is unusual, if not unique, in that it mourns, in anticipation, the poet's own death. Three different composers later set it to music. **GB**

> " *Go, and catch a falling star; get with child a mandrake root; tell me, where all past years are; or who cleft the Devil's foot.* "

John Donne
'Song'
c. 1598

These lines were probably written before John Donne met Anne More, his patron's niece. Their marriage was an act of career suicide for Donne, and these lines presage that impulsive disregard for convention, but also hint at the strange anomalies such disregard produces. In searching for meaning, we also seek to escape the horrors that social, political and religious constraints impose. It is the whimsy of this imagery, enjoining us to achieve the impossible, that is so intriguing and poignant: Donne finally managed to climb clear of the disgrace of his unsanctioned marriage, only to have to face the death of his beloved Anne during childbirth when she was only thirty-three years old.

The fanciful endeavours suggested by these lines contain an exaggerated vitality and curiosity. They are like Zen koans (riddles), at once nonsensical and profound. The past, like a falling star, is unreachable, and babies are not born from the roots of plants, however suggestively shaped. We cannot study the origins of Satan's cloven hoof without getting far too close to his demonic gaze. Yet the pictures these lines provoke plunge us into the possibilities of paradox and we can begin, like Donne, to question and even break the rules. **LW**

> " *The treason is done, the traitor is no longer needed.* "

Pedro Calderón de la Barca
Life Is a Dream
1635

One of the greatest Spanish dramatists of the Golden Age, Calderón wrote around one hundred full-length plays and seventy one-act pieces for performance in church. His most famous major work is *Life is a Dream*.

As this play begins, Prince Segismundo has been imprisoned in a tower since birth because his father is convinced that he would be a cruel and wicked ruler. Segismundo is later freed, but after he turns violent, his father sedates him, returns him to his tower and convinces him that his excursion was a dream. Segismundo is subsequently freed from his prison by a band of rebellious soldiers, whom he then leads against his father. Although the rebels prevail in battle, Segismundo spares his father, who in gratitude proclaims him king. In the last section of the play, Segismundo, by now having undergone a moral awakening, rewards the virtuous characters. But when one of the rebel soldiers asks what the reward will be for liberating him, Segismundo sentences him to life imprisonment in the same tower, adding the above words.

Segismundo's explanation of the rebel soldier's punishment suggests that treason is relative to the circumstances. Earlier in the play, Segismundo's father offered a similar thought on civil wars: 'In such battles, those who win are loyal; the losers, traitors.' The question of whether Calderón approved these sentiments or merely recorded them has left scholars divided. **GB**

"Not heaven itself upon the past has power; But what has been, has been, and I have had my hour."

John Dryden
The Twenty-Ninth Ode of the First Book of Horace
1685

Fantasies about time travel notwithstanding, it is impossible to change the past. The above quotation – from Dryden's English translation of a work by Horace, the Roman poet of the 1st century BCE – elegantly acknowledges that inescapable truth. As the preceding lines of the ode – 'Be fair, or foul, or rain, or shine,/The joys I have possessed, in spite of fate, are mine' – indicate, Dryden is affirming the value of past happiness, even in the face of present sorrow.

The sentiment occurs often in poetry throughout the ages. A humorous variant occurs at the end of Sydney Smith's rhymed recipe for salad: 'Serenely full, the epicure would say,/Fate cannot harm me, I have dined to-day.' A 20th-century equivalent was provided by American songwriters George and Ira Gershwin in their 1937 song 'They Can't Take That Away From Me.'

The opposite is also much in evidence, as for example in the verse of the 11th-century Persian Omar Khayyám (in Edward FitzGerald's translation): 'The Moving Finger writes; and, having writ,/Moves on: nor all thy Piety nor Wit,/Shall lure it back to cancel half a Line,/Nor all thy Tears wash out a Word of it.' **GB**

⦿ In 1688, John Dryden was appointed by King Charles II as the first official poet laureate of England.

History . . . is, indeed, little more than the register of the crimes, follies and misfortunes of mankind.

Edward Gibbon
Decline and Fall of the Roman Empire
1776

A modern equivalent of the above words, applied to journalism rather than to history, is 'If it bleeds, it leads' (c. 1982). The above quotation – perhaps the most famous by English historian Edward Gibbon – is excerpted from a longer sentence that reveals Gibbon's characteristic irony. Discussing the Roman emperor Antoninus (reigned 138–161 CE), Gibbon writes: 'His reign is marked by the rare advantage of furnishing very few materials for history; which is, indeed, little more than the register of the crimes, follies, and misfortunes of mankind.' The historian is thus praising Antoninus for his failure to provide any fodder for the historian. Gibbon is also alluding here to *L'Ingénu* (1767), a novella by his acquaintance Voltaire, which contains the thought: 'History is but the record of crimes and misfortunes.'

Modern historians often adopt or adapt Gibbon's description: Hugh Trevor-Roper entitled a volume of his reminiscences *Crimes, Follies, and Misfortunes* (1998). But they do not necessarily agree with their source. A common response to Gibbon is that history is also the register of the efforts to punish the crimes, correct the follies and alleviate the misfortunes of humanity. **GB**

⊘ The Colosseum during the period of Rome's decline, as imagined by 18th-century Italian painter Bernardo Bellotto.

" You can never plan the future by the past. "

Edmund Burke
Letter to a member of the National Assembly
1791

Anglo-Irish statesman Edmund Burke was here responding to a request from François-Louis-Thibaut de Menonville, a member of the revolutionary National Assembly in France, for him to amplify his *Reflections on the Revolution in France* (1790). The remark appears in the final paragraph of his letter, in which Burke criticizes the assembly for its diligence: 'They who always labour can have no true judgement,' he wrote, arguing that the assembly continually legislated without taking the time to assess the consequences of its previous actions.

But Burke was by no means suggesting that, in general, the past is no guide to the future. He was a historian himself, although his history of England from the time of Julius Caesar to the end of the reign of Queen Anne in 1714 stalled at the year 1216. In his political career as a Whig member of the British Parliament, he constantly deferred to established traditions and authorities, arguing that their persistence was testimony to their value. In *Reflections*, for example, he suggested that the leaders of the French Revolution were selfish and short-sighted, writing: 'People will not look forward to posterity, who never look backward to their ancestors.' GB

" England expects that every man will do his duty. "

Admiral Horatio Nelson
Flag signal at the Battle of Trafalgar
1805

This message was raised on the mast of Nelson's flagship, HMS *Victory*, just before the start of the Battle of Trafalgar, in the Atlantic Ocean, in which Britain took on the combined fleets of France and Spain. The men aboard all twenty-seven of the ships under the admiral's command cheered when they read it.

Nelson went to sea at age twelve, and worked his way up through the ranks. Despite seasickness and a dislike of authority, by the age of twenty he had become a captain. He exemplified the courage and patriotism of a military hero, and having lost his right arm and his right eye in different engagements, he embodied the battle-scarred warrior. A brilliant strategist, and one who had himself endured the privations suffered by ordinary seamen, he inspired complete loyalty.

This quotation derives much of its resonance from the man who said it: Nelson had done it all, and he didn't hide at Trafalgar. Instead of sheltering in the centre of the column, he led from the front. By 4pm the battle was won, but the hero had been shot dead. LW

❷ *The Death of Nelson* (1806) by US painter Benjamin West.

"Look back, and smile on perils past!"

Sir Walter Scott
The Bridal of Triermain
1813

Sir Walter Scott is widely credited as the originator of the historical novel – fiction that is based on real events for as long as the facts do not get in the way of the story.

In this narrative poem of his, the lowborn poet Arthur is wooing his aristocratic lover Lucy by telling her a tale about the exploits of Sir Roland De Vaux as he seeks to rescue Gyneth – illegitimate daughter of King Arthur – from her enchanted slumber. The above words occur in the introduction to the poem; Arthur is complimenting Lucy on crossing a stream, of which she was initially fearful, on her way to meet him. But Arthur is also alluding to the challenges that De Vaux will have to overcome in rescuing, wooing and winning Gyneth: first the threat of fear, then the potential snares of pleasure, wealth and pride. Since the latter obstacles also stand in the way of the love of Arthur and Lucy, owing to the class difference between them, Arthur is hinting that she ought to emulate De Vaux.

If there is a general moral to be found in Arthur's advice to Lucy, it is that dangers are not as frightening after they have been overcome – a thought echoed by 19th-century French novelist Honoré de Balzac, who wrote, '[O]ur worst misfortunes never happen, and most miseries lie in anticipation.' On the other hand, 20th-century US baseball player Leroy 'Satchel' Paige offered contrasting advice: 'Don't look back. Something might be gaining on you.' **GB**

"My days among the dead are past; Around me I behold, Where'er these casual eyes are cast, the mighty minds of old."

Robert Southey
'My Days Among the Dead Are Past'
1818

Robert Southey was a poet and a biographer of Horatio Nelson, John Wesley, Oliver Cromwell and John Bunyan. He was a scholar of European literature, particularly Portuguese and Spanish, and popularized the children's story of Goldilocks and the Three Bears in the first narrative version published in 1837. He was the British poet laureate from 1813 until his death in 1843.

'My Days Among the Dead Are Past' is a twenty-four-line, four-stanza poem about the author's relationship with those who came before him, to whom he refers as his friends. He claims to learn useful lessons, not only from studying the virtues and failings of the thinkers of the past, but also from direct discussions with them, which he claims to have daily. The trajectory of the poem is toward securing an everlasting future companionship with those same dead – 'My place with them will be' – through the immortality of his work, which will travel on 'through all Futurity.'

These lines of Southey are evidently still remembered today, but his work is generally out of fashion. Thus, the apparent certainty with which he here anticipates eternal fame may seem a little hubristic to modern readers. **JF**

Look on my works, ye Mighty, and despair.

Percy Bysshe Shelley
'Ozymandias'
1818

Born in England in 1792, Percy Bysshe Shelley is regarded as one of the finest of the Romantic poets. However, he struggled for recognition in his lifetime and was disowned by his aristocratic father for his atheism, socialism, and espousal of 'free love.'

On the eve of Shelley's emigration to Italy, he and his friend Horace Smith decided to write a sonnet each on the ruined statue of Ozymandias, as recalled by Greek historian Diodorus Siculus. Smith's poem is unremembered, but Shelley's became a classic. 'Ozymandias' describes the ruins of an ancient sculpture, its huge legs standing trunkless in a desert landscape. Nearby, the head lies shattered, half sunk into the sand. Ozymandias (Ramses II, pharaoh of Egypt), once king of kings, stands powerless. His works, designed to overawe other rulers, have disappeared, as has the ancient Egyptian empire itself: '...boundless and bare/The lone and level sands stretch far away.' The moral is that the monumental works of tyrants do not last, and their power is mocked by future generations who do not have to fear them. But Shelley also hints at an inner desert, in which all our achievements may prove futile in the face of our mortality. JF

⬥ Detail from *Shelley Composing 'Prometheus Unbound' in the Baths of Caracalla* (1845), by Joseph Severn.

An army marches on its stomach.

🔺 Portrait of the Emperor Napoléon at Fontainebleau (1814), by Paul Delaroche.

🔻 Napoléon on his way into exile in *The Eagle's Flight* (1857) by Hugues Merle.

Napoléon Bonaparte
Attributed
c. 1820

In the January 1904 issue of *Windsor Magazine*, M H Morrison began an article on 'The Army Cook-House and Field Kitchen' with the above sentence, which he described as a Napoleonic aphorism. But there is no evidence that Bonaparte ever said or wrote these words, although he offered the less picturesque observation that armies 'must feed themselves on war at the expense of the enemy territory'. Napoléon was especially concerned with supply because of the enormous size of his forces, which he complained he found 'naked and ill-fed'. But the importance of supply to military effectiveness was noted as early as the 4th century by Vegetius. Frederick the Great, king of Prussia in the mid-18th century, is sometimes credited with saying, 'An army, like a serpent, travels on its belly.'

Historian B H Liddell Hart provided two corollaries to this aphorism. In discussing the importance of meals in affecting committee planning, he suggested that 'History marches on the stomach of statesmen.' And about digestive disorders among German troops during World War I, he wrote: 'An army fights on its stomach, and falls if its stomach is upset.' **GB**

" The best of Prophets of the future is the past. "

Lord Byron is classed as one of the great English Romantic poets, but much of his work is more sardonic than that of near contemporaries, such as John Keats.

There are many ways of prophesying – by dreams, by cards, by numbers, by the stars – but the above quotation suggests the perhaps more rational approach of simply consulting the past and projecting its conditions and tendencies to the future.

Philosophical doubts about the value of the past as a guide to future performance were raised by English philosopher David Hume in the 18th century and reinforced by the American philosopher Nelson Goodman in the 20th century, but for the bulk of humanity – including historians – it seems like a commonsense guideline. The Renaissance political thinker Niccolò Machiavelli, for example, regarded it as accepted wisdom that '[W]hoever wishes to foresee the future must consult the past.'

In context, Byron was musing about the tragedies he proposed to write or hoped to finish, including *Sardanapalus* and *Cain*, both of which were published later the same year. He wondered why, at the height of pleasure, there is 'a certain sense of doubt and sorrow,' and attributed it to 'a retrospect to the past, leading to a prognostication of the future'. Concerned mainly with emotional experiences, he never developed the idea of a link between the past and the future. **GB**

" The world is weary of the past, O, might it die or rest at last! "

The above couplet occurs at the end of Shelley's verse drama about the Ottoman sultan Mahmud, who is supervising Turkish encroachments into Greece. It is spoken by a chorus of captive Greek women. By the end of the play, the Turkish attacks have failed. Saying, 'The world's great age begins anew' – which hints at the ancient Greek idea of eternal return – the chorus welcomes the prospect of a revived and renovated Greece, complete with new versions of the ancient figures of Greek mythology. But in the last six lines the chorus seems to realize that the cyclical nature of history entails not only the imminent revival of Greek freedom, but also the eventual return of Turkish oppression. This concluding couplet thus expresses a yearning for a break in the cycle of eternal return: for the end of the world. As it happened, for Shelley himself, this definitive ending was not far away: he drowned in the Ligurian Sea the following year.

Because the referent of 'it' is ambiguous, the couplet is sometimes interpreted as expressing a hope for the end – not of the world, but of the past, and by extension of the discipline that studies the past: history (compare 'History is bunk,' attributed to Henry Ford). **GB**

> *History, like love, is so apt to surround her heroes with an atmosphere of imaginary brightness.*

James Fenimore Cooper
The Last of the Mohicans
1826

History and myth are regular bedfellows, no matter the time or place. In his account of frontier life in late 18th- and early 19th-century America, James Fenimore Cooper helped propagate legends about the lives of homesteaders and Native Americans.

The Last of the Mohicans is the most famous novel in Cooper's series, *Leatherstocking Tales*, all five volumes of which explore the life of Nathaniel Bumppo, the child of white homesteaders who grew up among Delaware's Lenape tribe. It is set in 1757, during the Seven Years' War between France and Britain, when the two countries vied for control of North America. Through its blend of fact and sweeping, romantic fiction, *The Last of the Mohicans* blurred the distinction between history and myth and shaped the perception of an era dominated by iconic heroes. This line between reality and myth is explored elsewhere in popular culture, particularly in cinema, for example, in the Western *The Man Who Shot Liberty Valance* (1962). In discussing the veracity of an incident, a newspaperman opines: 'When the legend becomes fact, print the legend.' Cooper understood that reasoning all too well. **IHS**

> *History is a set of lies agreed upon.*

Napoléon Bonaparte
Memoirs
1829

The truth of this maxim is borne out in the experience of indigenous peoples everywhere (if Native Americans had written the history curriculum in the United States, it would have a very different slant). The phrase deliberately inverts 'History is nothing more than a convenient fairy story,' an earlier observation by 18th-century French historian Bernard Le Bouyer de Fontenelle.

A brilliant self-publicist, Napoléon well knew that military victories were not enough; he had to win hearts and minds as well. While his contemporaries wrote frequently tedious descriptions of their military achievements, the French emperor's memoirs contained thrilling tales of derring-do which he ensured appeared on the front pages of all his nation's newspapers. When elements of the royalist French press identified what he was up to, they responded with vitriolic articles that denounced him. Napoléon countered by setting up or taking over six newspapers and writing articles himself. This continued even after his exile, his memoirs 'adjusting' history in his favour.

Even in such a poor translation as this (it should read 'fables,' not 'lies'), this phrase presages many subsequent events, including the elimination of Chinese heritage by the Red Guards of Chinese leader Mao Zedong, and the propaganda initiatives of ISIS in Syria and contiguous nations. **LW**

> " *Nothing that was worthy in the Past departs; no Truth or Goodness realized by man ever dies, or can die.* "

Thomas Carlyle
Edinburgh Review magazine
1831

In an article entitled 'Characteristics' about Thomas Hope's *An Essay on the Origin and Prospects of Man* and Friedrich von Schlegel's *Philosophische Vorlesungen*, Carlyle urged that it is unnecessary to lament the past. 'The true Past departs not,' he wrote, adding the above words. In context he was disclaiming a possible inference from the recognition of the universality of progress: if it is inevitable that everything ceaselessly changes, from scientific knowledge to governmental systems, then are there any constants to guide humanity or to which humanity may aspire? Carlyle answers yes: only the superficialities of what is true or good vanish while the substance endures. Thus, Carlyle wishes to distinguish his intellectual position from, on the one hand, unrealizable nostalgia for the past and, on the other hand, unalloyed enthusiasm for the future.

While Carlyle's idea may seem comforting initially, there is room to wonder whether it exaggerates the importance of the future. If, for example, people lose interest in reading Carlyle, does that mean that he was never a worthy author, or is worthy only insofar as his works are similar to what appeals to readers now? **GB**

> " *Let us learn from the past to profit by the present, and from the present to live better in the future.* "

William Wordsworth
Attributed
c. 1838

Is there any point in knowing about the past? While historians might maintain that their subject is worth studying for its own sake, the above quotation implies that there may be a pragmatic reason for doing so, and it is perhaps not surprising that it frequently appears today in books offering personal financial advice. Yet it is not necessary to construe 'profit' and 'live better' in their narrowest, most materialistic senses, nor yet to regard this advice as applicable solely to the individual. Variations on the theme of the general importance of learning from the past to understand the present and predict the future are common. In 1938, for example, French sociologist Émile Durkheim wrote: 'It is only by carefully studying the past that we can come to anticipate the future, and to understand the present.'

This quotation began to appear around 1838, without attribution, as a filler in newspapers in the United States and Britain. It was often preceded by: 'Life is divided into three terms: that which was, which is, and which will be.'

The common modern attribution to Wordsworth is almost inexplicable, but perhaps stems from the fact that it precedes, again without attribution, a genuine quotation from the English poet in Tryon Edwards's *A Dictionary of Thoughts* (1891). **GB**

When the past no longer illuminates the future, the spirit walks in darkness.

Alexis de Tocqueville
Democracy in America
1840

On learning that the author of this quotation was an aristocrat, one might construe the words as a core principle of strong political conservatism. In his book, de Tocqueville's characterization of a despotic potential in democracy may well seem to confirm the impression that he resented the destruction of the ancien régime in his homeland of France. On the contrary, despite his noble heritage, de Tocqueville was a staunch defender of the democratic ideals of freedom and equality that the French Revolution had sought to establish.

From his travels in the United States, de Tocqueville was impressed by the manner in which democratic ideals had been adopted there with much greater success than in France and other European nations, where those ideals could emerge only by forcefully opposing the feudalism that had governed past societies. Precisely because the United States had no such traditions, its future 'spirit' could not be guided by the past. And for that reason, de Tocqueville warned of the need for vigilance, so that the despotic societies of the past do not re-emerge in the democratic form of an excessively powerful majority. **TJ**

◉ This portrait of Alexis de Tocqueville was painted by French Romantic painter Théodore Chassériau in 1850.

> " *No man who is correctly informed as to the past will be disposed to take a morose or desponding view of the present.* "

Lord Macaulay
The History of England
1848

The historian Lord Macaulay offers these words in the opening paragraphs of his book, having asserted that 'the history of our country during the last 160 years is eminently the history of physical, of moral, and of intellectual improvement' and dismissed the notion that the present represents the result of degeneration and decay from a golden age in the past.

Macaulay is not only judging England to have progressed since 1688 – the year of the Glorious Revolution, in which King James II was deposed by Parliament and replaced with William III and Mary II – but also announcing his intention to explain the historical events in terms of that progress. British historian Herbert Butterfield coined the term 'Whig history' in the 20th century to describe the approach to history that 'studies the past with reference to the present,' understanding the past as a march of progress towards today's state of enlightenment and evaluating historical actors as virtuous or vicious according to whether they helped or hindered that progress. Although unnamed by Butterfield, Macaulay, a Whig politician, was implicitly among the targets of his critique. **GB**

> " *History repeats itself, first as tragedy, then as farce.* "

Karl Marx
The Eighteenth Brumaire of Louis Bonaparte
1851–52

Karl Marx was a German political economist, philosopher, sociologist and revolutionary socialist. His central concern was to critique and actively oppose capitalism, and thereby make progress towards the establishment of a classless society. Although Marx's magnum opus, *Das Kapital* (1867), was a work of political economy, many of his writings have come to highlight conceptual insights on a wide range of topics, including art and literature. The work from which the above quotation is taken was his historical and empirical exploration of political phenomena.

In context, Marx's aphorism analytically connects the 1851 coup of Louis-Napoléon to the earlier coup by his uncle, Napoléon Bonaparte. The comparison is made via an allusion to the theory of German philosopher Georg Wilhelm Friedrich Hegel. The exact Hegel reference is unclear, but it likely refers to his argument that history teaches us that people and governments seldom, if ever, learn from history (and implicitly, that they repeat it).

That that should be the case struck Marx as ludicrous, because it does not have to be that way, and it would not be if humans were only prepared or better able to learn from experience. But they repeatedly show that they are incapable of such discernment. **JE**

❯ The 19th-century socialist thinker Karl Marx.

> # " *I do not pretend to understand the moral universe, the arc is a long one . . . But from what I see I am sure it bends toward justice.* "

Theodore Parker
Ten Sermons of Religion
1853

A phrase used by US President Barack Obama that appeared in *Time* magazine in 2009, during his first term of office in the White House, was, in fact, an adaptation of a much-quoted statement by social reformer Theodore Parker more than a century and a half earlier in a sermon entitled 'Of Justice and the Conscience.'

Parker was an important figure in the abolitionist movement against slavery. He was a Unitarian minister and transcendentalist who, believing that all men were essentially good, was convinced that abolition was inevitable in the fullness of time. Parker's words foreshadowed the American Civil War of the 1860s, but with slavery abolished in 1865, it was a justice he would not live to see: he died in 1860.

Just over one hundred years after the emancipation of African Americans from slavery, Martin Luther King, Jr paraphrased Parker's words in his landmark 'Where Do We Go From Here?' speech in 1967, before the Southern Leadership Christian Conference, when he declared: 'The arc of the moral universe is long, but it bends towards justice.' And for Obama, despite opposition, the reforms he saw as his mission would be achieved in time. **ME**

⬙ US President Barack Obama is one of many notable figures to have paraphrased Parker's quotation.

That sign of old age: extolling the past at the expense of the present.

Sydney Smith
Quoted in Lady Holland's memoir of her father
1855

It may not be too difficult to discern the truth behind this quotation. As we grow older, our remembered youth acquires a rose-tinted hue, and we become impatient with modernity, particularly as new methods and mores become difficult for us to grasp or accept.

Sydney Smith came up with many witticisms that are treasured by posterity but which did little to advance his career in the Anglican Church. Lord Byron once quipped that Smith's "jokes were sermons, and his sermons jokes," and no one in the English establishment would rush to promote to the rank of bishop someone who spoke of 'three sexes – men, women and clergymen'. Smith was nevertheless a popular speaker; he wrote regularly for the *Edinburgh Review*, and eventually became a canon of London's St Paul's Cathedral and a wealthy man. His politics inclined to the Whig – he opposed imperialism – but he did not support democracy. In her memoir, his daughter, Saba, who married Sir Henry Holland, sought to present a different side of her father – rather than a clever cynic, she portrayed him as a gentle, caring rural parson (who invented a back scratcher for the animals on his farm). JF

Sydney Smith wanted to be a lawyer, but his father insisted that he become a vicar.

"Time flies over us, but leaves its shadow behind."

⚅ Francisco Goya's painting *Time and the Old Woman* (c. 1808–12) captures the decaying effects of time.

Nathaniel Hawthorne
The Marble Faun
1860

The above epigram combines two proverbial aspects of time: the speed of its passage and its saddening effects. It is a possible reflection of a verse from the Apocrypha: 'Our time is a very shadow that passeth away' (Wisdom of Solomon 1:5).

At the centre of Hawthorne's novel is the ambiguity of why Donatello is, mysteriously, identical to the 2,000-year-old statue of the title that he so closely resembles. Early in the novel, the beautiful Miriam jokingly asks Donatello what a faun like him could 'know about the joys and sorrows, the intertwining light and shadow, of human life?' Later, Kenyon is visiting Donatello at his ancestral mansion for the first time. After Donatello says that he often stays up late watching the stars, Kenyon comments that he imagined him as engaged in simple pleasures during the day and sleeping soundly at night. Donatello replies that he might have done so when he was a boy, but he is a boy no longer, adding the epigram. Kenyon is unimpressed, smiling 'at the triteness of the remark,' but acknowledging to himself that Donatello must have formulated it on the basis of his own sorrows. **GB**

> " *These times of ours are serious and full of calamity, but all times are essentially alike. As soon as there is life there is danger.* "

Ralph Waldo Emerson
'Public and Private Education' lecture
1864

Ralph Waldo Emerson, US poet, essayist and philosopher, was born in Massachusetts. He studied at Harvard before serving as minister at the Second Church in Boston. After the death of his wife, he resigned his post and travelled to Europe, where he visited Thomas Carlyle, who profoundly influenced his thinking on social and political matters. On his return to the United States, he became involved in transcendentalism, and he edited the movement's journal, *The Dial*, from 1842 to 1844. Transcendentalism was opposed to scientific rationalism and encouraged reliance on intuition and experience. Emerson shocked many people with his unconventional religious views and his belief in 'the divine sufficiency of the individual'. His most famous essay, 'Self-Reliance,' published in 1841, developed the maxim 'Trust yourself.'

The above quotation speaks as directly to us today as it did to Emerson's original audience at the Parker Fraternity during the American Civil War, when the nation seemed to be tearing itself apart. But the deeper truth is that there is no absolute safety at any time or any place. Our times too are 'serious and full of calamity'. Just by being alive, we are hostages to fortune. **JF**

> " *History doesn't repeat itself, but it does rhyme.* "

Mark Twain
The Gilded Age: A Tale of Today
1873

This quotation has often been attributed to US author Mark Twain. Certainly, he did write something similar, in *Mark Twain in Eruption: Hitherto Unpublished Pages About Men and Events* – the remaining typescript from his published memoirs of 1924 – and he also reiterated the sentiment vividly in a novel he cowrote with Charles Dudley Warner, *The Gilded Age: A Tale of Today*: 'History never repeats itself, but the kaleidoscopic combinations of the pictured present often seem to be constructed out of the broken fragments of antique legends.'

In this view, while history does not actually repeat itself, events may echo (or rhyme with) previous occurrences – for example, the intervention of the United States and its allies in Afghanistan in 2001 did not exactly repeat the Soviet occupation of that country between 1979 and 1989, but one may discern similarities in the two campaigns.

The observation that events recur is as old as history itself, from the Book of Ecclesiastes in the Old Testament of the Bible – 'There is nothing new under the sun' – to Nietzsche's doctrine of eternal recurrence, and even to Machiavelli's consideration that the study of the past would reveal repeating patterns.

Twain's strong social conscience would have made him acutely aware that those in positions of power were most in need of this awareness. However, knowing how to read the entrails of history does not necessarily imply that such knowledge will be used to benefit anyone other than the one who knows. **LW**

"We are all in the gutter, but some of us are looking at the stars."

Oscar Wilde

Lady Windermere's Fan

1892

This moving observation on the human condition is made by the character Lord Darlington, who has just had his declaration of love for Lady Windermere rejected. He is sitting writing letters while his male companions engage in light-hearted banter, and his interjection causes some merriment. Nevertheless, it punctures the cynical atmosphere with a moment of sincerity. What links us is the bitter struggle to live; however, a few of us open our eyes to the sky and see that beauty can change everything.

At the end of the first performance of *Lady Windermere's Fan*, Wilde congratulated the audience on their good taste. He added that it persuaded him they thought 'almost as highly of the play as I do myself'. Having risen to prominence on the basis of his wit, Wilde died disgraced and bankrupt, despite his determination to live beyond the bounds of social mores. Most quotations from Oscar Wilde are at least mildly ironic. This one is oddly prescient. His life was as broad in scope as any Greek tragedy: he shone with brilliance but society could not bear his open challenge, and he was honoured only by posterity. **LW**

◭ Wilde's words are immortalized in street art above a takeout restaurant in Bristol, England.

◭ Irish wit and playwright Oscar Wilde photographed in 1882 by Napoleon Sarony.

> " *Things bygone are the only things that last: The Present is mere grass, quick-mown away; The Past is stone, and stands for ever fast.* "

▲ The vestibule of the ancient Roman baths at Herculaneum in Italy.

Eugene Lee-Hamilton
Sonnets of the Wingless Hours
1894

In the first eight lines of 'Roman Baths,' a Petrarchan sonnet in the above collection, English poet Eugene Lee-Hamilton describes a visit to the overgrown ruins of ancient Roman baths. Underneath these baths, rich mosaic decorations were later discovered. As is customary, the last six lines of the sonnet extract a moral, stated in the above tercet. The first line reiterates the theme of the sonnet. Since the past was already described as '[t]he only thing which can never decay,' it was necessary for Lee-Hamilton to avoid repeating himself: he cleverly managed it by dabbling in paradox. The second line alludes both to the grass that literally covered the baths and to the transitoriness of life, via a familiar phrase from the Bible, 'All flesh is grass' (Isaiah 40:6). The third line similarly alludes both to the stone of which the baths were constructed and to the permanence of God's word: 'The grass withers, the flower fades: but the word of our God shall stand for ever' (Isaiah 40:8).

Lee-Hamilton was a diplomat who turned to poetry after he fell victim to a cerebrospinal disease that left him paralyzed and in constant pain. **GB**

"Those who cannot remember the past are condemned to repeat it."

George Santayana
The Life of Reason
1905–06

Spanish-born American essayist, philosopher, poet and novelist George Santayana was founder of Harvard University's philosophical club and a cofounder of the literary journal *The Harvard Monthly*, as well as contributing editor and cartoonist for *The Harvard Lampoon*. He regarded himself as American, but in 1912 he returned to Europe, where he remained until his death in 1952. It was during his residency in the United States that he wrote his epic, five-volume *The Life of Reason*. The above quotation appears in volume one, *Reason in Common Sense*. It has occasionally been attributed to Edmund Burke, who wrote something similar in a 1790 pamphlet: 'People will not look forward to posterity, who never look backward to their ancestors.' The phrase suggests that progress alone is not healthy for society and that there must be an awareness, an ability to recall the past. If change is absolute, then there is a strong certainty that the same mistakes will be repeated. For society to change for the better, it is necessary to learn from the mistakes that have been made. Santayana's epic work, which was subtitled 'The Phases of Human Progress,' remained the key work in understanding his moral philosophy. **IHS**

◉ Santayana used to tear pages out of the book he was reading and take them out to read in the sunshine.

> " *The present contains nothing more than the past, and what is found in the effect was already in the cause.* "

La Leçon de Philosophie dans les Fleurs.

◉ Henri Bergson giving a philosophy lecture after his election to the Académie Française in 1914.

Henri Bergson
Creative Evolution
1907

In *Creative Evolution*, French philosopher Henri Bergson contrasts 'unorganized bodies' with 'organized bodies,' such as living beings. Unorganized bodies have no individuality of their own and are regulated by the law expressed in the above words. The fact that drawers can be removed from a chest, he suggests, shows that the pieces were separate all along. But the situation is different for living beings. The fact that a number of worms can be regenerated from the fragments of a single worm does not show that there was not a single worm in the first place. The argument here plays a role in Bergson's philosophy of biology. Neither mechanism nor teleology explains evolutionary novelty, he argues: creative evolution requires a 'vital impetus' ('*élan vital*').

The phrasing of Bergson's law of organized bodies is reminiscent of a medieval doctrine used by 17th-century French philosopher René Descartes in one of his arguments for the existence of God: the principle that there can be nothing in an effect which is not previously present in the cause. Later in his book, Bergson is explicit that the mechanistic view of life that he opposes derives from a strand of Descartes' thought. **GB**

> *Without words, without writing and without books there would be no history, there could be no concept of humanity.*

Hermann Hesse
Gertrude
1910

Early in life, Hermann Hesse developed a concept of humanity and a love of books and writing. German-born, he had Estonian and French-speaking Swiss as well as German ancestors. He lived in Basel, Switzerland, for part of his childhood, and eventually settled there in 1899, trading antique books. He had ambitions to be a poet, but his literary genius went unnoticed until he published the novel *Peter Camenzind* in 1904. German militarism troubled him, even in his adopted country, and many of his books were suppressed in Occupied Europe under Nazi rule and not republished until long after the German defeat in 1945. The Nazis sought to destroy anything in writing that challenged their own view of humanity and its history, so Hesse's internationalism and pacifism were natural targets for them.

The above quotation from *Gertrude* is sonorous but not necessarily easy to agree with. In Hesse's day, books were the chief way in which ideas were transmitted, but many societies had no written language. They did not have books to preserve their history, but that did not mean that they had no concept of humanity – books and culture often go together, but they are not necessarily interdependent. **JF**

> *The Past is like a funeral gone by The Future comes like an unwelcome guest.*

Edmund Gosse
Collected Poems
1911

By deprecating both the past and the future, the above couplet is in effect recommending living in the present. Indeed, the poem 'May-Day' continues by urging the reader to emulate birds and flowers that:

'. . .sifting all things, find the Present best,
And garnish life with that philosophy'.

Gosse's thought was not original: for example, in 1834, US poet and essayist Ralph Waldo Emerson wrote in his journal: 'With the past, I have nothing to do; nor with the future. I live now,' and Emerson himself may have been influenced by Buddhist scriptures. By selecting concrete emblems of past and future that are both familiar and disagreeable, however, Gosse achieved a memorable version, if lighter in tone, of the thought.

Nevertheless, Gosse was sufficiently concerned about the past to write a biography of Sir Walter Raleigh, the English courtier and poet of the late 16th and early 17th centuries, and about times to come to write a pamphlet entitled 'The Future of English Poetry'.

By his own account Gosse was not so enthusiastic about the present when he was eight years old. Then, according to his memoir *Father and Son* (1907), 'There was no past and no future for me, and the present felt as though it were sealed up in a Leyden jar [a device that stores static electricity]'. **GB**

"We two kept house, the Past and I . . . I tended while it hovered nigh, leaving me never alone."

Thomas Hardy

Satires of Circumstance

1914

Thomas Hardy, English poet and novelist, was born early in Queen Victoria's reign (1837–1901) but lived into the age of modernism in literature. Largely self-educated, he became skilled in classical poetic forms, which he used in his own poetry and which sometimes made his poems excessively formal for some tastes. His novels challenged social mores, and he was noted for his sympathetic portrayal of women. His own relationship with his first wife, Emma, went sour, however, and when she died in 1912, he was filled with remorse. His rediscovery of his youthful love for her inspired *Satires of Circumstance*, a collection of poems, including 'The Ghost of the Past', the source of the above quotation.

This poem of five eight-line stanzas is complex, subtle and open to interpretation. The subject ('I') at first lives closely with the Past in 'a spectral housekeeping/Where fell no jarring tone – perhaps in contrast to Hardy's 'housekeeping' (cohabitation) with his wife, which had often jarred badly. Then gradually, the Past recedes and becomes a 'fitful far-off skeleton/Dimming as days draw by'. If time heals all wounds, this may be the way it works. JK

⊘ Thomas Hardy regarded himself as a poet by temperament and a novelist only by necessity.

I realise that patriotism is not enough. I must have no bitterness or hatred towards any one.

Edith Cavell
Final words
1915

British nurse Edith Cavell was sentenced to death by firing squad in a German military court in 1915, for hiding Allied soldiers after the retreat from Mons during World War I. While working at a Red Cross hospital in Brussels, she nursed soldiers of both sides diligently, but establishing the secret safe route for hunted men through German-occupied Belgium to neutral Holland was to her mind a humanitarian act equal to caring for the wounded.

The day before her execution, she was visited by Reverend Stirling Gahan, British chaplain in Brussels, to whom she said the above words. Cavell was hailed in Britain as a war hero who died for her country. After the war she was given a state funeral in London, in May 1919, and a statue was erected in her memory.

Arrested in July 1915, Cavell was not executed until October. She spent the last ten weeks of her life quietly reflecting on her Christian beliefs. She had proved her patriotism by risking her life to save British soldiers from capture, but she realized this was not all her faith demanded of her: she forgave her executioners, refusing to feel bitterness towards them. JF

⊙ Edith Cavell, whose statue now stands just off Trafalgar Square in central London.

"The old Lie: Dulce et decorum est Pro patria mori."

⊘ Generally regarded as the greatest World War I poet, Wilfred Owen wanted to convey 'the pity of war.'

Wilfred Owen
'Dulce et Decorum Est'
1917–18

Wilfred Owen was one of several talented poets who served as soldiers during World War I and recorded in memorable verse the horrors that they witnessed. Like Siegfried Sassoon and Rupert Brooke, Owen fought on the frontline, where his experiences led him to despair at man's capacity for violence and the ruthlessness of the military hierarchy. Owen's most acclaimed work is 'Dulce et Decorum Est', which, borrowed from the Roman poet Horace, means 'It is sweet and honourable,' Horace's verse continues, 'pro patria mori' – 'to die for one's country.' Owen's poem was written in 1917, revised in 1918, and published in 1920. Owen died on 4 November 1918, seven days before the conflict's end.

Owen wrote the poem at Craiglockhart War Hospital in Edinburgh, where he had been sent to convalesce following a diagnosis of neurasthenia (shell shock). It is comprised of two sonnets that resemble the French ballade poetic form, albeit with breaks away from convention that serve to reinforce the terrible events he recounts. The first part takes place in the present and describes a gas attack. The second recalls the event and questions the notion of patriotism. **IHS**

"Human history becomes more and more a race between education and catastrophe."

H G Wells
The Outline of History
1920

Herbert George Wells, who was born in England in 1866, was best known as a writer of speculative fiction. His science-based futuristic novels included *The Time Machine* (1895), *The Invisible Man* (1897), *The War of the Worlds* (1898) and *The First Men in the Moon* (1901). Hugely popular at the time of their publication, his 'scientific romances,' as he called them, pioneered themes that would later be adapted for cinema with big-budget productions such as the 1953 Hollywood epic version of *The War of the Worlds*.

Wells's subject matter gradually moved to more conventional themes, with novels like *The History of Mr Polly* (1910), set in lower middle-class England before World War I. Already a committed socialist, Wells was prompted by the outbreak of war to take a more socially conscious path, with writing that reflected both his political and moral concerns, in speculative nonfiction about the future of society. In *The Outline of History* he voiced his deepest concerns generated by the disastrous conflict, about technological change running at a far faster pace than our understanding of one another, and the civilizing power of truly humanistic education. **ME**

◉ H G Wells wrote about the future of society in works such as *The Time Machine*, made into a popular movie in 1960.

> # *The history of men's opposition to women's emancipation is more interesting perhaps than the story of that emancipation itself.*

Virginia Woolf – a leading literary modernist of the 20th century – pictured during the 1930s.

❯ Suffragist Charlotte Despard gives an impromptu speech at London's Trafalgar Square (c. 1935).

Virginia Woolf
'A Room of One's Own'
1929

Virginia Woolf was born in London in 1882, and died in 1941, during World War II. Her life thus spanned a period of great social change in England, which is reflected in her writing. The extended essay 'A Room of One's Own' – based on lectures she had delivered at the University of Cambridge – employs a fictional narrator and narrative to examine women as both writers of, and characters in, fiction. Woolf explores the history of patriarchy and its deleterious effects on women's writing. The essay is particularly memorable for her invention of the tragic character Shakespeare's sister, whom the patriarchy bars from receiving the school education given to her male sibling and thus prevents from developing her genius.

It was Woolf's contention that 'a woman must have money and a room of her own if she is to write fiction'. Her particular interest was in the ways in which men opposed feminists as they pursued their ultimate objective – the full emancipation of women. In her work Woolf repeatedly highlights the effects of patriarchy, not only in women's experience, but also in the brutal aspects of imperialism and war. JF

> ## " We can only pay our debt to the past by putting the future in debt to ourselves."

John Buchan
Speech to the Boy Scouts Association
1939

John Buchan was born in Scotland in 1875. He is mainly remembered for his fast-paced action novels, including *The Thirty-Nine Steps* (1915), featuring patriotic and imperialistic heroes, such as Richard Hannay. But Buchan was also a war correspondent for *The Times*, a London newspaper, and a member of the British Parliament. He became Baron Tweedsmuir when he was appointed governor-general of Canada in 1935, a post which he held until his death in 1940. He was also Chief Scout of Canada during this time, and made the above remark in his annual address to the Boy Scouts Association in 1939. Prevented from giving the speech in person due to ill health, it was broadcast from his sickbed in Ottowa. Robert Baden-Powell, founder of the Scout Movement, described the address as 'one of the most inspiring that has ever been given to the scouts in Canada'.

But how much of a debt do we actually owe to the past? Since we cannot judge what future generations will regard as good, we cannot be sure that they will feel indebted to us at all. They will be influenced, certainly, but not necessarily indebted. Yet the intention of Buchan's words is clear: we should always act with one eye on the future, and what we do today will undoubtedly impact later generations, beneficially or detrimentally.

A man of his time, John Buchan believed that the debt his generation owed to the past was a positive one and that therefore the legacy they left future generations should be positive too. But if we doubt the former, can we ensure the latter? **JF**

> ## " Our image of happiness is indissolubly bound up with . . . our view of the past, which is the concern of history."

Walter Benjamin
On the Concept of History
1940

Walter Benjamin was a German Jewish philosopher and critical theorist. Known only to a limited audience during his lifetime, he became famous with the posthumous publication of his numerous works.

Although the above quotation is sometimes taken to mean that in order to understand the concept of happiness, it is necessary first to understand the historical context in which it occurred, his actual thought was: 'Our image of happiness is indissolubly bound up with the image of redemption. The same applies to our view of the past, which is the concern of history.' He is, therefore, not asserting a connection between happiness and the past, but between happiness and the past on the one hand and redemption on the other hand.

Although the theses in *On the Concept of History* are enigmatic, a metaphor later in the work is helpful in understanding the central theme of redemption. German philosopher and cultural critic Walter Benjamin imagines the angel of history, facing towards the past, but propelled by a storm, which 'is what we call progress,' towards the future: 'The angel would like to stay, awaken the dead, and make whole what has been smashed.' Using a different theological metaphor, he describes the present as endowed with a messianic power of recovering the past, which it is obliged to use. So the task of the historian, in Benjamin's view, is essentially redemptive. **GB**

"Nothing changes more constantly than the past; for the past that influences our lives does not consist of what actually happened, but what men believe happened."

Gerald White Johnson
American Heroes and Hero Worship
1943

Gerald White Johnson, who died in 1980, was a prolific journalist, historian, biographer, novelist and essayist, whose career spanned nearly three-quarters of a century. Born in 1890, he began writing professionally at the age of twenty years, joining the staff of local papers, including the *Lexington Dispatch* and *Greensboro Daily News*. After serving in World War I with the American Expeditionary Forces, he began a long affiliation with the *Baltimore Evening Sun* and *Baltimore Sun*, where he forged a reputation as a forthright humanist and liberal thinker.

Johnson retired in 1926 to concentrate on writing books, which he published on a regular basis. These mainly consisted of historical critiques and commentaries on contemporary US society. In an era when even a whiff of leftism was deemed unpatriotic, he made no apologies for his progressive stance on political and social issues. Always sceptical of the received wisdom of accepted sources, as voiced in the quotation from his 1943 book *American Heroes and Hero Worship*, he was described in an obituary in the *Greensboro Daily News* as 'a stirrer-upper, a writer who looked beyond his own time, a progressive voice in an often conservative wilderness'. **ME**

"History is written by the winners."

George Orwell
Tribune magazine
1944

George Orwell, the pen name of Eric Arthur Blair, was an English journalist, essayist and novelist. Prevalent in his work are the themes of opposition to totalitarianism and support for democratic socialism. He is best known for his allegorical novella *Animal Farm* (1945) and his dystopian novel *Nineteen Eighty-Four* (1949).

The above quotation is often misattributed to British politician Winston Churchill (who said to the House of Commons in 1948 that he wanted the past left to history as 'I propose to write that history') and also to German philosopher and cultural critic Walter Benjamin, who wrote that 'adherents of historicism actually…empathize with the victor'. However, it was Orwell who made the above remark in his 'As I Please; column in *Tribune*, a British democratic socialist magazine.

Orwell began the piece by recounting the tale of Sir Walter Raleigh who, after being unable to uncover the reason for a lethal quarrel he witnessed, is said to have burned the history of the world that he was writing in despair at ever being able to present an accurate version of events. This difficulty to establish the truth was something that Orwell found particularly worrying with regard to the contemporary political situation in Europe. He warned that the lies told by totalitarian regimes not only risked distorting the records for future historians, but attacked 'the concept of objective truth'.

In the quotation above, Orwell is acknowledging what was, for him, the uncomfortable truth that might is right – that the most widely disseminated accounts of the past will be those created by people who have thrived in the prevailing political climate, no matter how those conditions have been achieved. **JE**

> # "The most effective way to destroy people is to deny and obliterate their own understanding of their history."

George Orwell
Attributed
c. 1948

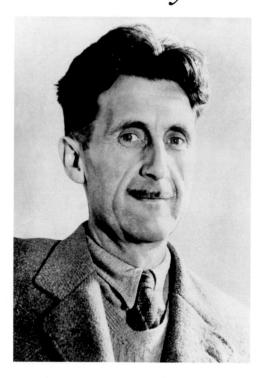

🔺 Born Eric Arthur Blair, George Orwell took the second part of his pen name from the River Orwell in East Anglia.

🔻 A still from the 1956 movie adaptation of *Nineteen Eighty-Four*.

George Orwell, the English journalist, essayist and novelist, was concerned with themes of social injustice, opposition to totalitarianism and support of democratic socialism. He is best known for his dystopian novel *Nineteen Eighty-Four* (1949), his allegorical novella *Animal Farm* (1945) and his nonfiction, which included *Homage to Catalonia* (1938), an account of his experiences in the Spanish Civil War.

The above quotation is often attributed to Orwell. It seems most likely to derive from paraphrasing of other Orwellisms, or a general impression of his work more broadly. It remarks on the power granted by establishing ideological control via the destruction of the oppressed's knowledge of themselves. Prominent among those who have reacted against this tendency are Muhammad Ali and Malcolm X, who in the 1960s changed their names because they believed that their previous names had been imposed on them by oppressive whites.

Regardless of disputes about the authorship of these words, they contain an important lesson: that we should guard carefully against attempts to dominate us by altering our history. JE

PARTY
AREA
2

BIG BROTHE

IS WATCHIN
YOU

"*It is a fair summary of history to say that the safeguards of liberty have been forged in controversies involving not very nice people.*"

● Felix Frankfurter in his Harvard classroom in 1939, the year he was appointed an associate justice to the US Supreme Court.

Felix Frankfurter
United States vs Rabinowitz
1950

After he sold four postage stamps with forged overprints (which increased their value to collectors) to an undercover federal agent, Albert J Rabinowitz was arrested. Government agents searched his office without a warrant and found 573 more forged stamps. Rabinowitz was subsequently indicted, tried and convicted of illegal possession of the stamps, but he appealed the conviction on the grounds that the search violated his rights under the Fourth Amendment to the US Constitution, which requires warrants for searches. The appeal court reversed the verdict, but the case was then appealed to the Supreme Court. The above quotation comes from Justice Frankfurter's opinion. Describing Rabinowitz as 'a shabby defrauder,' Frankfurter insisted that, nevertheless, principle as well as precedent required that the search be deemed unlawful. The majority of justices disagreed, however.

Rabinowitz was not the only dubious character involved in a legal case with broader implications. For example, Ernesto Miranda, namesake of the Miranda warning (right to silence) given by police in the United States to criminal suspects, was convicted of rape. **GB**

"For all at last returns to the sea ... the beginning and the end."

Rachel Carson
The Sea Around Us
1951

Born and raised in Springdale, Pennsylvania, Carson started out as an English major at Johns Hopkins University, then changed to zoology. She later worked for the US Bureau of Fisheries and found fame as a writer.

The above quotation is the final sentence of her best-selling book about marine biology. Her more famous environmental science work, *Silent Spring* (1962), highlighted the destructive effects of the pesticide DDT, but both books are relevant to this quotation. Carson maintained that we are part of a cyclical, integrated system: 'Oceanus, the ocean river, like the ever-flowing stream of time.' The quotation is both metaphorically and literally accurate: we are in and of the land and air, but we are predominantly made of water. The salty blood in our veins is a pulsing reminder that we evolved, as every creature did, from the sea. The ocean cradled us from our single-celled beginnings but like us, the land itself exists in flux and will return to the sea. Continents dissolve, particle by particle, in rivers. Soil is carried in the wind or forms nuclei for rain that runs into the ocean, and then materializes, just as our own bones are calcified, into the patterned forms of rock.

This is both comforting and humbling: we belong here, with all that surrounds and encompasses us. Yet it is also a reminder that we flourish or perish as an element of larger systems and that, therefore, we should respect this cyclical flow. **LW**

"The past is a foreign country: they do things differently there."

L P Hartley
The Go-Between
1953

These words form the opening sentence of Hartley's celebrated novel, which was filmed in 1970 in a version directed by Joseph Losey, scripted by Harold Pinter, and starring Alan Bates and Julie Christie. The narrator is recalling events that took place some fifty years earlier in the summer of 1900, when he was approaching his thirteenth birthday. The novel's themes include the problematic structure of British society and the origins and consequences of emotional detachment, all of which create a sense of being a stranger in a strange land. Another theme is how we use rites and signs to influence events, thinking that we are more powerful than we really are. This too is a symbol of a kind of cultural paradigm that looks foreign from the outside.

We are bound and directed by the past in ways that we could never be to a place separated from us by geographical distance. Yet Hartley's phrase has gained gravitas. Societies shift, behaviour shifts and to act differently is to manifest a different way of thinking. Culture is of its time, and we cannot hang on to things as they once were any more than we can return to the past. Hartley himself was something of an outsider, and his book concerns both being out of place, and, looking back, being out of time. Memory shifts depending on where you are looking from, and the past is transfigured each time we revisit it, reinventing itself in some more or less altered form. **LW**

> ❝ *That men do not learn very much from the lessons of history is the most important of all the lessons that history has to teach.* ❞

● The British-born writer Aldous Huxley applied for US citizenship but was refused because of his pacifism.

Aldous Huxley
Esquire magazine
1956

Aldous Huxley was born in 1894 into an aristocratic English family. He was related to many of the intellectual giants of the Victorian era, including Thomas and Matthew Arnold, Julian Huxley and Mrs Humphrey Ward. Famous for the dystopian novel *Brave New World* (1932), set in a totalitarian consumerist future society, he also wrote nonfiction. His interests were wide-ranging and included Greek history, neurology, psychology and pharmacology. He died in Los Angeles the day John F Kennedy was assassinated: 22 November 1963.

This quotation begins Huxley's essay 'A Case of Voluntary Ignorance,' in which he wryly critiqued the principle 'if you wish for peace, prepare for war,' first articulated under the Roman Empire. Observation of this maxim has resulted, he explained, in every civilized country spending almost half of every century at war. *The March of Folly* (1984), by US historian Barbara Tuchman, travels the same philosophical road, showing that 'the pursuit of policy contrary to the self-interest of the constituency or state involved' is an all-too-common historical phenomenon. But Huxley's comment is a counsel of despair. **JF**

"Progress may have been all right once, but it has gone on too long."

Ogden Nash
The New Yorker magazine
1959

The above quotation appears in a poem entitled 'Come, Come, Kerouac! My Generation is Beater Than Yours.' The author was addressing the Beat generation novelist and poet Jack Kerouac, whose jazzlike poetry was not to Nash's liking. A master of light verse, Nash intentionally completed the couplet with a rhyming line of dissimilar length and irregular meter: 'I think progress began to retrogress when Wilbur and Orville started tinkering around in Dayton and at Kitty Hawk, because I believe that two Wrights made a wrong.' His antipathy to air travel was sincere: after a difficult flight in 1937, Nash never flew again.

Regardless of the specific example of excessive progress, Nash's line expresses a mild degree of nostalgia that is psychologically plausible. Generally, owing to a phenomenon known as cognitive ageing (a normal consequence of ageing, distinct from dementia), learning is easier for the young and harder for the old. The young are thus poised to benefit from, and therefore to appreciate, progress, whereas the old, while perhaps appreciating progress in the past, find progress in the present to be uncomfortably hard to assimilate. **GB**

◉ The prolific American poet and humorist Ogden Nash, photographed in 1931.

" *Houston, we've had a problem.* "

James Lovell
Apollo 13
1970

One of the most famous quotations of modern times, the words uttered by US astronaut James Lovell on the Apollo 13 mission are often misquoted as 'Houston, we have a problem,' as in the movie *Apollo 13* (1995).

Apollo 13 was planned as the third manned landing on the moon, with a crew of John 'Jack' Swigert Jr, commander James Lovell, and Fred Haise Jr. But two days after the launch on 11 April 1970, an oxygen tank exploded onboard, causing an electrical failure. The crew reported back to command base in Houston, Texas; the conversation is now part of space exploration history:

'Swigert: I believe we've had a problem here.
Houston: This is Houston, say again, please.
Lovell: Houston, we've had a problem. We've had a main bus B undervolt.'

The seriousness of the situation was understated by the cool language employed. The damaged oxygen tank crippled the spacecraft's service module, upon which the command module depended. As a result the lunar landing had to be aborted. Anxious millions watched on television as the mission headed back to Earth in a semicrippled capsule with reduced heating, limited water and a damaged carbon dioxide removal system. Eventually, the astronauts splash-landed safely on 17 April, six days after blastoff. **ME**

◉ Flight controllers at Houston prepare to land Apollo 13.

" *The past is full of life, eager to irritate us, provoke and insult us, tempt us to destroy or repaint it.* "

Milan Kundera
The Book of Laughter and Forgetting
1979

We want to be master of the future, novelist Milan Kundera tells us early in his fifth novel, *The Book of Laughter and Forgetting*, so that we can change the past. It is through the manipulation of past events, or the recording and recollection of those events, that individuals and groups control how they will be regarded.

Milan Kundera remains one of the most famous writers of Czechoslovakia's Communist era. Although his early work featured a strong political slant, his novels steered clear of any party line, often employing satire and absurdism to explore the role of systems and the people who occupy them. *The Book of Laughter and Forgetting* was his first work to be published in France, where he moved in 1979 after his Czech citizenship was revoked, and he became a French citizen in 1981. It set the template of the books he subsequently wrote in exile. Here Kundera muses on all manner of subjects, through a series of short stories. The quotation comes from an account of Mirek, a loyal Communist Party member who has fallen out of favour, and compares the ability of regimes to rewrite history with his own attempts to eradicate a former lover from his life. **IHS**

"*It takes great courage to break with one's past history and stand alone.*"

⬥ Marion Woodman, the Jungian analyst and well-known writer on feminine psychology.

Marion Woodman
Addiction to Perfection: The Still Unravished Bride
1982

Woodman is here discussing women with compulsive eating disorders, such as anorexia. Her attitude towards the therapeutic role of groups, such as Overeaters Anonymous, is mixed. While she regards compulsive syndromes as solitary – 'Real compulsives carry out their rituals alone' – and she acknowledges that understanding from others is helpful in alleviating them, she also warns that such groups may have their own agendas. Moreover, whatever help they may provide, it is still up to individuals to find their own path to her 'healing archetypal pattern' (a phrase showing Woodman's debt to psychologist Carl Jung). The above words both acknowledge the difficulty of doing so, and salute those who succeed in doing so.

Woodman's is not a particularly original thought. In 1966, for example, an ad for a brand of men's pants showed a pod of peas over the slogan: 'Sure, it takes courage to break with the past. But what are you, a man or a green pea?' Whatever validity there is to Woodman's observation in the context in which it was offered, it is plausible to suppose that there are situations in which it would take greater courage to accept one's past. **GB**

"What we may be witnessing is not just the end of the Cold War ... but the end of history."

Francis Fukuyama
The National Interest
1989

The year 1989 saw the fall of Soviet-controlled Communism. The political rift between East and West, which had dominated geopolitics since the end of World War II, was healed. Over the next few years most countries in the former Eastern Bloc became democratic, and it was in this context that Fukuyama's essay 'The End of History?' appeared in this conservative journal.

Its title notwithstanding, Fukuyama's claim was not that history, or events that make up history, would cease to exist, but that liberal democracy had won out and would dominate in the future. Champions of Fukuyama's rhetoric believed that a world enveloped by capitalist democratic institutions would cease to wage war. However, critics were quick to note the essay's short-term perspective on human history. Since the events of 11 September 2001, it is viewed by many as a naive notion from a relatively peaceful period of history. Fukuyama has distanced himself from some of his ideas, albeit for different reasons to those of his critics, suggesting in *Our Posthuman Future* (2002) that human scientific development is the greatest threat to liberal democracy. **IHS**

⬧ The political scientist Francis Fukuyama, who argued that human history as a struggle between ideologies was at an end.

" *Clinging to the past is the problem. Embracing change is the answer.* "

Gloria Steinem
Moving Beyond Words
1994

For almost five decades Gloria Steinem has been a key feminist. Her life reflects the attitude behind her quotation, which appeared in her sixth published book: if you want things to change, you must act and not wait for change to happen to you.

After spending two years in India in the late 1950s, Steinem became a journalist. Her first major story, for *Esquire* magazine, was about contraception, followed by an article in 1962 on the way women have to choose between a career and marriage. Yet she claims not to have become a feminist until 1969, when she covered an abortion rally for *New York* magazine. As the feminist movement gained momentum in the early 1970s, Steinem rose to prominence as one of its leading voices, cofounding *Ms.* magazine in 1972. She became politically active, both in domestic politics and on the international stage. Her 1979 article on female genital mutilation raised public consciousness of the subject, and she has continued to campaign for a universal ban on the practice. **IHS**

◔ Writer, lecturer, political activist and feminist Gloria Steinem.

" *We'll be remembered more for what we destroy than what we create.* "

Chuck Palahniuk
Invisible Monsters
1999

At one point in this novel three people – the narrator, Seth and Brandy – are at the top of the Space Needle in Seattle. Brandy tells the narrator and Seth to '[s]ave the world with some advice from the future,' and they accordingly inscribe their advice on a series of postcards, which Brandy kisses and lets sail over the city. The above words are written by Seth on the fourth postcard, preceded by: 'Only when we eat up this planet will God give us another.' Seth's postcard thus combines acknowledgement and resentment of the environmental crisis. A similar sentiment appears in the novel for which Palahniuk is best known, *Fight Club* (1996), in which the narrator complains: 'For thousands of years, human beings had screwed up and trashed and crapped on this planet, and now history expected me to clean up after everyone.'

A scientific counterpart of the above quotation is suggested by the term 'Anthropocene,' which denotes the geological epoch in which human activity began to impact on the planet. There is disagreement about the starting date of the Anthropocene, but the first detonation of a nuclear weapon in 1945 is a prime candidate. **GB**

Politics & Society

> ## " *To fight and conquer in all our battles is not supreme excellence; supreme excellence consists in breaking the enemy's resistance without fighting.* "

Sun Tzu
The Art of War
C. 500 BCE

Sun Tzu was a Chinese philosopher, general and strategist during the Spring and Autumn period (c. 771–476 BCE) of ancient China. He is traditionally credited as the author of this classic manual of military strategy, a work that focuses on practical advice for winning conflicts. The principles in *The Art of War* have a far wider applicability, however, and have influenced Western peacetime thought as much as Eastern.

The above quotation asserts that a spectacular military performance on the battlefield is not the smart way to pursue policy. The best strategy is to weaken the enemy subtly and covertly, so that it is rendered incapable of resistance before a sword is unsheathed or a shot is fired. As Sun Tzu wrote in an earlier passage: 'The best thing of all is to take the enemy's country whole and intact.' Winning with minimal destruction not only is ethically more desirable, but also gives the victor a better outcome – fewer casualties mean more people to carry out the conqueror's will, the greater the remaining wealth to exploit and the less wartime damage to repair. The greatest consideration is to overcome the foe without fighting and to win without conflict. JE

⊘ A 19th-century Chinese artist's impression of Sun Tzu, the reputed author of *The Art of War*.

"Famous men have the whole earth as their memorial."

Pericles
'Funeral Oration'
430 BCE

Pericles was a general and the most notable orator and statesman of the Golden Age of Greece. He became ruler of Athens in 461 BCE, and remained in power until his death in 429 BCE. The end of Pericles's leadership coincided with the beginning of the Peloponnesian War (431–404 BCE), which was sparked by friction between an increasingly powerful Athenian empire and the adjacent Peloponnesian states (including Sparta).

We find the above quotation in the *History of the Peloponnesian War*, by Greek historian Thucydides, a contemporary of the Athenian leader. In this section of his speech, Pericles highlights the greatness of Athens 'as she really is,' arguing that it results from Athenians who 'knew their duty' and were willing to sacrifice their lives for Athens. As a consequence they won timeless praises and glory 'in men's minds,' because 'in people's hearts their memory abides and grows' forever as a source of inspiration. Thus, Pericles's famous quotation is proposing that those who die bravely for their city-state and its people are immortalized in the hearts and minds of the individuals inspired by them, and that that kind of memorial is greater than any headstone. JE

⊘ This idealized bust of Pericles shows him as a soldier–citizen. It is a Roman copy in marble of an earlier portrait.

> # "What I say is that 'just' or 'right' means nothing but what is to the interest of the stronger party."

Thrasymachus
Quoted in Plato's *Republic*
c. 380 BCE

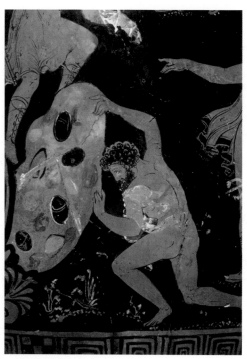

A detail of a Greek vase from the 4th century BCE depicts either Hercules or Sisyphus performing a feat of physical strength.

Thrasymachus (c. 459–400 BCE) was a Sophist philosopher in ancient Greece. In Plato's dialogue, he challenges Socrates on the nature of justice. The above quotation is the first of Thrasymachus's three considered definitions of justice. The others are that justice is no more or less than obedience to laws and that justice is nothing but the advantage of another. While the tension between the three definitions is a matter of continuing scholarly debate, the first is often treated as the central tenet of Thrasymachus's thought.

By saying, in effect, that justice and rightness are only what benefit the 'strong' over the 'weak,' Thrasymachus is challenging the notion that there is a reliable standard of morally or politically correct action beyond what benefits the powerful. Instead, he contends that power is the sole determinant of rightness and justice.

Thrasymachus's account is a powerful, normative challenge to debates over the nature of rightness and justice. In any society it is those who make the laws who hold the power, and it is therefore likely – perhaps even unavoidable– that they will legislate to their own advantage, and thus preserve the status quo. **JE**

"He who is to be a good ruler must have first been ruled."

Aristotle
Politics
C. 335 BCE

In *Politics*, Aristotle implies that the above quotation comes from another source, but it has since been widely attributed to the Greek philosopher himself. The statement occurs in the context of a discussion of political communities, which, it is suggested, are composed of two types of people: rulers and subjects.

Aristotle notes that age is an acceptable organic differentiation between those who rule and those who are ruled. Elders have a stronger claim to govern than the young – not only because of their longer experience of the world, but also, crucially, because they know what it is like to be governed. Their actions in power therefore will be influenced by their enhanced capacity to understand the concerns and issues of the ruled and to be sympathetic to their plight, while those who rule without ever having been ruled may be ignorant or indifferent to those whose lives they affect.

This is all sound in theory, but it may be objected that early experience of domination does not necessarily temper the behaviour of those who rise to power. Accession to power may change purpose – people who have been ruled and then gain power may decide simply to take whatever they can get for themselves and exploit those below them in the hierarchy, rather than act in the people's best interests. **JE**

"Man is by nature a political animal."

Aristotle
Politics
C. 335 BCE

Aristotle followed Plato and Socrates in discussing human nature, although his conclusions sometimes differed from theirs. One central defining element of humanity for Aristotle was the notion encapsulated in the above quotation, by which he meant that humans naturally develop increasingly complex communities, alongside characteristic divisions of labour.

By focusing on human beings as tending to form communities, Aristotle provided a firm challenge to the opposing notion that humans are individuals and individualistic, and that they can function satisfactorily in isolation and often choose to do so.

So powerful is the above quotation, and so influential has it since been, that few people today seriously argue that humankind prospers best in isolation. Individualism is seen as an important motivator, but few believe that detachment from society confers any blessings. Indeed, Aristotle's dictum is almost universally accepted as a matter of fact.

Once the premise of the dictum has been agreed, humankind can move on to detailed consideration of its social obligations within the political framework. If the formation of communities is natural, what should those social relations look like? What are our rights and obligations within such a society? We can continue to ask whether it is possible to reject society, and, if it is, what the implications are of so doing. **JE**

> *"Though bitter, good medicine cures illness. Though it may hurt, loyal criticism will have beneficial effects."*

Sima Qian
Records of the Grand Historian
C. 109 BCE

Records of the Grand Historian, also known as the *Shiji*, is a monumental work of historiography, completed by Sima Qian following the death of his father, who had begun the work. As a record of Chinese civilization over the previous twenty-five hundred years, the task would take about two decades to complete. But a few years after he had begun, Sima offended the Han emperor Wu (r. 141–87 BCE) by defending the character of a general who had defected to the enemy after suffering thousands of casualties when heavily outnumbered. Sima was castrated and imprisoned for three years.

After his punishments, Sima returned to work, and in keeping with the Confucian precept of avoiding direct confrontation with the authorities, he instead made veiled criticisms of certain figures in his biographical accounts. Thus, the above quotation aims to justify any unpalatable criticisms perceived in his writings. The remark is also relevant to loyalty in any important relationship. For example, rather than being an act of disloyalty, whistle-blowing is often motivated by loyalty to an organization's social responsibilities – clearly a higher authority than one's direct line manager. TJ

⬧ This engraving depicts a Chinese surgeon of the 1st century BCE, with assistants carrying his book and a medicinal gourd.

"We are just statistics, born to consume resources."

Horace
Epistles
21 BCE

As the pre-eminent Latin poet in the early period of the Roman Empire, Horace had established his literary reputation with his first book, *Satires*. One satire in the second book portrays the mythical Greek hero Ulysses, seeking to 'amass riches and heaps of money' after the many suitors of his wife, Penelope, had consumed all his goods while he was away fighting the Trojan War. In the first book of the *Epistles*, Horace returns to these same characters, but instead of satirizing them as morally corrupt, he adheres to Homer's account of their virtuous qualities, especially in extolling Ulysses for his strength of mind in resisting the entrapments of the Sirens and Circe. In contrast, Penelope's suitors are described as 'useless drones' who live only to 'consume resources'.

The above quotation suggests that all people are equally at the mercy of their continual need for resources, but Horace is certainly not counselling despair. On the contrary, Ulysses is shown to exemplify the moral virtues espoused by Epicurean philosophy, with its focus on living modestly, and avoiding the pursuit of 'empty' desires that can never be satisfied. Horace's advice is highly pertinent in today's consumer societies. TJ

This oil painting by Italian artist Camillo Miola (1877) imagines Horace at his country home.

Auberte the kynge of fra
ce was son of predis
tourhaunce he was
bethene Thomas Archbisshop of

"Will no one rid me of this turbulent priest?"

Henry II
Attributed
1170 CE

In 1162 the king of England appointed his friend Thomas Becket as the archbishop of Canterbury. He expected that Becket would allow him to avail himself of the Church's money. But Becket took his new responsibility seriously, refusing to hand over ecclesiastical funds, and thus provoked the king into making the above remark. On hearing the king's cry, four loyal knights immediately rode to Canterbury and stabbed the prelate to death before the altar of his cathedral in 1170.

The broad sequence of events is verifiably accurate, but there is a problem with the quotation – namely, there is no proof that Henry II ever said any such thing. It was probably a part of oral tradition for centuries, but the earliest written form of it appears in *History of the Life of King Henry the Second*, which was published in 1769, by the British statesman George Lyttelton.

A gap of almost six centuries between event and account is unusually long, but similar difficulties recur frequently in the study of medieval history – the earliest records are written many years after the events they purport to describe. **JP**

◀ Four knights carry out Henry II's request.

"In the kingdom of the blind, the one-eyed man is king."

Erasmus
Adagia
1500

This proverb is one of several thousand that Renaissance scholar Erasmus translated from Greek into Latin in his *Adagia*, where he also records an alternative version: 'Among the blind, the cross-eyed man is king.' The adage has a political meaning, suggesting that a relative disadvantage can become a source of power over those who are even more disadvantaged. But the richness of its analogy affords a much wider scope of interpretation and application. As Erasmus himself comments, if the blind are taken to represent the uneducated, then from their perspective 'one who is half-educated is considered very learned'. Erasmus also suggested that 'in tuneless company, the lark can sing'.

While the general meaning of the proverb serves as a reminder that power is relative rather than absolute, the metaphorical meaning of 'one-eyed' or 'cross-eyed' also permits a further layer of significance in the political interpretation, warning against the dangers of an uneducated public being manipulated by bigoted demagogues. Moreover, as the proverb can meaningfully apply to any form of social organization that strongly relies on, and rewards, leadership, it has extensive relevance throughout contemporary society. **TJ**

So long as the great majority of men are not deprived of either property or honour, they are satisfied.

Niccolò Machiavelli
The Prince
1513

An Italian Renaissance historian, philosopher and diplomat, Machiavelli is often described as the originator of modern political science, but he is nonetheless controversial, even today, for his apparent advocacy of immoral behaviour in pursuit of political power.

Perhaps a more charitable view is that Machiavelli was merely a chronicler of pragmatism in action. He seldom, if ever, recommended anything in particular; he merely reported what he had gathered from his own studies and from his personal observations.

The above quotation is an illustrative case in point. In all societies, throughout recorded history, it has been notable that ordinary people generally remain content with their lot for as long as they are not humiliated and can carry on their business more or less as usual. For example, after the Nazi invasion of many countries of Europe during World War II, resistance movements tried to undermine the occupying forces, but those who were not directly affected carried on as normal, not necessarily because they had any sympathy with Hitler, but because they felt powerless to stop him. Such people were not active collaborators. JP

I know I have the body but of a weak and feeble woman; but I have the heart and stomach of a king.

Elizabeth I
Tilbury speech
1588

This quotation is taken from the queen of England's famous address to her troops at the port of Tilbury, Essex, as they prepared themselves to repel an invasion by the Spanish Armada. Elizabeth was endeavouring to dispel any thoughts that her armed forces may have entertained that they were less effectively led by a female monarch than they would have been by a king. (She was the first undisputed queen regnant in British history.)

She draws attention to the fact that she has come before them with a minimal bodyguard; she places her trust in them. She then reassures them about her own powers with the above words and then adds that if anyone – not just the Spanish – attempts to invade England, she will herself 'take arms' and be the troops' 'general, judge and rewarder' of their virtues in the field.

What neither the monarch nor her subjects knew at the time was that the Spanish fleet, having been repelled from the Straits of Dover at the Battle of Gravelines the previous day, was on its way home by a circuitous route around the north of Scotland. JE

❯ Portrait of Elizabeth I (c. 1588), attributed to George Gower.

> **I want there to be no peasant in my kingdom so poor that he is unable to have a chicken in his pot every Sunday.**

Henry IV

Histoire du roy Henry le Grand
1589

King Henry IV of France (r. 1589–1610) has always maintained a reputation as a good king, but he was perhaps most notable for his cultivation of public opinion in pursuit of securing the throne for the Bourbon dynasty. His predecessors had been widely regarded as weaklings, but he portrayed himself as a man of action and described himself as a man with 'a weapon in hand and an arse in the saddle'.

Henry made prolonged, and largely successful, efforts to bring together the warring Protestants (Huguenots) and Roman Catholics within his country, although not everyone approved of his conciliatory policies: he survived two assassination attempts before he was stabbed to death by a third assailant, a fanatical Catholic.

This quotation appears in an account of the king's reign by Hardouin de Péréfixe, Archbishop of Paris. In 16th-century France, chicken was a luxury food item, so Henry's promise was of a standard of living well above subsistence level. And it was no empty promise: his subjects' wildest dreams were fulfilled. **JE**

◑ King Henry IV of France was also known as Henry of Navarre.

> **Friends, Romans, countrymen, lend me your ears.**

William Shakespeare

Julius Caesar
c. 1599

Julius Caesar tells the story of the betrayal and murder of the title character, a successful general who becomes leader of Rome. After Caesar has been in power for a short time, his allies start to fear that he will turn into a tyrant; they plot against him and stab him to death.

The above quotation begins the address made by one of the conspirators, Mark Antony, at Caesar's funeral. The speech outwardly praises those who plotted with him against Caesar, but implicitly criticizes them.

Shakespeare's writing is famously regarded as a model of rhetoric, because of its use of emotionally charged language. This opening line attempts to unite the mourners with one another and with the speaker himself. The speech is a model of how to manipulate a crowd through concealed flattery. By associating Romans, countrymen and friends, Mark Antony is deluding the audience into thinking that they are a tight unit, bound together by both patriotism and affection. He uses these traits to persuade those present to give him their full attention. Having gained it, he pours his subversive message into their ears and begins the process of outmanoeuvring the coconspirators, particularly Brutus and Cassius, his two fellow members of the triumvirate, in the struggle to fill the power vacuum left by the assassination. **JE**

"*A desperate disease requires a dangerous remedy.*"

Guy Fawkes
Attributed
1605

Guy Fawkes was one of a small group of Roman Catholic conspirators who tried to assassinate the Protestant King James I of England, along with members of both houses of the English Parliament, in what became known as the Gunpowder Plot. The aim of the leader, Robert Catesby, was to replace the king with the monarch's daughter, Princess Elizabeth, as a Catholic ruler. Fawkes was in charge of the explosives. The plot was thwarted on the night of 4–5 November 1605, when guards found up to twenty barrels full of explosives in a cellar beneath the Parliament building.

Fawkes is believed to have made the above remark on the following morning. For a while he refused to divulge the names of his fellow conspirators, but torture on the rack loosened his tongue, and most of those he identified were arrested. Fawkes was tried and convicted by a special court, and on 31 January 1606, he was hanged, drawn and quartered opposite the building he had tried to destroy. Three of his coconspirators – Thomas Wintour, Ambrose Rookwood and Robert Keyes – suffered the same fate. Catesby tried to escape but was shot dead while resisting arrest. JE

◎ Guy Fawkes (*left*) and coconspirator Robert Catesby.

◉ Engraving depicting the public execution of Guy Fawkes.

" *I will govern according to the common weal, but not according to the common will.* "

James I in the royal robes of state, holding the sceptre and orb that symbolized his office.

James I

Speech to Parliament

1621

The successor in 1603 to Queen Elizabeth I, James I – the first Stuart ruler of England, who was also King James VI of Scotland – was a committed advocate of royal absolutism. In an earlier speech to Parliament, he had referred to kings as 'God's lieutenants upon earth' who 'sit upon God's throne'. His insistence on the divine right of kings antagonized Parliament, creating the political climate that led to the English Civil War (1642–51).

James I is here stating some of the key demands of the divine right, namely that monarchs are subject to no earthly authority and that their authority to rule comes directly from God. He was the first English monarch who explicitly claimed this right.

James I means that he will rule for the good of his subjects ('weal' is 'wealth'), but that he will not be influenced by what people want ('the common will').

James I's idea that only he knew what was best did not play well with his subjects. After his death in 1625, his son Charles I persisted with the same policy. The rebellions against Charles's rule led to his deposition and execution in 1649. For the next nine years, England was ruled by Oliver Cromwell, Lord Protector. **JE**

"Love your neighbour, yet pull not down your hedge."

George Herbert
Outlandish Proverbs
1640

Proverbs that are popular in one generation may fall into disuse in the next, and either disappear altogether from active speech or become increasingly difficult to understand as their colloquialisms become archaic. Other sayings remain in common parlance, but only in part. For example, most modern native English speakers know the expression 'Give a dog a bad name,' which refers to the difficulty of losing a bad reputation, even an unjustified one, but few know the whole quotation, which is: 'Give a dog a bad name, and hang him.'

George Herbert's lovely collection has preserved several such sayings that might otherwise have been lost. The above remark is one of the axioms he recorded that addresses broadly political matters – for example, that relations between the owners of adjacent properties are notoriously fragile.

Elsewhere in Herbert's anthology there is plenty more of the same. For example, 'A fair wife and a frontier castle breed quarrels' alludes both to physical proximity (this time of contiguous states) and to sexual rivalry. Another great one that is ripe for revival is: 'Honour and profit lie not in one sack.' **JP**

George Herbert was an English cleric, a poet and a collector of idiomatic expressions.

"Man to Man is an errant wolf."

Thomas Hobbes
De Cive
1642

English philosopher Thomas Hobbes strongly influenced the history of political thought, particularly in his *Leviathan* (1651), which developed some of the themes outlined in the earlier *De Cive* (*On the Citizen*), the source of this quotation. *De Cive* is the first of a trilogy of works by Hobbes with human knowledge as their subject, along with *De Corpore* (*On the Body*, 1655) and *De Homine* (*On Man*, 1658).

'*Homo homini lupus*' ('man is a wolf to man') was a well-known saying in the tradition of political theory. It was originally found in Plautus's comic play *Asinaria* (195 BCE), and later countered by Seneca the Younger, who wrote that 'Man is something sacred for Man' (c. 65 CE). In the dedication to *De Cive*, Hobbes writes that there is truth in both assertions – 'Man to Man is a kind of God' accurately describes relations between citizens, while 'Man to Man is an errant wolf' reflects the attitudes of cities to one another.

Although Hobbes is often taken to mean that humans are predators of other humans, his actual point was that they might act fairly to those within their own societies, but think nothing of endangering peoples outside the societal boundaries. Hobbes is here referring to the potential threats that human beings may pose to one another. An obvious example is that of the slave trade, which had its origins in African chieftains using men and women captured from other tribes for bartering purposes. When the European colonizing powers required manpower, it was easy for them to exploit this pre-existing system. Both the chieftains and the Europeans respected their own communities but were a scourge on those existing outside them. **JE**

"The bigger the hat, the smaller the property."

English proverb
Unknown
c. 1650

The above phrase is now better known as an Australian expression. It occurs in exactly this form in the novel *The Merry-Go-Round in the Sea* (1965), but author Randolph Stow makes no claim to have coined it. Among the numerous variations in Antipodean culture is 'The smaller the property, the wider the brim,' as recorded in Dymphna Cusack's *Picnic Races* (1962). The saying is also found in American English: in *The Fighting Edge* (1922), William MacLeod Raine uses the expression, 'The bigger the hat, the smaller the herd.'

In each and every form, the meaning is the same: that the more extravagant the claim, the less impressive the underlying truth. Boastfulness is generally construed as an overcompensation for a sense of lack. Whether or not the person in question actually appears to be lacking in reality – in personal attributes or material assets – is almost immaterial. It is more significant that the wearer of the exaggeratedly large hat is assumed to have less to be proud of than modest people, who prefer not to call attention to themselves and are content to belittle their achievements in their public discourse.

The expression also raises the question of how much an observer can accurately infer from outward displays of wealth – one might, for example, assume that a man who comes to a business meeting in a Rolls-Royce automobile is very rich. But perhaps that is the impression he is trying to create, in order to conceal the fact that he lives in a tumbledown shack. The saying is a warning that things are seldom as they appear. It is important to remember, for example, that some of the world's most impressively booming economies have done so only by accepting eye-watering levels of debt. **JE**

"The law locks up the man who steals the goose from the common, but leaves the greater criminal loose who steals the common from the goose."

English convict saying
Unknown
c. 1650

The English medieval system of landholding included some land in each village that was kept 'in common'. Poor villagers who had no land of their own could keep a cow or some poultry on the common, where everyone's livestock shared the grazing. By 1500, recurrent episodes of bubonic plague had drastically reduced the population, and agricultural land was no longer farmed co-operatively, but parcelled into individual holdings. Under pressure from falling rents, landowners shut off the common land and farmed it themselves, often displacing people, as well as livestock. This process became known as 'enclosure'; each individual land enclosure required a separate Act of Parliament.

From 1600 onwards, the rural population rose sharply, and lack of common land became a problem. Hunger often resulted in people poaching livestock from what had been common land but was now 'owned' by the landlords. Robbery, even of the pettiest kind, was severely punished – by death or, later, by transportation to Australia when it became a penal colony. Political radicals opposed the Enclosures and sought reform of the justice system, including reduced penalties for theft. JF

⚓ A ship full of convicts sets sail from England for Australia. Their sayings became rooted in the fledgling nation's identity.

"In the moment of crisis, the wise build bridges and the foolish build dams."

Nigerian proverb
Unknown
c. 1650

In common with other proverbs, the origins of this saying are lost in the past. One of its meanings is that we need to be open-minded about solutions to problems, and seek new ideas rather than shoring up old ones. The proverb has been quoted in response to various situations, however: both literally, to suggest that development money is better spent on bridges than on dams, because large-scale dam building too often has caused the destruction of communities, whereas bridges open up communications between them; and metaphorically, to support the idea that bridges enable people to move forward, to travel somewhere new, whereas dams only hold back the tide of history.

The proverb is not as straightforward as it may seem. For one thing, crisis implies urgency – and construction works tend to be long-term projects. For another, it is not always wiser to build bridges than dams. When a storm surge is forecast on the coast, or heavy rain in the hills, it is wise to check that your flood defences are in order. The Dutch legend of the boy who put his finger in the dyke to prevent the water from farther opening the breach casts him as a hero, not as a fool. **JF**

In such condition there is no place for industry, because the fruit thereof is uncertain ... and the life of man solitary, poor, nasty, brutish and short.

Thomas Hobbes

Leviathan

1651

English philosopher Thomas Hobbes strongly influenced the history of political thought, particularly through the work from which the above quotation is taken, in which he advocated the need for an absolute sovereign to ensure peace. *Leviathan* was written in France, to which Hobbes had fled to escape the turmoil of the English Civil War.

Hobbes's theory develops from a set of strong arguments regarding human nature and the kinds of threats to individual welfare in the absence of a strong state. He argues that the state of nature of humanity is characterized by every individual living under threat – the 'war of every man against every man,' in which anyone could hurt or kill anyone else, motivated by desire or self-interest. This is the core of Hobbes's analysis – that positive industry is impossible under such conditions, as one's accomplishments or other pursuits can always be destroyed by another's violent interventions. While Hobbes's proposed solution – the rule of an absolute monarch – was controversial (as was his dark picture of human nature), his theoretical work was instrumental in the development of modern political science. JE

⊘ The title page of a revision of Thomas Hobbes's *Leviathan*, published in 1652, one year after the first edition came out.

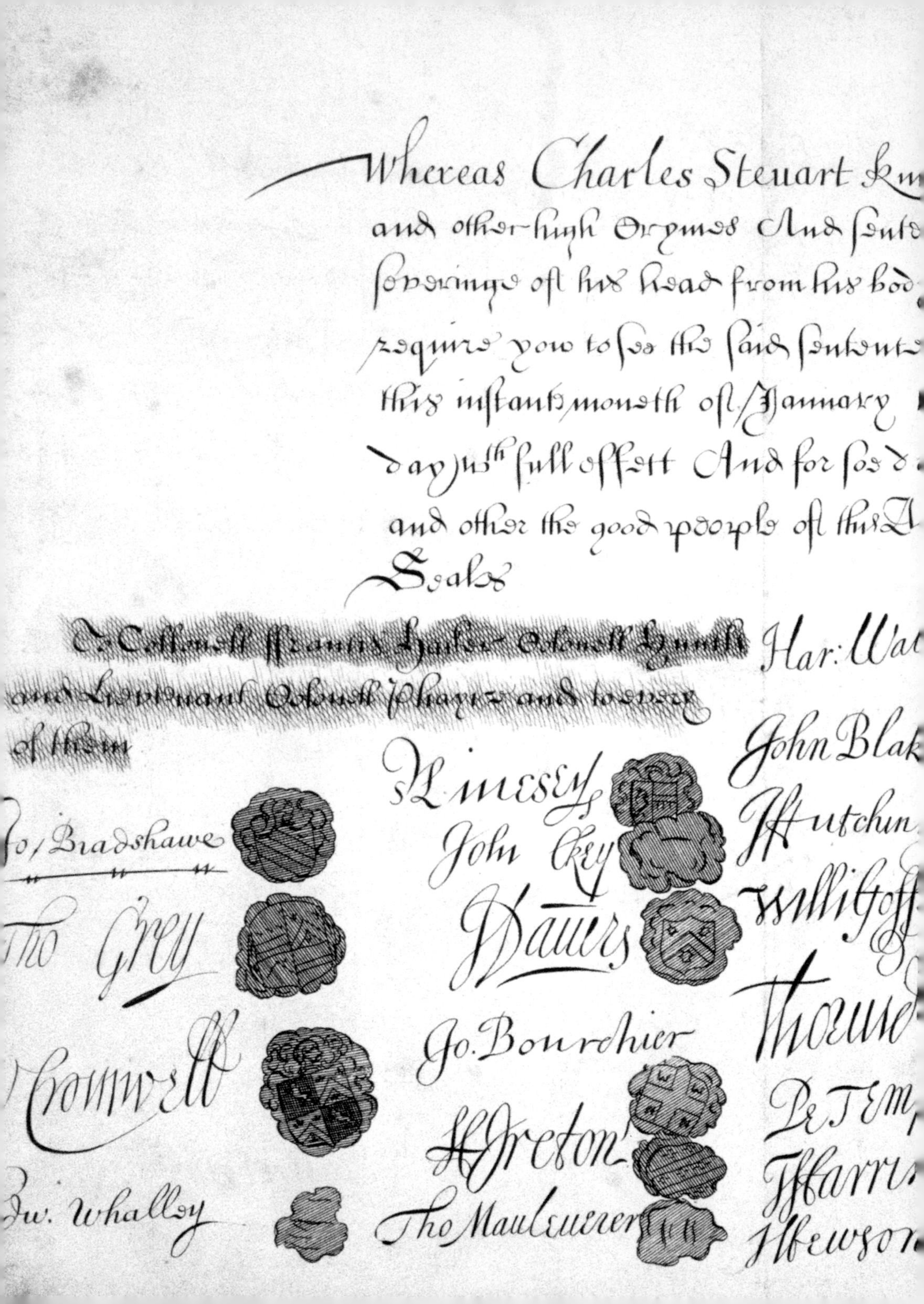

Whereas Charles Steuart Kinge

and other high Crymes And sente

sovrainge off his head from his bod

require you to see the said senten

this instant month of January

day)wth full effect And for soe d

and other the good people of this A

Seales

~~Co Collonell ffrancis Hacker Colonell Huncks~~ Har: Wal

~~and Lievtennant Colonell Phayre and to every~~

~~of them~~

Jo/ Bradshawe

Tho Grey

Cromwell

Ew. Whalley

Kinesey

John Okey

Dauers

Jo. Bourchier

H Ireton

Tho Mauleuerer

John Blak

Hutchin

willigoff

Thomas

De Tem

ffarri

Hewson

Necessity hath no law.

Oliver Cromwell
Speech to the First Protectorate Parliament
1654

This dictum is of ancient origin, and has been expressed in many forms, but its political meaning was highlighted when notably invoked by Cromwell in defending his assumption of power as Lord Protector of the Commonwealth, after the abolition of the English monarchy. As one of the regicides who signed the death warrant for King Charles I, Cromwell argued that his acceptance of the highest political office was necessary to ensure the future stability of government.

Even while arguing that the welfare of the populace must take precedence over any law, Cromwell acknowledged that the principle of necessity may be abused. The philosopher Immanuel Kant later made the same point, but he argued that such a drastic act as the execution of Charles I could never be a necessity, even if it prevented the citizens from suffering serious abuses. Nevertheless, Kant and earlier scholars, such as Thomas Aquinas, recognized that imminent threats to life or safety would sometimes require breaking the law. The fact that such a discretionary principle is now commonly applied in judicial reasoning shows that the law itself recognizes that its authority is not boundless. TJ

◔ Copy of a portrait of Cromwell (1654) by Sir Peter Lely, which the sitter demanded should show him with 'warts and all'.

◔ Copy of the death warrant of King Charles I (1649).

"God is usually on the side of the big squadrons against the small."

Roger de Rabutin, Comte de Bussy
Letter to the Comte de Limoges
1677

This is the best-known expression of a proverbial sentiment, although 'squadrons' is sometimes replaced by 'battalions'. The earliest version of the same idea is found in Book IV of the *Histories* by Tacitus, the Roman author of the 1st century CE – '*Deos fortioribus adesse*' ('The gods are on the side of the stronger'). In the 18th century, Voltaire gave his own variation: '*Dieu n'est pas pour les gros bataillons, mais pour ceux qui tirent le mieux*' ('God is on the side not of the big battalions, but of the best shots'). Most recently, Jean Anouilh provided another take in *L'Alouette* (*The Lark*, 1953), his play about Joan of Arc: '*Dieu est avec tout le monde. . .Et, en fin de compte, il est toujours avec ceux qui ont beaucoup d'argent et de grosses armées*' ('God is on everyone's side. . .And, in the last analysis, he is on the side of those with plenty of money and large armies').

The fatalism that overhangs this idea is widely accepted, but it is not universal. For example, the Book of Ecclesiastes in the Old Testament of the Bible states that '[t]he race is not to the swift or the battle to the strong'; nevertheless, as Dashiell Hammett reputedly added, 'that's the way to bet'. **JP**

In my mind, there is nothing so illiberal and so ill-bred, as audible laughter.

Lord Chesterfield
Letters to His Son
1748

Philip Stanhope, fourth Earl of Chesterfield, was a British statesman. He is best remembered today as the author of more than 400 letters to his illegitimate son, also named Philip, in which he offered advice on a vast range of topics, particularly on how to behave like a gentleman.

One of the problems with advice, as Chesterfield himself noted in one of these letters, is that it 'is seldom welcome; and those who want [need] it the most always like it the least'. Another difficulty is that words that are wise when presented in the form of general precepts – for example, 'An injury is much sooner forgotten than an insult' – may seem pompous when addressed by a parent to a child, by Age to Youth.

As a consequence, most subsequent readers have admired Chesterfield's letters for both their style and their substance, but perhaps quietly thanked their stars that they were not the original addressee. Most readers, but not all: Samuel Johnson told James Boswell that in his opinion, Chesterfield's letters 'teach the morals of a whore, and the manners of a dancing master' – in other words, that the kind of manners that Chesterfield tried to instil were not worth cultivating. **JP**

⊘ This portrait of Lord Chesterfield (1769) was painted by an associate of English painter Thomas Gainsborough.

"Man alone consumes and engulfs more flesh than all other animals put together. He is, then, the greatest destroyer, and he is so more by abuse than by necessity."

George Louis Leclerc, Comte de Buffon
Histoire Naturelle
1753

At around the same time as Denis Diderot published his *Encyclopédie* in twenty-eight volumes, with contributions by numerous authors, the Comte de Buffon published his *Histoire Naturelle*, which was created with far less assistance. Buffon planned fifty volumes, but died after completing only thirty-six. Nevertheless, the work is monumental, and its narrower scope – just natural history rather than the whole of human knowledge – enabled Buffon to consider the relationship between humans and animals in depth. He did not restrict his treatment of the subject to a mere description, but drew various conclusions with ethical implications.

The above quotation comes amid observations about the extent to which humans have made 'domestic slaves' of animals, bred them in recklessly high numbers, and indulged an insatiable appetite for hunting. The words are often cited in support of vegetarianism, in spite of the fact that Buffon concludes that such a diet is too insubstantial. But Buffon's criticism was directed against the 'immoderate appetite of the rich man', and is therefore relevant to modern concerns about increasing wealth and demand for animal products. **TJ**

"After us the deluge."

Madame de Pompadour
Attributed
1757

Jeanne Antoinette Poisson, Madame de Pompadour, was the mistress of Louis XV, king of France, from 1745 until her death from tuberculosis in 1764 at the age of forty-two years. Well educated, with a talent for music and drama, Jeanne Antoinette was married at nineteen, and shortly after founded a Paris salon that was attended by various luminaries, including Voltaire. She became the king's mistress within weeks of meeting him and was installed in the royal palace of Versailles.

Her divorce soon followed, and the king purchased her a title. Madame de Pompadour wielded enormous influence, albeit unofficially. In 1755 she and a prominent Austrian official brokered peace between their countries. The resulting alliance with Austria, and then with Russia, drew France into the Seven Years' War. The country fared badly during this period, losing its territories in America to the British and in 1757, it lost the Battle of Rossbach to Prussia.

According to Madame du Hausset's *Mémoires* (1824), it was after the Battle of Rossbach that Jeanne Antoinette made the above comment to her lover in order to mollify him. The expression '*après nous le déluge*' conveyed a belief that should revolution topple the monarchy, it would not only be the monarchy that would suffer. Instead, the order imposed by the king and his authority would disappear and France would descend into chaos. When Jeanne Antoinette added the line, 'I care not what happens when I am dead and gone,' she was telling the king that existence without the monarchy would be awful and the revolutionaries were welcome to it. **IHS**

❯ Portrait of Madame de Pompadour (c. 1758) by François Boucher.

In this country it's good to kill an admiral from time to time in order to encourage the others.

⬥ Portrait of Voltaire by Nicolas de Largillière, painted in 1718.

Voltaire
Candide
1759

Not many French aphorisms have made it untranslated into English, but this is one of them, at least in part: any punishment that is regarded as unjust, and which frightens those who, in different circumstances, might have had to endure it themselves, may prompt the comment that it was '*pour encourager les autres*' ('to encourage the others').

Voltaire's satirical shot at the English was occasioned by the execution in 1757 of Admiral John Byng for his failure to recapture the Mediterranean island of Minorca from the French during the Seven Years' War (1755–64). Byng had faced overwhelming opposition, and his death caused international outrage.

Between the guilty verdict by the court-martial and the execution, the House of Commons tried to intercede on Byng's behalf. William Pitt the Elder told King George II that the populace was 'inclined to mercy'. The monarch, unmoved, replied: 'You have taught me to look for the sense of my people elsewhere than in the House of Commons.' George's attitude oddly reflects another remark of Voltaire in a letter of 1766: 'When the masses get involved in reasoning, all is lost.' **JP**

Our greatest glory is not in never falling, but in rising every time we fall.

Oliver Goldsmith
The Citizen of the World
1760

Oliver Goldsmith was an Anglo-Irish author, best known for his novel *The Vicar of Wakefield* (1766) and his play *She Stoops to Conquer* (1771). The above quotation is taken from a fictional work that took the form of a series of letters, supposedly written home by a Chinese visitor to London named Lien Chi Altangi.

The basic idea of a foreigner in a strange land was full of satirical possibilities, which Goldsmith exploited to maximum effect. The naive Chinese man thinks that the people buried in Westminster Abbey are so honoured because they led virtuous lives rather than because they were rich. When he is accosted by a group of ladies in the street, he assumes that they are keen to learn about life in China; they are, in fact, prostitutes. Lien's questions about British foreign policy lead him to the conclusion that the British desire for fur leads them into disastrous overseas military involvements.

Goldsmith's text is peppered with sayings, such as the one above, that imitate the manner of Confucius. His target is British life, but Lien is not allowed a position of moral superiority. He is criticized, too, for deserting his family, who, in his absence, are sold into slavery. JE

Goldsmith.

◈ A 19th-century engraving of Oliver Goldsmith by J W Cook.

"Man was born free, and everywhere he is in chains."

Jean-Jacques Rousseau
The Social Contract
1762

Rousseau was one of the most influential thinkers of the Enlightenment. He is best known for two books: his *Discourse on Inequality* (1755) and *The Social Contract*, the latter of which is the source of the above quotation. Both of these works became vastly important in modern Western political theory. In addition, his *Confessions* (Part I, 1782; Part II, 1789) are among the world's greatest autobiographies.

The Social Contract is a bridge between Rousseau's *Discourse on Inequality* (a descriptive account of the origins of inequality and the State) and his prescriptive account of how governments can secure freedom. Rousseau recognizes that while human nature is inherently free, in real life, human beings are often subject to a number of limitations on their freedom. Thus, in practice, conditions erode or violate liberty.

Rousseau proceeds to analyze how we may break out of that vicious circle. This quotation is therefore a commentary on the contradictory nature of contemporary civic life – that every human being is born free but is reined in to a greater or lesser extent by a wide range of constraints – some legal, some social, some real, some imagined. **JE**

❸ Rousseau in Jeaurat de Bertry's *An Allegory of the Revolution* (1794).

"Man will never be free until the last king is strangled with the entrails of the last priest."

Denis Diderot
'Les Éleuthéromanes'
1772

In the quotation above, Diderot, never one for half measures, makes his feelings about the monarchy and the Church perfectly clear. Like much of his writing, the quotation's source was published after his lifetime, although the line has also been attributed to Jean Meslier, a Catholic priest who, after his death, was discovered to have been the atheist who wrote a 633-page octavo manuscript, 'Testament.' In this work Meslier refers to a man who 'wished that all the great men in the world and all the nobility could be hanged, and strangled with the guts of the priests'.

The man in question was almost certainly Diderot. A prominent figure during the Enlightenment, he was best known in his lifetime for cofounding the *Encyclopédie* in 1751. His aim with this work was to 'make good the failure to execute such a project hitherto, and should encompass not only the fields already covered by the academies, but each and every branch of human knowledge'. The first volume was published to acclaim, but the courts held up the second one, levelling accusations against the book's seditious and anti-religious entries. The work continued to be a thorn in the side of the Establishment but, like this quotation, was also a symbol of a new freethinking world. **IHS**

"Patriotism is the laſt refuge of the scoundrel."

Samuel Johnson
The Life of Samuel Johnson by James Boswell
1775

In his 1774 pamphlet 'The Patriot,' Johnson left readers in little doubt about his view that politicians who appeal to patriotic feelings are disingenuous. His criticisms of false patriotism stemmed from the great value that he found in what he regarded as genuine patriotism. He observed that the true patriot is motivated by concern for the public good. Those who resort to patriotic pronouncements with the ulterior motive of self-advancement are, in his view, 'hypocrites of patriotism'.

A year after the pamphlet's publication, Johnson's biographer, James Boswell, recorded his subject making the above remark, which, he noted, was uttered suddenly, and 'in a strong and determined tone'. Boswell then pointed out that Johnson here meant 'pretended patriotism,' which is a 'cloak for self-interest'.

This quotation is not, as it is sometimes taken to be, a blanket condemnation of patriotism in any form. There is no doubt that Johnson regarded patriotism as a force for good in a country, able to unify its people in ways that religion, for example, cannot. In the first edition of his *Dictionary* (1755), Johnson defined 'patriot' as 'one whose ruling passion is the love of his country' – there's nothing opinionated or judgmental there. However, in the fourth edition, which was published in 1773 and included significant revisions, something gave him cause to add the more negative observation that the term 'is sometimes used for a factious disturber of the government'. **TJ**

"Government, even in its beſt ſtate, is but a necessary evil; in its worſt ſtate, an intolerable one."

Thomas Paine
Common Sense
1776

The quotation above comes from the opening page of *Common Sense*, a seminal pamphlet in the lead-up to the American War of Independence. Author, philosopher and political thinker Thomas Paine was an English colonist who was destined to become one of the Founding Fathers of the United States. He emigrated to the American colonies in 1774, just as revolution against British rule was fomenting. In the context of the colonist population at the time, *Common Sense* was proportionally the best-selling American title in history, with 150,000 copies (the equivalent of 15 million with today's population) distributed in the first few months of 1776.

Paine sees the establishment of any government as a 'necessary evil,' a useful device to spell out the colonists' need to govern themselves. In the pamphlet he goes on to argue how Britain simply could not be trusted to deal with the colonies fairly, with its record of having imposed unjust taxes and so on. The purpose of the pamphlet was not just to set out the argument for independence, but to motivate the populace into action. *Common Sense,* published anonymously in January 1776, achieved this aim magnificently: on 4 July of the same year, the thirteen colonies adopted the Declaration of Independence and became the United States of America. **ME**

My people and I have come to an agreement which satisfies us both. They are to say what they please, and I am to do what I please.

Frederick II of Prussia
Attributed
1785

Frederick II ruled Prussia, a powerful kingdom in what is now eastern Germany. During his reign, parts of Prussia that had been ruled by neighbouring countries were regained, and the country became a strong military power. A change of leadership in Russia – removing an enemy at a critical juncture – helped to make this happen, and Frederick's father had built up Prussia militarily and economically. He also owed much to his mother, sister of Britain's George II, who had imbued him with the cultural ideals of the Enlightenment.

European monarchies of the 18th century, particularly those of Catholic countries such as France and Austria, tended to dominate their people intellectually and economically, frowning upon independent thought and action. Frederick, however, while expecting his ministers to follow his lead, believed in benevolent despotism, as this quotation, from *Life of Frederick the Great* by T B Macaulay (1859), testifies. For Frederick, free expression was a safety valve for his people's private ideas and discontents; it was acceptable as long as it did not translate into concerted action that would interfere with his governing decisions. **JF**

⚫ Portrait of Frederick II of Prussia, painted eighty-four years after his death by Wilhelm Camphausen in 1870.

It would be an endless task to trace the variety of meannesses, cares and sorrows, into which women are plunged by the prevailing opinion, that they were created rather to feel than reason. "

Mary Wollstonecraft
A Vindication of the Rights of Woman
1792

Mary Wollstonecraft was arguably the first feminist. In her pamphlet *A Vindication of the Rights of Men*, published anonymously in 1790, she attacked the prevailing view of society founded on the subordination of women. Denied education or rational pursuits, Wollstonecraft said, women were obliged to focus on charming men into looking after them – it was this argument that she developed further in *A Vindication of the Rights of Woman*, published two years later.

Wollstonecraft was no stranger to love and attraction, in spite of her fierce advocacy of female rationality. In France during the Reign of Terror, she fell in love with an American and had his child, but the relationship failed. In 1796 she found happiness with William Godwin, whom she married, but she tragically died at the age of thirty-eight, after giving birth to their daughter, also called Mary, the author of *Frankenstein* (1818). Godwin's posthumous publication of his wife's candid autobiography caused a scandal, and for generations her voice was not heard. It may be argued that, despite two centuries of feminism, many women remain too preoccupied with their outward appearance. JF

The only thing necessary for the triumph of evil is that good men do nothing. "

Edmund Burke
Letter to William Smith
1795

A classic case of a very popular and familiar quotation being misattributed, the most famous use of the line was by US President John F Kennedy, addressing the Canadian Parliament in 1961. In his speech Kennedy declared: 'At the conference table and in the minds of men, the free world's cause is strengthened because it is just. But it is strengthened even more by the dedicated efforts of free men and free nations. As the great Parliamentarian Edmund Burke said, "The only thing necessary for the triumph of evil is for good men to do nothing."'

However, although this is the most quoted statement associated with the 18th-century British politician, for a long time there was no clear evidence as to its exact source. Indeed, *The Oxford Dictionary of Quotations*, while judging it to be the most popular quotation of modern times in a poll conducted by the editors, ran the line in its Misquotations section, with the comment 'Attributed (in a number of forms) to Burke, but not found in his writings.' Nevertheless, alternative evidence was presented in the fourteenth edition of *Bartlett's Familiar Quotations* in 1968, when the words were credited to Burke, having been found in a letter he wrote to William Smith in January 1795.

Regardless of the quotation's origin, its sentiment certainly reflects the character of the philosopher-statesman: Burke fought several political battles against injustice and the abuse of power over the course of his career. ME

Never interrupt your enemy when he's making a mistake.

Napoléon Bonaparte
Statement to his marshals
c. 1805

Napoléon Bonaparte was a French general and political leader who became France's first emperor. A coup in 1799 placed Napoléon in the position of First Consul, and in 1804 the French Senate declared him emperor of the First French Empire, a position he held until his defeat and exile in 1814. He escaped and succeeded in an 1815 coup before defeat after a few months' rule.

While the wording of the above quotation varies, it is always attributed to Napoléon and is thought to be a remark he made to marshals while discussing a battle of 1805. Other wordings include 'Never interrupt your enemy when he is in the process of destroying himself.' The meaning is the same: always allow an enemy to make a mistake. The logic is simple; if your enemy is going to fail in their own plans, perhaps by making a poor tactical decision, executing a poor strategy, or simply failing in what they are attempting to do, you should allow them to fail. In that way, they will potentially exhaust resources that otherwise will be devoted to hurting you. Secondarily, their failure in what they are doing may diminish their strength or reveal shortcomings in their defences that you can exploit. JE

◬ Napoléon in exile on the remote island of St Helena, where he was sent after being defeated at the Battle of Waterloo.

"Next to a battle lost, the greatest misery is a battle gained."

△ *Arthur Wellesley, 1st Duke of Wellington*, painted in 1815 by Sir Thomas Lawrence.

Arthur Wellesley, 1st Duke of Wellington
Attributed
1815

The Battle of Waterloo was arguably Wellington's finest hour. It was also the bloodiest battle of his military career, in which a number of his closest friends were killed or maimed. Arthur Wellesley, 1st Duke of Wellington, had built up an enviable reputation as a general during the Napoleonic Wars, especially in the Iberian campaign (1807–14, often called the Peninsular War), but until 1815, he had never faced Napoléon himself. He had his chance when Napoléon escaped from exile in Elba and swept across France. Napoléon attacked Wellington's multinational army not far from Antwerp, in Belgium, and for hours the outcome of the battle was in doubt. Wellington described it to one of his officers as 'the nearest-run thing you ever saw in your life'.

Wellington's point was that whether you win or lose a battle, the human loss is bound to be severe. He made the quoted remark to Lady Frances Shelley soon after the Allied army had retaken Paris, as she noted in her diary. On an earlier occasion he had said to an acquaintance, 'War is a terrible evil'. Military genius though he was, he had no illusions about the human cost of a battle, even when it is won. **JF**

War is nothing but the continuation of politics with the admixture of other means.

Carl von Clausewitz
On War
1832

Clausewitz was a distinguished Prussian general whose study of military strategy, from which the above quotation is taken, has been required reading for army officers of every country since its first publication.

At the heart of Clausewitz's thinking was a reaction against the theories of the generation that preceded him, who believed that the conduct of war was rigorously structured and subject to codifiable rules. This was quite alien to his own experience in the French Revolutionary and Napoleonic Wars, in which Prussia had suffered catastrophic defeats. During these campaigns, Clausewitz had found that war was mad and whirling and that victory depended on numerous factors in addition to armed might, among them blind chance and individual genius. In short, Clausewitz was a Romantic and as close to the heart of the Romantic movement as Ludwig van Beethoven and William Wordsworth.

The idea that war is politics by other means has never been discredited or contradicted – most people agree with Winston Churchill's remark that 'To jaw-jaw is always better than to war-war' and that the latter breaks out only after the failure of the former. JP

⊘ This portrait of Clausewitz (1830) was painted by Berlin academician Karl Wilhelm Wach.

"The proletarians have nothing to lose but their chains."

Karl Marx and Friedrich Engels
Communist Manifesto
1848

The *Communist Manifesto* is a short pamphlet – just twenty-three pages in the original, German-language edition – that provides a conspectus of history, from medieval feudalism to contemporary capitalism, which, the authors contend, consists of a series of class struggles. It goes on to predict that these conflicts will inevitably end with the overthrow of the status quo by the workers, who will abolish private property and 'raise the proletariat to the position of ruling class'.

The work was a slow burner. It found little favour with the reading public after the failure of the European revolutions of 1848, but towards the end of the 19th century, there was a gradual revival of interest, and the *Manifesto* formed the bedrock of Communism as it spread across much of the world and took root in several countries, most notably Russia.

Part of the attraction of the *Communist Manifesto* is its sense of the dramatic. It begins portentously – 'A spectre is haunting Europe – the spectre of Communism' – and ends with the words in the above quotation, followed by: 'They have a world to win. Working men of all countries, unite.' **JP**

> *I can offer you neither honour nor wages; I offer you only hunger, thirst, forced marches, battles and death. Anyone who loves his country, follow me.*

Giuseppe Garibaldi
Attributed
1849

Born in Nice (now in France) in 1807, Garibaldi became a revolutionary as a young man. He took part in a failed coup in the Italian state of Piedmont in 1834, after which he fled to South America to escape execution. Italy at that time consisted of a number of tiny city-states dominated by the great powers of the region, France and Austria. Attempts to throw off the influence of these imperialist powers began in 1848 and continued until Italy became a single country in 1861. Garibaldi's long campaign to unite Italy, known as the Risorgimento, showed that revolutions are not always quick or easy to carry through. The zeal, determination and perseverance of Garibaldi inspired revolutionary movements across the world. He was the first person to use guerrilla tactics against formal armies.

Attributed in *Garibaldi* (1882) by Giuseppe Guerzoni, Garibaldi's inspirational speech was made in July 1849 when he left Rome, which was under siege by the French army. Garibaldi suggests that any true patriot would undergo suffering and deprivation for the good of their country. Winston Churchill issued a similar rallying call to the British political Cabinet on 13 May 1940. **JF**

> *Let every one mind his own business, and endeavor to be what he was made.*

Henry David Thoreau
Walden
1854

Thoreau was a leading light of transcendentalism, a movement that placed more faith in 'insight' than logic and reason. Ralph Waldo Emerson wrote of Thoreau that '[h]e was bred to no profession; he never married; he lived alone; he never went to Church; he never voted; he refused to pay a tax to the State; he ate no flesh; he drank no wine; he never knew the use of tobacco; and, though a naturalist, he used neither trap nor gun'.

The book from which the above quotation is taken – its full title is *Walden; or, Life in the Woods* – is a collection of eighteen essays about the author's simple life on the shores of Walden Pond in eastern Massachusetts. Set within that seemingly unambitious framework is a work of deep contemplation, a philosophical treatise on the nature of many components of life, including work, relaxation, self-reliance and individualism. *Walden* also set the modern standard for nature writing.

One might remark that not a lot happens in *Walden*; most of the action takes place in the author's mind, in his far-ranging contemplations rather than in the outside world. Even so, the work is nevertheless endlessly fascinating as the product of an intelligent mind communing with itself and attempting to reach the truth about the society from which Thoreau had absented himself. Nor is *Walden* great for the facts that it contains; its reputation rests simply on the writing, and Thoreau is a model of prose style. **JP**

"You may fool all the people some of the time; you can even fool some of the people all the time; but you cannot fool all of the people all the time."

⚊ President Lincoln receives Native American chiefs from the Southern Plains in March 1863.

⚊ Lincoln makes the Gettysburg Address in 1863.

Abraham Lincoln
Attributed
1858

There is considerable doubt about whether the sixteenth President of the United States ever really made this remark, but the generally (although not universally) accepted consensus is that he said it in a speech at Clinton, Illinois, on 8 September 1858, during his unsuccessful campaign for election as the Republican candidate for the US Senate. Unfortunately, the words do not appear in the transcript of this address, and the earliest attribution to Lincoln appears in a biography by N W Stephenson that was published in 1923, almost seventy years later. In the meantime the same remark was also attributed to Phineas T Barnum, the circus showman, and creator of 'The Greatest Show on Earth.'

However, as we may see elsewhere in the present volume, even the best quotations benefit from a respected source. In a famous scene in *The Fortune Cookie* (1966), Billy Wilder's movie about a plot to defraud an insurance company, Jack Lemmon, at the heart of the intended scam, finds this quotation in the cookie that accompanies a Chinese take-out meal. The irony works for as long as the attribution is to Abraham Lincoln; Phineas T Barnum would never have cut it. **JP**

"Finality is not the language of politics."

Benjamin Disraeli
Speech to the House of Commons, London
1859

When Disraeli made this remark, he was Chancellor of the Exchequer in the second of the Earl of Derby's short-lived minority British Conservative governments, which ran from February 1858 to June 1859.

Many of Disraeli's most famous spoken utterances and written aphorisms tended to be wit for the sake of wit alone – *l'art pour l'art* – rather than attempts to persuade the listener of eternal verities. Here, however, he finds a memorable and economical formulation of the serious idea, often expressed in other forms, that politics is the art of the possible, with the warning that few windows of opportunity remain open for long.

The context of the quotation was a long speech on government plans for giving the vote to more British people than ever before. The speech was given in the period between the two Reform Acts, which introduced wide-ranging changes to the electoral system of England and Wales. The first Act, in 1832, had been a small step towards the Chartists' ultimate goal of universal suffrage. The second, in 1867, was passed into law shortly before Disraeli himself, a lifelong proponent of extending the right to vote, became Prime Minister in February 1868.

Disraeli preceded the above quotation with the words: 'We have sought to offer to the country, in the hope that it will meet with its calm and serious approval, what we believe to be a just and – I will not say a final, but – conclusive settlement.' Clearly, he knew that there was more to be done, but he took the pragmatic view that Rome was not built in a day. **JP**

"A man who has nothing for which he is willing to fight . . . is a miserable creature, who has no chance of being free."

John Stuart Mill
Fraser's Magazine
1862

John Stuart Mill was an English political economist, feminist, civil servant and philosopher. The son of Scottish philosopher and political economist James Mill, J S Mill is noted in philosophy for his book on inductive logic, *A System of Logic* (1843), and for his works advocating individual liberty, including *On Liberty* (1859). He also authored a defence of a variant of utilitarianism that distinguishes between the qualities of pleasures.

In his essay 'The Contest in America,' first published in *Fraser's Magazine* in 1862, Mill discusses war. His prime insight is that while war is ugly, it is not the ugliest thing for a people. Mill contrasts wars that degrade a people, where humans are used as a disposable means towards some powerful person's benefit, with wars that are freely participated in to advance rightness, goodness and justice. The above quotation criticizes people who prioritize personal safety to the extent that there is no cause for which they would risk it. Mill goes on to assert that such people cannot be free unless their freedom is fought for by better people than themselves. In short, Mill is defending wars fought for noble causes and criticizing people who refuse to get involved. **JE**

"Politics is the art of the possible."

Otto von Bismarck
Interview with Friedrich Meyer von Waldeck
1867

Otto von Bismarck (Otto Eduard Leopold, the Prince of Bismarck) served as a conservative statesman and Prime Minister in Prussia and was the founder and first Chancellor of the German Empire. He is credited with managing foreign affairs to preserve peace in Europe.

Bismarck delivered the above remark in an interview of 1867, describing politics (in full) as 'the art of the possible, the attainable. . .the art of the next best'. Bismarck saw no fault in resorting to compromise if it would help to achieve lasting political success, and he rejected all-or-nothing idealism and its wrongheaded attempts to make 'the impossible' happen. His advocacy of seeking pragmatic solutions to achieve the 'next best' thing expressed his understanding that major goals are often achieved incrementally, and by circuitous routes, rather than by short, decisive acts.

Bismarck's search for pragmatic possibilities was reflected in his career-long emphasis on diplomacy. His great achievements were the unification of Germany, maintenance of German hegemony and prevention of wars between European powers that would surely have undone everything he was trying to accomplish. Bismarck believed in practical politics, in paying attention to the contexts, possibilities and limits that condition political activity. His approach was an implicit critique of 'idealism' in politics; by extension the quotation urges caution and attentiveness in all human discourse. It is ironic that one of Hitler's greatest battleships was named for him. **JE**

"I am tired . . . My heart is sick and sad. From where the sun now stands, I will fight no more forever."

Chief Joseph of the Nez Percé people
Surrender speech
1877

The quotation above is from a famous speech made on 5 October 1877, by Chief Joseph, a leader of the Nez Percé (Pierced Nose) Native American people, which had been forced from its native territory by the US federal government. Tribesmen resisting the encroachments of the European settlers had become engaged in a war with the US Army, but after many battles, Chief Joseph saw no option but to surrender. Although the translated speech was purportedly a verbatim transcription of Joseph's words, its authenticity has been questioned, as it may have been written from memory. Also, the literary ambitions of the transcriber, Charles Wood, may have tempted him to embellish the speech. Whether or not that was the case, Joseph's speech in Washington two years later was to display much of the same poignant sincerity, an indication that the words were his.

Joseph had repeatedly argued against resorting to war, but the Nez Percé had been forced to defend themselves from the pursuing army. Joseph's surrender had no dishonour, and his words expressed dignity in representing the unjustly defeated party. Likewise, his honest admission of being tired, having a sick and sad heart, and wishing never to fight again were all sentiments that expressed a longing for peace. His words have resonated with many others battling injustices. **TJ**

"Power tends to corrupt and absolute power corrupts absolutely."

⊘ Historian and member of Parliament Sir John Dalberg-Acton was given the title Baron Acton of Aldenham in Shropshire in 1869.

Lord Acton
Letter to Bishop Mandell Creighton
1887

Mandell Creighton was a theologian who rose through the ranks of the Church of England to become the Bishop of London. John Dalberg-Acton, the First Baron Acton, was a Roman Catholic historian, politician and writer. In 1887, Creighton was a professor at Cambridge University and Canon at Worcester Cathedral. The third and fourth volumes of his *History of the Papacy* were published that February. They focused mainly on Sixtus IV, Alexander VI, and Julius II. In his historiographical approach, he steered clear of any condemnation.

Creighton, inviting Acton to review the texts for the *English Historical Review*, was surprised by what he saw as a vituperative reaction to his work. The exchanges that took place over subsequent weeks pitted Creighton's relativist approach against Acton's normative stance. To Acton, the conditions or environment should not have such a drastic impact upon those holding positions of moral authority. His famous quotation appeared in one of his responses, concluding that '[g]reat men are almost always bad men, even when they exercise influence and not authority'. Creighton eventually accepted that the Papacy's power had frequently been abused. **IHS**

"Practical politics consists in ignoring facts."

Henry Brooks Adams

The Education of Henry Adams

1907

Henry Brooks Adams was a US historian, educator, novelist and journalist. He was the great-grandson of John Adams, the second President of the United States, and grandson of John Quincy Adams, the sixth President. Henry was best known in his lifetime for his nine-volume chronicle of the history of the United States during the administrations of Thomas Jefferson and James Madison. His memoir, the Pulitzer Prize-winning *The Education of Henry Adams*, was published posthumously.

The quotation above pertains to John Adams, whom Henry describes as never liking to deny an evident fact. This observation is followed by the words of the quotation. Henry suggests that politicians have a desire for facts, but also show a tendency to ignore them for pragmatic political purposes. The author also notes that 'education and politics are two different and often contradictory things'. In essence, the quotation chides politics itself for being antithetical to facts. But to whose detriment? Henry Brooks Adams is asking, if such is the nature of politics, can we challenge this tendency within the system as it exists or must we transform the system more dramatically to force facts to be acknowledged? JE

⊘ Henry Brooks Adams, US novelist, academic and member of the distinguished Adams political family.

"The country is governed for the richest, for the corporations, the bankers, the land speculators and for the exploiters of labour."

Helen Keller
The Manchester Advertiser
1911

Helen Keller was a prolific US author, lecturer and political activist. An illness when she was nineteen months old had made her deaf and blind, and she learned to communicate via sign language with the help of her longtime teacher, Anne Sullivan. In addition to being the first deaf-and-blind person to earn a Bachelor of Arts degree, Keller was an outspoken feminist and Socialist and was a member of the Socialist Party of America and the Industrial Workers of the World.

The above quotation, from a letter by Keller on women's suffrage in *The Manchester Advertiser* (1911), pointed an accusing finger at Britain's gross class inequality. With reference to suffrage under extreme class inequality, she asked, 'What good can votes do you?' and continued, '[T]his wrong lies at the bottom of all social injustice, including the wrongs of women.' She concluded that 'the few own the many because they possess the means of livelihood of all,' despite 'free and equal' elections. For Keller, Britain was too dominated by the capitalist class, and she argued that, in the context of Britain's extreme class inequality, a 'democratic' government was democratic in name only. JE

"Justice and judgement lie often a world apart."

Emmeline Pankhurst
My Own Story
1914

In *My Own Story*, an account of her life and activism as a leading figure in the suffragette movement, Emmeline Pankhurst recounts an incident in her childhood. In the 1860s a group of Fenians – campaigners for Irish independence from England – attempted to rescue comrades from a police van by blowing off the doors with a firearm; in so doing, they accidentally shot and killed a police officer. Arrested and charged with murder, they were executed at a public hanging. Pankhurst comments on the story in the above quotation, which she puts forward as one of the terrible facts of life. The distinction it draws would inform her entire life as an activist for women's rights, particularly after the suffragette movement acknowledged the futility of peaceful protest and began to find more militant ways of gaining the world's attention.

Pankhurst worked for women's rights from a young age. In 1918, at the end of World War I, the Representation of the People Act allowed women over the age of thirty who met a property qualification to vote – this affected only 40 percent of the total population of UK women. It was not until 2 July 1928, just a few weeks after Pankhurst's death, that the government passed the Equal Franchise Act, and the minimum voting age for women was reduced to twenty-one years. **IHS**

❯ Pankhurst addresses listeners from a London balcony in 1914.

"*Democracy is beautiful in theory; in practice it is a fallacy.*"

Benito Mussolini
The New York Times
1928

Speaking to Edwin L James of the *The New York Times*, Benito Mussolini introduced the quotation above by asserting that 'democracy is talking itself to death'. The Italian saw himself as a man of action and was impatient with what he saw as futile discussion. He had worked as a journalist in the Socialist press when young, but abandoned the party in protest at its opposition to World War I. In 1919 he founded the Fascist Party, recruiting many unemployed war veterans, whom he organized into armed militias known as the Blackshirts. In 1922 Italian democracy was in chaos, and he took the opportunity to form a government. Sweeping away democratic institutions, he became a dictator: Il Duce ('The Leader'). He was eventually executed in 1945.

But Mussolini's words are often quoted today because modern democracy has not altogether lived up to its promise. The influence of money on the electoral process, the triumph of extremism and gridlock in governance caused by opposing and uncompromising political factions have all reduced democracy's appeal. Ominously, perhaps, Mussolini's interview was concluded by his telling James: 'You in America will see that some day.' **JF**

⊘ Mussolini, shown here in the 1920s, believed that effective governance flowed from a strong leader's undisputed will.

"You must be the change you wish to see in the world."

Mahatma Gandhi
Attributed
c. 1930

Although the above quotation is widely attributed to Mahatma Gandhi, there is no evidence that the words came from him, or that its related story is true. Neither does it appear in the ninety-eight volumes of the authorized collection of Gandhi's works. The story is that a woman approaches Gandhi and asks him to help wean her son off sugar. He tells her to come back in a week. She returns, and this time Gandhi speaks to the boy about his sugar intake. Curious, she asks the Indian leader why he did not speak to the boy on their first visit. Gandhi responds that he had first to wean himself off sugar before being able to set an example for the boy.

As a man who lived his life by example, in his religious belief, political thought and day-to-day activity, Gandhi adhered to the idea that to fight for a cause is to embody it. In chapter six of his work *Ethical Religion* (1907), Gandhi wrote: 'A man is but the product of his thoughts. What he thinks, he becomes.' Subsequent publications, such as the essay 'Partners in Conflict Resolution' by Stella Cornelius in *Building a More Democratic United Nations* (1991), use the quotation to help explain Gandhi's philosophy. **IHS**

◬ Gandhi, knowing that humankind commonly says one thing but does another, sought to unify his teachings and his actions.

" *The only thing we have to fear is fear itself.* "

President Roosevelt speaks at the podium during his inaugural address in Washington, DC, on 4 March 1933.

Franklin D Roosevelt
Inaugural address as US President
1933

Franklin D Roosevelt was elected President of the United States at a time when the nation was struggling with the Great Depression. The famous quotation above was penned not by Roosevelt but by a close adviser who added it to his speechwriter's final draft. However, the notion of fearing fear itself was not new, having been expressed in publications over the previous two decades, even appearing in US newspapers and advertisements. Much earlier, the 16th-century essayist Michel de Montaigne had written 'the thing I fear most is fear'.

The panic selling that precipitated the Wall Street Crash of 1929 had shown the compounding and ultimately paralyzing effect of fear. In his speech, Roosevelt described the fear as 'nameless, unreasoning, unjustified terror'. It was to combat this fearful mood and restore the nation's self-confidence that he was to introduce the government's vast reconstruction projects that would become known as the New Deal for America.

Today's prevalent fear of terrorism highlights the importance of the quotation. Terrorists work to arouse a continual, heightened sense of fear that can be resisted only if people refuse to succumb to it. **TJ**

"Democracy means the opportunity to be everyone's slave."

Karl Kraus
Half-Truths and One-and-a-Half Truths
1935

Born in 1874 in a part of the Austrian Empire that is now the Czech Republic, Karl Kraus was a Jew who converted to Christianity as a young man. He wrote in many different genres: drama and satire, essays, aphorisms and poetry. He opposed racism and capital punishment and was a stern critic of sloppy grammar and imprecise prose. A pacifist for most of his life, he believed that World War I (in which Austria was allied with Germany) was fought for spurious reasons, attributing its outbreak to people in authority not saying or writing what they meant: 'Diplomats lie to journalists,' he said, 'and believe these lies when they see them in print.'

Kraus wrote: 'An aphorism never coincides with the truth: it is either a half-truth or one-and-a-half truths.' That is certainly true of his quotation above about democracy, which focuses ironically on the egalitarianism that democracy often lauds but rarely delivers. Other examples of Kraus's sharp and often provocative aphorisms include 'Psychoanalysis is that mental illness for which it regards itself as therapy' and 'The devil is an optimist if he thinks he can make people worse than they are.' Make of those what you will. **JF**

⊘ Kraus, seen here in 1928, looked to socialism, especially in China, to produce a better political system than democracy.

> " *Liberalism is extremely harmful in a revolutionary collective. It is a corrosive which eats away unity, undermines cohesion, causes apathy and creates dissension.* "

Mao Zedong
Combat Liberalism
1937

Mao Zedong was the founder of the People's Republic of China following the success of the Chinese Communist Revolution. He governed as the chairman of the Communist Party of China from its initial establishment in 1949 until his death in 1976. Politically, he was responsible for initiating the Great Leap Forward (and its associated famine) and the Cultural Revolution. As a theorist he is also notable for works such as *On Guerrilla Warfare* (1937) and 'On Contradiction' (1937).

In the book from which the above quotation is taken, Mao criticized liberalism for its tendency to reject the 'ideological struggle' and to stand only for 'unprincipled peace'. By 'liberalism,' Mao was referring to what he saw as a culpable tendency in people to let the ideological differences between them slide – to fail to address them adequately, to address them only quietly or lightly and privately, or to critique them for personal reasons rather than for reasons of common fairness. Mao cautioned individuals to reject and oppose 'liberal tendencies' where they find them. He believed that simply 'agreeing to disagree,' as liberals characteristically did, potentially harmed and undermined revolutionary projects. **JE**

> " *The end may justify the means as long as there is something that justifies the end.* "

Leon Trotsky
'Their Morals and Ours'
1938

Leon Trotsky was a founding leader of the Red Army, a Soviet politician, and a Marxist revolutionary and theorist. He joined the Bolsheviks prior to the October Revolution of 1917 and quickly rose to the top. After leading opposition to the rise of Stalin, Trotsky was removed from power and later expelled from the Communist Party and the Soviet Union. He continued to oppose Stalin's regime until his assassination in Mexico in 1940.

Trotsky published his article 'Their Morals and Ours' in the Socialist Workers' Party's *New International* magazine as a response to increasing dissatisfaction on the international left with the Socialist revolutionary project, and particularly its morality and conduct. Trotsky's quotation – which has also been worded as 'a means can be justified only by its end. But the end in its turn needs to be justified' – relates to classic arguments in moral philosophy regarding the relationship between means and ends.

In essence Trotsky is arguing that means can only be justified if their ends are also justified. Importantly, by using the word 'may' rather than 'does,' he allows for the possibility that even those ends that are justified do not necessarily justify their means. In short, justified ends are a necessary, but not a sufficient, condition for the justification of means. By drawing this distinction, Trotsky was taking a softer line than Stalin, who ultimately withdrew from justifying his ends at all. **JE**

"War is like love, it always finds a way."

Bertolt Brecht
Mother Courage and Her Children
1939

Brecht was born in the medieval city of Augsburg, in Germany, in 1898. He studied medicine and philosophy before serving as a medical orderly during World War I, an experience that turned him into a lifelong pacifist. After the failure of the Socialist revolution in Germany in 1919, he began writing plays, many in collaboration with the composer Kurt Weill.

His increasingly Marxist views forced him to flee Germany after Hitler came to power in 1933, and he wrote *Mother Courage and Her Children* in exile in November 1939, just after the outbreak of World War II. Set in 17th-century Europe during the Thirty Years' War (1618–48), it depicts life and loss for one family in the shadow of an interminable war, in which Mother Courage's children are killed one by one.

Brecht's wry comparison of war to love unhappily still rings true. However much humankind attempts to find ways to circumvent, outlaw or otherwise prevent war, the urge to make war appears to be as deeply embedded in the human psyche as the urge to make love. Further, it is in pursuit of love and war that humankind shows its greatest determination and ingenuity; technological advances, for example, have been shown to occur more rapidly in wartime than in peacetime. The two world wars, Cold War confrontations, and armed insurrections against dictatorship and oppression of the 20th century have given way to the terrorism and fragmented, bitter local conflicts of the 21st century. Unfortunately, Brecht offers no solution to the vexing problem. **JF**

"Live simply so that others may simply live."

Mahatma Gandhi
Attributed
1939

Few individuals have as many uncorroborated quotations attributed to them as Mahatma Gandhi. Since his assassination in 1948, a whole industry has grown up around him – some working to explain his thinking, others attempting to commandeer him in support of their own agendas. Many of the quotations in circulation reflect a specific viewpoint or philosophy that was espoused by him – one may have been plucked out of thin air, another is a genuine quotation transformed to reinforce a point someone was making. The above quotation has appeared in various forms, including the version 'The rich must live more simply so that the poor may simply live.' Either way, the meaning is that living one's life fairly and modestly gives others the chance to live to a standard that they too deserve.

However, material welfare is only part of the equation. As Gandhi stated in his famous 'Quit India' speech to the British in Bombay (now Mumbai) in 1942, 'In the democracy which I have envisaged, a democracy established by nonviolence, there will be equal freedom for all.' Gandhi was asserting that a true democracy depends upon universal equality, and without equality selfishness reigns supreme. Moreover, the path society should follow is marked out by truth, and truth, as Gandhi wrote in the weekly journal *Young India*, is unassailable. 'An error does not become truth by reason of multiplied propagation, nor does truth become error because nobody sees it. Truth stands, even if there be no public support. It is self-sustained.' For Gandhi, India had to embrace historic truth to escape its colonial past. **IHS**

> # "*I and the public know, what schoolchildren learn: those to whom evil is done, do evil in return.*"

○ Auden was here photographed in the course of making a radio programme for US broadcaster CBS in c. 1940.

W H Auden
'September 1, 1939'
1939

Wystan Hugh Auden was an Anglo-American poet known for his verse on love, politics, and cultural themes. He wrote 'September 1, 1939,' the source of the above quotation, on the occasion of the start of World War II. The poem's structure follows that of W B Yeats's 'Easter, 1916,' which had taken as its subject the Irish war of independence from Britain.

Auden's poem begins by expressing the decline of hope as prospects for peace decline and the 'odor of death' permeates the night. In the quotation, Auden is referring to the origins of the onset of World War II. He states, in effect, what everyone knows: that when evil is done to people, they reproduce evil in return. Auden's meaning is a matter of interpretation, but he could be implying that Hitler is reproducing evil that was done to him, or more generally, to Germany. He also may be implying that those wronged by Hitler are likely to reproduce evil themselves. While in context the poem relates to Germany and the events surrounding the onset of World War II, the quotation is a general acknowledgement that people who are victims of evil often reproduce the evil done to them. **JE**

I have nothing to offer but blood, toil, tears and sweat.

Winston Churchill
Speech in the House of Commons
1940

On 30 September 1938, British Prime Minister Neville Chamberlain returned from Germany carrying the Anglo-German Declaration and the Munich Agreement, a non-aggression pact signed in the light of Germany's occupation of Czechoslovakia. With it, Chamberlain declared 'peace for our time.' It did not last long. On 1 September 1939, Germany invaded Poland and both Britain and France declared war. On 10 May 1940, after the allied retreat from Norway, Chamberlain stepped down as Prime Minister and was replaced by Winston Churchill, then the First Lord of the Admiralty.

On 11 May the Royal Air Force began a campaign of bombing raids on German cities, and on 13 May Churchill addressed the House of Commons. The speech he made was a rallying cry to the nation, outlining the hardship that was to come, and his complete commitment to seeing Britain victorious. The quotation above was an echo of a speech Churchill had made in 1931, but more crucially, it paraphrased a similar call made in 1849 by Giuseppe Garibaldi, the revolutionary Italian leader and one of Churchill's heroes, as well as a speech made by Theodore Roosevelt in 1897. **IHS**

⊘ Churchill, here addressing a crowd in 1939, was adamant that Britain should not countenance German expansionism.

> **"** *All animals are equal, but some animals are more equal than others.* **"**

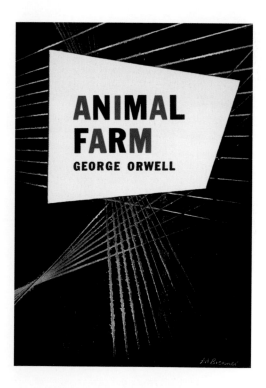

ANIMAL
FARM
GEORGE ORWELL

⊘ The front cover of the first US edition of George Orwell's novel *Animal Farm*.

George Orwell
Animal Farm
1945

Eric Arthur Blair, whose pen name was George Orwell, was an English journalist, essayist and novelist. Prevalent in his works are the themes of social injustice, opposition to totalitarianism and support of democratic socialism.

Orwell's best-known works are the dystopian novel *Nineteen Eighty-Four* (1949) and the allegorical novella *Animal Farm* (1945). The quotation above derives from the latter work, in which animals conspire to take control of their farm from humans, establishing 'Animalist' commandments to prevent the reproduction of the oppressive behaviour of the humans. But as time goes by, the pig Napoleon (an allegory of Stalin) gradually transforms these principles in order to monopolize his power. Thus, the quotation is a degraded, hierarchical version of the seventh, final principle of Animalism, that 'all animals are equal.' The new version establishes that the formal equality among animals must coexist with a recognition that some animals are superior to (or 'more equal' than) others. Orwell is parodying Communist 'workers' equality' under Stalin, where the Soviet Union is formally 'of the worker' and 'democratic,' but where Communist Party chiefs exercise absolute control. **JE**

> ❝ *The secret of success is to offend the greatest number of people.* ❞

George Bernard Shaw
Days with Bernard Shaw
1949

Stephen Winsten was a member of the 'Whitechapel Boys,' a group of young Jewish writers who were raised in the East End of London. A leftist politically and a conscientious objector during World War I, his worldview reflected that of one of the most famous subjects he wrote about, George Bernard Shaw. Winsten and his sculptor wife, Clara Birnberg, lived as neighbours of the Shaws in the English county of Hertfordshire.

In addition to an acclaimed biography of the social reformer Henry Salt, Winsten published four books about Shaw: the edited collection *G B S 90: Aspects of Bernard Shaw's Life and Work* (1946), *Days with Bernard Shaw* (1949), *Shaw's Corner* (1952) and *Jesting Apostle: The Private Life of Bernard Shaw* (1956). The quotation above comes from the second and best-known work, a conversational account of the time Winsten spent with Shaw prior to the acclaimed playwright's death.

Days with Bernard Shaw is famous for its collection of delicious aphorisms and bon mots delivered by Shaw, who was a noted wit. Winsten's intention in writing the book was not merely to deliver a book-length collection of Shaw's funniest lines, but to clear up any misapprehension the public might have had regarding his views on all aspects of life. Even so, some of the comments, such as this quotation, remain provocative and open to interpretation. Winsten commented: 'So much of what he has written and spoken has been misinterpreted,' adding, 'Not, of course, that Shaw cares a ha'penny about this.' **IHS**

> ❝ *Free will and determinism are like a game of cards. The hand that is dealt you represents determinism. The way you play your hand represents free will.* ❞

Norman Cousins
Attributed
c. 1951

Norman Cousins was editor of *Saturday Review* for more than thirty-five years, during which time he broadened the magazine's focus from pure literature to literature and current affairs, thereby doubling its circulation.

Cousins was a lifelong campaigner for world peace. His work behind the scenes in bringing the United States and the Soviet Union to the negotiating table resulted in 1963's Limited Test Ban Treaty. He was also a vociferous opponent of US military involvement in Vietnam.

A prolific author as well as an editor, Cousins wrote *The Good Inheritance: The Democratic Chance* (1942), which criticized the US government for failures in social policy, but remained optimistic about the nation's capacity to right every wrong. Other publications included *Modern Man is Obsolete* (1945), reflections on the Atomic Age, and *The Pathology of Power* (1987), about how the creation and use of destructive weapons were moving beyond the control of individuals and into that of corporations. Cousins would later become adjunct professor of psychiatry at the University of California at Los Angeles. The above quotation comes from a *Saturday Review* article entitled 'A Game of Cards.' **IHS**

"*Ideas are more powerful than guns. We would not let our enemies have guns; why should we let them have ideas?*"

Stalin's avuncular exterior belied a total ruthlessness in suppressing any questioning of how he ran the Soviet Union.

Joseph Stalin
Attributed
1952

For decades the quotation given above has been indiscriminately attributed to Joseph Stalin, even though there is no documented evidence that he even uttered words to the same effect. At the same time it neatly encapsulates a principle by which he ruled. The Soviet dictator was notorious for the extensive purges he conducted against people who did not share his ideas and for his brutal repression of millions belonging to many different ethnicities. He would do whatever was necessary to weaken any threat to his absolute power, including the introduction of harsh criminal penalties to deter the spread of counter-revolutionary ideas.

The belief that ideas are more powerful than weapons has been expressed in many forms since antiquity. It is a variation of the adage that 'the pen is mightier than the sword.' The first version, appearing in sayings collected by the Assyrian scholar Ahiqar (500 BCE), has it that the 'word' is mightier. Stalin would have known that, historically, new ideas have had the power to inspire social revolutions and topple regimes, so even if the quotation was only one of his paranoid thoughts, the idea it expresses is powerful and resilient. **TJ**

"If you don't want a man unhappy politically, don't give him two sides to a question to worry him; give him one. Better yet, give him none."

Ray Bradbury
Fahrenheit 451
1953

US science fiction, horror' and fantasy writer Ray (Raymond Douglas) Bradbury is best known for his dystopian novel *Fahrenheit 451* (1953), as well as two science-fiction story collections, *The Martian Chronicles* (1950) and *The Illustrated Man* (1951).

Fahrenheit 451 is set in a future US society where the authorities have initiated a large-scale book-burning campaign. Book ownership is illegal, and the burnings are intended to control who possesses knowledge. The above quotation from the novel encapsulates the viewpoint of all authoritarian regimes. It acknowledges that there are at least two sides to any question and that giving intellectual and political choices to the people carries the risk that they will become discontented with the political state of affairs. In practical terms the way to deny people choice is to restrict the information they possess, minimize their anger, skew their interpretation of events and limit their sense of what might be possible. In their ignorance they are more likely to think as the authority wants them to. Thus, effective social control relies on pursuing a strategy of restricting the flow of information to the public. JE

⬥ Cyril Cusack (*left*) and Oskar Werner incinerate literature in the François Truffaut movie *Fahrenheit 451* (1966).

"It is better to be defeated on principle than to win on lies."

Arthur Calwell attends the Banco Court in Sydney for the swearing in of a Chief Justice of New South Wales in 1960.

Arthur Calwell
Attributed
1960

Arthur Calwell was a member of the Australian House of Representatives from 1940 to 1972 and leader of the Australian Labor Party from 1960 to 1967. On 21 June 1966, he was shot while in his car as he was leaving a meeting. He was virtually unscathed, but he thus became only the second target of attempted political assassination in Australia's history.

The above quotation, attributed unsourced to Calwell, discusses the relationship between politics and truth. People are suspicious that politicians are prepared to lie or say anything to get elected, but Calwell here asserts that it is better to tell the truth and risk defeat than it is to score political victories under falsehoods. He is admonishing politicians who lie, just as he is promoting and valuing truth-telling more than the acquisition of political power.

In a world where the populace is often cynical about the veracity of politicians (and where political statements are often taken to be little more than lies fuelled by opinion polls), Calwell's attributed aphorism reminds us that we have a duty to prioritize the truth over personal self-aggrandizement and lust for power. JE

" *The job of a citizen is to keep his mouth open.* "

Günter Grass
Attributed
c. 1960

Günter Grass, best known as the author of the picaresque novel *The Tin Drum* (1959), and winner of the 1999 Nobel Prize in Literature, was for most of his career regarded as the moral conscience of postwar Germany. He was a social democrat (a mild left-winger) whose works were always politically committed: *Local Anesthetic* (1969) was about the Vietnam War; *The Rat* (1986) was about nuclear Armageddon; and *A Broad Field* (1996) was a fictional examination of the reunification, six years previously, of East and West Germany.

In 2006, Grass surprised the reading public by stating, just before the publication of his memoirs, that his military service during World War II had not been as a conscript in a German air defence unit, as he had previously claimed, but in the Waffen-SS, Hitler's elite fighting force, which initially recruited from among the most fervent Nazi sympathizers. He was henceforth demoted as a writer and as a moral authority.

The above remark comes from before that fall from grace and remains quotable regardless of the speaker's war record. The sentiment is broadly the same as that expressed by Pastor Martin Niemöller – that if we do not speak out when others are victimized, there will be no one to speak out for us when it is our turn. **JE**

" *A revolution is a struggle to the death between the future and the past.* "

Fidel Castro
Speech
1961

Fidel Castro was the political leader of Cuba from 1959 to 2008. The above quotation was delivered in his speech on the second anniversary of the Cuban Revolution, in which Marxist–Leninist forces had overthrown the right-wing dictatorship of General Fulgencio Batista.

The underlying idea is that revolution is not a once-and-for-all occurrence. It is not that everything was wrong, and the revolution fixed it. In Castro's scheme of things, revolution is constant: at any given moment in the history of any political entity, the past is outmoded, and redundant, and the only hope lies in tomorrow, which cannot begin until today becomes yesterday.

Such radical rhetoric concerned Cuba's neighbours, particularly the United States, which became alarmed when Castro nationalized all Cuban commerce and industry and expropriated American businesses.

After a bungled attempt to oust Castro (the Bay of Pigs fiasco), Washington severed diplomatic and trade links with Havana, and Castro's main trading partner became the Soviet Union. Following the arrival of Russian-made nuclear warheads on the Caribbean island, the world teetered on the edge of nuclear war. **JE**

> # *My fellow Americans, ask not what your country can do for you – ask what you can do for your country.*

◔ Kennedy and his wife, Jackie, arrive before the inaugural parade in 1961.

◑ Kennedy delivering his inaugural speech.

John F Kennedy
Inauguration address
1961

The United States today has a reputation for not only being a place where basic rights to life, liberty and the pursuit of happiness are held sacrosanct, but also for policing the world to ensure that other countries are of like mind. The seeds of this decidedly nonisolationist mentality may be found in John F Kennedy's inaugural address, in which he made it known that the United States would do whatever was necessary to 'assure the survival and the success of liberty' – by which he meant upholding the principles of the Bill of Rights, such as the freedom of speech, the right to a fair and speedy trial by jury, and a federalist system of government.

In this fifteen-minute speech, the new president encouraged his fellow Americans to unite against the common enemies of humanity: disease, poverty, tyranny and war. He also sent a clear message concerning ending the arms race with the Soviet Union, and his hope for peace in the Nuclear Age. His words in the quotation above came near the end of the address, and they stress the other-centredness of the human condition and the fact that we are all codependent citizens of the world. **JP**

"Freedom is never more than one generation away from extinction."

"For of those to whom much is given, much is required."

Ronald Reagan
Address to the Phoenix Chamber of Commerce
1961

John F Kennedy
Speech
1961

This is one of the speeches that defined Reagan's political career. He was a mildly successful Hollywood actor whose presidency of the Screen Actors Guild in the 1940s revealed his skill as a negotiator and figurehead. Originally a liberal Democrat, he swung to the conservative right in the 1950s because of his fear of a Communist insurgency in the United States, particularly in Hollywood. (He famously said, 'I didn't leave the Democratic Party. The party left me.') In the early 1960s he became one of the more famous members of the National Rifle Association. He appeared at Barry Goldwater's nomination for the Republican ticket during the 1964 presidential election. Three years previously, he had addressed a Chamber of Commerce in Phoenix, Arizona. His statement, which he would recycle for his 1967 California gubernatorial speech, stressed the fragile nature of democracy from a libertarian standpoint: 'We didn't pass it on to our children in the bloodstream. It must be fought for, protected, and handed on for them to do the same, or one day we will spend our sunset years telling our children and our children's children what it was once like in the United States where men were free.' **IHS**

US President John F Kennedy included these words in a speech to the Massachusetts Legislature on 9 January 1961. He had a habit of misquoting, misattributing and mangling other people's words, generally out of his own store of remembered (or misremembered) quotations, though on occasion he was perfectly capable of inventing his own pithy and pertinent remarks. The origins of some of these half-quotations have never been run to earth. The above quotation, however, is a reference to chapter twelve of the Gospel according to St Luke in the New Testament of the Bible; written originally in Greek, it has been variously translated.

In Luke's Gospel, Jesus delivered this piece of wisdom in the context of a servant, expected to carry out his master's wishes while waiting watchfully for that master's return. Kennedy, however, used the words to speak about the responsibility of leadership. Leaders, he said, would be judged by 'the high court of history' according to four attributes: courage, judgement, integrity and dedication. Many people feel that Kennedy himself possessed all four of these, which is why he is remembered as a great leader of the Western world. **JF**

If you're not ready to die for it, put the word 'freedom' out of your vocabulary.

Malcolm X
The Chicago Defender
1962

Cited by biographer Peter Goldman in *The Life and Death of Malcolm X* (1973), the above quotation originally appeared on 28 November 1962, in *The Chicago Defender*, one of a handful of American newspapers published specifically for an African American readership. As such, it was at the forefront of the civil rights struggle and other campaigns on behalf of black America.

Among black activists in the early 1960s, Malcolm X was a highly controversial, and divisive, figure. Whereas the civil rights movement called for an end to segregation across the United States – and equal educational, legal and voting rights – Malcolm X promoted black supremacy.

Born Malcolm Little in 1925, while in prison in the late 1940s, he converted to the Muslim faith and became a member of the Nation of Islam, a separatist 'Black Muslim' organization. Leaving jail in 1952, Malcolm X, as he now dubbed himself, became spokesman for the group and its leader, Elijah Muhammad. At the time of the *Defender* quotation, Malcolm X was becoming disillusioned with the overt racism of the Nation of Islam – which he subsequently left in 1964; he was assassinated by three of its members in 1965. **ME**

⊘ Malcolm X was shot dead while he was preparing to make a speech at the Audubon Ballroom, Manhattan, New York.

" *Only crime and the criminal, it is true, confront us with the perplexity of radical evil; but only the hypocrite is really rotten to the core.* "

Hannah Arendt
On Revolution
1963

Johanna 'Hannah' Arendt was a German-born American political theorist. She escaped from Europe after the rise of Hitler, and eventually became a US citizen. Arendt is best known for her coverage of the 1961 trial in Jerusalem of Adolf Eichmann, one of the architects of the Nazi 'Final Solution.' It was in reference to him that she coined the famous phrase 'the banality of evil.'

In the book from which the above quotation is taken, Arendt contrasts the American and French Revolutions of the late 18th century. Her overall view, uncommon in her lifetime, was that the former was a success, the latter a catastrophe.

In her analysis of the hypocrisy of French Revolutionary leader Maximilien Robespierre, Arendt demonstrates that crime and the criminal are complex topics and that the relationship between the two is even more entangled, but that, in the final assessment, the criminal is – or, at least, may be – redeemable. However, for redemption to occur, the wrongdoing must be acknowledged. Since hypocrites do not admit their mistakes, they are worse than even the basest criminal, because they do not admit the error of their ways. JE

◉ Hannah Arendt was a philosopher who did not like to be described as such, because she thought the term was restrictive.

Leadership and learning are indispensable to each other.

John F Kennedy
Speech (undelivered)
1963

The above quotation was part of the speech that US President John F Kennedy intended to deliver to the Dallas Citizens Council at the Trade Mart in Dallas, Texas, on the evening of 22 November 1963. However, on that day, he was shot in the head as he rode through the streets of the city, and he died later in hospital.

In his draft script – 2,500 words, planned to run for around fifteen minutes – Kennedy moved from education, as referenced in the above remark, to a broader consideration of the US role in realizing what he termed 'the ancient vision of peace on earth, good will toward men'. This led into a section that celebrated the recent diplomatic triumph over the Communist Soviet Union, which had been forced to climb down after a confrontation with the United States over the supply of intercontinental missiles to Cuba.

The president would have gone on to say: 'That must always be our goal, and the righteousness of our cause must always underlie our strength. For as was written long ago: "Except the Lord keep the city, the watchman waketh but in vain."' (Here, he is quoting from Psalm 127 in the Old Testament of the Bible.) JE

◉ President Kennedy sets out on his final journey through Dallas in an open-top limousine.

I have a dream that my four little children will one day live in a nation where they will not be judged by the color of their skin but by the content of their character. "

Martin Luther King Jr
Speech
1963

Martin Luther King Jr's stirring speech from the steps of the Lincoln Memorial at the climax of the civil rights movement's March on Washington for Jobs and Freedom, 28 August 1963, referenced the US Declaration of Independence, the US Constitution, Lincoln's Gettysburg Address and the Emancipation Proclamation that ended slavery one hundred years previously.

King had fought hard and long in the civil rights struggle, particularly in the racially segregated Southern US states, where he led many civil disobedience demonstrations through the late 1950s and early 1960s. The Washington march was to rally mass support for the civil rights legislation proposed by President John F Kennedy, and a quarter of a million participants, black and white, made the gathering a historic success.

The oration, which became known as the 'I Have a Dream' speech, was shown on live TV. After King made the various references to US history, singer Mahalia Jackson shouted from the crowd, 'Tell them about the dream, Martin.' King launched into the partly improvised, passionate conclusion from which the above sentence, one of the speech's most quoted lines, was drawn. **ME**

◔ Civil rights leaders head the march to the Lincoln Memorial in Washington, DC in 1963.

❷ King on the platform from which he made his historic speech.

"A week is a long time in politics."

Harold Wilson
Attributed
1964

This is a phrase that has gained currency over time. It is an acknowledgement that modern living is fast and that there is no speed limit in modern politics. Whatever success a politician achieves on Monday might be forgotten within days, and an event soon after might even destroy a promising political career by Friday. Constant media coverage has only increased the pace of events. Pundits jockey with one another to gain the upper hand, and nothing is sacred in the race for a good story. Politicians are pilloried for the slightest mistake, and the excuse that they are human is one that rarely registers with the electorate as TV newscasters, newspaper editors and opposition parties bay for the blood of anyone remotely involved.

It is believed that Harold Wilson was the first politician to use the quoted phrase. A Labour politician, he was Prime Minister of Britain from 1964 to 1970 and from 1974 to 1976. During his time in power, he initially oversaw a period of economic stability, but the 1960s ended with him sending British troops into Northern Ireland. His second period of office was less stable. He took charge of a minority government, and the economy was in sharp decline. He suddenly resigned on 16 March 1976, and was replaced by James Callaghan. He is believed to have made the comment during the 1964 sterling crisis, but when interviewed about it in 1977, he could not remember having said it. **IHS**

"In politics, if you want something said, ask a man; if you want something done, ask a woman."

Margaret Thatcher
Speech
1965

The future first female British Prime Minister, Margaret Thatcher, made this famous remark to members of the National Union of Townswomen's Guilds during a speech on the topic: 'Woman – No Longer a Satellite.' Although it would be another fourteen years before she took the top job in UK politics, Thatcher was already making her mark as a woman to be reckoned with.

After winning the 1979 general election, and returning the Conservative Party to power, Thatcher quickly gained a reputation worldwide for her uncompromising politics and tough leadership style – leading one Soviet journalist to dub her 'the Iron Lady,' a highly appropriate nickname that stuck with her for the rest of her political career.

Her wide-ranging, free-market policies, which became known as Thatcherism, divided the nation as no other British leader had done in the postwar years, and even members of her own administration often found her a challenge to work with. She did not suffer fools gladly, and the (mainly male) members of her Cabinet were known to tread carefully in her presence. However, feminists complained that, despite her avowed support of women in the workplace, she did little to improve their opportunities or prospects. **ME**

"Men are not the enemy, but the fellow victims. The real enemy is women's denigration of themselves."

Betty Friedan
Christian Science Monitor
1967

Betty Friedan was a leading activist in the US women's movement, who helped to establish the National Organization for Women in 1966 and National Association for the Repeal of Abortion Laws (NARAL) in 1969. A wife and mother herself, she opposed the social constraints that prevented mothers from working. In *The Feminine Mystique* (1963), she explored ways women might find personal fulfillment outside traditional caring roles and inspired American feminism's second wave.

Unlike more radical feminists, Friedan refused to demonize men. Controversially, she portrayed the female sex as surrendering to social forces that reduced them to subordination, believing in their own inferiority, and therefore reinforcing their existing image.

Today's women are less likely to defer to men or to yield head-of-the-household status to their male partners. Yet the workplace glass ceiling remains: men's careers still run a higher trajectory and attract better pay. Is it self-denigration or a weary desire for peace that prevents female self-assertion? Perhaps, as Friedan says, 'The only way for a woman, as for a man, to find herself, to know herself as a person, is by creative work of her own.' **JF**

"The revolution is not an apple that falls when it is ripe. You have to make it fall."

Che Guevara
Che Guevara Speaks
1967

Ernesto 'Che' Guevara was an Argentine Marxist guerrilla leader, revolutionary, military theorist and physician. On the basis of his experiences in the Cuban Revolution, he wrote the book *Guerrilla Warfare* (1961), in which he developed the pre-existing *foco* theory, one of the central tenets of which is that mass insurrections can be precipitated by the carefully targeted actions of just a few agents provocateurs.

Since the writings of Marx and Engels, Socialist, Communist and anarchist radicals have discussed strategies for the overthrow of capitalism. The above quotation connects to many abiding questions of revolutionary strategy. Some orthodox Marxists posit that economic crises and contradictions will organically create revolutionary conditions and social upheaval – that, sooner or later, capitalism will destroy itself. By contrast, Che is here arguing that capitalism will not topple unless it is pushed.

In 1967, Che became involved in an insurrection against army regulars in Bolivia. He was captured and shot dead by government agents, and buried with others in an unmarked grave. Thirty years later, his remains were discovered and removed to Cuba, where there is now an official memorial to him. **JE**

"Revolution is the festival of the oppressed."

Born in Australia, Germaine Greer became one of Britain's strongest advocates of feminism.

Germaine Greer
The Female Eunuch
1970

Every revolution should have a manifesto or a declaration of intent. In the case of second-wave feminism, which arose out of the cultural shifts of the 1960s and became a political force in the 1970s, there were several such documents to choose from. They were written by a diverse group of women, including Betty Friedan, Gloria Steinem, Mary King, Erica Jong and Germaine Greer.

Greer's book, from which the above quotation is taken, became a cause célèbre for the feminist movement and turned the journalist – already well-established on the satirical magazines *Oz*, *Private Eye* and *Suck* – into a household name. She even appeared on the cover of *Life* magazine, where she was described as the 'Saucy Feminist That Even Men Like'. Greer eschewed equality between the sexes, instead favouring liberation, asserting difference and 'insisting on it as a condition of self-definition and self-determination' between men and women. She engaged publicly with the gender debate, arguing that nothing short of a revolution in attitudes would bring change. Most famously, she opposed Norman Mailer, an ardent critic of the feminist movement, in a public debate in New York. **IHS**

"When I give food to the poor, they call me a saint. When I ask why they are poor, they call me a Communist."

Hélder Câmara
Attributed
1970

Hélder Câmara was the Brazilian Roman Catholic Archbishop of Olinda and Recife from 1964 to 1985. He was an advocate of liberation theology and is today remembered for his social work for the poor – he was sometimes known as 'the bishop of the slums' – and for his political advocacy of human rights and democracy.

The above remark is quoted in *Helder, the Gift: A Life that Marked the Course of the Church in Brazil* (2000) by the priest Zildo Rocha. Câmara was never one to toe the official papal line. He called on fellow churchmen to live lives of poverty, so that they knew what it was like. He was also a vocal critic of several Vatican doctrines, notably Rome's ban on birth control, which he first described as 'a mistake' and later as 'a torture'. With regard to violence, Câmara stressed that he did not practise it himself, but he was not necessarily opposed to it, if it was employed sparingly to combat injustice.

The latter view was not only unpopular with the Pope; it also made Câmara an object of suspicion for the government of Brazil, which, throughout his time as archbishop, was a military dictatorship masquerading as a two-party system. **JE**

⊘ Hélder Câmara was an outspoken critic of both his government and his employers.

" The measure of a country's greatness is its ability to retain compassion in times of crisis. "

Thurgood Marshall
Furman vs Georgia
1972

Thurgood Marshall was an Associate Justice of the Supreme Court of the United States, appointed by President Lyndon B Johnson. Marshall served from 1967 to 1991 and was the court's first African American justice. Prior to being a judge, Marshall was notable for his successes in arguing before the Supreme Court; he was part of the victorious team in *Brown vs Board of Education* (1954), the case that led to the ruling against separate schools for black and white children.

The above quotation followed the ruling that the application of the death penalty differed so much from one US state to another that it was effectively arbitrary, and therefore unconstitutional. Marshall – a passionate opponent of capital punishment – wrote the above in his concurrence with the proposed ruling.

Furman vs Georgia led to a moratorium on the death penalty throughout the United States, which lasted until *Gregg vs Georgia* in 1976 reaffirmed the constitutionality of the punishment. The first state to conduct an execution after its reintroduction was Utah, which carried out the death sentence (by firing squad) on Gary Gilmore in January 1977. JE

" Hope will never be silent. "

Harvey Milk
Attributed
c. 1975

Harvey Bernard Milk was an American politician, most notable for being the first openly gay person elected to public office in California (he served on the San Francisco Board of Supervisors). Milk remained in office for nearly eleven months and was responsible for the passage of an important gay rights ordinance for the city. On 27 November 1978, Milk and Mayor George Moscone were assassinated by Dan White, a city supervisor who wanted his job back after having resigned.

The above quotation is widely attributed to Milk, though it is unsourced. However, hope was a theme that reappeared consistently in Milk's life, activism and political career. In a famous speech he noted that his election was not only a political victory for people who were oppressed due to their sexual orientation, but also one for those oppressed on account of their race, age and so on. It was one of Milk's fundamental ideas that people must fight against what oppresses them because in so doing they give others hope – and without hope, life is not worth living. As he expressed it, 'It means hope to a nation that has given up, because if a gay person makes it, the doors are open to everyone.'

Harvey Milk was an inspiration for the dispossessed. He was memorably played by Sean Penn in Gus Van Sant's movie *Milk* (2008). JE

❯ Milk outside his camera shop on the day of his election in 1977.

"Well-behaved women seldom make history."

Laurel Thatcher Ulrich
American Quarterly
1976

This line first appeared in a journal essay entitled "Vertuous Women Found." Once it took root it was not unusual to see it on T-shirts, mugs, posters, and bumper stickers. Its author was a professor at Harvard, a historian who focused on early America and women.

The phrase perfectly summed up Ulrich's study of pious, well-behaved colonial females, described by Cotton Mather (Puritan minister, campaigner, and staunch supporter of the Salem witch trials) as "the hidden ones." Unless they caused some upset, women's only noted presence during this period was to appear in the odd eulogy. Speaking out almost certainly guaranteed them notoriety, as well as entry into some historical document other than a death record.

Ulrich's phrase was eventually embraced by women's groups and took on another life. The author herself would return to it in 2007, when she used it as the title of a book that looked at key texts by three women—Christine de Pizan, Elizabeth Cady Stanton, and Virginia Woolf. Her reason for revisiting it was pragmatic: "[B]ecause of the popularity of the slogan, it offers an opportunity to reach out to those who might not take a history course, and encourage them to ask new questions about the nature of history." **IHS**

"An eye for an eye only ends up making the whole world blind."

Mahatma Gandhi
Attributed
1982

This striking statement is made in *Gandhi* (1982), the inspirational movie directed by Richard Attenborough, but it is not certain that Gandhi actually said this, though it certainly encapsulates his philosophy. Some credit scriptwriter John Briley with the words, but the original source may be Louis Fischer's 1950 biography of the Indian leader. Fischer summed up Gandhi's nonviolent views in very similar terms, although he did not attribute the words to Gandhi or say when they were spoken. Martin Luther King Jr.'s book *Stride Towards Freedom* (1958) gave another version of the same aphorism, recalling its roots in the Bible: Exodus 21:24 commands that vengeance be limited to "an eye for an eye and a tooth for a tooth, no more." But Jesus revolutionized this by telling his disciples not to resist an evil person, but to turn the other cheek.

Since King admired Gandhi, it is possible that he had read Fischer's book and acquired the idea from it. Jesus's take on it was undoubtedly the background to the nonviolence of King's civil rights campaign, from the Montgomery, Alabama, bus boycott onward, as well as inspiring pacifists for 2,000 years. **JF**

Weightlessness is a great equalizer.

Sally Ride
NOVA
1984

Twenty-one years after Valentina Tereshkova left the Earth's atmosphere, on June 18, 1983, Sally Ride became the first American woman to fly into space. A PhD physics graduate, she was one of 8,000 applicants who answered a Stanford University student newspaper ad for potential astronauts. She joined NASA in 1978, as the Space Shuttle program was preparing its first launch. She was a member of the crew on the second flight by Challenger, the seventh shuttle flight. Her impressive credentials notwithstanding, at the preflight press conference Ride alone was asked questions like "Will the flight affect your reproductive organs?," "Will you become a mother?," and "Do you weep when things go wrong on the job?" Her response was, "How come nobody ever asks [Captain] Rick Hauck those questions?"

She returned for a second flight in 1984 and was one of the lead investigators into the 1986 Challenger disaster. She left NASA in 1987 to return to a research position at Stanford. In 2001 she founded Sally Ride Science, an organization aimed at popularizing science. The above quotation highlighted Ride's belief that in science there is no gender imbalance. **IHS**

◬ Sally Ride eating a meal during a space flight onboard the Challenger shuttle.

"Truth is not merely what we are thinking, but also why, to whom, and under what circumstances we say it."

Václav Havel
Temptation
1985

Václav Havel was a Czech writer, philosopher and politician, who was President of Czechoslovakia from 1989 to 1992, and then after the 'Velvet Divorce' from Slovakia, the first President of the Czech Republic from 1993 to 2003. He first came to prominence in the Prague theatre world as an absurdist playwright, the author of works such as *The Garden Party* (1963), and was also the leader and founder of the Civic Forum, which opposed the Communist regime in Czechoslovakia.

Temptation is a Faustian play, set in a Cold-War era Communist country. The above quotation critiques the notion that the 'truth' of a claim is merely what it says: that is, its factual content. Several factors determine whether or not a claim may be misleading when spoken (even if it is still 'technically' true); these include the purpose of the statement, the audience and the circumstances of the utterance. In short, a number of deceptive rhetorical strategies can be brought into play to bias the impact or effect of a 'technically' true spoken thought. The strategies are capable of effectively amplifying or silencing what the claim purports to say or of transforming its interpretation. Consequently, 'truth' in speechmaking hinges on more factors than are usually acknowledged. **JE**

"We must always take sides. Neutrality helps the oppressor, never the victim."

Elie Wiesel
Nobel Peace Prize acceptance speech
1986

Born a Jew in Romania, Eliezer 'Elie' Wiesel was captured by the Nazis, but survived the death camps of Auschwitz, Buna-Monowitz and Buchenwald. After liberation, he resolved to honour the memory of the millions who had been murdered in the gas chambers by telling the story of the Holocaust, first as a journalist in France and later as a writer and a university professor in the United States. Of his many books, he is most famous for *Night* (1958), an account of his teenaged experience of trying to look after his father in the concentration camps, when he realized with horror that any notion of truth, honour or morality was equally at risk of annihilation.

In his Nobel Peace Prize acceptance speech, Wiesel reflected on the lessons he had learned from his life under the Nazis. Having survived World War II, he 'swore never to be silent when and wherever human beings endure suffering and humiliation'.

Silence, in Wiesel's view, 'encourages the tormentor, never the tormented. Sometimes we must interfere'. He continued: 'When human lives are endangered, when human dignity is in jeopardy, national borders and sensitivities become irrelevant. Whenever men or women are persecuted because of their race, religion or political views, that place must – at that moment – become the center of the universe.' **JE**

Civilized people must get off their high horse and learn with humble lucidity that they too are an indigenous variety.

Alain Finkielkraut
The Undoing of Thought
1988

Alain Finkielkraut is a French essayist whose work often critiques the impact of multiculturalism and relativism on Western values. In 2014 he was elected to the Académie Française, the central council in all matters relating to the upkeep of the French language.

In *The Undoing of Thought*, Finkielkraut expresses the fear that 'civilization' will be eroded by multiculturalism – that universal values will collapse if relativism denies us the ability to have values whose meaning is independent of context – for example, he approves of the French government's ban on the Muslim headscarf because he believes such clothing is inimical to French culture.

The above quotation occurs in a passage criticizing French anthropologist Claude Lévi-Strauss, who believed that so-called 'civilized' minds are no different from the minds of so-called 'indigenous' peoples the world over. Finkielkraut sees the world rather differently. In his view: 'Multiculturalism does not mean that cultures blend. Mistrust prevails. . .parallel societies are forming that continuously distance themselves from each other. . . When hatred of culture becomes itself a part of culture, the life of the mind loses all meaning.' **JE**

⊘ Alain Finkielkraut is a French left-wing intellectual whose views attract controversy.

"People always say that I didn't give up my seat because I was tired, but that isn't true ... No, the only tired I was, was tired of giving in."

Rosa Parks
My Story
1992

When forty-two-year-old African American Rosa Parks refused to give up her bus seat to a white man in Montgomery, Alabama, on 1 December 1955, it triggered a wave of protest that led directly to the birth of the civil rights movement. After the 'white' section of the bus was filled, a white man demanded her seat – when she refused, the driver called the police and Parks was arrested for breaching segregation laws. She was convicted four days later, and the black community began a boycott of the city buses that lasted 381 days. It was coordinated by the newly formed Montgomery Improvement Association, led by a newcomer to the district, the young Martin Luther King Jr.

Opposition included the firebombing of churches and King's home, but the US Supreme Court ruled that segregation was unconstitutional; the boycott was called off on 20 December 1956. King's leadership of the action made him a major voice in the emergent civil rights movement. In 1996, Rosa Parks received the Presidential Medal of Freedom from President Bill Clinton, and in 1999 she was named as one of *Time* magazine's 'Heroes and Icons of the 20th Century.' **ME**

⬣ Rosa Parks sitting down on a bus became one of the most important political events in US history.

> # *The most common way people give up their power is by thinking they don't have any.*

Alice Walker
Attributed
2004

Alice Walker is an influential and prolific American novelist, poet and activist. After she was blinded in her right eye as a child, her sharecropper parents bought her a typewriter. She is acclaimed for her epistolary novel *The Color Purple* (1982), which focuses on the lives of African American women in the Southern United States in the 1930s, during which period they were caught between a racist white culture and a patriarchal black one. The book was adapted into a movie by Steven Spielberg in 1985, and a musical produced by Oprah Winfrey and Quincy Jones in 2004. Walker is also notable for coining – in *In Search of Our Mothers' Gardens* (1983), an essay collection – the term 'womanist' to describe distinctively black feminism.

Walker's political activism is oriented around critiques of racism, sexism, class society and other systems of oppression. The above quotation – from *The Best Liberal Quotes Ever: Why the Left is Right*, an anthology compiled by William P Martin – challenges the hopelessness that is sometimes felt by oppressed people. It is a powerful expression of the wise old saying that one must never surrender or despair. JE

⌖ Alice Walker had a good education in spite of the insistence of her parents' landlords that people like her did not need one.

"The most intense hatreds are not between political parties but within them."

Phillip Adams
Attributed
2005

Phillip Adams is an award-winning Australian journalist, filmmaker and broadcaster. He is an inveterate controversialist, especially as the regular presenter of the radio show *Late Night Live*.

The above quotation, however, reads less like a provocation than a plain statement of fact. In Adams's native country, Prime Minister Julia Gillard was unceremoniously ousted in 2013 by Kevin Rudd, who, in addition to being a member of the same political party, had recently promised that he would never attempt to usurp her. In Britain in 1962, Prime Minister Harold Macmillan sacked six members of his Cabinet, suddenly, in what became known as 'the Night of the Long Knives' (a satirical reference to the event of the same name in Nazi Germany in 1934).

There are numerous US examples. In 1804, Vice President Aaron Burr killed Founding Father Alexander Hamilton in a duel. During the Civil War, Confederate President Jefferson Davis and General Joseph E Johnston blamed each other for everything that went wrong; and in the 1960s fellow Democrats Robert F Kennedy and Lyndon B Johnson hated each other with a passion. **JE**

⊘ Phillip Adams believes that there are few enemies more dangerous and treacherous than a political ally.

"Neanderthals fighting over some damn hill."

Carlos Santana
The Universal Tone
2014

It is easy to ridicule the utterances of many pop stars about world peace as banal and meaningless. Cynics may ask how many lives have been saved by John Lennon's 'Give Peace a Chance' or how many conflicts have been ended by Tom Paxton's or Melanie Safka's 'Peace Will Come.' But in his memoir, Mexican American guitarist Carlos Santana broke the mold decisively. The above quotation concludes a passage that begins:

'To this day I detest anyone who tries to indoctrinate others into hating people because they are different and trying to get ahead and uplift themselves. I detest it as much as I did when some Mexicans were trying to get me to hate gringos. That's what they tried to tell me in Tijuana, and I didn't buy into that lie either. We're all people. The other stuff – like flags, borders, third world, first world – that's an illusion. All this stuff keeps us stuck in the same place where we were 10,000 years ago.'

The band Santana – which specialized in rock with a Latin feel and Afro Cuban rhythms – had major hits in the 1960s and 1970s, both with singles, such as 'Black Magic Woman' and 'Oye Como Va,' and with the albums *Abraxas, Santana III* and *Caravanserai*. JP

Carlos Santana at his 1996 induction into the RockWalk on Sunset Boulevard, Hollywood, California.

> *It does not matter what's the colour of your skin, what language do you speak, what religion you believe in. It is that we should all consider each other as human beings.*

Malala Yousafzai
Nobel Peace Prize acceptance speech
2014

⬥ Kailash Satyarthi on being awarded his Nobel Peace Prize.

⬥ Malala Yousafzai acknowledges the audience at the award ceremony in Oslo, Norway.

Born in 1997, Malala Yousafzai was a teenager in the Swat Valley of Pakistan when the Taliban invaded the area from neighbouring Afghanistan, imposed strict Islamic laws that prevented girls from being educated and trained them to become suicide bombers.

This did not play well with Malala, the daughter of a liberal educator who named her after a 19th-century Afghan opponent of British invaders. She agitated against the occupiers so vehemently – both in speeches such as 'How Dare the Taliban Take Away My Basic Right to Education?' and in a widely read blog for the BBC – that there was an attempt on her life: in October 2012 she was shot in the head by a Taliban gunman.

Seriously wounded, Malala was airlifted to Britain, where she gradually recovered, and reached a wider audience than ever before. On her sixteenth birthday in 2013, she addressed an audience of 500 people at the United Nations in New York City. In 2014, Malala Yousafzai was one of two recipients of that year's Nobel Peace Prize. Her fellow laureate was Kailash Satyarthi, the Indian social reformer who campaigned against child labour and advocated the universal right to education. JE

Philosophy

ИН-
ЖИЛ,
ИН-
ЖИВ,
ИН-
БУДЕТ ЖИТЬ!

ВЛ. МАЯКОВСКИЙ.

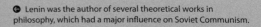 Lenin was the author of several theoretical works in philosophy, which had a major influence on Soviet Communism.

"A journey of a thousand miles begins with a single step."

Laozi
Tao Te Ching
C. 550 BCE

The thrust of the above quotation is that when something needs to be done, it is as well to start immediately. Among numerous viable equivalents is the old English proverb: 'Mighty oaks from little acorns grow.'

Of the supposed author of the Chinese remark, the first philosopher of Taoism, little is known for certain. Some people doubt that he ever existed, but the more widely held view accepts the account of his life in the *Shiji* of Sima Qian, a Chinese historian of the 1st century BCE. According to this biographical sketch, Laozi was a scholar at the court of the Zhou dynasty emperors. There is, however, general agreement that the *Tao Te Ching* cannot be the work of one man alone; the book was compiled over many years by more than one, and probably numerous, authors.

Sima Qian relates that late in life, Laozi met the young Confucius, who praised the old man in poetical terms, comparing him to a dragon that flies high on the wind and clouds. There is no external corroboration that any such encounter ever took place, but Confucians venerate Laozi as a saintlike figure. **JP**

"I cannot teach anybody anything; I can only make them think."

Socrates
Attributed
C. 425 BCE

Although the ancient Greek Socrates never wrote anything, the transmission of his teachings and style of inquiry through two of his students, Plato and Xenophon, cemented his status as a founder of Western philosophy.

The above quotation, widely attributed unsourced to Socrates, relates to the ability to transmit knowledge to others as a teacher. It roughly refers to Socrates's metaphorical depiction of himself in *Theaetetus* (c. 369 BCE) – a dialogue between Socrates and Theaetetus about the nature of learning, written down by Plato – as a 'midwife' of knowledge, helping others to give 'birth' to the wisdom they already have (and attributing no innate wisdom to himself). In this sense, Socrates sees himself not as teaching (transmitting knowledge to people that they did not have), but rather as encouraging them to use their minds to discover what they already knew at some level. Consequently, such commentary in *Theaetetus* supports the first claim of the above quotation (that Socrates cannot actually teach anybody anything new) and may possibly support the latter (that he is only enabling them to think through problems for themselves). **JE**

"Man is the measure of all things."

Protagoras
Attributed
c. 420 BCE

Protagoras was a pre-Socratic philosopher, identified by Plato as one of the Sophists, a group of teachers for hire for young nobles and statesmen in ancient Greece. In addition to being immortalized by Plato in dialogues, Protagoras is traditionally believed to have authored a number of now-lost works, such as *On the Gods*, *On Virtues* and *On Ambition*.

The above quotation, attributed in Plato's *Theaetetus* (c. 369 BCE), is the one for which Protagoras is best known. It is because of this phrase that Protagoras is credited for founding philosophical relativism – the notion that, in effect, all points of view are equally valid. These words are often followed by noting that people are the measure 'of the things that are, that they are, and of the things that are not, that they are not' – in other words, that each individual's claim to truth is relative to that individual and his or her perception. While little of Protagoras's work has been passed down, philosophical relativism has provided a robust intellectual challenge, against which most stronger philosophical claims of knowledge must contend, whether regarding epistemology, ethics or political philosophy. JE

◈ *Democritus and Protagoras* (1663–64) by Salvator Rosa, the 17th-century Italian painter, poet and printmaker.

In much wisdom is much grief: and he that increaseth knowledge increaseth sorrow.

The reputed author of Ecclesiastes was King Solomon. This engraving is by 19th-century French artist Gustave Doré.

Old Testament
Ecclesiastes
C. 400 BCE

The book of Ecclesiastes is traditionally attributed to Solomon, King of Israel, who is reputed also to have been the author of the Book of Proverbs and the Song of Solomon. However, Solomon lived in the 10th century BCE, and the language of Ecclesiastes is the Aramaic-influenced Hebrew of around 600 years later.

Ecclesiastes is something of an anomaly within the Old Testament; it contains few references to God, and the sentiments expressed in it have more in common with the roughly contemporaneous Greek philosophy of Epicureanism than with the Abrahamic religions.

The overriding theme throughout Ecclesiastes is the power of fate and the futility of struggling against it. There is 'a time to every purpose under the heaven,' 'a time to be born and a time to die,' and the stoical observation that 'one generation passeth away, and another generation cometh: but the Earth abideth for ever'. Since 'all is vanity,' the work advises that 'a man hath no better thing under the sun, than to eat, and to drink, and to be merry'.

Many people say that knowledge is power, but here is a reminder that it may also be painful. **IHS**

" *I know that I do not know.* "

Socrates
Attributed
399 BCE

Ancient Greek philosopher Socrates engaged a large number of people of his day in a wide range of debates. He was reputedly a man of great integrity and a skilled orator. However, at the age of seventy years, he was accused of impiety and corruption of the youth, put on trial, convicted and executed by being forced to drink hemlock, a deadly poison. The scene is memorably represented in *The Death of Socrates* (1787) by French painter Jacques-Louis David.

A central element of Socrates's reputation is his attributed claim to know nothing, as quoted by Plato in the *Apology*. This is often paraphrased in a number of ways, including the above variant (although some scholars have argued that it was never said in this form). Whichever way it is phrased, the quotation relates to Socrates's consistent emphasis during his trial that he is aware of the limits of his own knowledge. This is a considerable theme in accounts of Socrates's debates and dialogues, which often involve asking an interlocutor targeted questions in an attempt to encourage them to arrive at a deeper answer to the question in hand or to doubt their prior certainty. Even if reliable accounts of this quotation are somewhat hard to pin down, the words accurately reflect Socrates's approach to intellectual discussion in his emphasis on understanding the limits of one's own knowledge. **JE**

" *The unexamined life is not worth living.* "

Socrates
Attributed
399 BCE

Socrates wrote nothing, but his character and philosophy have been affectionately preserved in the work of his pupil, Plato, a prolific author. The *Apology* from which the above quotation is taken is the latter's account of Socrates's defence (an old meaning of 'apology') when he was on trial for his life.

The background is this: Socrates was a classic eccentric, whose offbeat take on contemporary events was easy to satirize (as Aristophanes did in his comedy *The Clouds*), but which nevertheless exerted a strong influence on the Greek society in which he lived.

When this influence was thought to have become too strong, the people of Athens arraigned Socrates on the vague and probably trumped-up charge of corrupting the youth of the city. The philosopher defended himself doughtily, but the people found him guilty. At first, the court offered him the possibility of exile, but he declined that option and was executed by being forced to drink hemlock.

Socrates was willing to face martyrdom for knowledge and the pursuit of wisdom. In effect, the above quotation reflects his choice – it is stating that if one's life is not spent being self-reflective and critical, then it is not worth living (by implication, that it is better to die than to live such a life, or at least, that one's continued life is irrelevant if spent in ignorance). **JE**

" Great wisdom is generous; petty wisdom is contentious. "

Zhuangzi
Zhuangzi
c. 3rd century BCE

Zhuangzi was a foundational Chinese Taoist philosopher, who lived during the Warring States period (475–221 BCE). He is the author of the *Zhuangzi*, which is considered to be one of the two foundational texts of Taoist philosophy (along with Laozi's *Tao Te Ching*). The *Zhuangzi* is a large collection of parables, anecdotes and fables, and it promotes being carefree and following 'the way' by following nature.

The above quotation is a rendering of a statement attributed to the philosopher from 'The Chapters' of the *Zhuangzi* ('The Chapters' are considered to be Zhuangzi's own writings). The text itself is complex and contains many seeming contradictions, yet while translation compounds the text's ambiguity, Zhuangzi's words emphasize the difference between 'great' and 'lesser' understanding. Whereas the former highlights that wisdom is expansive, the latter is limited and subject to the misunderstandings and partial views that cause conflict. Ambiguities aside, this passage reminds us that having only partial information is a marker of lesser understanding and that attaining ever more complete understanding is a sign of a wise individual. **JE**

" There is nothing so absurd but some philosopher has said it. "

Cicero
De Divinatione (On Divination)
44 BCE

It is the 'been there, done that' of philosophical statements. In essence, as René Descartes would put it in his 17th-century treatise 'On Divination: 'One cannot conceive anything so strange and so implausible that it has not already been said by one philosopher or another.'

The Latin source of Cicero's quotation takes the form of a dialogue between the author and his brother, Quintus. The first of its two books contains Quintus's defence of the practice of divination. He adduces cogent, if not ultimately persuasive, reasons in support of the merits of haruspicy (divination by examining the entrails of sacrificial animals), augury (divination by the flight of birds), astrology and other oracles.

The second volume presents Cicero's refutation of it all, at the end of which the author declares: 'Just as it is a duty to extend the influence of true religion, which is closely associated with the knowledge of nature, so it is a duty to weed out every root of superstition.' Having said that, he and Quintus agree to follow the traditional Socratic method and make no final verdict on the matter in hand, but rather leave readers to make up their own minds. **IHS**

"*Things are not always what they seem.*"

Phaedrus
Fables, Book IV
c. 50 CE

Gaius Julius Phaedrus was a Roman fabulist and Latin author, and he is notable for being the first writer to translate entire books of fables into Latin (including those known collectively as *Aesop's Fables*). In addition to his impact on Western literature for his translations and authored fables, he is well known for his influence on Jean de La Fontaine, whose own fables made a considerable impression on fabulists across Europe.

The above philosophical quotation refers to the frequent difference between reality and appearance. Although it is easy to take for granted the outward appearance of the state of things – the causes and effects of events and objects, or the meaning of communication and arts, for example – this phrase reminds us that the evident face-value meaning or state of affairs is not always the true one. Sometimes the real meaning, state or causation is hidden, and therefore it takes critical and careful thought to discern the real intention. In effect, Phaedrus's words remind us to not take knowledge for granted and to approach life thoughtfully rather than wander blindly through it and risk being misinformed and misled. JE

⊘ A detail from *The School of Athens* (1509–11), a fresco by Italian Renaissance artist Raphael.

> " *Reserve your right to think, for even to think wrongly is better than not to think at all.* "

Hypatia
Attributed
400 CE

Hypatia was the last great philosopher of the classical era, and the first woman to have a major impact on the science of mathematics. Her philosopher father, Theon, encouraged her studies, and she studied in Athens and Rome. When she returned to her native Alexandria, Egypt, she became head of the city's Neoplatonic school, where she taught mathematics and astronomy and imparted the knowledge of Plato and Aristotle.

Although the above quotation is generally credited to Hypatia, it has also been attributed to Theon. Hypatia also remarked: 'Life is an unfoldment, and the further we travel, the more truth we can comprehend. To understand the things that are at our door is the best preparation for understanding those that lie beyond.'

Hypatia had strong views and expressed them trenchantly; inevitably, therefore, she made enemies. The historian Socrates Scholasticus noted in his *Ecclesiastical History*: 'On account of the self-possession and ease of manner which she had acquired in consequence of the cultivation of her mind, she not infrequently appeared in public in the presence of the magistrates.' Hypatia was murdered when a feud between the Governor and the Bishop of Alexandria descended into citywide chaos. **IHS**

> " *You can take comfort in the likelihood that what is now making you miserable will also pass away.* "

Boethius
The Consolation of Philosophy
523 CE

Boethius was a Roman senator who rose to the high rank of consul, and later held a powerful administrative post. However, his good fortune came to an abrupt end when he was imprisoned and sentenced to death on suspicion of treason. Boethius was well versed in ancient Greek philosophy, from which he found consolation in the year before his execution by writing *The Consolation of Philosophy* in the form of a dialogue with the personified figure 'Philosophy.'

Dismayed and depressed by his reversal of fortune, Boethius's complaints are forcefully rebuked as Philosophy explains that fortune necessarily entails change. He is not consoled by these 'high-sounding phrases' but comes to appreciate their meaning when he is reminded of his life's happy moments. No subsequent misfortunes can erase the memories of such happiness; even though it must inevitably come to an end, so too must the unhappy times. In this manner Philosophy teaches Boethius to recognize that his own mistaken beliefs are the ultimate cause of his sufferings. **TJ**

❷ The opening page of a 1494 edition of Boethius's masterwork.

Quid hác láncéas métancás ad fléc éna pumsét accéas

Quid me félie toácaos láchisa amét

Cy commence Boece son premi
er liure p maniere de dyaloque en me
tr es et en proses compile et translate a
la consolation des desolez et a la retra

ctation de ceulx qui trop se adherdent
empeschent des biens temporelz.
Et en cestui premier metre parle Boece
cóme homme dolent et fort desole

SANCTVS THOMAS DEAC

ERITAE
MEDITA
BITVR GVT
VR MEVM ET
LABIA MEA
DETESTABVN
TVR IMPIV~
PROVERBIO~

MVLTITVD
INIS VSVS
QVE IN RE
BVS NOMI
NANDIS S
EQVENDV P
HILOSOPHV
CÊSET CÕMVNÊ

E HIC
LVMÊ
CLESIE

HIC ADIN
OMNEM VIÃ DISCI

"Philosophy is the handmaiden to theology."

St Thomas Aquinas
Commentary on Boethius's *On the Trinity*
1257–58

Thomas Aquinas was a strong-willed character. He decided to join the Dominicans, a relatively recent order, instead of the Benedictines, with which his mother's family was associated. As a result he was abducted on his mother's orders, imprisoned in the family's castles and sent a prostitute to derail his vow of celibacy.

Philosophical conclusions, for Aquinas, could not contradict those of the Church. If philosophizing found that something in the 'sacred doctrine' did not accord with reason, Aquinas's conclusion was that our capacity to reason was insufficient: faith trumps doubt. Philosophers like to think they question "all the way down," while theologians see this as allowing the servant (reason) to dominate the master (faith). Albert Einstein later warned of the dangers of promoting the intellect to the status of a god: 'It has, of course, powerful muscles but no personality. It cannot lead, it can only serve; and it is not fastidious in its choice of a leader.' Even as a philosopher, it is hard to argue that each field, however scientific, does not take some basic truths on faith. **LW**

◀ Thomas Aquinas is flanked by Aristotle and Plato.

"Entities should not be multiplied unnecessarily."

William of Ockham
Quodlibeta
c. 1324

English scholastic philosopher William of Ockham was a Franciscan monk of the 14th century with some controversial views, one of which – that Pope John XXII, the current ruler of the Holy See, was a heretic – got him excommunicated.

Less controversial was the above quotation, which is known as 'Ockham's razor.' In academic terms it means that 'plurality should not be assumed without necessity'; in common parlance, it means that whenever there is more than one possible solution to any problem, the simpler or the simplest is most likely to be correct. We should cut away all irrelevant matter – hence 'razor.'

In fact, William of Ockham was not the first person to think of this: the credit should go to his contemporary, French bishop Durandus of Saint-Pourçain, but as we may see throughout the present volume, it is one thing to make a good remark and quite another to get the credit for it from posterity.

Modern US philosopher Alan R Baker has suggested that the true use of Ockham's razor lies in discussing metaphysical theories, when 'superfluous ontological apparatus' are employed. **IHS**

"To be, or not to be, that is the question."

This 19th-century portrait by Thomas Lawrence depicts John Kemble in the role of Hamlet.

William Shakespeare
Hamlet
c. 1600

Widely considered the greatest English-language author, William Shakespeare was a poet, playwright and actor, and he remains one of the most influential writers of all time. One of the playwright's most notable tragedies, *Hamlet* is set in the Kingdom of Denmark. It is a dramatization of Prince Hamlet's revenge on his uncle, Claudius, who, after murdering Hamlet's father, seized the throne and married his mother – Queen Gertrude.

Hamlet's musing 'to be, or not to be…' is the opening phrase of one of the character's best-known soliloquies. In it, Hamlet is contemplating the option of suicide. He acknowledges the difficulties and pains of life, but also recognizes that the outcome of death – what comes after life – is uncertain. By considering suicide as a response to tragedy, Hamlet is debating how best to deal with the turmoil of life. Thus, the phrase 'to be, or not to be' more generally signifies the problems of existence; more specifically, it refers to the issue of how we deal with great adversity. Do we continue to struggle, or do we choose to end our lives? And what is at stake in that choice? JE

"Life's but a walking shadow, a poor player that struts and frets his hour upon the stage, and then is heard no more."

William Shakespeare
Macbeth
c. 1606

Macbeth is the dramatic tragedy of a Scottish general pushed by his own ambition, and by that of his wife, to murder the king following a prophecy that he will become King of Scotland. After the murder, he has to continue escalating the violence and tyranny to cover his deeds until he meets a tragic end. *Macbeth* chronicles some of the potential negative consequences of personal quests for power.

In the above quotation, spoken by Macbeth in one of the most significant soliloquies in the play, Shakespeare is primarily discussing the fleeting nature of existence. Macbeth has just lost his powerful wife, and he is alone in the political and bloody turmoil that they created together. His ambition is ebbing away to leave behind nothing other than pessimism and despair. His words refer to life's brevity and futility – life is destined to end too soon – 'a poor player that struts and frets his hour upon the stage, and then is heard no more'. In this way, life is rendered meaningless – it is merely a 'walking shadow', with no substance, and after the struggle for purpose and impact is passed, one's life just stops, silenced forever. JE

This illustration by A E Jackson from c. 1910 portrays the three witches in Act IV, Scene I, of *Macbeth*.

" *I think, therefore I am.* "

René Descartes
Discourse on Method
1637

● Copy of a portrait of René Descartes that was painted in 1649.

❯ Illustration from Descartes' *De Homine* (1662), showing sensory perception of an image and muscular action.

A Latin philosophical proposition (*'Cogito ergo sum'*), translated into French to reach a wider audience (*'Je pense, donc je suis'*) and rendered in English in the form reproduced here, this assertion forms the basis of modern Western philosophical thought, and the epistemological argument underpinning the essence of knowledge and belief. It appears in the French philosopher's treatise on the development of natural sciences, which also explores questions of morality and the existence of God.

It is in the exploration of existence and the notion of doubt that Descartes reaches the conclusion that if we doubt, we cannot question the fact that we exist, stating, 'I observed that, while I thus wished to think that all was false, it was absolutely necessary that I, who thus thought, should be somewhat.' The very fact that we doubt that we exist means that we do exist.

Descartes returned to the proposition in *Meditations on First Philosophy* (1641), albeit in the shorter form of 'I am, I exist.' The Latin equivalent appeared in his *Principles of Philosophy* (1644), in which he stated that this knowledge 'is the first and most certain [knowledge] that occurs to one who philosophizes orderly.' **IHS**

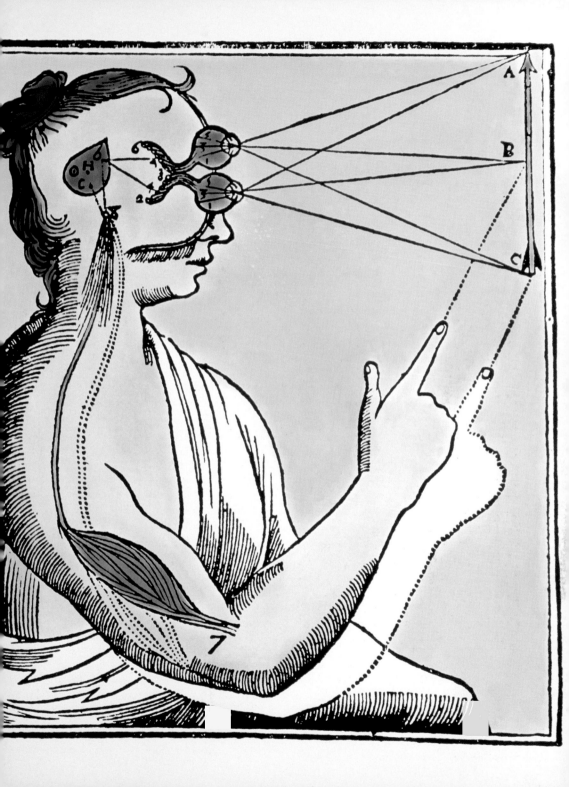

" Philosophy triumphs easily over past evils and future evils; but present evils triumph over it. "

François de La Rochefoucauld
Reflections; or Sentences and Moral Maxims
1665–78

The above quotation – Maxim 22 – by French writer and philosopher François de La Rochefoucauld will resonate with many people. La Rochefoucauld was a firm believer in the power of philosophy, but he also asserted that although it could be used to theorize about past events and to predict future ones, it had little purpose when it came to explaining current events. This is because a large part of philosophy is about pondering what lies ahead and debating the reasons for past events, but the present is something that is not open to discussion of this nature. Hindsight and foresight are useful tools, but they cannot be applied to current events. In this maxim, La Rochefoucauld seems to be suggesting that the present always has the potential to take us by surprise.

The philosopher wrote many maxims, memoirs and letters and has been described as the epitome of the accomplished 17th-century nobleman. He was also a respected soldier who fought bravely in the siege of Paris before his exile in 1643. Although La Rochefoucauld was renowned for his clear-sightedness, he was a man who neither condemned nor praised his fellow human beings, but instead simply depicted the times in which he lived. **TH**

" If men were born free, they would, so long as they remained free, form no conception of good and evil. "

Baruch Spinoza
Ethics: Part IV
1677

The above quotation is Proposition 68 from Spinoza's philosophical treatise and masterpiece *Ethics*, which was published posthumously. In it he rejected the notion of free will, because he believed that if human beings have free will, they will be motivated by personal desires.

Spinoza was a Sephardic Jew whose ancestors had fled from Portugal to Amsterdam in the late 15th century. His upbringing was a traditional Jewish one, but at the age of twenty, he began studying with Franciscus van den Enden, a former Jesuit, and a free thinker who was later condemned as an atheist. This association worried the Amsterdam Jewish community, and the situation was compounded when Spinoza disputed his sister's claim to their father's inheritance in a civil court as opposed to a Talmudic court. As a result he was excommunicated from the Jewish congregation. For the rest of his life, Spinoza worked as a lens grinder, student and writer, but he did not take up the prestigious teaching posts that he was offered. His admirers are many, and his legacy far-reaching: he influenced Hegel, who said that a philosopher is 'either a Spinozist or not a philosopher at all'. **TH**

"Man differs more from man, than man from beaſt."

John Wilmot, Earl of Rochester
'A Satyr Against Reason and Mankind'
1679

The difference between humans and beasts is, according to most authorities, the presence of souls in the former and the absence of them from the latter. John Wilmot's argument is that the rest of living existence is free of this gift or curse, yet this does not create the gulf we might imagine. Humans are not exclusive, he argues. It is the capacity to reason that has divided humanity: we do it in such differing degrees that we quickly lose any common purpose.

Wilmot's life was divided between domesticity and debauchery. He loved the country but could not resist the court scene. Likewise, he saw parallels between the attempts by humans to bear themselves up with philosophical arguments and to allow themselves to go with instinct. Humans can choose, and their choices create such variation in motivation and outcome that they cease to be able to mutually identify. Yet if they chose Wilmot's 'right reason,' they would find common sense. Eating when you are hungry or sleeping with someone when you feel like it are better uses of rationality than the complex differentials to decide the particulars of appropriate behaviour. The waste of time, effort and intellect on moral approbation is shamefully divisive given that we, in common with 'beasts,' should all be striving for survival and happiness. **LW**

"Philosophy is nothing but discretion."

John Selden
Seldeniana, or, The Table-Talk of John Selden, Esq.
1689

An English jurist, historian, antiquarian, politician, Hebraist, Orientalist and polymath, Selden was admired by leading intellectual contemporaries, such as poet John Milton and playwright Ben Jonson. He was an erudite man, and his opinion on matters of law and the constitution carried considerable weight when he was at the peak of his career. Among his most influential judgements was that a single nation should be allowed to rule the oceans – this was against the prevailing view that the seas should be free to all. His controversial views sometimes irked the Church authorities, and, more dangerously, the King of England, Charles I: Selden started out as a Parliamentarian, and was twice imprisoned for this affiliation, but later became a Royalist.

The above quotation comes from a collection of Seldon's sayings recorded by his secretary, Richard Milward, which was published thirty-five years after the speaker's death. The book covers topics as diverse as witches and the Pope; while some of the content is serious, some of it is bon mots, as one would expect from a book titled *Table-Talk*. Selden's words are in the context of suggesting that when 'men comfort themselves with philosophy,' it is because they have 'digested those sentences and made them their own'. Adopting a philosophy gives them the freedom to justify what they think or do 'upon the matter'; they will adopt the philosophy that suits their opinions or actions. **CK**

" *All is for the best in the best of all possible worlds.* "

Reiner aber kan sich als der in dergleichen beßer einbilden, wie Unglück gewesen, und eine herrliche bedencket, Sache es was für sey, einen

unaus- wenn sprechli- sie damals chen Trost er gewesen, in und die Seinigen von Ihren Nöhten empfun- einer solchen Anstalt, den haben würden."

G. W. Leibniz über Versicherung

⊙ Gottfried Leibniz was not only a renowned philosopher but also a respected mathematician and political adviser.

Gottfried Leibniz
Theodicy
1710

A long-standing question that has preoccupied philosophers and theologians is why God allows evil in the world. German philosopher Leibniz believed that there was a rational purpose in God's design that necessarily made this world the 'best of all possible worlds'. Granting that God is both perfectly benevolent and omnipotent, this implies that he must have had a 'sufficient reason' for permitting evils in the world he created. As these imperfections are part of a much greater universe, Leibniz argued that they must therefore contribute to completing the best possible world that an omniscient and omnipotent God could have created.

While Leibniz's argument accepted evil and suffering as necessary in God's grand scheme of things, it offered little comfort to those who suffered. As a result, the above quotation is more commonly associated with *Candide* (1759), wherein Voltaire mocks Leibniz through the character of Dr Pangloss, who repeatedly states that whatever disaster has happened, or will happen, must all be for the best. Pangloss himself is the victim of constant calamities, through which Voltaire satirizes a view of Creation that he evidently finds absurd. **TJ**

"What do we perceive besides our own ideas or sensations?"

George Berkeley
Of the Principles of Human Knowledge
1710

George Berkeley was born in County Kilkenny in Ireland, but he moved in 1720 to England. As a Christian, Berkeley frequently wrote against freethinkers. He was also a distinguished mathematician and wrote an important work on calculus. His last work, *Siris* (1744), is wide-ranging, covering science, theology and philosophy. Contemporary philosophers study Berkeley because of his views on perception, the difference between 'primary' and 'secondary' qualities, and the importance of language.

The above quotation is a challenge to the philosophies of John Locke and Isaac Newton. Berkeley's theory, called 'immaterialism,' states that material objects, such as tables and chairs, exist only in the minds of the people who see them: 'For what are [these] objects but the things we perceive by sense?' He expands on this notion by suggesting that it is contradictory that such things should exist unperceived. His first important work – 'An Essay Toward a New Theory of Vision' (1709) – was not successful initially, so he rewrote it and published it as a dialogue: *Three Dialogues between Hylas and Philonous* (1713). Philonous represents the mind; Hylas, matter. **TH**

◈ John Smybert painted this portrait of Anglo-Irish philosopher George Berkeley in 1727.

"We should weep for men at their birth, not at their death."

Montesquieu
Persian Letters
1722

In this epistolary novel, in which two fictional Persian noblemen visit France and write home about the habits of the indigenous population, the words above can be read in two ways: either life is brutal, and we are better not born at all into this vale of tears, or mourning death is simply self-indulgence – we should rejoice that those we love have reached a higher plain.

In early 18th-century France, life for all but the privileged few (of whom Montesquieu was one) was often torturous, and relieved only by death. A similar sentiment had been expressed by 13th-century Pope Innocent III, who wrote: 'Man was formed of…the filthiest seed. . .born to toil, dread, and trouble. . .born only to die.' Under such circumstances, which were largely unchanged 500 years later, birth might be an occasion of mourning. Death, on the other hand, should bring joy to the faithful, who believe that those we love will be united with God.

The idea that life is pain is nothing new: it is expressed in various forms in every language throughout the ages. But this is one of the most succinct, and therefore quotable, versions. **LW**

A wise man, therefore, proportions his beliefs to the evidence.

David Hume

An Enquiry Concerning Human Understanding
1748

Wisdom is commonly associated with knowledge gained through experience. However, as Scottish philosopher David Hume suggested in his discussion of miracles, it is the ability to assess the nature and quality of our experiences that constitutes true wisdom. While Hume was a staunch defender of empiricism as the only means by which to gain knowledge, he recognized that the evidence we use to form and maintain beliefs is often derived from unreliable sources, such as the testimony of others. In contrast, the laws of nature have themselves been established from our long, repeated experience of their reliable operation, so beliefs based on these laws are warranted to the highest degree of probability.

In stressing the high degree of repeated evidence required to justify a belief in any phenomenon, Hume's argument about miracles showed probability to be of crucial importance for drawing wise conclusions about matters in science and everyday life. For that reason it also implied a kind of personal and public duty involved in holding and espousing beliefs, and this has led to a distinct and continuing field of inquiry about the 'ethics of belief.' TJ

⊘ This pencil, chalk and watercolour portrait (c. 1764) by Louis Carrogis captures Hume's contemplative nature.

"Live your life as though your every act were to become a universal law."

⬥ Kant's extensive works helped to establish a new era of philosophical thought.

Immanuel Kant

Groundwork of the Metaphysics of Morals
1785

Kant is considered a central figure to the development of modern philosophy. His most notable works include *Critique of Pure Reason* (1781), *Critique of Practical Reason* (1788) and *Critique of Judgement* (1790). He is one of the central figures in moral philosophy promoting deontological (rule-based) ethics, which derive the rightness of acts independently from their resulting consequences.

Kant's theory revolves around what he considered the single moral obligation: the 'categorical imperative.' The above quotation is from the first formulation of the categorical imperative, which argues that an act is right if it is universally right in all circumstances, irrespective of consequences or context of the proposition, from its logical properties alone. We should thus avoid acting according to any maxims that, if universalized, would generate logical contradictions. While the Kantian approach to ethics is simultaneously influential and critiqued, it reminds us not to perform actions from our personal standpoint and interests, which only 'work' because we are the only ones performing them. JE

All truth passes through three stages. First, it is ridiculed. Second, it is violently opposed. Third, it is accepted as being self-evident.

Arthur Schopenhauer
Attributed
c. 1818

Arthur Schopenhauer was a German philosopher best known for his work *The World as Will and Representation* (1818). He is also known for his metaphysical and ethical system, which is often interpreted as an example of pessimism in philosophy.

The above quotation in its exact phrasing is often attributed to Schopenhauer, but most frequently without source information – it almost certainly does not exist in the philosopher's magnum opus of 1818. However, Schopenhauer is appropriately credited for being among the first to refer to 'stages of truth' in the *The World as Will and Representation*, where he states: 'To truth only a brief celebration of victory is allowed between the two long periods during which it is condemned as paradoxical, or disparaged as trivial.' Although it is likely that the above quotation did not come from Schopenhauer, its meaning is clear: new statements of truth are first derided, then challenged, before finally gaining credibility as a new common sense. Regardless of the misattribution, such a quotation encourages readers to question established narratives regarding truth and falsehood. **JE**

⬤ Schopenhauer has been cited as an influence by Richard Wagner and Sigmund Freud, among many others.

"Whatever is reasonable is true, and whatever is true is reasonable."

Georg Wilhelm Friedrich Hegel
Elements of the Philosophy of Right
1821

Georg Wilhelm Friedrich Hegel was a 19th-century German philosopher whose systematic theory about the process and development of human knowledge has been subject to extensive debate. This is partly due to the lack of clarity that can sometimes be exacerbated in translations of Hegel's writings or lectures. The meaning of the above quotation can perhaps be grasped more clearly by the common, alternative translation: 'What is rational is actual, and what is actual is rational.' As Hegel is describing the formation of ideas, an idea becomes rational (reasonable) only when manifested in some actual (true) material form. In this way the mind gives objectivity to what was previously 'only an idea,' and that idea, in turn, can then be perceived as rational.

As the above quotation is from *Elements of the Philosophy of Right*, in which Hegel sets out his political theory, it has sometimes been misinterpreted to support political conservatism by implying that any established constitution must be more rational than any imagined alternative. On the contrary, Hegel's theory highlights the dynamic power of the mind in creating ideas that can direct the progress of social and political institutions. **TJ**

"Man is what he eats."

Ludwig Feuerbach
The Natural Sciences and the Revolution
1850

In its simplest sense, 'Man is what he eats' amounts to the observation that all human beings are essentially composed of the substances they consume. This basic idea had been recognized by writers and thinkers centuries before German philosopher Ludwig Feuerbach expressed it in such concise terms. Despite its apparent simplicity, he intended the aphorism to explain how a prodigious variety of cultural practices throughout history have emerged from this basic need for sustenance.

In keeping with Feuerbach's materialistic rejection of mind–body dualism, mental functions must also be affected by the nutrients that the body digests. Since the very nature of human thought and emotion is the product of these chemical substances, Feuerbach believed that a true understanding of human nature could proceed only by scientific investigations into the material foundations of mental phenomena. His renewed focus on humanity's corporeal nature influenced aspects of Karl Marx's emerging theory of historical materialism. But it has proven a more fertile basis for research in anthropology, and most notably in behavioural neuroscience. **TJ**

❯ Rabelais's character Gargantua gorges himself on food.

> " *It is better to be a human being dissatisfied than a pig satisfied; better to be Socrates dissatisfied than a fool satisfied.* "

J S Mill in a cartoon by caricaturist Spy (Leslie Ward), published in *Vanity Fair* magazine in March 1873.

John Stuart Mill
Utilitarianism
1863

Mill was an English political economist, feminist, civil servant and philosopher. His intellectual development was significantly influenced by his being the son of Scottish philosopher and political economist James Mill, and the close friend of the founder of modern utilitarianism, Jeremy Bentham. Mill was particularly notable in philosophy for his works defending political liberty (*On Liberty*, 1859) and for a variant of utilitarianism that distinguished between the qualities of pleasures.

In his account of utilitarianism (from which the above quotation derives), Mill advocates a distinction between higher and lower pleasures, arguing against notions that the 'greatest happiness' to be pursued is purely hedonistic. Instead, while satisfaction derived from these sources is not entirely devoid of value, Mill is promoting pleasures such as the pursuit of knowledge, art and music. Although his method of choosing which pleasures are 'higher' or 'lower' may be controversial, it is a thought-provoking argument that human beings are capable of developing higher and more complex capacities and enjoyments, and thus political and moral actions should facilitate those enjoyments. **JE**

"There is no fixed and constant authority, but a continual exchange of mutual, temporary, and, above all, voluntary authority and subordination."

Mikhail Bakunin

'What is Authority?'

1871

Bakunin was a Russian political philosopher whose writings provided much of the basis for anarchism – the belief that governments are unnecessary (and self-serving and generally malign) and that every individual should be accountable only to him- or herself. His views differed profoundly from those of the Communist Karl Marx, and the two men fell out badly over the correct way to proceed towards world revolution.

The essay from which the above quotation is taken continues thus: 'This same reason forbids me, then, to recognize a fixed, constant and universal authority, because there is no universal man, no man capable of grasping in all that wealth of detail, without which the application of science to life is impossible, all the sciences, all the branches of social life.'

Bakunin's other famous remarks were 'The urge for destruction is also a creative urge,' and in a possibly lighter vein, 'Everything will pass, and the world will perish, but [Beethoven's] *Ninth Symphony* will remain.' His most famous work was *An Appeal to the Slavs* (1848), which called for a free federation of the peoples of Eastern Europe. **JP**

"Beauty is in the eye of the beholder."

Margaret Wolfe Hungerford

Molly Bawn

1878

Hungerford was a prolific Irish Romantic novelist whose works were popular throughout the English-speaking world in the late 19th century. Her novels are now largely forgotten, but she achieved immortality through the above quotation, which is now universally ascribed to her, even though she seems to have taken it from previously established proverbial usage. Moreover, there are many earlier versions of the same idea, probably dating back to the 3rd century BCE, when a similar aphorism (in Greek) was attributed to Plato. The idea that it expresses, that appreciation of beauty is a personal matter that is not necessarily shared by everyone, was already proverbial by 1600 and can be found in, among other places, William Shakespeare's *Love's Labour's Lost* (c. 1597), and later in Benjamin Franklin's *Poor Richard's Almanack* (1759).

If it is true that the opinion of the person looking (rather than the appearance of the person being looked at) is what creates beauty, does this explain why members of both sexes (women more so than men, but this may be a result of endemic patriarchy) try so hard to appear attractive? Many are willing to change their appearance if those whose opinions they value suggest it, for it is the compliments of others that please them, rather than the sense of being attractive to themselves. The proverb gives prominence to cultural currency, too: some find beauty in a modern work of experimental painting or an art installation, whereas others see only a few splashes of paint or an unmade bed; and ideas of feminine beauty, as evidenced by portraiture, change radically over time. **JF**

"That which does not kill us makes us ßronger."

Friedrich Nietzsche
Twilight of the Idols
1889

Nietzsche was a German philosopher whose work has been deeply influential in Western philosophy. He is renowned for his theory of aesthetics, his rejection of religion and notions of objective truth, and his advocacy for the creation of the self and external world in one's own chosen ideal image.

Twilight of the Idols, from which the above quotation derives – sometimes as 'That which does not destroy me, makes me stronger' – was written in a little over a week while Nietzsche was on holiday in Sils Maria. Functioning as a sort of introduction to Nietzsche's work, the book highlights the contributions of Roman thinkers. It also emphasizes the philosopher's focus on the concept of 'transvaluation of all values': affirming, rather than condemning, life. The above quotation, from the aphoristic Maxims and Arrows section, is prefaced by the words 'Out of life's school of war,' thus signalling, in context, that there are oppositional circumstances and conflicts in the world, but that if one survives the hardship (overcomes it rather than succumbs to it), one emerges from it stronger than before. **JE**

◉ *Friedrich Nietzsche* (1906) by Norwegian artist Edvard Munch.

"Truth is the objeĕ of philosophy, but not always of philosophers."

John Churton Collins
Attributed
c. 1900

The brilliant career of John Churton Collins began unpromisingly with the emigration of his father, an 'improvident Gloucestershire doctor,' to Australia, where he immediately died. His widow was left with three young children. Collins's ferocious intellect was soon evident, and it ensured him a place at King Edward's School in Birmingham, from where he went on to study at Oxford University. His ambition was no less than the reform of the university system, and his target, the 'infectious complicity' of academic institutions. Against this background, his statement about philosophers (quoted in Aphorisms in the *English Review* of April 1914) implies criticism of those who fail to take seriously the task of academia, to understand what is valuable to the regeneration of humanity.

Collins was described by the poet Alfred, Lord Tennyson, as 'a louse on the locks of literature'. His efforts at academic reform were largely successful, but the personal cost could not have been higher. Collins's body was found lying in a ditch outside Lowestoft, Suffolk, after he had presumably committed suicide: the ultimate act of despair at a world unable to bear the truth. **LW**

" Time: that which man is always trying to kill, but which ends up killing him. "

Herbert Spencer
Attributed
1902

Herbert Spencer was an English philosopher, sociologist and political theorist of the late Victorian and early Edwardian eras. He was well known as a proponent of evolution, having coined the term 'the survival of the fittest' after reading *On the Origin of Species* (1859) by Charles Darwin. Spencer is both noteworthy and controversial for being a central figure in social Darwinism, which extends to society the concept of 'the survival of the fittest,' opposing humanitarian efforts for their perceived inhibiting role on natural evolutionary processes. The phrase implies that those who succeed and fail in society do so because they are, respectively, the most and least suited for survival, de facto justifying social inequality.

The above quotation is often attributed (unsourced) to Spencer, and the words are a play on the phrase 'killing time,' which refers to wasting time or finding a way to pass the time. Spencer's phrase relates to the fact that although people, at first, may attempt to 'kill time,' eventually time, instead, will kill them all. The latter insight is a clear reference to our inevitable mortality. Since we must, as entities, die, time is our ultimate enemy – we can never kill time, but time inevitably kills each and every one of us. **JE**

" A man is literally what he thinks. "

James Allen
'As a Man Thinketh'
1903

James Allen was a British author whose inspirational and philosophical books and poetry helped to start the self-help movement. He is best known for his work 'As a Man Thinketh,' a literary essay on the power of thought to produce and transform circumstances in one's own life. The title comes from the Book of Proverbs in the Old Testament of the Bible: 'As a man thinketh in his heart, so is he.' After Allen's death in 1912, his widow, Lily, kept his memory alive and ensured that his writings remained in print and reached the widest possible audience.

Allen precedes the above quotation with an examination of the Book of Proverbs passage. He argues that the phrase reflects 'the whole of man's being' and also affects the entirety of human circumstance and experience. He follows this by stating that a man is actually nothing other than what he thinks, 'his character being the complete sum of all his thoughts'. In essence this means that the person – one's virtue, character traits, that is, one's self – is the aggregate of thoughts. As a consequence, it is implied in context that people have a choice: one can disregard the conscious control of thoughts, becoming a product of circumstance (and outside determination and creation), or one can take conscious control over one's own thoughts and, by doing so, take responsibility for one's own self-creation, character and circumstances. **JE**

" There is only one thing that a philosopher can be relied on to do . . . contradict other philosophers. "

William James
Speech at the World Peace Congress
1904

The above quotation comes from a speech delivered by US philosopher and psychologist William James at a banquet held on the closing day of the World Peace Congress in Boston, Massachusetts, in October 1904. His remarks were subsequently published in *The Atlantic Monthly* in December the same year.

At the time James delivered his speech, he was an active member of the faculty of Harvard University and acknowledged as one of the world's leading thinkers. His comment constitutes the opening lines of his speech at the banquet and is suitably witty for such an occasion. However, the aim of the event was serious: the World Peace Congresses were run by the forerunner of the League of Nations, the Inter-Parliamentary Union, and it was the primary forum for the peace movement before World War I.

James went on to point out that although ancient philosophers 'defined man as the rational animal,' he remains an animal, albeit 'the most formidable of all beasts of prey'. James then considered the psychological roots of war and explained why there would always be wars – because humans are bellicose by nature. **CK**

" Life is the art of drawing sufficient conclusions from insufficient premises. "

Samuel Butler
The Note-Books of Samuel Butler
1912

Samuel Butler was an English author. Two of his best-known works are the satirical utopian novel *Erewhon* (1872) and the semiautobiographical novel *The Way of All Flesh*, published posthumously in 1903, which reacts against hypocrisy in the Victorian era. He is also known for his prose translations from Greek of the *Iliad* and the *Odyssey* of Homer.

The above quotation, from Butler's posthumously published notebooks, is one of the author's thought-provoking and humorous takes on life. He is analyzing life as, on the one hand, giving 'insufficient' premises to make decisions – we are rarely given all the knowledge we need to succeed in life and determine our course of action. On the other hand, we hope to draw 'sufficient conclusions' and take the available information to make the best inferences, choices and responses under the circumstances. And this is not a science but rather an art – we cannot, with certainty, come to the right conclusions, but we can try to develop the 'best' approach, and reach the best possible outcomes within these serious limitations. In essence, Butler is implying that life does not give people the perfect information about the right thing to do, but it does give them the ability to make the appropriate choices within the confines of their circumstances. **JE**

ЛЕНИН —
ЖИЛ,
ЛЕНИН —
ЖИВ,
ЛЕНИН —
БУДЕТ ЖИТЬ!

ВЛ. МАЯКОВСКИЙ.

"A lie told often enough becomes the truth."

Vladimir Lenin
Attributed
c. 1917

Vladimir Ilyich Lenin was a Russian politician, theorist, and Communist revolutionary. He was head of the Russian Soviet Federative Socialist Republic from 1917 to 1924 and of the Soviet Union from 1922 to 1924. He ruled a Russia that had become a one-party Socialist state. Of his written works, he is notable for *The Development of Capitalism in Russia* (1899), *What Is to Be Done?* (1902), *Imperialism* (1917), and *The State and Revolution* (1917).

The above quotation is almost certainly an unsourced misattribution to Lenin—similar phrases have also been ascribed to Joseph Goebbels. Regardless of authorship, it most literally (and cynically) means that the constant repetition of evident falsehoods transforms them into truth—in other words, established truth may at times be only repeated falsehood. Less cynically, it may merely mean that a lie told often enough appears true, or that it can be taken for truth, and in this regard, promotes a healthy skepticism of supposed common sense rather than the radical skeptical position that truth is merely agreed-upon falsehood. Lies can be accepted as truth, thus calling into question established dogma. JE

Lenin in 1917, when he became the first head of the Soviet state.

A Russian propaganda poster from 1967: "Lenin Lived, Lenin Lives, Lenin Will Live Forever!"

" *Wherefore one cannot speak, thereof one must be silent.* "

Ludwig Wittgenstein
Tractatus Logico-Philosophicus
1921

Wittgenstein was one of the most original thinkers in the history of philosophy, and much of his originality consisted in showing that very history often amounted to the futile pursuit of nonsense. In his first publication, *Tractatus Logico-Philosophicus*, Wittgenstein described as nonsense all those propositions that fail to factually 'picture' the world. Therefore, even a statement such as 'green is a colour' is nonsensical as both nouns refer to mental concepts rather than represent real objects. Because this suggests that only scientific propositions can ever make sense, then entire areas, such as aesthetics and ethics, are rendered meaningless. And precisely because thoughts on such topics are meaningless, 'one must be silent' about them.

Many readers of the *Tractatus* have observed that Wittgenstein made much of the distinction between saying and showing. Most importantly, this means that what cannot be adequately expressed in language can nevertheless be shown. For this very reason, by exposing the limits of language, Wittgenstein's insight has most notably inspired visual artists in their attempts at expressing the ineffable. **TJ**

In philosophy, it is not the attainment of the goal that matters, it is the things that are met with by the way.

Havelock Ellis
The Dance of Life
1923

British essayist and physician Havelock Ellis was a pioneering sexologist, notable for his seven-volume *Studies in the Psychology of Sex* (1897–1928) and his advocacy for an open and nonjudgemental approach to many sexual practices and desires that were deemed to be taboo in their time. In *The Dance of Life*, Ellis promoted the recognition of life as an art, and the development of the self through a variety of arts and practices, such as dance, thought, writing, religion and morality. He also engaged with *The Philosophy of 'As If'* (1911) by German philosopher Hans Vaihinger, which argued that a large array of human knowledge consists of 'fictions' that can only be pragmatically justified – instead of asking if something is true, it is better to ask whether it is useful or not to act as if it were true.

Critiquing Vaihinger's writing, Ellis argues that the work failed to answer its own question, but that it is still useful as a support for struggling spiritual believers. Therefore, the quotation above refers to the fact that a work may have positive (if unintended) consequences, and even if it fails at answering its own enquiry, there may be valuable insight nonetheless. JE

⊘ Seen here in 1932, Havelock Ellis is best known for his controversial studies of human sexual behaviour.

> ❝*The truth is often a terrible weapon of aggression. It is possible to lie, and even to murder, with the truth.*❞

Alfred Adler
The Problems of Neurosis
1929

Adler was an Austrian psychiatrist and the founder of individual psychology, a holistically oriented psychotherapeutic method that emphasizes the concepts of self-determination, the unity of the self and the importance of the environment of the patient. Adler's work was an attempt to critique the more mechanistic views of humanity that he saw as characteristics of the output of Sigmund Freud.

The above quotation addresses the long-standing notion of 'the truth' as a universally good, unproblematic description of things as they are. Adler was discussing the actions of a patient who had a sudden crisis of conscience, and revealed to her husband that she had been having an affair for the last twenty-five years. He noted that this was not a case of a mere guilt complex, but was rather her use of the truth to hurt her husband: '[It] was quite clearly an attack upon the husband who was no longer obedient.' This realization is followed by the above quotation, which notes how the truth can be used as a 'terrible weapon' in misleading or hurtful ways, to the point of causing grievous injury, even death, as a consequence of the truth being known. **JE**

> ❝*Man is condemned to be free.*❞

Jean-Paul Sartre
Being and Nothingness
1943

Sartre was a French philosopher, activist and playwright, most notable as a central figure in 20th-century existentialism and Marxist thought. One of his major works, *Being and Nothingness*, strongly argues the proposition that an individual's existence precedes his or her essence – that is, people create for themselves contra-belief systems that posit a human essence prior to empirical life.

The above quotation relates to the notion that human beings are not responsible for their origination – they enter the world not of their own volition – yet are inescapably responsible for every one of their subsequent choices. In other words, they are forced into a situation in which they are culpable for their actions, and must carefully choose them, yet they did not elect to be in that situation.

Sartre is here acknowledging that we have a deep and unchosen responsibility in this existence, but that it is one that we did not ask for; it was forced upon us. This is the moral quandary that underlies the notion that existence precedes essence, in that there is no recourse outside the self for the objectively correct mode of living for which we are responsible, but rather we must take our radical freedom seriously.

Thus, in philosophical terms at least, freedom is not necessarily the great goal that it is often held to be: it may be an imposition rather than a desideratum. **JE**

"Man is the only creature who refuses to be what he is."

Albert Camus
The Rebel
1951

French-Algerian philosopher and journalist Camus is best known for his novel *The Stranger* (1942) and his book-length essay *The Myth of Sisyphus* (1942), in which he explores the concept of 'the absurd', referring to the conflict we face from our desire for meaning in the context of an indifferent universe. He is also renowned for *The Rebel* (1951), an exploration (and critique) of revolutionary political violence.

In *The Rebel*, Camus discusses rebellion from a philosophical standpoint. On the one hand, although our world is often taken to have no inherent rationality or meaning and is often unjust, we still struggle and rebel. While Camus acknowledges that the reasons for rebellion (and potential justification for political violence) would have to be studied from an elaborate examination of historic examples, most generally, rebellion emerges because 'Man is the only creature who refuses to be what he is.' Humanity refuses to be stuck in conditions and limitations (including repression). Simultaneously, another implication of this quotation is that humanity's inability to abide limitations means that humanity is unable to simply 'be' and be satisfied. JE

Albert Camus in 1952, five years before he was awarded the Nobel Prize in Literature.

" *If we want things to stay as they are, things will have to change.* "

GIUSEPPE DI LAMPEDUSA

The Leopard

Giuseppe Tomasi di Lampedusa
The Leopard
1958

From the acclaimed historical novel *The Leopard*, the above quotation reflects the strategic thinking of a young aristocrat seeking to maintain his privileged lifestyle, which is threatened by the social and political upheavals of 19th-century Sicily. With Garibaldi's troops on the verge of overthrowing the Bourbon kingdom that had long ruled the island, the nephew of the fictional Prince of Salina fears that he and his family will lose the wealth and privileges of their noble class. Therefore, he informs his uncle that he is joining Garibaldi's nationalist volunteers, and later marries the daughter of the local mayor, whose support for Garibaldi has considerably increased his wealth and social status.

At first, the prince dismisses his nephew's reasoning as paradoxical, but very soon he comes to understand that self-preservation is possible only by making often radical changes. The novel ends with the image of the prince's faithful dog reduced to a rug, and like the serval that is the family's heraldic symbol, survival demands the ability to adapt quickly to changing environments. The wisdom of this quotation applies forcefully to environmental threats such as global warming. **TJ**

⬤ Book cover for the English language version of *The Leopard*, published in 1960.

The soul is the effect and instrument of a political anatomy; the soul is the prison of the body.

Michel Foucault

Discipline and Punish: The Birth of the Prison

1975

Foucault was a French philosopher, philologist and social theorist. His body of theoretical work addressed issues pertaining to the relationship between knowledge and power and how they are used to control individuals in daily life. *Discipline and Punish*, one of his major theoretical works, analyzes the evolution of Western penal systems.

Foucault critiques the development of institutions and practices designed to 'discipline' the populace, particularly convicted criminals. The goal of such an exercise of power is not to restrict or punish, but to create individuated, productive, law-abiding people through impositions on the body, among other means. The above quotation relates to the ways in which disciplinary power endeavours to conform individual agency to practices that benefit those enacting power. This new, controlled, individual subjectivity conforms or, one might say, imprisons the body and its future practices – it is the story of a self whose agency is reformulated from the outside and internalized. Thus, the words relate to Foucault's larger project of identifying the ways power is used to transform human agency from the outside. **JE**

◉ A photograph of Foucault in 1967, when he was establishing his reputation as an influential but controversial thinker.

> *" The Structure of language determines not only thought, but reality itself. "*

Ruth Nanda Anshen
Biography of an Idea
1986

The above quotation is often misattributed to Noam Chomsky, but that seems at odds with his normal position as a critic of the idea that language determines, or limits, the perception of reality. It is, in fact, the work of American philosopher Ruth Nanda Anshen.

This theory of linguistic relativity was largely developed by Benjamin Lee Whorf. A familiar example is the claim that the Inuit language has numerous words to describe various forms of snow. It originated from research by anthropologist Franz Boas in 1911, and Whorf contributed to popularizing the claim, but it has since been debunked.

Chomsky's criticisms of linguistic relativity are best explained through his analysis of Whorf's claim that the language of the American Indian Hopi lacks the concept of time as a past–present–future continuum, as opposed to speakers of European languages. Chomsky noted that, in English, the future is only distinguished from the past and present by the use of modal terms expressing notions of possibility (could), obligation (must), intention (will), etc. So by Whorf's own measures, English speakers would have no concept of the future. Chomsky's criticisms have undermined Whorf's theory, but more modest claims about the perception of colour have since provided some support to the theory of linguistic relativity. TJ

> *" There is a great deal of pain in life and perhaps the only pain that can be avoided is the pain that comes from trying to avoid pain. "*

R D Laing
Did You Used to be R D Laing?
1988

Ronald David Laing was a Scottish psychiatrist who wrote extensively on the subject of psychosis. His work was influenced by existential psychology and was unique for taking the expressed feelings of patients as having validity in their experiences, rather than discounting them as effects of a mental illness or disorder. Laing was long associated with the anti-psychiatry movement.

The above quotation relates to Laing's belief that it is normal and natural that much in life works against the well-being of individuals – there is a 'great deal of pain,' and that pain is inevitable. The implication is that we could make our lives better by ceasing attempts at avoidance of pain: we should accept the imperfections of existence and learn to roll with life as it is. It reminds us that, while life is sometimes a challenge, we can improve ourselves through learning to embrace, or at least to withstand, the tribulations and sufferings that it brings rather than be frustrated by fruitless attempts to avoid anything that is bad. JE

❯ Laing compared mental anguish to a shamanic journey.

Religion

The circle of hell from Dante's *Divine Comedy*, as depicted in a 19th-century fresco in Villa Massimo Lancellotti in Rome.

"Be still, and know that I am God."

Psalm 46
Book of Psalms
c. 1000 BCE

To be 'still', in the Hebrew sense of *rapa*, means both to slow down or cease movement, and to weaken, as a soldier might succumb to exhaustion at the end of a long battle. These words are an exhortation to cease in our constant struggle to avoid paying attention to what is happening right now. We are told that our continuous engagement with future and past makes it impossible for us to see that we are alive for no other purpose than to experience being alive. The wonderful ambiguity of the above phrase in what it is actually referring to – who is this 'I' who is God, exactly? Is it me? Is it you? – demands that we consider the quotation as an invitation to perceive without thinking. (The Christian interpretation pushes the thought into the mystical beyond, to refer to a transcendent omnipotence that is related to us only through grace; the Zen interpretation sees it as a reflection of emptiness, a *koan*.)

To be wholly silent and inactive forces us to face our mortality, our greatest fear. To own and acknowledge this abyss – to meet it without additional illusions, false promises of eternal hereafters, covenants that hide our true purpose – is simply the most courageous thing we can do. Out of this arises compassion, pure and endless. What we are in the midst of is not judgement or demand, but acceptance, deep and loving, of ourselves. **LW**

"Under the shadow of thy wings shall be my refuge, until this tyranny be over-past."

Psalm 57
Book of Psalms
c. 1000 BCE

David was a legendary king of the Israelites, known for brutally slaying thousands of Philistines, including Goliath. However, he also wrote hundreds of psalms praising the glory of his god. Most of us know Psalm 23 and its reference to walking through 'the valley of the shadow of death'. As a warrior and devout believer, David often appealed to his god in times of violent battle.

However, the above psalm relates to an earlier event in David's life. David had tried to kill the jealous King Saul, who was set on revenge. David, appealing to God to provide him safety in his shadows, took refuge in a cave. David later emerged from the cave and into the light, just as God's grace saves his believers from darkness. David prostrated himself before Saul asking for his forgiveness, which both Saul and the Lord offered. It was on that day and during their confrontation that Saul predicted that David would become king.

This psalm has inspired adventurers and echoes the hero's journey: going down into darkness and then emerging from his trials enlightened and free. **DK**

❯ The opening page of a *Book of Psalms* (1470) depicts King David.

" *Ye, though I walk through the valley of the shadow of death, I will fear no evil; for you are with me.* "

🔊 A 19th-century painting titled *The Voice of the Lord* by James Tissot depicts a visionary experience.

Psalm 23
Book of Psalms
c. 1000 BCE

The psalms make up a kind of religious songbook, with many of them traditionally attributed to King David, who ruled ancient Israel around 1000 BCE. Scholars now believe that they were written over at least five centuries and therefore reflect the religious needs of people at different times. This verse is Psalm 23:4, one of the most famous, which begins: 'The Lord is my shepherd.' It expresses trust in Israel's God Yahweh (Jehovah) who acts like a shepherd leading his people to good pastureland, imagery that would have been evocative for a pastoral people such as the ancient Israelites.

The words translated as 'the shadow of death' may mean simply 'deepest darkness' or 'deep shadow,' since in the Old Testament darkness and death are often associated. The valley may also be taken metaphorically – as John Bunyan portrayed it in his allegory *A Pilgrim's Progress* (1678) – as a place of terror and demons. It may also be seen as symbolic of the inevitability of each human being's death, fear of which can cast a dark shadow over a life. But it may be a real valley, a deep ravine infested by armed robbers in biblical times, still seen along the mountain road from Jerusalem to Jericho. **JF**

Birth is suffering, ageing is suffering, illness is suffering, death is suffering.

Buddha
Dhammacakkappavattana Sutta
510 BCE

Siddhārtha Gautama, often referred to as Buddha, was a sage who lived and taught in northeastern India some time between the 6th and 4th centuries BCE, and whose teachings formed the intellectual foundations of Buddhism. After attaining enlightenment following meditation under a bodhi tree, the Buddha discovered the Four Noble Truths: life contains suffering; the origin of suffering is attachment to desire; ending this attachment ends suffering; and following the noble Eightfold Path is the key to ending attachment.

This quotation constitutes the First Noble Truth of suffering (*dukkha*) and forms part of the first teaching given by Buddha after enlightenment. It refers to the fact that many unavoidable and natural aspects of existence are experienced as painful or difficult – as suffering. Even in the absence of extensive or particular misfortunes, many aspects of life involve potential loss and pain. We need to enhance our ability to deal with suffering by getting to its source, and by learning to overcome that source. As the First Noble Truth underlying the vast edifice of Buddhist philosophy, this line is perhaps the foundational touchstone of Buddhism. JE

The monumental bronze statue of Tian Tan Buddha, also known as the Big Buddha, at Lantau Island in Hong Kong.